Interviews With Brief Therapy Experts

INTERVIEWS WITH BRIEF THERAPY EXPERTS

Michael F. Hoyt, Ph.D.

USA	Publishing Office:	BRUNNER-ROUTLEDGE
		A member of the Taylor & Francis Group
		325 Chestnut Street
		Philadelphia, PA 19106
		Tel: (215) 625-8900
		Fax: (215) 625-2940
	Distribution Center:	BRUNNER-ROUTLEDGE
		A member of the Taylor & Francis Group
		7625 Empire Drive
		Florence, KY 41042
		Tel: 1-800-634-7064
		Fax: 1-800-248-4724
UK		BRUNNER-ROUTLEDGE
		A member of the Taylor & Francis Group
		27 Church Road
		Hove
		E. Sussex, BN3 2FA
		Tel: +44 (0) 1273 207411
		Fax: +44 (0) 1283 205612

INTERVIEWS WITH BRIEF THERAPY EXPERTS

1 2 3 4 5 6 7 8 9 0

Printed by Edwards Brothers, Ann Arbor, MI, 2001.
Cover design by Ellen Seguin.

A CIP catalog record for this book is available from the British Library.
⊚ The paper in this publication meets the requirements of the ANSI Standard Z39.48-1984 (Permanence of Paper).

Library of Congress Cataloging-in-Publication Data
Hoyt, Michael F.
    Interviews with brief therapy experts / Michael F. Hoyt.
        p. cm.
    Inlcudes bibliographical references and index.
    ISBN 1-58391-353-X (alk. paper)
    1. Brief psychotherapy. 2. Psychotherapists—Interviews. I. Title.

    RC480.55 .H682 2001
    616.89′14—dc21

                                                                00-069669

ISBN 1-58391-353-X (case)

To My Colleagues

One afternoon the last week in April
Showing Kai how to throw a hatchet
One-half turn and it sticks in a stump.
He recalls the hatchet-head
Without a handle, in the shop
And go gets it, and wants it for his own.
A broken-off axe handle behind the door
Is long enough for a hatchet,
We cut it to length and take it
With the hatchet head
And working hatchet, to the wood block.
And there I begin to shape the old handle
With the hatchet, and the phrase
First learned from Ezra Pound
Rings in my ears!
"When making an axe handle
    the pattern is not far off."
And I say this to Kai
"Look: We'll shape the handle
By checking the handle
Of the axe we cut with—
And he sees. And I hear it again:
It's in Lu Ji's *Wen Fu*, fourth century
A.D. "Essay on Literature"—in the
Preface: "In making the handle
Of an axe
By cutting wood with the axe
The model is indeed near at hand."
My teacher Shih-hsiang Chen
Translated that and taught it years ago
And I see: Pound was an axe,
Chen was an axe, I am an axe
And my son a handle, soon
To be shaping again, model
And tool, craft of culture,
How we go on.
                    —Gary Snyder ("Axe Handles," 1983)

I want to warn you not to copy me, but to work out your own method. Our people tell us to be original. If you can watch the method, though, and the way I go about it, maybe that will give you some thoughts about what to follow, what it's all about. Then you work out your own substance, your own songs, your own prayers and things to go with it.

—Rolling Thunder (quoted in Boyd, 1974)

A married couple came before the old rabbi to settle an argument. He listened to the first spouse and then said, "You're right." He then listened to the second spouse, and again said, "You're right." A student attending the proceeding then spoke: "Rabbi, I've been listening. First you told one person they were right, and then you told the other person they were right. They can't both be right." To which the rabbi replied, "You're right, too!"

—Yiddish Folk Tale

And my voice goes everywhere with you, and changes into the voice of your parents, your teachers, your playmates and the voices of the wind and the rain.

—Milton H. Erickson, M.D. (quoted in Zeig, 1988)

CONTENTS

PREFACE

The volume in hand comprises a dozen interviews conducted with brief therapy experts. Previously published in various books and journals, they are collected here in one place for the first time. The roster of participants includes some of the field's most influential innovators as well as a number of leading students and critics. The interviews were conducted to explore technical, theoretical, and ethical aspects of the theory and practice of brief therapy, the "conversation" or "interview" format allowing a give-and-take spontaneity that is especially congenial for talking about "talking therapy."

Each interview provides a platform to explicate the thinking of a particular person or to explore aspects of a perplexing problem. As readers familiar with Jay Haley's (1985) three-volume *Conversations with Milton H. Erickson, M.D.* or Richard Simon's (1992) *One on One: Conversations with the Shapers of Family Therapy* know, friendly interlocutory dialogue can be particularly useful for an in-depth probing of issues.[1] Questions can be asked, answers can be explored, responses can be revisited and reflected upon. The "inter-view" process is also two-way. As perceptive readers of this unique collection will note, at times various parallel processes emerge within the dialogues—process mirrors content, form follows function, the medium becomes the message.

Specific introductions open each chapter. Four of the interviewees (Robert Goulding, Donald Meichenbaum, Paul Watzlawick, Michael White) have been honored as faculty at the world-renowned Evolution of Psychotherapy conferences, and all the participants have made contributions that rightly earn the label "expert." Chapter 1, "On the Importance of Keeping It Simple and Taking the Patient Seriously: A Conversation with Steve de Shazer and John Weakland," features de Shazer (the co-origina-

---

[1]I read somewhere that Albert Einstein's mother used to ask little Albert every day when he came home from school, "Did you ask any good questions today?" I also take inspiration from Terry Gross' lively "Fresh Air" interviews on National Public Radio and Roy Firestone's (1993) "Up Close and Personal" ESPN television *tête-à-têtes* with leading sports figures.

tor of Solution-Focused Therapy) and his mentor Weakland (of Mental Research Institute fame) discussing the work of Milton Erickson, the importance of closely attending to the client's worldview rather than imposing one's own obfuscating theory, and the role of strategy and collaboration.

Chapter 2, "Welcome to Possibilityland: A Conversation with Bill O'Hanlon," elaborates ways of using brief therapy and solution-oriented therapy methods to help clients expand their perceived options and to move safely into more desirable ways of being, with a special focus on assisting persons suffering aftereffects from sexual abuse and other trauma. O'Hanlon (who now calls his evolving approach "Possibility Therapy") emphasizes the importance of acknowledgment and validation as a first and essential (and often overlooked) part of brief therapy. The discussion of the *narrative* and the *experiential* senses of self is particularly fascinating within the context of recent controversies regarding "true" and "false" recall of abuse.

Chapter 3, "On Ethics and the Spiritualities of the Surface: A Conversation with Michael White and Gene Combs," also emphasizes the importance of listening for the client's experience. Rather than focusing on the theoretical and technical aspects of Narrative Therapy (which White co-originated), however, our discussion centers on the spirit that informs the work—the values of caring, compassion, and service, the importance of constructing a path with love. An exercise is also included to help readers recognize and resist ways in which their conscious purpose and commitment to psychotherapeutic work may be undermined by common pathologizing discourses.

Chapter 4, "Cognitive-Behavioral Treatment of Posttraumatic Stress Disorder from a Narrative Constructivist Perspective: A Conversation with Donald Meichenbaum," also addresses issues in the treatment of persons who have been abused. Like the other interviewees, Meichenbaum (one of the originators of Cognitive Therapy) is extraordinarily articulate and informed, drawing on an extensive clinical and research background. In our discussion, he, too, focuses on the importance of the therapeutic relationship being collaborative and the need for careful attention to language, and addresses ways (including some cultural nuances) of helping clients to get "unstuck" by continuing their telling of the story until they construct a narrative that allows them to move forward, beyond the trauma.

Chapter 5, "Contact, Contract, Change, Encore: A Conversation about Redecision Therapy with Bob Goulding," reports an interview done near the end of Goulding's life. In addition to discussing his views regarding key aspects of effective psychotherapy, Goulding (the co-originator of Redecision Therapy, a treatment approach that grew out of the Transactional Analysis theory of Eric Berne) describes aspects of his personal and professional development, assigning special importance to his training with Fritz Perls and his long-term collaboration with Mary Goulding as the turning points of his life and career.

Chapter 6, "Constructing Therapeutic Realities: A Conversation with Paul Watzlawick," presents some ideas about constructivism and the Mental Research Institute strategic interactional approach from MRI's chief theoretical architect. Watzlawick comments on some of the figures that most influenced him (including Thomas Szasz, Hans Vaihinger, and Heinz von Foerster), discusses the subjective nature of "second-order" reality and the importance of the client coming to a new way of looking (a "therapeutic reality"), and explains his views regarding influence and informed consent.

Chapter 7, "Solution Building and Language Games: A Conversation with Steve de Shazer (and Some After Words with Insoo Kim Berg)," again features the ideas of the chief developer of Solution-Focused Therapy. Some of the history and minimalist elegance of the approach is explored, with special attention to the way language can be used to construct therapeutic solutions. As a bonus, at the end of the conversation Insoo Berg (co-developer of the Solution-Focused approach) joins us and provides some perspective on her perspective.

Chapter 8, "Postmodernism, the Relational Self, Constructive Therapies, and Beyond: A Conversation with Kenneth Gergen," addresses some of the evolving problems of living and doing therapy in these postmodern times, including issues of character and integrity, relational responsibility and conflict resolution between competing value systems, and the possibilities of relatedness and the limits of narrative. A major contributor to the social constructionist movement, Gergen eloquently portrays both the potentials and challenges that lie ahead.

Chapter 9, "About Constructivism (or, If Four Colleagues Talked in New York, Would Anyone Hear it?): A Conversation with Scott Miller, Barbara Held, and William Matthews," is an account of a discussion that took place at the "Brief Therapy: Lasting Impressions" conference held in New York during August 1998. A spirited exchange emerges as we discuss empiricism, pragmatism, and what may be meant by the term *reality*.

Chapter 10, "Brief Therapy and Managed Care: A Conversation with Michael Hoyt," reports an interview done with me as subject (conducted by Matt Carlson). While fuller accounts of my own thinking can be found elsewhere (Hoyt, 1995, 2000), I take the liberty of including this here because of the numerous references I make to the contributions of other interviewees, and because our discussion about how the incursion of managed care may be influencing the practice of therapy—for better or worse—is very relevant to the brief therapy field.

Chapter 11, "Honoring Our Internalized Others and the Ethics of Caring: A Conversation with Karl Tomm and Stephen Madigan," is a highly personal look into the development and application of Tomm's ideas about ethics and the social construction of self. From the beginning of the exchange, in which he "opens space" by inquiring about *our* interests, his degree of self-revelation and soul-searching are extraordinary.

Chapter 12, "Direction and Discovery: A Conversation about Power and Politics in Narrative Therapy with Michael White and Jeff Zimmerman," concludes the volume. We explore the concepts of *power* and *collaboration*, White (who also appears in Chapter 3) explicates some of his thinking about post-structuralism and responds to quotations I present from various critics, and we have an extended discussion about some of the personal experiences that have influenced our thinking and development—including White asking me about my interest in asking questions!

The term *brief therapy* can mean many different things. As Jay Haley (1995, personal communication), Paul Watzlawick (Chapter 6), and Steve de Shazer (Chapter 7) all told me, the term *brief* was originally used simply to distinguish the approach from those (usually psychoanalytically influenced) that set out to be *long-term*. Efficiency became the watchword; and there were lots of theories and no one overarching method. Thus, as Bill O'Hanlon comments in Chapter 2, *brief therapy* has come to mean, generically, any therapeutic approach that is problem-driven; that is focused on resolving the presenting complaint, with the therapist responsible for creating and maintaining the focus. In this sense, as O'Hanlon notes, *brief therapy* includes psychodynamic, solution-oriented, problem-focused, lots of family therapy, systemic and interactional approaches—all having a goal-directed emphasis on resolving the presenting problem.

In addition to meaning "efficient" and "to the point," *brief therapy* is also used sometimes to refer particularly to time-sensitive intervention based on certain (social constructionist) theoretical principles, not on the length of treatment. Directly or indirectly, these approaches—which are sometimes loosely associated with the work of the famous psychiatrist-hypnotherapist Milton Erickson (with Gregory Bateson and the word *epistemology* waiting in the wings)—involve a wide variety of creative methods that operate at the level of cybernetics and hermeneutics, strategies and "language games," all more-or-less intended to influence how clients interact and construe ("story") their experience.[2] Several of the interviewees in this book knew Erickson and studied his work closely, and Erickson's appreciation of how language shapes our sense of reality

---

[2] For a brief history of brief therapy, see Hoyt (1995, pp. 291-294); for an overview of the narrative function of "storying," see *Some Stories Are Better than Others* (Hoyt, 2000).

and his ideas about more fully utilizing clients' own competencies and resources can be seen to prefigure discussions about client "empowerment" and "open the space" for considerations about therapist activity and the role of influence and power, "intervention" and different types of therapeutic tasks and "homework," the use of language in the creation of "therapeutic realities," and so on.

Some of our interviewee-experts might at first question being subsumed under the *brief therapy* rubric (since their work does not derive from the Ericksonian tradition and was not developed primarily to address length-of-treatment issues), and a few might even be uncomfortable about being called "expert" (or at least would want to clarify what is meant by the term *expert*, what it might say about therapeutic power relations and therapist-client roles). It is safe to say, however, that while they may differ in their therapeutic approaches, all the interviewees focus on ways to enhance the effectiveness of treatment—with careful attention to the uses of language, to the interplay between intrapsychic and interpersonal factors, and to issues of influence and respect for clients' competency and autonomy. "By comparing . . . views," as Joseph Campbell (quoted in Larsen & Larsen, 1991, p. 215) put it, one "may calculate for the parallax." There are many fascinating nuances and contrasts, and readers will find much to ponder.

A few words about method: When preparing for an interview, I generally immerse myself in the particular person's writings, supplemented by attending workshops they may teach and/or watching videotapes of their work, reading secondary sources (what others have said about them), and also discussing their work with colleagues. I take detailed notes, cull a few key quotations, and organize a loose outline of primary and secondary questions. After the interview is done, the tape is transcribed and the typescript is circulated to all participants for further elaboration and polishing. Footnotes are also inserted to provide fuller scholarly exposition.

Most of the interviews were done face-to-face; a couple (Paul Watzlawick, Kenneth Gergen) were conducted with back-and-forth mailings. All are lively and often witty; some are quite poignant and personal. In two instances (Karl Tomm and Stephen Madigan; Scott Miller, Barbara Held, and Bill Matthews), the conversations were held before a "live" audience at a professional conference. In one instance (the conversation with White and Combs), I had a very comprehensive interview schedule in hand but, in response to a mutual desire for a more relaxed communication ("How about if we just talk?" Michael asked) I literally tossed the sheaf of papers over my shoulder as we began. What resulted is much more alive and to the heart of the matter than what would probably have occurred had I persisted in asking an endless series of academic questions.

Except in the case of the Karl Tomm and Stephen Madigan conversation (Chapter 11), last names are used throughout the following transcripts to identify speakers. As in the original 1998 publication (in *The Handbook of Constructive Therapies*), we honor Karl's request to use first names to reflect the more personal tone of our meeting.

Each interview is full of information and able to stand on its own. There is also some "exchange" or "synergy" (as well as controversy) between chapters as participants explore the same issues and also occasionally respond, directly and indirectly, to questions and quotations drawn from the writings of other interviewees. Watzlawick, and White and Zimmerman, for example, respond to some of Held's and Matthews' characterizations of their work being "anti-realist"; I quote Gergen to Held; White demurs (if not eschews) being labelled a "constructivist," and he and de Shazer embrace post-structuralism; and White responds to some issues raised by Tomm and by de Shazer. Meichenbaum references the work of White, Gergen, and O'Hanlon; and while not explicitly citing one another, Goulding, de Shazer, and O'Hanlon all highlight the importance of careful listening, clear goals, and focusing on client strengths.

Some readers might prefer to work through the book from front to back, or turn immediately to a particular discussion. Every chapter has its value and, read like a reflecting team (see Andersen, 1991; Friedman, 1995), the whole is intended to be greater than the sum of its parts. The interviewees are all extraordinarily articulate and insightful. I am grateful to my colleagues for their willingness to participate and for their expertise and enthusiasm. Readers are invited to pull up a chair.

☐ References

Andersen, T. (Ed.) (1991). *The Reflecting Team: Dialogues and Dialogues about the Dialogues*. New York: Norton.

Firestone, R. (1993). *Up Close: And in Your Face with the Greats, Near-Greats, and Ingrates of Sports*. New York: Hyperion.

Friedman, S. (Ed.) (1995). *The Reflecting Team in Action: Collaborative Practice in Family Therapy*. New York: Guilford Press.

Haley, J. (Ed.) (1985). *Conversations with Milton H. Erickson, M.D.* (Volumes 1–3) New York: Triangle Press.

Haley, J. (1995). Personal communication.

Hoyt, M. F. (1995). *Brief Therapy and Managed Care: Readings for Contemporary Practice*. San Francisco: Jossey-Bass.

Hoyt, M. F. (2000). *Some Stories are Better than Others: Doing What Works in Brief Therapy and Managed Care*. Philadelphia: Brunner/Mazel.

Larsen, S., & Larsen, R. (1991). *A Fire in the Mind: The Life of Joseph Campbell*. New York: Doubleday.

Simon, R. (1992). *One on One: Conversations with the Shapers of Family Therapy*. New York: Guilford Press.

CHAPTER

On the Importance of Keeping It Simple and Taking the Patient Seriously: A Conversation with Steve de Shazer and John Weakland

The solution of problems and the problems of solutions have long been the focus of attention for John Weakland and Steve de Shazer. One of the contributors of the original double-bind hypothesis (Bateson, Jackson, Haley, & Weakland, 1956), Weakland (who passed away in 1995—see Cade, 1995) was Codirector of the Brief Therapy Center at the Mental Research Institute in Palo Alto, California. He was coauthor of *Change: Principles of Problem Formation and Problem Resolution* (Watzlawick, Weakland, & Fisch, 1974), *Counseling Elders and Their Families: Practical Techniques for Applied Gerontology* (Herr & Weakland, 1979), and *The Tactics of Change: Doing Therapy Briefly* (Fisch, Weakland, & Segal, 1983). de Shazer is Senior Research Associate at the Brief Family Therapy Center in Milwaukee, Wisconsin. Like Weakland, he is a major figure in the development of brief therapy and the shift toward a constructivist perspective. His books include *Patterns of Brief Family Therapy* (1982), *Keys to Solution in Brief Therapy* (1985), *Clues: Investigating Solutions in Brief Therapy* (1988), *Putting Difference to Work* (1991), and *Words Were Originally Magic* (1994a).

Originally appeared, with changes, in M. F. Hoyt (Ed.) (1994), *Constructive Therapies, Volume 7* (pp. 11–40). New York: Guilford Press. Used with permission.

The following conversation took place during the afternoon of December 3, 1992, in Phoenix, Arizona, where we were all participating in the Fifth International Congress on Ericksonian Approaches to Hypnosis and Psychotherapy (see Zeig, 1994).

Hoyt: I think it's appropriate that we're meeting here at the Erickson conference, especially since the theme is "The Essence of the Story." And that was the first thing that I wanted to ask. What do you think is the essence of being a brief therapist?

de Shazer: My first immediate thought is that "essence" is a muddling word. Because when you talk "essence," that means you also talk something about "nonessence." And you've got me, Michael. That, to me, is unanswerable because of that.

Hoyt: Maybe I should take out the question about the essence and ask it the other way. What is brief therapy?

de Shazer: Oh, shit. I think that made it worse! *[laughter]*

Weakland: About the essence, I'll say one thing. It's leaving out a whole lot of stuff that a great many people otherwise think is essential.

de Shazer: Right.

Hoyt: Well said. It's leaving out what many people think is essential, but obviously isn't.

Weakland: Yeah, I guess that it's about *simplifying*. That's probably the essence, if there is such a thing.

Hoyt: What's the Ericksonian essence in your work?

Weakland: When I get to the Ericksonian essence, it has really nothing to do with technique. It has nothing to do with theory. It mainly had to do with Erickson was very curious, and he was a hell of an observer, and he looked and listened to other people, and he finally had the guts to draw his own conclusions. That basically is what I think was the essence of Milton and comes at a much deeper level than what he did specifically.

de Shazer: I guess my point again is around this point of "essence." When you start to look for the essence of Erickson's work or brief therapy, you're always in danger of forgetting the "nonessential" stuff. You automatically point to something that is nonessential when you say something is essential. Automatically. And you're in danger then of sticking something into the "nonessential" box that will prove, in the long run, to be just as essential as anything else has been.

Weakland: You're always in danger of being too sure of yourself beforehand. You're equally in danger of not having the nerve to go with what you think is best.

de Shazer: So I think it's a very slippery category because of that. A not-very-useful way of thinking. You can't afford to box things off into this "nonessential" box, because over and over it has proved to be that things we thought were not essential at one point were things that later turned everything around.

Weakland: Also, you can't—it's very similar—but you can't really do the same with big and little, or at least what seems to me to be big things often seem to other people to be little things and vice versa.

Hoyt: In your own experience, what did you put in the nonessential box that you then brought back?

de Shazer: I started off trying to construct a theory, in the formal sense of the term, looking at Erickson's published cases and there's all these goddamn cases that didn't fit the theory. I mean, the theory worked very well. There were five major patterns. That worked just fine. I simplified it. But, nonetheless, there was always pile number six, which usually contained more cases than the other five. But we thought, you know, it's only a matter of figuring out how the theory works in these other cases.

Weakland: We're going to whittle down that residual category until it's no bigger than all the rest and go from there.

de Shazer: I started off, essentially, looking for the essence, a very grand theory. And there are always these weird cases. And then I tried doing my form of brief therapy. And I could get most of my cases to fit into these five patterns, but, goddamn it, even by deliberately trying, I couldn't get all of them to fit. So I swept it off to the side, remembering that all theories are incomplete and incorrect, and that it's okay. It's just that the "weird cases" pile kept growing over the years.

Weakland: That brings a terrible thought to mind. It couldn't have been very far away, but I never saw it this clearly. I have done a certain amount of reading in physics. I never got rid of my original scientific bent. Besides, they have things to say that make more sense than most of the psychologists. And poor old Einstein struggled for many late years looking for the grand, unified theory, and he left a number of other people who were doing it. And I read *Infinite in All Directions* by Freeman Dyson [1988], and I was moved to sit down and write Dyson a letter pointing out that it's never going to happen, because you're putting together new interrelated observations; you're always building new observing tools and taking new angles of observation, so you're always going to have more stuff to interrelate. Therefore, you will never reach the end. Dyson didn't answer. And now that I think of it, we're in the same fix.

Hoyt: The more we know, the more ways we can theorize it, but it doesn't necessarily mean . . .

Weakland: We may simplify certain things, but we are never going to reach an endpoint that will encompass everything, unless we just completely stop doing anything.

Hoyt: My question really is backwards. Rather than asking what's the essence, meaning pulling all this data together into one, it may be more useful to realize the uniqueness of the experiences.

de Shazer: Yeah. Yeah. I think the way I see it now is that every session is somehow a unique event, and that the main thing the therapist has to do is listen and keep it simple. And if you do it, I think, the clients will tell you what to do.[1]

Hoyt: That reminds me of my favorite Einstein story. I read that his mother, when he would come home from school each day, would say to him, "Albert, did you ask any good questions today?"

Weakland: This enterprise of therapy is a bitch of a job, because in a number of respects you have to go two directions at the same time, although they stay in close relation to each other. I'm not so sure that this isn't really the essence of living in general, but you have got to have some idea what you're about in a session, but you have to always be prepared to hear something that will tell you that you're headed the wrong way. You have always got to be making contact with your clients, but you've always got to preserve enough distance so that you're not seeing things exactly the same way they are or you're no good.

---

[1]In his paper, "Essential, Non-Essential: Vive la Différence," de Shazer (1994b, pp. 248–249) reports: "In order to reread Erickson's case examples as though for the first time, I needed to adopt a reading strategy that would allow me to not drag along all of my previous readings that involved the pursuit of a Theory. . . . To aid me in this rereading, I decided to interpret these case examples as stories—not as exemplary lessons, but as pure stories. Thus, I read them as if they were fiction, which meant that I was no longer taking the distinction between 'literature' and 'science' very seriously at all. . . . As I continued to read using this strategy, I started to see myself and Haley and even Erickson-the-author in much the same relationship to these tales as the Baker Street Irregulars have to the Sherlock Holmes adventures. . . . It then dawned on me that the Erickson-the-clever stories, like the Sherlock Holmes stories, actually underdevelop or underrealize all the other characters that appear in the stories, particularly the clients. Often, these other characters, like inspector Lestrade, no matter how important to the story itself, are just cardboard cutouts. We have little or no idea about their contributions to the therapeutic endeavor.

"However, as you and I know, and as Erickson and Haley also know, in order to have a therapeutic enterprise, there needs to be both therapist and client. As I reread my own cases from this point of view, I came to realize what clever clients I have had. Most of the ideas for 'unusual interventions' in the miscellaneous pile in fact came from the clients themselves! Fortunately, we were cleverly listening when they told us what to do.

"To reread my own case stories using the persona of clever-clients unfortunately forces the therapist-in-the-story to appear to be incredibly stupid. Undoubtedly, we therapists could not learn as much from de Shazer-the-stupid as we did from Erickson-the-clever. Maybe we all need to remember systems theory here and reread these stories with an interactional focus, which would lead us to the idea that clever therapy depends on having clients and therapists cleverly working together in clever ways."

de Shazer: You've got to know where you're going.

Weakland: Yeah. So that you're doing things that are in a sense contradictory or at least headed in opposite directions over and over again. And, I think, probably in a lot of other ways that one could spell out. Maybe the essence is to be ready to live with uncertainty.[2]

de Shazer: Exactly. And incompleteness.

Weakland: Yeah. And that is the last thing that most people want to do.

de Shazer: Or, as Wittgenstein says, "You've got what you've got, and that's all there is." Just take what you've got, no matter how incomplete and inconsistent and incoherent it appears. You've got what you've got.

Hoyt: It isn't even especially this field, but this is one of many fields that people want closure or want *the* answer—fast answer, slow answer, brief answer, long answer.

de Shazer: Ten steps.

Weakland: Yeah. That's right. That's the sort of thing I meant. That's the sort of thing that will sell.

de Shazer: Completely muddleheaded. The widest variety of unnecessary and unuseful divergences from figuring out what the hell to do.

Hoyt: Many of the different methods that are called techniques or steps may be creative and clever, but they don't seem necessary and may just be imposing . . .

Weakland: Clouding the waters. Some are nice stories, a combination of nice stories and eight to ten steps, and you can just go out and follow them. It's a great sales job.

---

[2]In his written report that came out of the "Ericksonian Methods: The Essence of the Story" conference where this conversation took place, Weakland (1994, pp. 288–290) wrote: "[I]n a world, perhaps especially a professional world full of the search for fixed answers, Erickson was a lifelong opponent of dogma at any level. This is, he was opposed to the construction of or adherence to grand theories. Over and over, when asked general questions, he would respond instead with another concrete example. Equally, however, although he was a very practical man, he rejected the limiting premises implicit in accepting the received popular wisdom uncritically. He was continually saying and doing things that appeared contrary to 'common sense.' It is perhaps especially significant—for this is where many opponents of dogma make a large exception—that he clearly was not eager even to establish a new dogma of his own. . . . In my judgment, the key to all this is Erickson's emphasis on *observation*. . . . Erickson looked at and listened to others (and also himself) carefully. Then he made his own judgments about what to believe and do, based primarily on his distillation of such firsthand experience. But he was ready, secondarily, to listen to 'authorities' in the same way—that is, not as sources of truth but as also expressing views, whose value and relevance he would judge for himself. I see his stance as a profoundly individualistic one, yet that of an individual in contact with, not in isolation from, others. Moreover, and perhaps even rarer and more difficult, he proposed that his patients and students do likewise—examine things more widely and deeply, then decide for themselves. We might see this as his one dogmatic principle."

de Shazer: Those ten steps won't lead to stories like that. *[laughter]*

Weakland: You mean, they don't come from the same place? [laughter] You see, thinking about first-order and second-order change, although it is useful to diagram or explain certain things, it does not help you help people make specific changes in the midst of practice.

de Shazer: There is this group that I call the "weird case" pile. The ones that don't fit the theory.

Weakland: That's where the potential instruction is.

de Shazer: Yeah. It's these "weird cases" that don't fit the theory . . .

Weakland: All right, then we're more similar than I thought, but I didn't start with anything like a theory. What I started with was lost in the world and saying, "What the hell is going on out there?" And I didn't understand what was going on in the "normal world," so called, let alone the world of problems.

de Shazer: Reading Erickson's papers, my initial response was, "What the fuck is going on here? He's got to be crazy."

Weakland: Oh, God, when I first went down to talk to him, my main reaction was, "That is interesting, but I can't make a fucking bit of sense out of it."[3]

Hoyt: Do you remember when you began to see it? Was there a moment or watershed where it clicked?

Weakland: Oh, no. It was very gradual. One of the simplest stories he told, one of the plainest stories he told, it was 20 years I began to think about that again and thought about what it was, which was simply the story about Erickson and the headwaiter and his son and the son's friend who weren't dressed properly. Remember that story?

Hoyt: Recount it, please.

Weakland: It was in San Francisco. And Erickson was there for one of those traveling roadshows that they used to put on. And his son was working somewhere near the city, and Erickson invited him to come down and have dinner with him one night. And he came down with a young friend. They went down to the dining room. The two young men were dressed quite casually and, when they got to the doorway of the dining room, the headwaiter said, "I'm sorry, sir, you cannot come in. The two young men with you are not dressed properly for the dining room." And Erickson said, "But I am a guest in this hotel and these two young men are my guests." And the headwaiter said, "I'm sorry, sir, but the two young

---

[3]Transcripts of many conversations with Erickson (involving Weakland, Haley, and Bateson) are available in Haley (1985).

men are not dressed properly according to our rules here. I cannot admit you." And Erickson said, "But I am a guest in this hotel and these two young men are my guests." And this went on very civilly for several more rounds, at which point, suddenly the headwaiter said, "Would you come this way, please," and took them to a nice table and seated them. I can get it, but I don't understand it. I can get it, but don't understand it. The sense I finally made out of it, which wasn't long ago, was . . . well, I connected it up with some things that finally we'd gotten clear on and that helped me to at least get some grasp. Erickson was not arguing. There was no confrontation. There was just a statement of fact. He did not argue with the headwaiter's statement. He just made his statement of fact. He did not escalate; he didn't change the volume of his statement. He just repeated it. But he was clearly prepared to repeat it essentially forever if necessary. And, I'm assuming that meanwhile the pressure was growing on the head-waiter to get on with his business. But the main point was he made no confrontation, no argument; he just stated a fact and kept on stating it. So, but how come . . .

de Shazer: So, how come . . . that sounds like more of the same of something that's not working.

Weakland: What's the difference? Well, somebody, I think it was Bateson somewhere, said we have to consider the role of time in these things. That was changing.

de Shazer: Ah. That was changing. And there may have been some other things about the situation . . .

Weakland: There may have been some people piling up . . .

de Shazer: Ah, the line behind them! This is the whole point I suppose: exceptions. And here's an exception of some sort. Now the easiest thing to do with exceptions is to sweep them under the rug and forget 'em.

Weakland: Furthermore, that's a time-honored procedure in many a field . . .

de Shazer: That's how you keep your theory pure . . .

Weakland: Including the cases of cancer that go into remission.

de Shazer: Right. For 20 years.

Weakland: Including the "flights into health" that plagued the field of analysis for so long.

Hoyt: "Flukes." "Flight into health." "Let's not talk about that one."

de Shazer: Right. Keep your theory pure, you see.

Weakland: But it's always those exceptions that seem most interesting. That's probably another example of how my mind is bent.

Hoyt: Well, here's an exception that I've been struggling with. I'll read you the quotation. It's in the Preface to *Putting Difference to Work* [de Shazer, 1991, p. xiii]. Steve, you say, "You do not need to know what a problem is in order to solve it." Yet, John, you're giving a workshop [at the Ericksonian Congress] called "What's the Problem?" Why ask, "What's the problem?" if you don't need to know what the problem is?

Weakland: Why not? It doesn't always get in the way of resolving it.

de Shazer: Yeah. You just don't need to know what it is.

Weakland: In a sense, you never know what it is.

Hoyt: Is the problem the problem they're stating?

Weakland: It's, "What do you see as a problem?"

Hoyt: Steve, you wouldn't ask that at the beginning . . .

de Shazer: Not usually.

Weakland: I wouldn't usually talk too much about solutions, but I might. I don't think you necessarily need to know what the problem is. I happen to think it's one way to go that can be very simple and productive, and will fit with the inclinations of most of your clients. So why not?

de Shazer: I think it's not necessary. And I use the word "necessary" very strongly. It's not necessary.[4]

Hoyt: How do you deal with patients, though, that come in, and they're more traditionally oriented and they feel they need to tell their story, and they need to present their problem, give their history, portray their tale?

de Shazer: I guess that I have to tell you, frankly, I don't get many of them. My hunch is that it is more of a therapist's concern about what they think the client thinks. I've found that, basically, my clients tend to be veterans, and they've told these stories before. And if I can get in and break into that story with exceptions questions, or a miracle question, we can get beyond it very, very quickly.

Weakland: Okay, then you're saying or implying that a lot of your clients have told that story enough so they're tired of telling it and finding it doesn't go anywhere.

de Shazer: Yeah.

Weakland: All right. But let me give you a further answer to my title. It's not aimed at solution-focused therapists. It's aimed at conventional

---

[4]To highlight this contrast, de Shazer, Berg, Lipchik, Nunnaly, Molnar, Gingerich, and Weiner-Davis (1986) entitled an early paper on solution-focus "Brief Therapy: Focused Solution Development" to parallel an early paper by Weakland, Fisch, Watzlawick, and Bodin (1972) entitled "Brief Therapy: Focused Problem Resolution."

therapists who think they know better than the client what the problem is. That's where it's really aimed.

de Shazer: Oh, that's the problem, all right. That's a problem.

Hoyt: The psychoanalyst David Malan [1976], in his work on short-term psychodynamic therapy, writes about "valuable false solutions," where, in his model, the patient is doing something useful but not addressing an "underlying" or "more important" issue. Have you ever had instances where someone takes a solution and you feel that solution is going to be so limiting to them or hurtful to them that you'll try to talk them, maybe not out of the solution but try to get them to expand their options?

de Shazer: Hum . . . I don't think so.

Weakland: When they're saying it's okay, even though I don't think it might be, as long as they say they think it's okay, and they can convince me that they think it's going to stabilize and continue to be okay, then that's okay.[5]

de Shazer: Malan still implies that he knows best . . . And if we want to get into that frame, that's probably true with every case, then. *His* thing.

Hoyt: "Do it my way." That's "The Art of Psychoanalysis," Haley's [1969] satiric paper—the attitude that, "We still haven't addressed this deep enough, long enough, the way I think you should."

Weakland: Yes.

Hoyt: Yvonne Dolan, who gave a wonderful presentation the other day, has emphasized in some of her work with clients [Dolan, 1991], how important it is to let them tell their experiences, to validate and hear their history. And Cory Hammond the other day was talking about the importance he saw for abreaction with PTSD folks and MPDs.

de Shazer: I have no idea what these initials mean.

Hoyt: Multiple Personality Disorder and Post-Traumatic Stress Disorder.

de Shazer: Okay.

Hoyt: Is there a time when people need to talk through their feelings with the therapist? "Working through," some people would call it.

Weakland: Oh, yeah. I'll give you an answer to that in my framework.

---

[5]de Shazer (1991, p. 112) has described the general characteristics of well-formed goals, the features of solutions that affirmatively answer the question, "How will we know when to stop meeting like this?" They are: (1) small rather than large; (2) salient to clients; (3) described in specific, concrete, behavioral terms; (4) achievable within the practical contexts of clients' lives; (5) perceived by the clients as involving their "hard work"; (6) described as the "start of something" and not as the "end of something"; and (7) treated as involving new behavior(s) rather than the absence or cessation of existing behavior(s).

If somebody has kept it all to themselves, then to talk to a therapist is a new behavior.

de Shazer: Right.

Weakland: And then it can be useful. If they've talked to three other therapists, let alone six relatives and 42 in-laws, then it don't amount to shit.

de Shazer: Then, it's problem talk; it's problem-maintaining behavior already.

Hoyt: It's stabilizing rather than progressive.[6]

de Shazer: Yes. I guess that I'm going to go more indirectly on an answer for that. Some years ago, we talked to a whole bunch of people that had terminal diagnoses, cancer, from six months to 15 to 20 years before. So they should have been dead a long time. And a common feature we found running throughout the cases was that they didn't talk to other people about the cancer.

Hoyt: They didn't create a social world that would reinforce destruction.

de Shazer: Yeah, one of them told me very plainly that she got up and went back to work the next day after she got this terminal diagnosis.

Weakland: By God, that's interesting. You'd never find this out from reading Bernie Siegel [1986].

de Shazer: We didn't have enough cases, and I couldn't get the funding, but . . .

Hoyt: If there's one exception, one . . .

Weakland: It opens the door, but the people who control the money and things won't recognize that it opens the door.

de Shazer: They all had goals. They all went back to work. They all followed doctor's orders—until they stopped taking doctor's orders.

Hoyt: I saw a tape of Norman Cousins describing an interview with a woman who was eight years after her diagnosis. She was a nice, little, blue-haired old lady, very polite. And she said, "The doctor told me that I had six months to live." And Norman Cousins said, "And what did you say to him then?" And she said, "I told him to go fuck himself!" *[laughter]*

de Shazer: To me, that fits the stereotype of these successes. We had this one, her husband had a terminal diagnosis of some sort. So she had been

---

[6]Drawing on the work of Gergen and Gergen (1983, 1986—see Chapter 6, this volume), in *Putting Difference to Work* de Shazer (1991, p. 92) describes three narrative types: (1) *progressive* narratives that justify the conclusion that process is being made toward goals, (2) *stabilizing* narratives that justify the conclusion that life is unchanging, and (3) *digressive* (or *regressive*) narratives that justify the conclusion that life is moving away from goals.

nursing him. And then she got her terminal diagnosis. And she said to the doctor, "I'm going to outlive that son-of-a-bitch." And she did . . . by 15 years. *[laughter]* Or another one of these. She was lying in the hospital and had just gotten this terminal diagnosis. And the Cancer Institute people come in and say, "I'm sure you're wondering, `Why me?'" And the woman says, "No, actually, I'm not. Why not me?"

Weakland: Because it makes exactly the same sort of logical sense.

Hoyt: Yeah. I see taking history as being very destructive, most of the time. That is, so many people look at the past, and it's problem talk. The emphasis is on history and diagnosis of problems, rather than the future or the resources.

Weakland: I've been more and more convinced that every one of these things is quite unique.

Hoyt: Other than the money, what's the biggest impediment? How do you get people to make the shift, get mental health professionals to see it?

de Shazer: Well, I think that I have a somewhat facetious answer and that is that they're not "mental health," they're "mental illness" professionals. It's not a mental health industry; it's a mental illness industry.

Weakland: Yes.

de Shazer: We're in doublespeak.

Hoyt: Yes.

de Shazer: But I'm rather puzzled by this in some ways.

Weakland: Would part of that be that people, therefore, that get into it, by and large need dependents?

de Shazer: I think they need to see themselves as being wrapped up in something important.

Weakland: Certainly, one line of that is, "Those poor, damaged people need me."

de Shazer: Right.

Hoyt: Meaning, "and I'm not one of them."

Weakland: That, too.

Hoyt: And, "I'm different. I'm one of the healthy, wise ones."

Weakland: Yeah. "Even if I was one before, now I have surmounted that and can bring help to them."

de Shazer: What I also think is involved, on another level entirely, is the misapplication of the scientific metaphor to this field. I don't know why Freud abandoned other metaphors. But I've been reading Freud. In his 1915 "Introductory Lectures on Psycho-Analysis," Freud says, "The only thing there is, is the talk between doctor and patient." That's the only thing there is. That's all psychoanalysis is. Then he forgot that by the end of the third page, but he talked about that for several paragraphs.[7]

Weakland: It might have changed the course of history.

de Shazer: So it was becoming medical, becoming scientific—to me, in an inappropriate way, because that science then got captured by this positivistic mode of science, which we now call "science," which is a very small part of something that might be called science. Science was quite different 200 years ago. And, in our world, research has narrowed down to this A versus B business. And all that complicates the picture.

Weakland: By and large, I have a strong impression that it is only people like psychologists and sociologists who are concerned to be "scientific." Scientists aren't concerned about this. They go ahead and do their work.

Hoyt: They're interested in answers.

Weakland: They're interested in problems and answers, and maybe even in procedures, but they don't sit around thinking about "scientific."

de Shazer: Right.

Weakland: They don't seem to be worried about it.

de Shazer: Yeah. But it becomes necessary to worry about it if you have a misapplied model. So if you are applying some theory of oranges, and you have apples in your hand, then you've got to really worry about your theory, you see.

Hoyt: Let me stay with this idea. In training people, what stumbling blocks do you see people having in learning to be solution-focused?

Weakland: Are we getting fresh people or trained, already "properly" trained people?

Hoyt: What are the stumbling blocks with each of those two?

Weakland: Getting fresh people, it's a helluva lot easier.

de Shazer: Yeah, usually. I can train an engineer in a relatively short period of time, or a computer scientist.

Hoyt: So what's the baggage that "mental illness" professionals need to let go of?

---

[7]Freud's words (1915/1961, p. 17): "Nothing takes place in a psycho-analytic treatment but an interchange of words . . . the patient talks . . . the doctor listens. . . . Words were originally magic and to this day words have retained much of their ancient magical power. By words one person can make another blissfully happy or drive him to despair. . . . Words provoke affects and are in general the means of mutual influence among men. Thus we shall not depreciate the use of words in psychotherapy and we shall be pleased if we can listen to the words that pass between the analyst and his patient."

Weakland: I'd say that, just to begin with, there's a body of "knowledge" and a point of view that goes along with it, both of which have been acquired at considerable cost and, therefore, people have got a large investment in it.[8]

de Shazer: And people don't, we haven't trained ourselves to pay attention to what works.

Weakland: That is true.

de Shazer: And even people who have been in the field for a long time and have lots of "experience" get married to their theories, as we all do. But they won't pay attention to what works. Even stuff they do. So I think that what's really difficult, to me, with the older, more experienced practitioners, usually, is that they know all this stuff about what works but they don't know they know it. And they get hung up on looking at what doesn't work. It's good to know what doesn't work, but it's really helpful to know what does.

Hoyt: I think this may be a benefit of this managed-care movement that's come in—even though it has some problems, there is the idea of accountability [Hoyt, 1995]. They're not going to pay therapists for long, inefficient treatment. In some way, people are going to have to start looking at what works and what doesn't work. Even if all the altruistic reasons don't motivate people, being told, "We're only going to pay you if it works," may bring people around.

de Shazer: Judgments of what works are good. Who's making the judgments? I hope it's the clients.

Hoyt: I hope so. That's a good point.

de Shazer: I think we have enough evidence from various research projects that therapists are very bad judges of what works. You contributed to that literature and so have I.

Weakland: That's the other end of the thing I'm talking about. It's, "We know better than they do."

Hoyt: I was actually the principal investigator on the single-session therapy project with Moshe Talmon and Bob Rosenbaum [Hoyt, Rosenbaum, & Talmon, 1992; Rosenbaum, Hoyt, & Talmon, 1990; Talmon, 1990]. And we asked people, "In terms of the problem that you came in

---

[8]In his essay "Myths about Brief Therapy; Myths of Brief Therapy," Weakland (1990) describes some of the assumptions and belief systems that constrain practice and often promote unnecessary complexity. In a related vein, Hoyt (1985, 1990, 1995) has discussed some of the factors—including the belief that "more is better," theoretical obligations, financial payoffs, emotional entanglements, and reactance against being required to work briefly—that may interfere with efficient practice.

with, are you satisfied or unsatisfied? What do you see as different?" And so it was really client-centered, rather than us giving a rating.

Weakland: That's what makes the difference.

de Shazer: It's really amazing to think that you have to ask the customer about whether he got what he wanted or not.

Weakland: Just within the last six months, I've seen a flyer come from some analytic-connected institution in the [San Francisco] Bay Area, in which one of the workshops is titled—let's see how close I can reproduce it—"Resolving the Problem of Desire for Early Termination."

Hoyt: I saw that, too.

Weakland: It's dealing with a problem that clients have without even knowing they have it, and it's important to cure that one, or nothing else can be cured.

Hoyt: It's to keep them in.

de Shazer: Must prevent "flight into health," because they're flying around there with their eyes closed, and they never know what they're going to run into!

Hoyt: Do you notice any gender differences? In your clinic, do women want longer or do men want longer therapy?

Weakland: Oh, I've noticed gender differences everywhere.

de Shazer: My father told me all about that. He still notices and he's 85!

Weakland: My father didn't tell me a thing, but I notice some myself.

Hoyt: People have come up to me at workshops and said—I've heard this on several occasions—"Brief therapy is more of a masculine energy or a male endeavor. It's fixing things. It's problem-solving. It's not relationship and nurturing and holding and unfolding."

Weakland: And you're asking us questions about what's the difficulty in getting people trained in working this way?

de Shazer: You've got your answer. Just like every client, you've got your answer already.

Weakland: My God, we've got all this garbage, and they're acting like it's serious.

Hoyt: I think it's a confusion of their interests and the client's interests.

de Shazer: I hear some of that sometimes, too. And I usually try to have a tape of Insoo [Berg—de Shazer's wife and colleague] along with me in my workshops. And she's pretty obviously different genderwise, if nothing else. And then they get a little puzzled by that, the people who ask this question, they get a little puzzled. And then they say after I've puzzled

them by showing Insoo's tapes, then they say, "What you two do doesn't even look like therapy."

Hoyt: So you've heard that too?

Weakland: I see people come up with all sorts of cockamamie ways of saying, "Can I somehow keep from having to take this seriously?" Which I assume means it's making some sense to them, but they're scared of it somehow.

de Shazer: That's a pretty common reaction, actually. When people watch our tapes, they frequently find what we do to be unbelievable. I always start my workshops with, "You've got to be skeptical. And you probably can't be more skeptical than I am, and I'm going to remind you to be skeptical, if anybody starts to go too far in the other direction." I always start with this. "If somebody had told me about this model 15 years ago, I would have called the men in the white coats. This can't work. And every day I'm surprised, but it does work. And I still am. It's not logical in some way."

Hoyt: I think the simpler you keep it, the more the client's resources can be utilized, and so it's ultimately respectful to let them access what they have.

Weakland: It's a helluva lot more respectful than knowing better than the client what ails them, which I think is the most basic comparison. And it's what the whole damn other psychiatric and psychotherapeutic scheme is based on.

Hoyt: What taught you this? Was there a moment when you got it?

Weakland: Jesus, how did I find that out? I think I found that out—I must have gotten primed some by Milton, but I didn't recognize it, and by getting tired by what I knew of psychodynamics. But I think what really did it for me was time with the early family therapists where we started out with something that we thought was new and different. And within five years, I was starting to read articles like "After Only a Year of Family Therapy, the Nature of the Problem Was Becoming Clarified." And I thought, Jesus Christ, we've gone and copied the worst thing about the analytic movement at several times their pace. And that's what pushed me toward brief therapy. And, in brief therapy, one of the main things was, "What's the present problem?" and stopping looking around and behind and under it and second guessing. That's the real thing. I think that's as close as I can come.

Hoyt: How would you contrast that to long-term therapy?

Weakland: The essence of long-term therapy is to create the illusion that you can make life not be one damn thing after another.

Hoyt: Steve, was there something where you got the power of cooperation, the power of empowerment?

de Shazer: I guess it was when we started to listen to the clients and take them seriously, actually. And that was the discovery at some point, and I don't know when it was anymore, but I know it dawned on us in about '82 or started to dawn on us.

Weakland: Let me interrupt one second. After he tells you this, you need to go back and ask him one thing, because he said something that sounded very plain and simple, but I think it's very complicated what it means.

Hoyt: Let him tell this, and then you ask him.

Weakland: I may forget it. But the phrase is, "Listen to the clients and take them seriously." So ask him about that later.

Hoyt: Continue.

de Shazer: Somewhere about '82, we started to—let's see, what was the word I want to use—*discipline* our observations around what clients were telling us were their criteria for improvement and success. And what they said was strikingly different from what even we, as brief therapists, thought it should be. And it was amazing, the "trivial" things they said made the difference sometimes, and that they weren't connected to whatever goddamn complaint they brought in. They'd list 12 criteria for measuring that things were better since the previous session, and 11 of them had nothing to do with the complaint. And it all seemed to me, up to that point, that the job of the therapist was the presenting problem and resolving that. That's the job. Plain and simple. Well, yeah, except if the client doesn't think it's resolved; in other words, it's not resolved. And the strangest things resolve "problems." They all fit the rule in that they're doing something different or at least seeing something different, which is doing something different.

Hoyt: We saw that in our single-session project, where not only did the main complaint problem get solved, but 60 or 70% of the patients also described what we called "ripple effects" with other problems clearing up or improving.

de Shazer: In our telephone calls to them later on, we found strikingly more oddball things that we couldn't possibly have predicted. And we learned that we couldn't predict anything.

Hoyt: Despite that, are there categories of patients that you've found your approach doesn't work with?

de Shazer: I wish there was a category like that.

Hoyt: Then you could predict it and say . . .

de Shazer: Then I'd have a project I could send John to work on. *[laughter]* John would love to have a project like this, wouldn't you? I would love to have a project like that. I would like to say, "This is a special category of something. And this is a 'something.'"

Hoyt: Anorexics or tall people or something.

de Shazer: Yeah, something that we could identify as a "something." And there seems to be no way to get at that. I have not found it in 25 years.

Hoyt: How about the category being people who have desire for long-term therapy or long-term relationship with the therapist—it may not be "therapy."

Weakland: Even that, I think if you assembled what you thought was a bunch of them and started to talk to them a little bit, you would probably find your category falling apart. Rather rapidly.

de Shazer: Yeah. We'd have more exceptions to the rule than examples of the rule. I think, for me anyway, our practice suggests that the sooner you can ask the miracle question,[9] the less likely you're going to get into that trouble. The sooner you can get an answer, of course.

Weakland: And the next thing you know, somebody is going to call up and immediately after they say "Brief Family Therapy Center," they're going to ask the miracle question.

de Shazer: Well, I don't think it'd work that way, because you have to respond properly. It's not the one step.

Weakland: He's still holding on to some threads of complexity.

Hoyt: When you say "respond properly," what's your thought behind that? Is there a certain thing that makes it "properly"?

de Shazer: No, it really depends on the client and what they're telling you. You have to respond properly for them. You have to take it seriously. There's a case I had recently, he's a borderline street person and long-

---

[9]The Miracle Question: "Suppose that one night, while you were asleep, there was a miracle and this problem was solved. How would you know? What would be different?" (de Shazer, 1988, p. 5) A number of other elegantly simple techniques designed to focus on the construction of useful solutions include the "Crystal Ball Technique" (de Shazer, 1985, pp. 81–92; after Erickson, 1954) which has patients visualize successful, complaint-free futures; and various "skeleton key" interventions, such as the "First Session Formula Task (de Shazer, 1985, p. 137), which tells patients: "Between now and the next time we meet, I would like you to observe, so that you can describe to me next time, what happens in your [family, life, marriage, relationship] that you want to continue to have happen." Rather than tailoring each intervention to the particular client, a generic or invariant task is assigned that paradoxically directs the client toward his/her/their own individual strength, success, and solution.

term drinker. And I asked him the miracle question. And we had this wonderful discussion for 25 minutes, and he sticks really, really nicely to the topic; what the miracle might be and what he might be doing the day after and all these other things. And I'm going with this and trying to expand it to his wife and so on. And then I asked him one of our scaling questions where a 10 stands for, "He'd do anything to get this miracle to happen" and a zero, "Well, if it happens, it happens." And I say, "Where are you on this?" And he says, "Oh, zero." That's when I said to myself, "Oh, no. Now what?"

Weakland: And he says, "Can't you give me a 0.5?" *[laughter]*

de Shazer: Right. Then he says he could not possibly stand the idea of winning $35 million in the lottery. $250,000, that he could handle. But not $35 million. He wouldn't know what the hell to do. So what's the first step? That "zero" meant something entirely different to him than it meant to me. "Oh, no, I'm not going to get my expectations that high." That's what that meant to him.

Weakland: "Well, suppose you woke up one morning and half a miracle would have happened while you were asleep. What would you notice? What would tell you that half a miracle had happened?"

de Shazer: Or, in another version, there was this guy in Leipzig recently— he was already in therapy—so I somehow got into asking him scaling questions starting with, "Are things better?" And we talked that around several times and using a scale from –10 to 0, he'd gotten up to –5 some- times. And we explored when they were. And then I asked the miracle question; he couldn't answer. He had no idea. And so I said, "Well, maybe this miracle brings you up to –5."

Hoyt: Brings you to where you are.

de Shazer: Well, he reached –5 once in a while. And he says, "Wow, yeah, and it also happens sometimes when . . . " And he went on to tell us about two more times in his life when he gets to –5. He describes his trip to Cologne, which was a wonderful place for him. He'd never been in the old west part of Germany. He'd never gotten out of the East Zone before in his life. And as he describes this, I say, "You know, –5 sounds an awful lot like 0 to me." Okay, so there's this half-miracle. Sounds good enough.

Hoyt: And he's happy?

de Shazer: Oh, yeah. He said he could stay at –5 forever and it would be okay.

Hoyt: You wanted me to ask about "listening to clients and taking them seriously."

Weakland: Yeah. I think that sounds very simple, but I don't think it is simple. I think we've made a beginning on that right here. I think it's a very complicated operation.

de Shazer: Yeah, it is. It's so easy to read into . . . you've got to watch out for this. People, therapists in particular, I guess, are taught to read between the lines . . .

Hoyt: "Listen with a third ear . . . "

de Shazer: Diagnosis, interpretation, understanding.

Weakland: "Perceptiveness."

de Shazer: Yeah. To me, however, the danger of reading between the lines is that there might be nothing there. So you've just got to listen to what the client says. So just stick on the lines of things. The client says that getting out of bed on the south side makes for a better day than getting out on the north side. Well then, goddammit, tell him to get out of bed on the south side. As crazy as it sounds.

Hoyt: If it works, don't fix it. Do more.

de Shazer: Yeah, do more of it. I had one sort of like that. He moved the bed over so he couldn't get out on the north side. He'd run into the wall trying to get out on the north side of the bed. That would be a different challenge to have, instead of a perceptivity training, to have a "simplicity training" or "beginner's mind"—a "denseness" training.

Hoyt: "Keep it simple."

de Shazer: "Stupidity training."[10]

---

[10]In an interview conducted elsewhere (Duvall & Beier, 1995, p. 72), Michael White and Insoo Berg had the following exchange while discussing a piece of solution-focused therapy work that Insoo had done:

White: I had a sense that you had taken in the complexity. And you had come out at the other end of that complexity with a message that was economical and, I think, quite profound. Now, how is it possible to share with the people who consult you about your work, how is it possible for them to know about that complexity that you are able to take in and somehow process and come out with the sort of messages that you do? My guess is the same about Steve's [de Shazer] work. From what I know of Steve, he's a philosopher and my guess is that he's able to grasp the complexities of the world, despite the fact that he represents himself as a minimalist therapist. I think that he's a minimalist in his message.

Berg: Yes.

White: But that message is informed by his grasp of the complexity.

Berg: Right.

White: Now that complexity, the grasp of that complexity, I don't think is possible without some consciousness of the sorts of issues that we're talking about here.

Berg: Right.

Hoyt: Maybe the fact that you weren't trained in psychology originally . . .

Weakland: That's a great help.

de Shazer: I think that my training in music helps.

Weakland: Ask him a little more about "taking it seriously," because I have this feeling that doesn't just mean one simple thing, that may mean maybe a lot of variations on that point. Taking it seriously. And I got your example; that's clear. But don't think it always means the side of the bed, that sort of thing.

de Shazer: Probably not.

Hoyt: What else would you think about "seriously"?

Weakland: Well, I think of an interview I had with a couple who came in to see me very concerned about their daughter who was anorexic. She was 30 years old, married with kids, but anorexic. They were very anxious about her, practically couldn't sit still. I had this one interview, after which I was going to be away the next week. Dick [Fisch] saw them the next week. I came back, and Dick started out telling about something disastrous, but he was putting me on. The truth of the matter was, they came in looking and sounding very, very different. And we were both up in the air about what the hell had happened. So I listened to the tape and I'd gone over it again since, and I had another interview with them. And the three sessions were all we had. We wouldn't have needed to have the third, really. So, I tried to figure out what the hell had happened in the interview that I had with them. Basically, I think all that happened was, or the main thing that happened was, I listened to them and I took it seriously, but I took it seriously in a certain way. I was clearly listening to and appreciating their concerns, but I wasn't getting excited. I think that's the main thing. There were a couple other things that went along with that like they'd been running around from one doctor to another. I suggested that "Certainly you may want to look for further doctors, but since the ones you've been finding have generally been unsatisfactory, you might want to give it a little more consideration before your next decision on a doctor for her." And I proposed that we could meet in two weeks, since I wouldn't be there, but if they wanted they could meet with somebody else, which was two steps more concretely of the same sort as my general behavior. And as far as I could see, that was it.

Hoyt: You took your sail out of their wind. *[laughter]*

Weakland: At least, I kept my wind out of their sail.

Hoyt: Yeah, okay. You didn't get on board and go with that problem.

Weakland: No. But at the same time I didn't tell them, "Look, folks, you're making too much out of it. Calm down," or any of that sort of shit.

de Shazer: Exactly. A counterexample of taking it seriously is when clients come in and tell you, "This is the problem. And it's a big, heavy, monstrous problem." To you, it looks trivial. And you go and tell these people about all these other people who have more problems, or bigger or more awful ones.

Weakland: Yeah. Yeah.

de Shazer: That's a counterexample.

Hoyt: "You think you've got a problem . . . "

de Shazer: Yeah. A client tells you they've got a problem, then they've got a problem, and you better take it seriously. You also better take it seriously if they tell you they ain't got a problem. That's the other part of it. He comes in and somebody sent him because he drinks too much. He says he doesn't drink too much or it's not a problem. Leave it alone. Take it seriously.[11]

Weakland: You're not going to deal with denial.

de Shazer: I'm going to deny the denial. You start to mess with that and you'll never work with him. Certainly, you'll never work with the drinking. If you help him get something out of therapy . . .

Hoyt: What I'm getting from what you're saying is it's best to accept that what the patient is communicating about is accurate. And it's our job to figure out what it's accurate about.[12]

Weakland: That's an interesting way of putting it, rather than converting them.

de Shazer: I'm not even sure about the last part . . . just, "it's accurate."

Hoyt: It's accurate.

de Shazer: Yeah. It's accurate. And that's all there is.

Hoyt: But if we're going to be of service to them, not just to take them seriously and listen, what do we add beyond listening?

de Shazer: The seriously. Taking them seriously. See, I think a lot of people listen, but they don't take them seriously.

Weakland: I think that's probably true.

de Shazer: For example, we recently heard a therapist [at the conference we were attending] who reported some nice stories. From the stories, it's clear the therapist listened. But from some of the instructions and steps that then got presented, it is clear the clients aren't being taken seriously.

---

[11]Solution-focused ways of working *with* the problem drinker are discussed at length in Berg and Miller (1992) and Berg and Reuss (1998).

[12]This is a paraphrase of a statement from Schnarch (1991, p. 344).

Weakland: Is it possible that, once again, maybe not as blatantly as some places, we've got a therapist who is doing one thing, and describing it quite differently?

de Shazer: My experience of this is, yeah, he does a marvelous job at storytelling, but the theory, the rule-making theory construction stuff is not his ballgame. He's telling us all these rules and steps and stuff he's never done.

Weakland: Okay, but what I'm saying is he doesn't have to tell us the rules one way or the other. What he ought to be telling us is how he does what he does.

de Shazer: I was thinking, sitting there, during a couple of these stories—show us two segments of videotape.

Hoyt: At least, let us decide what really happened rather than filtering it through a . . .

de Shazer: Or, at least, all the points could be made with two videos of about seven minutes each.

Weakland: You don't get either the appreciative audience nor the keynote speaker's fee for 15 minutes of videotape.

de Shazer: I know, that's why I don't get those jobs.

Weakland: I seldom get them either, partly because I get up there and I don't have any answers, and I'm struggling with questions in my mind. And I'm not "inspirational," as they say.

Hoyt: I think this touches on the "respectfully" and the "seriously," in a way. In the *Difference* [de Shazer, 1991, p. 33] book, you say, "The use of strategy and tactics, meant to suggest careful planning on the part of the therapist, implies at the very least that the therapist and the client are involved in a contest." And you, John, in your Foreword to the book, you stated your disagreement, saying: "At a specific level, I do not think that use of the term 'strategy' necessarily implies a contest between therapist and client; indeed, I would propose that de Shazer carries on his therapeutic conversations strategically" [Weakland, 1991, p. viii]. What's up?

Weakland: Simple. My view is somewhat different, at least from the views that Steve expressed there. My view is expanded a little bit more in the paper at Tulsa last summer [Weakland, 1993], in which I talk about what I mean by "strategic."[13]

---

[13]In his paper "Conversation—But What Kind?" Weakland (1993, p. 143) wrote: "Just as one cannot *not* communicate, one cannot *not* influence. Influence is inherent in all human interaction. We are bound to influence our clients, and they are bound to influence us. The only choice is between doing so without reflection, or even with attempted denial, and doing so deliberately and responsibly. Clients come seeking change which they could not

de Shazer: There's no disagreement with what you mean. It's the word. It's the extra baggage the word carries with it that I'm objecting to.

Hoyt: The word "strategic"?

de Shazer: Yeah.

Hoyt: What is the extra baggage?

de Shazer: It's the military metaphor that's attached to it.

Weakland: Oh, but I cannot be responsible for what a bunch of other people are attaching to things always.

de Shazer: It comes with it automatically. That's why I like the word "purposeful," rather than "strategic."

Hoyt: Were you aware of the military . . . ?

Weakland: I was not aware, if that is what he is referring to.

de Shazer: That's what I'm referring to. Trying to refer to.

Weakland: Well, it wasn't referred to sufficiently clearly in that quotation.

de Shazer: That could be.

Hoyt: You said a "contest" in strategy. Do you mean a "combat" in the way of military?

de Shazer: Yeah, contest, military.

Hoyt: It's like when people talk about their "therapeutic armamentarium."

Weakland: I never do that.

Hoyt: Other people do.

Weakland: Well, what am I going to do then with all of the words that formerly were good words and people have done similar things with them so that they all aren't worth a shit anymore?

de Shazer: You have to keep making up new ones.

Weakland: Then they'll do the same thing again.

Hoyt: It's hard to be politically correct in these times.

---

achieve on their own; expertise in influencing them to change usefully seems to us the esseence of the therapist's job. Therefore, we give much thought—guided, of course, by what a client does and says—to almost every aspect of treatment: To whom we will see in any given session, to the timing of sessions, to what suggestions we will offer as to new thoughts and actions, to responses we make to clients' reports of progress or difficulties encountered; and especially not just to the content of what we say, but to how we will phrase it. This strategic emphasis, however, does not mean that we propose or favor any arrangement in which a therapist has all the power, knowledge, control, and activity, while the patient is just a passive object of therapeutic actions—if indeed this were possible, which is very doubtful."

de Shazer: We want to be politically incorrect.

Weakland: I'm going to have to move to France and put it up as a project to the French Academy.

de Shazer: We have always this competition of winning/losing that gets attached to "strategy," because of this, the implication of underhanded dealings, the backroom dealings, the dirty guys behind the mirror, and so on. Which I think all come out of this military "strategic" word.

Weakland: That's where I would disagree. I think they are there, and I think they get attached to that word, but I don't think they come out of it. I think they come out of something much deeper, which is that therapists want to have power without acknowledging it, influence without acknowledging it. They want to be in there, superior and influential, with perfectly clean hands. And as long as that's the case, they will corrupt the hell out of any word you use.

de Shazer: Yeah, probably. That's probably true. And it's probably true with every word, absolutely. So if the word is easier to hear—I'm using the word "purposeful"—it's less distracting than the word "strategic." When I stopped using the word "strategic" and started using the word "purposeful," I got into less problems with my audience.

Weakland: Okay.

Hoyt: It's more "user friendly." It doesn't set off the "Is this manipulation? Is this somebody getting over on someone?"

de Shazer: Right. It's clearly manipulation. It's got purpose behind it.

Hoyt: Okay. In terms of listening to them seriously, that's what I was trying to get at. The purpose is to take them seriously, but the purpose is still to have influence?

de Shazer: No, the purpose is to reach their goal. And it's therapists . . .

Hoyt: Is this one of those kinds of binds that we started talking about, like connection versus independence? It's like in one way, we're empowering them, but we're influencing them.

Weakland: We care about influence. Yeah, but that's okay. This is the old hypnotic argument, where on the one side you have all those people who say, "You hypnotize somebody, you make them dependent." And on the other side is, "It depends on what you do with the hypnosis with the subject." You may use it to empower them. You may make them dependent, but it's not inherent in "hypnosis." Just as there's nothing inherent in "influence." It depends on what kind of influence it is.

de Shazer: There's always influence.

Weakland: Sure.

de Shazer: You can't not influence.

Hoyt: Is there an inherent language paradox here? To "influence someone" implies having a power over them, but you want to influence someone to be more powerful.

de Shazer: I think that in any conversation, everybody is influencing everybody else.

Weakland: Always.

de Shazer: And "power" is a bad concept.

Weakland: I think "power" is a bad concept because it is generally not very useful. But I don't think that it is an idea that will corrupt the world like Bateson seemed to think toward the end.

de Shazer: No, I agree that the idea of unilateral control is not possible.

Weakland: No, that's true.

de Shazer: Stalin proved that.

Hoyt: But constructing a reality that's going to make a difference is different than power; it's constructing.

de Shazer: And it takes at least two people to construct a reality. One person, by himself, might construct this reality, but it would probably be a psychotic one. It takes two to make it a viable reality.

Hoyt: If you mean a social reality.

de Shazer: Yeah.

Weakland: Is there any other?

de Shazer: There is no other.

Hoyt: Semantically, there's not. But what I do in my head is real in my head, to me.

de Shazer: Yeah. But I don't know about. . . . See, that's the whole point.

Hoyt: You know the one about the three baseball umpires that are disputing? This is my favorite constructivist story. The first one says, "I call 'em as I see 'em." And the second guy says, "Well, I call them as they are." And the third guy says, "They ain't nothing until I call 'em!" And that's, I think, what we're saying. Until we call them, it's not. Things come into reality by being said.

de Shazer: Right. Wittgenstein goes into all this stuff about the slipperiness of a private language. You can't depend on it. You can't count on it. You can't count on anything inside until you bring it out, test it out. Then, as soon as you do that, you're changing it.

Hoyt: Where is our field going? Do you have any prediction? Any sense of it?

de Shazer: I'm no good at predicting. I know that. I've proved that to myself beyond a shadow of a doubt.

Weakland: I may make an attempt at describing where it is, if I get geared up between now and April, or at least where I see it is. Where it's going, I don't think I'd try that.

Hoyt: Where do you think it is?

Weakland: Well, in terms of some things we know and some confidences we have, at the best, it is a helluva long way from the old days; but in terms of how it has become bureaucratized, stupefied, taken over, the extent to which people are willing to accept, both practically and intellectually, a sort of second or third place role for it, it's gone way the hell downhill. People work in a hospital at a level more or less that of a nurse in relation to the doctor, that sort of thing, when it should be changing the fundamentals of the whole field.

de Shazer: I think that we see some . . . there is some more, maybe a warped picture. There's more change to the whole field in Europe than there has been in the United States. There's more influence of systems theory in Europe. They take it a little more seriously. Well, like, family therapy became a method in the United States. Brief therapy is a method on the menu.

Weakland: I see the main change having taken place when things just got far enough so you could begin to sell family therapy and make some sort of a living at it.

Hoyt: That was the beginning of . . .

Weakland: That was the beginning of, "Let's see where we can make a quick sale. Let's `establish standards,' certifications, freeze them." I mean, once you've established them, you've largely frozen them, whether you do that deliberately or not.[14]

de Shazer: Narrow the pool of potential influence in the field, by saying, "Well, you are left-handed, you can't come in. We don't allow left-handed people any more."

Weakland: And worse yet is if you're left-minded.

de Shazer: Yeah.

---

[14]In a discussion conducted elsewhere (Hoyt, 1997, p. 198), Jay Haley made a similar observation:

Haley: I don't think this is a good time to start being a first-generation therapist. When I went into therapy, you could hang out a shingle. There was no licensing. All you needed was referrals and the people paid you. It was so simple then compared with how complex it sounds today.

Weakland: Say a little more about what goes on in Europe. Usually, all I hear is what I hear from Paul [Watzlawick], and mainly what Paul will say is, "A great deal is going on that you should know about." We say, "We're open." Then he says, "But you don't read German."

de Shazer: There's lots going on in Germany that nobody knows about. I think that there's more within the various mental health professions. There's more influence of systemic thinking, rather than in family therapy being one approach on the menu. There's less rigidity about some of these things. I have to go in another direction somewhat. In the United States, I think that brief therapists are still seen as a radical nut fringe. On one hand and simultaneously on the other, we're both archconservative and archradical. And family therapy has become this something that is organized and run by this organization over there. And hypnosis is organized and run by this organization over here. And somehow these two are different. I don't know how, but anyway. In Europe, although they have separate societies—there's an Ericksonian Society and so on and so on—there seems to be a wider variety of people who are in these various societies, and they don't seem to have any feuds (this is a general rule; there are exceptions) the same as they are in the United States about territory and right and wrong. There are some other feuds, but they're different. There are some right and wrong difficulties, but there's no such thing, for instance, as a one-model allegiance. It's an allegiance to a way of thinking.

Hoyt: Maybe that's even a reflection of multiculturalism, all the different languages and . . .

de Shazer: Well, I can just stick within Germany and say that. So I don't know that it's that. I think that they take the idea of general systems theory more seriously. Not completely, but more seriously. And I think John and I are pretty radical on that. We probably took it more seriously than most people, word for word sometimes.

Hoyt: Is there something about "American character," to use that broad stereotype, that makes people here want simple answers or ten-step programs? Or 12-step? [laughter]

de Shazer: Or 12-step or 5-step. I'm not sure I'd go that direction in describing the difference. I think that our psychotherapy business became overattached to the medical establishment. Part of it is that, and then it becomes this organization stuff. [Murray] Bowen was right. We shouldn't have organized at all. If nothing else, one thing I've always agreed with him about, maybe the only thing I've agreed with Bowen about, is we shouldn't organize this field. Don't do it! And he was saying—well, I don't know when he started saying that—but the first time I heard it, I agreed completely. Don't do it! Don't do it!

Hoyt: I don't know how we're going to take it back. I think, if anything, we're getting more organized in the managed-care movement and the licensing bureaus and the different schools of therapy and the certification and education business.

de Shazer: And it's all the same kind of thing. And the Europeans, they like to have these little certificates, too. But it's educational, rather than job training.

Weakland: Now, why are the psychiatrists in Europe doing therapy instead of giving pills and doing esoteric biochemical and brain anatomy research?

de Shazer: I'm not sure. Obviously, it's not all of them, but more than I meet here in the United States. I think they see themselves as doctors, and they're healing. I suspect medical training is different. These guys all, the ones I'm thinking of in particular, see themselves as healing, and they're afraid of medicines. They stay away from pills.

Hoyt: In the front of [Furman and Ahola's] *Solution Talk,* Carlos Sluzki [1992] writes a Foreword, and he has sort of a warning. He talks about, if you really take the solution approach, how radical it is. He puts it in the tradition of antipsychiatry and R. D. Laing and David Cooper.

de Shazer: I'm anti antipsychiatry, too.

Hoyt: But he says, if you really take this seriously, it's going to raise hell in traditional institutions. How you talk about people, what you chart, what you do; the whole egalitarian versus authoritarian structure breaks.

de Shazer: I agree completely.

Weakland: Oh, yeah, if you take our version seriously, that would happen.

de Shazer: Any version.

Weakland: And frankly, I think that's what should happen.

Hoyt: I wanted to ask you just a couple more questions. My question is, What's your cutting edge? What are you interested in now? What are you investigating? What's got you excited?

Weakland: Not a helluva lot, to tell you the truth. I'm tired. I've been seeing things going the way we've been talking about for many a year, and I've been putting my oar in to try to see things go differently. And I feel like I've been swimming upstream against a current that's probably faster than my stroke is.

Hoyt: What would you want people to take from your work?

Weakland: What would I want them to take from my work? I think that's fairly simple. Which is you look around the world, try to understand behavior, look at how people are dealing with each other first, and don't get away from that until you've given it a good look.

de Shazer: Don't let the theory get in the way. Theories will blind you.

Weakland: Also, don't let the theory that "everything is individual" get in your way. Don't let the theory that "everything is genetic" get in your way. Look at what the hell people are doing right here and now where you can look at them.

de Shazer: Don't even let the theory of "everything is not individual" get in your way.

Weakland: Okay. Fair enough.

de Shazer: It might be individual this time.

Hoyt: What in Zen they would say, "Have a beginner's mind."

de Shazer: Yeah.

Weakland: I think this emphasis is still fair because it is very plain that the medical way of looking and the individual psychology way of looking have gotten tremendous emphasis and support compared to anything that's gone with looking at the way people deal with each other on all fronts.

de Shazer: Absolutely. They also say in Zen, "Before enlightenment, a mountain is a mountain. After enlightenment, a mountain is a mountain."

Hoyt: What mountains are you climbing?

de Shazer: John's swimming this river; I'm climbing a mountain.

Weakland: He's got a better deal. Unless it's a new volcano, that mountain isn't rising up as he's climbing.

de Shazer: But some of the side trails are so interesting.

Weakland: That's always a possibility.

de Shazer: And you go back down to see something.

Hoyt: There's also the pleasure in climbing, not just to get to the top.

de Shazer: And I like to take a walk around it now and then. I don't have any particular place I'm going.

Weakland: I think you asked the question. I'm not excited about this, but there's a couple things I'd like to see happen. I would like to see a few more young people interested in things I'm interested in that would be likely to hang around our Institute. And I would like to see three, two, or even one person on our board of directors who would read that little piece by Carlos [Sluzki] and be in favor of it. I might think there might be some future in the Institute.

de Shazer: You know, 22 years ago, we could have had a Brief Therapy conference in Palo Alto, and we could have all fit into a VW bus. We'd need a little bigger bus now. It's grown faster than the population growth curve. But I think it's important for the field for there to be some outside to the field. And I think you've done it and our group has done it. We've been outside and inside simultaneously. We've been out in the margins. Not quite family therapy. And we're not quite brief therapy, MRI style, and you're not quite brief therapy, Milwaukee style. We're sort of always around the edge of things. Well, Insoo says I'm completely untrained, which is true. And John's completely untrained.

Weakland: Well, yeah.

de Shazer: And the field has to keep somebody out there; there has to be an outside, somebody in the margins. Family therapy would not have been an idea, much less a fact, if there had not been some outsiders. You, Jay [Haley], Gregory [Bateson]—untrained therapists.

Hoyt: Do you see these outsiders today?

de Shazer: Well, they're being legislated out of existence.

Weakland: Because they're trying, certainly working very hard, giving them a bad time, if there are any out there.

de Shazer: I'm looking for them. You've got to get those people. You've got to keep getting them in somehow, so they can take a look at things. If you legislate everything and train everybody in the orthodoxy, then you're closing out. You've got to kill the field in order to save it, so to speak.

Weakland: This is one time I think that might be apt.

Hoyt: Are you writing another book?

de Shazer: Am I writing a book? Yeah, sure. I'm always writing a book.

Hoyt: What's your next thought? What's it on?

de Shazer: I have no idea.

Weakland: He'll tell you that after it gets written.

de Shazer: Yeah, when it's done. My basic writing method is to sit down and write, and it's free form, so to speak, in my own way of doing free form. And then I edit. Chop, chop, cut, paste. So I really don't know where it's going.

Weakland: By God, that explains some things.

Hoyt: You'll see when you get there. You may have a solution without knowing the problem. What would you want people to take out of your work, Steve, if you wrote no more?

de Shazer: I know what I don't want, and that's for anybody to develop some sort of rigid orthodoxies. I'm afraid of that. I'm always afraid of that. For me, it's a big point of concern. That there's a right way to do this and this. And to see my descriptions—and they've done this to me; I've probably done this to myself—to see my descriptions as prescriptions. So what I'd like, I suppose, is what I said earlier about listen and take them seriously. The "take them seriously" part. That's what I want people to take out of it is to take it seriously. And I suppose that the break between "problems" and "solutions," certainly that part. But I ain't dead yet.

Weakland: Well, I'll tell you what I'd like to leave as a message: "Stay curious." And everybody is rushing like hell to try to get away from that.[15]

de Shazer: Or, to put it another way, if the choice is between the therapist or the client being stupid, it should be the therapist. *[laughter]*

Hoyt: Well, gentlemen, I think we've done it. I thank you both.

References

Bateson, G., Jackson, D. D., Haley, J., & Weakland, J. H. (1956). Toward a theory of schizophrenia. *Behavioral Science, 1,* 251–264.

Berg, I. K., & Miller, S. D. (1992). *Working with the Problem Drinker: A Solution-Focused Approach.* New York: Norton.

Berg, I.K., & Reuss, N.H. (1998). *Solutions Step by Step: A Substance Abuse Treatment Manual.* New York: Norton.

Cade, B. (1995). John H. Weakland (1919-1995): An obituary. *Journal of Systemic Therapies, 14*(3), i–iii.

de Shazer, S. (1982). *Patterns of Brief Family Therapy: An Ecosystemic Approach.* New York: Guilford.

de Shazer, S. (1985). *Keys to Solution in Brief Therapy.* New York: Norton.

de Shazer, S. (1988). *Clues: Investigating Solutions in Brief Therapy.* New York: Norton.

de Shazer, S. (1991). *Putting Difference to Work.* New York: Norton.

de Shazer, S. (1994a). *Words Were Originally Magic.* New York: Norton.

de Shazer, S. (1994b). Essential, non-essential: Vive la différence. In J.K. Zeig (Ed.), *Ericksonian Methods: The Essence of the Story* (pp. 240–253). New York: Brunner/Mazel.

de Shazer, S., Berg, I., Lipchik, E., Nunnally, E., Molnar, A., Gingerich, W., & Weiner-Davis, M. (1986). Brief therapy: Focused solution development. *Family Process, 25,* 207–222.

---

[15]In closing his paper, "Erickson's Essence: A Personal View," Weakland (1994, p. 291) made some observations that also might be applied to himself: "In the end, I think the essence of Milton Erickson's work is based on his personal qualities. So I would like to conclude by pointing to three such qualities that I see as fundamental to all he did. This requires going beyond the usual bounds of professional discussion. However, I hope we might follow his example somehow, even though I cannot say how these qualities might be taught to others, nor even how he acquired these qualities himself.

"First, Erickson was and remained a man with a great curiosity about life; he wanted to look at and reflect on everything that came into his view. Second, he had a wide and deep sense of humor, which I see as central for his ability to combine engagement and detachmnet even in very difficult and distressing situations. Finally, and I believe most important of all, a point that needs no documentation: In both his professional and personal life, Milton Erickson was a man of great courage."

Dolan, Y. M. (1991). *Resolving Sexual Abuse: Solution-Focused Therapy and Ericksonian Hypnosis for Adult Survivors*. New York: Norton.

Duvall, J. D., & Beier, J. M. (1995). Passion, commitment, and common sense: A unique discussion with Insoo Kim Berg and Michael White. *Journal of Systemic Therapies, 14*(3), 57–80.

Dyson, F. J. (1988). *Infinite in All Directions*. New York: Harper & Row.

Erickson, M. H. (1954). Pseudo-orientation in time as a hypnotic procedure. *Journal of Clinical and Experimental Hypnosis, 2, 261–283*.

Fisch, R., Weakland, J. H., & Segal, L. (1983). *The Tactics of Change: Doing Therapy Briefly*. San Francisco: Jossey-Bass.

Freud, S. (1961) Introductory lectures on psycho-analysis. In J. Strachey (Ed. and Trans.), *The Standard Edition of the Complete Psychological Works of Sigmund Freud* (Vol. 15–16, pp. 3–463). London: Hogarth Press. (original work published 1915)

Gergen, K. J., & Gergen, M. J. (1983). Narratives of the self. In T. R. Sabin & K. E. Scheibe (Eds.), *Studies in Social Identity*. New York: Praeger.

Gergen, K. J., & Gergen, M. J. (1986). Narratives form and the construction of psychological science. In T. R. Sabin (Ed.), *Narrative Psychology: The Storied Nature of Human Conduct*. New York: Praeger.

Haley, J. (1969). The art of psychoanalysis. In *The Power Tactics of Jesus Christ and Other Essays*. New York: Avon Books.

Haley, J. (Ed.), (1985). *Conversations with Milton H. Erickson, M.D. (Vols. 1-3)*. New York: Triangle Press.

Herr, J. J., & Weakland, J. H. (1979). *Counseling Elders and Their Families: Practical Techniques for Applied Gerontology*. New York: Springer.

Hoyt, M. F. (1985). Therapist resistances to short-term dynamic psychotherapy. *Journal of the American Academy of Psychoanalysis, 13*, 93–112. Reprinted in M.F. Hoyt, *Brief Therapy and Managed Care: Readings for Contemporary Practice*. San Francisco: Jossey-Bass, 1995.

Hoyt, M. F. (1990). On time in brief therapy. In R. A. Wells & V. J. Giannetti (Eds.), *Handbook of the Brief Psychotherapies* (pp. 115–143). New York: Plenum. Reprinted in M.F. Hoyt, *Brief Therapy and Managed Care: Readings for Contemporary Practice*. San Francisco: Jossey-Bass, 1995.

Hoyt, M. F. (1995). *Brief Therapy and Managed Care: Readings for Contemporary Practice*. San Francisco: Jossey-Bass.

Hoyt, M.F. (1997). Unmuddying the waters: A "common ground" conference. *Journal of Systemic Therapies, 16*(3), 195-200. Reprinted in M.F. Hoyt, *Some Stories are Better than Others: Doing What Works in Brief Therapy and Managed Care*. Philadelphia: Brunner/Mazel, 2000.

Hoyt, M. F., Rosenbaum, R., & Talmon, M. (1992). Planned single-session psychotherapy. In S. H. Budman, M. F. Hoyt, & S. Friedman (Eds.), *The First Session in Brief Therapy* (pp. 59–86). New York: Guilford.

Malan, D. H. (1976). *The Frontier of Brief Psychotherapy*. New York: Plenum.

Rosenbaum, R., Hoyt, M. F., & Talmon, M. (1990). The challenge of single-session therapies: Creating pivotal moments. In R. A. Wells & V. J. Giannetti (Eds.), *Handbook of the Brief Psychotherapies* (pp. 165–189). New York: Plenum. Reprinted in M.F. Hoyt, *Brief Therapy and Managed Care: Readings for Contemporary Practice*. San Francisco: Jossey-Bass, 1995.

Schnarch, D. M. (1991). *Constructing the Sexual Crucible: An Integration of Sexual and Marital Therapy*. New York: Norton.

Siegel, B. S. (1986). *Love, Medicine and Miracles*. New York: Harper & Row.

Sluzki, C. E. (1992). Foreword. In B. Furman & T. Ahola, *Solution Talk: Hosting Therapeutic Conversations* (pp. v–ix). New York: Norton.

Talmon, M. (1990). *Single Session Therapy*. San Francisco: Jossey-Bass.

Watzlawick, P., Weakland, J. H., & Fisch, R. (1974). *Change: Principles of Problem Formation and Problem Resolution.* New York: Norton.

Weakland, J. H. (1990). Myths about brief therapy; myths of brief therapy. In J. K. Zeig & S. G. Gilligan (Eds.), *Brief Therapy: Myths, Methods, and Metaphors* (pp. 100–107). New York: Brunner/Mazel.

Weakland, J. H. (1991). Foreword. In S. de Shazer, *Putting Difference to Work* (pp. vii–ix). New York: Norton.

Weakland, J. H. (1993). Conversation—But what kind? In S. G. Gilligan & R. Price (Eds.), *Therapeutic Conversations* (pp. 136–145). New York: Norton.

Weakland, J. H. (1994). Erickson's essence: A personal view. In J. K. Zeig (Ed.), *Ericksonian Methods: The Essence of the Story* (pp. 287–291). New York: Brunner/Mazel.

Weakland, J.H., Fisch, R., Watzlawick, P., & Bodin, A. (1974). Brief therapy: Focused problem resolution. *Family Process*, 13, 41–68.

Zeig, J.K. (Ed.) (1994). *Ericksonian Methods: The Essence of the Story.* New York: Brunner/Mazel.

Welcome To Possibilityland:
A Conversation with Bill O'Hanlon

Perhaps best known as the senior author of the classic *In Search of Solutions: A New Direction in Psychotherapy* (O'Hanlon & Weiner-Davis, 1989), Bill O'Hanlon is affiliated with Possibilities in Santa Fe, New Mexico. A peripatetic and much-acclaimed workshop presenter, O'Hanlon is also an accomplished songwriter and guitarist, avid computer techie, and Milton Erickson's former gardener.

O'Hanlon's great energy, enthusiasm, and evolving therapeutic interest and expertise are reflected in the range of his many publications, including *Taproots: Underlying Principles of Milton Erickson's Therapy and Hypnosis* (O'Hanlon, 1987); *Shifting Contexts: The Generation of Effective Psychotherapy* (O'Hanlon & Wilk, 1987); *An Uncommon Casebook: The Complete Clinical Work of Milton H. Erickson, M.D.* (O'Hanlon & Hexum, 1990); *Rewriting Love Stories: Brief Marital Therapy* (Hudson & O'Hanlon, 1991); *Solution-Oriented Hypnosis: An Ericksonian Approach* (O'Hanlon & Martin, 1992); *Love Is a Verb* (O'Hanlon & Hudson, 1995); *A Brief Guide to Brief Therapy* (Cade & O'Hanlon, 1993); *A Field Guide to PossibilityLand: Possibility Therapy Methods* (O'Hanlon & Beadle, 1994); and *Evolving Possibilities: Selected Papers of Bill O'Hanlon* (O'Hanlon & Bertolino, 1999). He has also produced a computer program, *Brief Therapy Coach* (O'Hanlon & Schultheis, 1993) and a videotape, *Escape from DepressoLand: Brief Therapy of Depression* (O'Hanlon, 1993a). His recent books, *Invitation to Possibility-Land: An In-*

Originally appeared, with changes, in M.F. Hoyt (Ed.) (1996), *Constructive Therapies, Volume 2* (pp. 87–123). New York: Guilford Press. Used with permission.

tensive Teaching Seminar with Bill O'Hanlon (Bertolino & O'Hanlon, 1999; also see Bertolino & Caldwell, 1999), *Solution-Oriented Therapy for Chronic and Severe Mental Illness* (Rowan & O'Hanlon, 1998), and *Do One Thing Different: And Other Uncommonly Sensible Solutions to Life's Persistent Problems* (1999) report some of the latest refinements in his continuing search for what works.

The following conversation took place in Orlando, Florida, on February 26, 1994, where we were serving as faculty members at the New England Educational Institute Winter Symposium:

Hoyt: What's the distinction between *brief therapy, solution-oriented therapy,* and *possibility therapy*?

O'Hanlon: There's a whole bunch of types of brief therapy. *Brief therapy* is pretty clearly therapy that's focused, and the therapist helps provide the focus. It's usually focused on problem resolution, and it's goal-oriented. There are lots of theories—psychodynamic, solution-oriented, problem-focused, lots of family therapy approaches, systemic approaches, interactional approaches—that one can use to do brief therapy within that framework. That's what most of the brief therapies have in common. They are problem-driven; they are focused on resolving the presented problem that the person brought in; they are goal-oriented; and the therapist is responsible for creating and maintaining those focuses.

Solution-oriented therapy is more than a brand of brief therapy or just therapy that tends to be brief. It's different. Solution-oriented therapy has mainly a focus on the present towards the future, and not so much a focus on the past. It's focused on what people do well and their resources. It comes out of an Ericksonian bias that people have resources and competency, [and] that there are ways to deliberately focus them on those resources and access those resources and evoke them during treatment.[1] The therapist can actively do that, and the therapist again actively creates and maintains a focus on the present towards the future and on resources and solutions—both past solutions, present resources and solutions, and future possibilities for solutions.[2]

---

[1] Erickson's words: "Patients have problems because their conscious programming has too severely limited their capacities. The solution is to help them break through the limitation of their conscious attitudes to free their unconscious potential for problem solving" (Erickson, Rossi, & Rossi, 1976, p. 18).

[2] Bertolino and O'Hanlon (1999, p. 30) write: "Steve de Shazer is considered the developer of solution-*focused* therapy, and Bill [O'Hanlon] is considered the codeveloper [see O'Hanlon & Weiner-Davis, 1989] of solution-*oriented* therapy. (Although it appears that a man named Don Norum was really the originator of solution-based therapies in 1978.) These two approaches are consistently lumped together and understood to be the same. However, this is a misperception as there are distinct differences between these approaches." O'Hanlon (1998, pp. 138–139) further explicates: "It became clear to me that because the

Possibility therapy, for me, is where all this comes together with brief and solution-oriented therapy—what I now typically call "possibility therapy" in my approach with the aftereffects of sexual abuse. I think what bothered me a bit about the articulation of brief therapy and solution-oriented therapy is that brief therapies seem to give short shrift to feelings, to people's felt experience and sense of themselves, their own experience. What I think Carl Rogers [1951, 1961] and followers of Rogers did long ago was talk about and really articulate and emphasize how important it is for people to have a sense of being *heard, acknowledged,* and *validated.* I think that's done in brief therapy a lot—the kind of solution-oriented, problem-oriented, problem-focused, interactional stuff that's the tradition I come from—but it's not articulated.

Hoyt: Literally validated, the truth of their experience—that what's happened to them has happened to them?

O'Hanlon: Oh, no, no. I'm talking about much more their felt sense of where they are now, their sense of who they are now and how they are now, and their ideas about the past. Being *acknowledged,* that's different from *validated.* I'm going to use the words a little differently, and we'll talk about the difference because that's part of the model or approach.

Milwaukee [de Shazer's] approach put such a value on minimalism, it left out several elements that I found crucial in my therapeutic work. The first was that there is no significant discussion of the importance of the validation of emotions in the Milwaukee approach. Because the emphasis is so much on 'solution talk,' sometimes clients have the sense that the therapist is minimizing or not attending to the problem. . . . Another difficulty I see with the Milwaukee approach is its tendency to be formulaic. . . . Another concern I have about the Milwaukee approach is that it studiously ignores political, historical, and gender influences on the problem (as well as the inner worlds of physiology and biochemistry) as being irrelevant to the process of therapy, since all one has to do is develop solutions and solution-focused conversations. . . . In contrast, in possibility therapy, while I take care not to bring in extraneous material and inquiries, at times these areas are crucial for both the therapist's understanding of the issues and felt experience of the client and for the development of solutions."

The interviews with de Shazer (see Chapters 1 and 7) reported herein were conducted prior to my interview with O'Hanlon, so I was not able to ask Steve to respond specifically to these comments. As quoted in Chapter 1 (p. 21), however, de Shazer commented: "A client tells you they've got a problem, then they've got a problem, and you better take it seriously. You also better take it seriously if they tell you they ain't got a problem. That's the other part of it. He comes in and somebody sent him because he drinks too much. He says he doesn't drink too much and it's not a problem. Leave it alone. Take it seriously." In the same interview (p. 29), de Shazer also made clear: "Don't let the theory get in the way. Theories will blind you," and went on to say: "I know what I don't want, and that's for anybody to develop some sort of rigid orthodoxies. I'm afraid of that. I'm always afraid of that. For me, it's a big point of concern. That there's a right way to do this and that. And to see my descriptions—and they've done this to me; I've probably done this to myself—to see my descriptions as prescriptions." (For some recent statements related to these issues, also see G. Miller & de Shazer, 1998, 2000.)

But I would say that the possibility therapy approach that came clearer to me is making sure that you balance that acknowledgment and validation with the directiveness or non-directiveness that goes on with the opening of possibilities. So you're not moving on so quickly that the person gets a sense of "Wait a minute, don't you want to hear about what I feel or what I think or where I am now or where I've been?"—so that you don't minimize or invalidate that, or give the person short shrift in terms of that. You really give them a sense that they've been heard; that their experiences have been acknowledged; that who they are has been valued and validated. And then, as soon as you're clear that they've got that, then you invite them and you can do it sort of simultaneously, invite them into a future with possibilities.

Hoyt: How does that juxtapose with the idea of brief therapy being quick or moving forward?

O'Hanlon: I think you have to be better at acknowledging people in brief therapy, because if you don't you're going to get that bounce-back effect—where they respond, "Wait a minute, you didn't really hear me, and I'm not going to cooperate with you."[3] I think brief therapists have always had to be really good at quickly meeting people where they are and acknowledging and validating. They are much more active in doing that than most longer-term therapists, who have the sense that they have to develop the relationship over time. Brief therapy is much more like, as Nick Cummings [1990] wrote about the GP [general practice] model, that basically you're not going to go to your general physician or family practice physician and say, "Let's you and I sit down for six or seven sessions, develop a little relationship, and then we'll get on to what I'm here for." You come in, you're hurting, and while you're working on what you're hurting about—either getting reassurance or getting some help to change it—the trust develops, the relationship develops. But if your physician

---

[3]This "rush to be brief," as Lipchik (1994) calls it, can be especially stimulated when an artificial, Procrustean limit is preimposed. O'Hanlon (1991, p. 108) has made his view clear in this regard: "Another thing that has become clear to me over the past ten years is that time-limited therapy is different from brief therapy. . . . I am a brief therapy evangelist, to be sure, but above and beyond that, I am an advocate of respecting clients. Therefore, I stand opposed to time-limited therapy. I certainly influence my clients in the direction of completing therapy briefly, but I also attend to their responses and let those influence me. What some clients have taught me over the years is that they won't complete their therapy briefly. Not that they are resistant or dependent, but that therapy takes differing amounts and lengths of time for different people. Erickson used to see people for sessions lasting three or four hours or for 15 minutes. Modelling that, I have completed therapy with some in one session and I have completed therapy with others in 3 years of regular sessions. My experience is that the vast majority of people will complete their therapy in a relatively short time, 3 or 4 sessions, and a few, perhaps 5%, will take longer."

doesn't hear you, then you're going to be frustrated. And that's part of the source of frustration with physicians sometimes. You have a sense they haven't really listened to you, they haven't heard you, they haven't taken you seriously. If that happens, you'll be less satisfied. But you don't spend a lot of time working on the relationship—you say, "Forget it. I'm going to go find somebody who will listen to me and who will acknowledge and validate me."

Hoyt: That also gets at the concept of "resistance." The idea that "They are not seeing it the way we think they should; therefore, they are being resistant," as opposed to us recognizing the validity of their experience.

O'Hanlon: This is a point that's been made by many therapists, I think, and especially more directive brief therapists. What we've called "resistance" has been a mix of a lot of things. Sometimes people bring certain issues that no matter how you approach them it's going to be difficult, you know, those so-called "borderline" or "characterological" issues, they are going to be challenging for people. There are ways to minimize that challenge. But I think some of the things that showed up as "resistance" were related to therapists' just not listening to people, not acknowledging them, not validating them, not taking them seriously.[4] And I think that people naturally respond to that with resistance. When therapists are trying to drive them in a direction they don't want to go, they show up as "resistant." When we think it really exists over there, it may be a function of the interaction.

Hoyt: It's not really resistance, it's that they are being noncompliant: meaning they are not complying with our vision of their reality.

O'Hanlon: That's right, or what we think they should do or feel. They are being pushed in a direction they don't want to go, so they push back. So I think that piece about making sure that you acknowledge and validate and value people that Rogers articulated influenced me a lot in the beginning of my career. Then I went into much more directive kinds of therapy. I learned family therapy, then I learned from Bandler and Grinder [1975, 1982], who later called their approach NLP [neurolinguistic programming], and then I learned Gestalt therapy along the way, then Ericksonian therapy, and brief, and solution-oriented therapies as the years went on. All of those really emphasize the directiveness of the therapists, and they didn't so much emphasize the nondirective aspects.

Hoyt: They are all based on a foundation of careful listening.

O'Hanlon: Careful listening, but they didn't articulate the *respectful* aspect so much. So I think, especially with the aftereffects of abuse, that

---

[4]The theme of taking the patient *seriously* was also a key in the de Shazer and Weakland interview reported in Chapter 1 of this volume.

you have to be very careful about that, because people can be very sensitive to being minimized or invalidated or not heard about that. We've certainly had a lot written and said about how society minimizes or denies or invalidates those kinds of experiences or people who have been abused, or blames some people who have been abused. So I think it's especially important for that to be articulated in the brief or solution-oriented therapy approaches. So I wanted to find some theory or some way of describing what I did that was more of a reflection of what I did. So possibility therapy is like the mutant child of Carl Rogers and Milton Erickson, in that it really places an emphasis on validating and valuing people and acknowledging their experience, the felt experience, and who they sense they are; *and* it also keeps the possibilities open for change.

Hoyt: With sexual abuse survivors, beyond reflecting and clarifying, what are some of the things you do?

O'Hanlon: I think if that's all one does, it's going to take a long, long time. It's going to be a pretty tortuous process, typically. So I think there are some things that one can bring from more directive and focused approaches and brief therapy approaches that can facilitate moving on and not being stuck.

Hoyt: Such as?

O'Hanlon: I think I need first to just articulate a little bit of my understanding of the aftereffects of sexual abuse trauma especially, but trauma generally, and how it's similar to traditional models of PTSD [posttraumatic stress disorder] and sexual abuse treatment, and how it's different from those—very different. I went to graduate school in marriage and family therapy, and I got my degree in that, and I went into a child development and family studies department where I got my degree at Arizona State. They made me learn all this stuff about child development— Kohlberg and Piaget and Vygotsky and all these people—and I quickly forgot it as soon as I got out of graduate school, and it never helped me with raising my kids or anything. But I remembered a few things over the years, and one of the things that I remember is that Piaget showed through experiments that all kids are born Buddhists. What do I mean by that? All kids seem to be born with this sense of nondifferentiation with the world. They glom everything together: "I am the world; you are the world; we're all together; and I don't make a distinction between me and parents, generally, and the chair that you're sitting in." After a while, in this culture, we turn kids from Buddhists into personalities. That is, we give them the sense that you sit over there in that chair, I sit over here in this chair, and we're both different from the chair.

So we start to distinguish the world, and so we develop a sense of boundaries. My boundaries end at my bag of bones typically, you end at your bag of bones, as Bateson [1972] said; that was one of his favorite phrases, "bag of bones." Some cultures give you the sense that you are the environment. Their boundaries are different. But in our culture, typically we have a sense that our boundaries end at our bodies and that's it—that I may have some connection with you, but basically you're separate from me. So, they have really good external boundaries. I have a sense that I end here and that you begin there. And I have maybe different parts of myself, but they are very diffuse internal boundaries. I have a shy part, but it's not really a personality, it's not really a separate part of me, it's just me—an expression of me that's a little different from my ham part that gets up on stage and teaches workshops. And I have a musical part and I have certain memories, but I have a sense those are *my* memories. What I think holds that inner stuff together and the boundary together is that we make a distinction between ourselves and the world, and we create a narrative: "Here's my story, here's me." And we do that when we go over the scrapbooks with our family members and they say, "That was you when you were four years old." I don't remember being there, but sure, okay, I'll accept that. We develop a sense of continuity of our lives and where we came from, what happened then, what happened then, what happened then, and how it led us to this. We develop a sort of coherent story with some noncoherent parts or parts that don't quite fit in, but a generally coherent story about ourselves, and a sense of where the story is going. So that's how this fits in with the narrative idea.

Hoyt: And that's the sense of "self."

O'Hanlon: That's right, a *narrative* sense of self, I think. We're going to talk about another sense of self as well. That's the narrative self or personality identity that one constructs.

Hoyt: Some parts may not fit in well, but there's a general sense of "This is Bill."

O'Hanlon: Yes, this is me, and there are parts that I don't like too well, that don't fit in well, but generally they're me.

Hoyt: Walt Whitman once said, "I am large, therefore, I have contradictions."[5]

---

[5]Whitman's actual words (from "Song of Myself" in *Leaves of Grass*, 1892/1993):

Do I contradict myself?
Very well then I contradict myself,
(I am large, I contain multitudes.)
    [Stanza 51]

In the same poem [Stanza 21], he also says:

I am the poet of the Body and I am the poet of the Soul,
The pleasures of heaven are with me and the pains of hell are with me,
The first I graft and increase upon myself, the latter I translate into a new tongue.

O'Hanlon: Yeah, and that will become very relevant to some of what I want to talk about next. So, when people are intruded upon physically or experientially earlier on, before they develop a coherent narrative of self—there is that "mystification" process that R. D. Laing [1967] talked about, where you tell the person what they are feeling or thinking; or "mind reading," as Virginia Satir [1967] called it.[6] I remember a story that I heard about Jay Haley—it may be apocryphal. One time he wanted to go out, and his wife wanted to have their 10- or 11-year-old daughter put on a sweater because she thought it was cold outside. The 10- or 11-year-old didn't want to put on the sweater. So mother and daughter were arguing. Haley leaned against the door jamb. He knew, "Don't triangulate." He knew enough not to get in between, and he let them argue it out. But finally he wanted to go, so he turned to the daughter and said, "Put on your sweater. Your mother's cold." So that's the opposite of that intrusion. He basically said, "Just do the behavior; you don't have to feel the feelings." Instead there are the parents who say to the kid who is kind of cranky, "Say, you know, you're really tired. You're so cranky, you're really tired." When it's time for the kids to go to bed in my house, I say, "You go to bed. *I'm* tired."

Hoyt: He didn't violate her with the misattribution, "You are cold."

O'Hanlon: Right, or tell the person, "You're sleepy," or "You're upset or angry," or whatever. That kind of stuff. That kind of mystification or attribution of experience goes on a fair amount along with sexual abuse, I think, and physical abuse: "You really like this. This feels good," when the person is not liking it or doesn't feel good, most of the time. And so, when that physical intrusion or experiential intrusion happens early on, the person often doesn't develop a really good sense of identity, or some pieces get left out of the identity story that are actually in a person's experience. I'm going to talk about the *experiential self,* or as Rogers called it, the "organismic self," and also the *narrative self,* the identity self, the self-image, the self-identity, the one that one constructs "who I am." When one gets intruded upon early on, I think some parts get left out of that identity story; they are never included in the narrative for one reason or another. We dissociate—that's well established. We dissociate, but not only do we dissociate, we disown. We say, "It's not me." As Gestalt used to say, "Don't say *it,* say *I.*" They were trying to get you to reown some things that you call the "it." Georg Groddeck [1923/1976] years ago wrote a book called *The Book of the It,* that was about the "it-ness" of some aspects of our experienced self. It was about other things, too, but I think the nice thing in that the *id* translates from German to English as the *it.* It really meant "the alien within," if you will. So, I think we develop that alien within our experience. So it's *dissociate, disown,* and—the third thing

---

[6]Or "mind fucking," as Fritz Perls (1969) was wont to say.

is critical—*devalue*. I don't experience it, I dissociate from it; and it's not me, I disown it; and it's bad, or I'm bad if I experience it.

Hoyt: It reinforces the dissociation.

O'Hanlon: So far, this is pretty much straightforward trauma theory. We dissociate, disown, but somehow devalue ourselves or the experience, and don't include it within the boundaries of our defined self or narrative self. We identify with certain aspects of our experience and disidentify with other aspects, and devalue those other aspects and dissociate those other aspects. When that happens, I think there are one or two aftereffects or sometimes both. One is that the symptoms that show up some time later are either *inhibited* kinds of symptoms or the opposite polarity, *intrusive* symptoms.[7] Inhibited symptoms are when you've got control of the rheostat and you turn it all the way down; the person is sexually numb, doesn't have any memories. It's like the "negative symptoms" of schizophrenia, as they are sometimes called, when there's lack of affect. Something's missing from the person's experience; it just goes missing altogether—when they would have thought they would have responded sexually or emotionally, they are just flat; they don't feel anything, sense anything; they don't remember anything, there are gaps in their memories. That's an inhibited kind of symptom. Or it's intrusive—flashbacks, not inhibited memory at all, intrusive memories, or compulsive behavior. Compulsive masturbation, or what Patrick Carnes [1983, 1989] calls "sexual addiction." It becomes a compulsive sexuality instead of nonsexuality or no sexual feelings.

Hoyt: Why would someone become compulsive if it's devalued, disowned, put away?

O'Hanlon: Precisely because it's devalued, disowned, put away. "It" goes out of relationship with your self, with your experiential self. Rogers actually had a theory that relates to this. He used to draw these two circles (or at least the way I was taught, there would be two circles). One would be the self-image, and one would be the organismic self, the experiential self, the one that actually has physiological sensory experience. And he thought that when they are far apart, the person is incongruent, and it results in neurotic behavior—for example, the guy who comes into your office and pounds on your desk, yelling, "I'm not angry." Instead of valuing one or another, Rogers would say, "I hear you saying you're not angry, and I see you pounding on the desk, and I hear you raising your voice." Not judging or valuing, but just validating both parts. Not saying

---

[7]Horowitz (1986) has characterized "stress response syndromes" as alterations between phases of "denial" and "intrusion." For a comprehensive review of the PTSD literature, see Meichenbaum (1994—also see Chapter 4, this volume).

one is right or one is wrong, like "You're really angry," or "Okay, your guy doesn't get angry." He wouldn't take either of those sides. He'd validate both sides, and he felt that under the warmth of that acknowledgment, the two sides, the two circles move more together and are able to merge. The closer they're together, the more congruent the person is. He had the idea that they are never going to be totally together, totally congruent, but you can get them closer together and, therefore, symptomatic experience and behavior diminishes.

It's as if the person is living in a house with a bunch of other people, and they decide there's a roommate there that they don't get along with. "Let's get rid of the bad roommate." So they throw the roommate out, change the locks. The roommate comes and pounds on the door for a while, and they say, "Don't let him in, just ignore him, he'll go away." After a while, it seems like he's gone away, because he stops pounding on the door. He slumps against the door and is tired; he can't keep it up any more; and the roommates figure, "Good, we've gotten rid of him." So he seems to go away until a day later, a year later, 5 years later, 20 years later, all of a sudden he decides, "I live there, my stuff's in there, I'm getting back in," and he crashes through the front window. That's flashbacks, or that's sexual compulsiveness. Something cues off that wakes the sleeping roommate outside the door and says, "I'm getting back in there, I belong there. I'm in your experiential life and, damn it, you're going to deal with me." So, something, you may be reading something that reminds you of the sexual abuse that you've had, or you may have been watching something on television. You go into therapy; a therapist may say, "Do you think you were abused, given your symptoms?" or whatever. And, boom, this flood of memories come back. Who knows? Something cues it off. Or, it's been happening for years, and the missing roommate has been crashing in through the window or has just gone missing for a while.

Hoyt: Or there may be some innate drive to integrate, to make whole.

O'Hanlon: It could be that finally when you get to a good enough place and you're ready to deal with it, who knows? I'm not precisely sure why, but that's typically the point that people come to see us—when they are being bothered by something. Either something's missing, inhibited, or something's intruding or making them feel compulsions. The idea is that it's out of relationship with your experiential organismic itself. And because it's out of relationship, it's like that movie *Dr. Strangelove.*

Hoyt: With the hand that keeps coming up?

O'Hanlon: Yeah. It's the hand, I think, that's clearly dissociated, devalued, and disowned, because it's a gloved, metallic kind of hand. And it's the hand, I think, that can push the button to start a nuclear war. This brilliant Cold War scientist, who is supposed to be modeled on Herman Kahn, is giving these lectures about how we can win a nuclear war, and all the time the hand is creeping up trying to choke the character (played by Peter Sellers), and the character is always pulling the hand back down. There's that sense that that hand is out of relationship with the rest of him, who is this cold intellectual. But that hand is like the disowned, devalued, dissociated part of people. Typically I find it's either sexual sensations or experience, sexual excitement, memories, anger, sadness—body feelings all together or some part of the body. Those are the typical things that I find that people have dissociated and disowned and devalued in the aftereffects of abuse. So one of those things or several of them have gone out of relationship with the person. So if it's part of your body, or your body, maybe you'll start slicing yourself up with a razor. That's how it shows up in a compulsive, intrusive way. Or you don't feel your body at all. No body. You keep running into things because you don't know where your body is, that kind of thing. So far this description sounds like fairly standard posttraumatic stress theory, especially post-sexual-abuse kind of stuff. The difference is in how do I think it can be treated? The standard idea is "You never really experienced it in the past because you dissociated from it. So in order to really heal from it, you have to go back and reexperience what you really didn't experience the first time. So you have to relive and remember the trauma." This is an "unexperienced experience" model. Typically age regression is used, with the therapist's encouragement to really reclaim and integrate those aspects of yourself that you dissociated, devalued, and disowned.

Hoyt: In a way, this is Freud's [1914/1958] idea of "remembering, repeating, and working through"—that what we don't experientially complete will continue to press, that the Gestalt will be there until it's completed. What we resist persists.

O'Hanlon: Right. That's the idea of the traditional treatment. What I'm suggesting is that there is an alternative, and actually the way that this occurred to me is that I've worked on this solution-oriented/brief therapy/possibility therapy wave for years. I've been hearing clients talk about sexual abuse since the mid-'70s, maybe 1974, when I started doing therapy. Also, I was sexually abused when I was younger. More recently, people have been bringing sexual abuse issues as the primary presenting problem. Before I knew much about what sexual abuse treatment experts were doing, I dealt with it in the ways that I typically did therapy, and then after about five years I got to thinking, "You know, I ought to go and find out what other people are doing, read a little more stuff." Most of what I read was very psychodynamic and not to my liking, and I started going to more workshops and I thought, "You know, I am not doing this right. My clients seem to be getting better, and I'm not having them age-regress and I'm not having them relive the experiences, but they seem to be doing fine and they tell me it's helpful in resolving their problems." I started to be bothered that there seemed to be a monolithic approach out there, like there is typically to drug and alcohol problems: it's the Twelve-Step model or nothing else. I started to think, "Wait a minute. There's an alternative here that should be spoken about." Not everybody has to age-regress. Some of my clients do, but it's the minority of my clients that age-regress and relive it with my support and help, and that takes a long time. It's a tortuous process. Usually people decompensate and get a lot worse during that process; often they get more suicidal, more self-injurious, feel worse about themselves. If they are in relationships, their relationships are strained by either lack of sexual contact, because at that point they are so into the memories that it's very hard for them to have a sexual experience that's present; they flashback too much, so the partners are upset. Or, they are just acting out a lot more or are a lot more disturbed, so it takes a special partner to really support them through that process.

Hoyt: What distinguishes the people who needed to age-regress and re-experience it fully from those people who were able to get well without it?

O'Hanlon: I have no clue—that's the first answer. I say that the therapy that I do is sort of like the sport of curling. I'm sweeping in front of people, opening possibilities, while I'm acknowledging and validating them, and I'm inviting them from the present into the future. Sometimes as I do that, they zip back to the past and start to relive and reexperience their abuse or remember it in very vivid ways. If that's what they do, I better go back there and sweep in front of them and support them in doing that. So, I would say my pragmatic answer is the people that do that seem to need to do that, and most people don't, and the people that don't, don't.

Hoyt: The people who don't, have you seen some long-term follow-up?

O'Hanlon: Yes.

Hoyt: That's convinced you that they don't really need to?

O'Hanlon: That's right. That it isn't just a "Band-Aid," as people sometimes say about brief therapy—that it really doesn't last. I've been able to do that with enough people so I'm convinced.

Hoyt: Some therapists hold the view that people need to fully reexperience and abreact; otherwise, they will be sealing over and be very likely to relapse, and these will be the people who later will be back, not having really resolved the problem. Yet many people report the other experience: that they are able to do the work, finish, and don't seem to have a relapse.

O'Hanlon: Sure, and I'm sure that it's possible that some people do the work and then it gets undone or whatever; it's not finished, or it shows up again because it wasn't done; or the piece that they did was done and they come back for something else. I'm sure on the other side one can say that with some of those longer-term abreactive approaches, we can see some of them in which the people don't survive or they don't get better; they just keep reliving it and seem to be stuck in the experience. So I think you've got to balance that. I would be wary of anybody who said everybody has to do it without age-regressing or catharting, because that seems to me much more a function of the therapist's beliefs than the client's needs.

Hoyt: Even if they don't age-regress or cathart, I think there is still a place for emotion and affect as part of the validation. If we slide past that without letting the person express their pain and validate it, it may not be the age regression that is missed, but that they haven't been heard.

O'Hanlon: Yeah, I think that's an important point. And the other thing is, sometimes acknowledging the details of the abuse without having to go back and live it and reexperience it emotionally, I think is another issue. Sometimes it is very important for people to speak about their abuse to another person or write about it or speak publicly about it. That seems to be an important part for some of my clients of what they do to come to terms with it—and we'll get back into this—and bring it into their sense of identity, their narrative about themselves. That seems to be part of that renarration process. That's different from reliving it or catharting. And I think you made a good distinction there. When they express emotion, it would be disrespectful to say, "I don't do emotions. I'm a brief therapist."[8] Really validate them as people and value them as people and make room for those emotions. But don't say, "Oh, good, now we're getting someplace. Go with it and get back into it."

Hoyt: As though the emotions are the goal more than anything else.

O'Hanlon: That's right. The idea that the expression of emotion is automatically curative is a dubious proposition. Anybody who has done a lot of marital therapy knows you can hear a lot of expressions of emotions and it's not necessarily curative.[9]

Hoyt: You mentioned that it may be the need of the therapist or the therapist's countertransference, their theory belief. You also mentioned in passing that you had had a sexual abuse experience in your own per-

---

[8]See Miller and de Shazer (in press).

[9]For more discussion of O'Hanlon's views regarding marital therapy issues, see Gale and Newfield (1992), Hudson and O'Hanlon (1991), and O'Hanlon and Hudson (1994).

sonal life. I don't want to probe into that more personally than you want, but what I want to raise is a point about what some people call "countertransference"—that therapists working with abuse victims have to be open to the experiences that are going to be stirred in themselves. Otherwise, we oftentimes have trouble validating people's experience because we're busy invalidating our own experience.

O'Hanlon: Guarding against our experiences.

Hoyt: So, in a way, one has to have done the work with oneself to be clear enough to hear so that we can let the other person be who they are; otherwise, we're going to restimulate our stuff in a way we don't want.

O'Hanlon: Sure, or in the other way—if we've actually come to terms and resolved it in some particular way, assuming that our clients are going to do it in the same way. It's like the AA [Alcoholics Anonymous] model saying, "I went through AA, so you're going through AA because that's the way that worked for me." Maybe there are other ways that people can stop drinking. It's important to be able to provide those alternatives, rather than saying this is the only way to do it. If I went through a regressive cathartic therapy and it was greatly helpful for me, or long-term therapy was and I loved it and thought it was great, it may not be that that's what my clients need. And it doesn't have to invalidate that long-term, wonderful therapy you went through. That's the caution of what I've called "theory countertransference."[10]

Hoyt: Because if you're talking about the idea of a narrative theory of repression, then there's also the possibility of countertransference repression—that I'm going to collude with you to keep this from your story because it's too close to my story, or will interfere with me believing in my story.

O'Hanlon: I think we're talking about two different ideas. One is sort of unfinished stuff of the therapist that might get in the way. The other one is an attachment to a theory or a method that might get in the way.

Hoyt: One is much more a personal problem, and the other is more theoretical.

O'Hanlon: That's right—getting attached to a certain theory. Or, "I learned it in graduate school or this was helpful for me personally," so it's a little more of a personal issue there. But I think those are two different concerns and possible traps that I'm trying to warn against. What I'd like to say is one of the bottom lines, one of the basic ideas that I want to get across here is *variability*. In agriculture, they have this idea that if you

---

[10]Advocating openness to various possibilities, O'Hanlon (1991; Hubble & O'Hanlon, 1992) has warned against "theoretical countertransference" and "delusions of certainty."

only have one strain of a crop, like the Irish potato or whatever, there's a potential for agricultural disaster because you don't have enough biodiversity. I think in therapy methods it's the same way: If there's not enough diversity in therapy approaches available, you're going to be in-validating and minimizing some people. When all the therapy theories were written by straight heterosexual white middle-class or upper-class men, it didn't bode well for other experiences being validated. I think the same thing about the sexual abuse aftereffects. Where there's only one way to do it—the unexperienced experience model, age regression, ca-tharsis, working through—then it's going to work wonderfully for the people for whom that really fits, and it's not going to have room for the other people; so I want to speak for an alternative that's worked for me and my clients. The alternative is valuing, going like brief therapy does for change through the door of the present problem or complaint. That is, instead of going globally after it, by "working through" the aftereffects of sexual abuse or going after the memories, get specific.

Because I do hypnosis, sometimes people come to me: "Can you hyp-notize and help me remember?" No. Number one, I'm not a good direc-tive hypnotist. I'm more of a permissive hypnotist, so I don't say, "Go back through the pages of time—you're five years old now and you will remember." It gives me the creeps, that stuff, anyway. It's too intrusive and too directive for my tastes. And the other thing is that I don't think typically it's helpful to remember that way. Some people do and some people will remember through hypnosis, and that's fine. But typically in both situations, whether they come for hypnosis or whether they don't, go through the door of the presenting complaint. I focus on the question: What are they complaining about? That is, when someone comes in and says, "I think I was sexually abused," or "I know I was sexually abused," or "I was sexually abused and I want to work on this," I say, "Okay, what's bothering you now? That is, what's your concern? What's your complaint? What do you want to resolve?" That makes it more brief, more focused, and you have some sense of when you get there. So typically they're going to complain about one thing or another. They are going to say, "Well, it bothers me because when I start to have sex with my partner, I go numb. I get scared right before I have sex, and I can push myself through that, but then I get numb."

Hoyt: So, "What are the particular impairments or residuals?"

O'Hanlon: "What's bothering you now? And how will you know when that's resolved?" That's the goal-oriented part: "How will you know when we've actually resolved it?" "Well, when I have sex with my partner and I'm there during the experience and I actually experience sexual sensa-tions, and I don't go away any more, I don't get numb, I don't age-regress and feel like a little kid being raped." Okay, that's a pretty good hint. We are starting to clarify what the goal is and how you'll know when you're done. Again, it's going back to that GP-model physician. You come in with a concern, and either you want reassurance that you don't have a brain tumor or cancer or something, and sometimes we can give reassurance: "Yes, a lot of people have been sexually abused, you're not strange, you're not out of the ordinary." And many people have these kinds of worries about themselves or experiences with themselves. Sometimes they think they were to blame; sometimes they think they should have been able to stop it even though they were a child; sometimes they had sexual sensations during the abuse, and then they feel guilty because they think they enjoyed it. We can normalize a lot of that stuff, like the book *The Courage to Heal* [Bass & Davis, 1994] can. You read that and you think, "I'm not so weird; other people experience this, too," so sometimes that's our function, to normalize and reassure. Like your physician would say, "It's going to pass in a couple of days; it's just a simple flu. It doesn't mean you have meningitis. I've checked for the warning signs and you probably don't have it. But if it persists, call me back." Sometimes we go for reassurance and sometimes we go for change. What are people complaining about and what do they want? Those are the things that typically drive brief therapy and goal-focused therapy. So that's the door in, because I find that when you go in through that door, that's where the dissociative, devalued, disowned parts are. How do I work in a present to future-oriented way rather than a past way? By valuing the person and valuing the part. So the part comes back into the person's experience by helping them acknowledge it and by me acknowledging it.

Hoyt: Can you give a brief example of valuing the person and the part?

O'Hanlon: Yeah. I had a person who came to see me who was dissociated to the point of multiplicity, multiple personality. During one of the conversations that we had in therapy, a part showed up, a personality that had never showed up—before. It was very hostile; as is often the case in multiple personality, there's a hostile, angry part. And that part was "Astoroth," the devil. Astoroth, when Astoroth emerged, basically started growling and threatening me and her, threatened to do terrible things to my genitals (I won't detail it here), and threatened to do terrible things to her, and threatened that therapy will get nowhere: "I will do everything I can to stop it. I'm going to defeat you. I'm more powerful than you. I'm more powerful than her." I said, "Okay, thank you for sharing." I was a little surprised because he emerged very quickly and he was gone as quickly as he came, and she was back, and she was disturbed by this—she was "Wow, what happened?" She said, "I think that that's the part that the people who tortured me put in me, the devil. So do you think you could do an exorcism?" Just for a second, I was thinking, "You know, I've never done an exorcism, and I have a priest friend who would probably do this; that would be kind of neat." Just for a second I thought that. Then I thought, "No, wait a minute. I think Astoroth *is* her. I don't want to get rid of Astoroth—that's her." My idea is that it is part of her experience, and I don't want to devalue or throw it out; it's the missing roommate thing. So I talked to her a little bit about it. I said, "Let's go a little farther. I think that's you." She said to me, "Me? No, thanks."

So over the next couple of sessions, Astoroth came out and visited with me—at first threatening me, and then I would say, "Well, what's going on? Why do you want to do this?" And I would talk to Astoroth like I would if a client came in and said, "I want to go out and kill everybody." Basically, Astoroth became my client, if you will. As Astoroth and I started talking—I'm kind of lively in therapy and can be humorous—and Astoroth, despite his hostility, liked my jokes, he would find himself laughing despite himself. So I'd say, "I got you, didn't I? You laughed at that one." He and I would start to joke together. For a devil, he had a pretty good sense of humor! *[laughter]* So we started to become friendly, and he started telling me, "I have to kill her to protect her." I said, "Okay, we have to protect her, but if you kill her you'll die too, and that seems kind of weird," and we talked about all that, and the strange logic of that. And then we found that that was some decision he'd made or she'd made a long time ago, and that we could retalk about that decision in light of current reality, and he got a lot more cooperative. He thought I was his ally after a while, not his enemy, so we started working together. She still didn't want have anything to do with him; she didn't want to touch him with a 10-foot pole. But he became less threatening to her, and after a while she was willing to approach him, and they started to develop a conversation—an internal and external dialogue—and they started to get along a little better. He became her real protector inside instead of torturer and threatener, and then he turned into a scared little girl which she protected, and then the scared little girl turned into her over time. So under the conversation in which Astoroth isn't blamed, isn't devalued, and isn't kicked out, if you will, *that* Astoroth starts to become part of her ongoing narrative of who she is and turned into her. So that's a sense of it. She didn't regress to do that.[11]

---

[11]Milton Erickson also accepted the fact that the client had different parts and focused on working with them. As Grove and Haley (1993, p. 183) report: "In Erickson's approach, the goal was not to try and merge the personalities or to search for additional personalities. The goal was to persuade the personalities to communicate directly with each other and to. . . . collaborate and make a positive contribution to the life of the total person." Grove (1993, pp. 16-17) elaborates: "There are several advantages to this orientation. By approaching secondary personalities as real individuals with their own independent needs

Hoyt: You provided enough of a container and made friends with parts of herself so she could, one might say, "metabolize."

O'Hanlon: That's a nice analogy. And I guess the difference between the traditional model is—the way to metabolize in the traditional model is you have to go back. In possibility therapy, you value the aspect, like anger was valued. You do not value some expressions of anger. You do value some expressions of anger, that's different. You know, she wanted to hurt me; that wasn't any good, I didn't want that. The containment, as you say, is the behavioral containment, saying, "It's not okay to hurt yourself, it's not okay to hurt me; it's not okay to hurt the body; it's not okay to hurt other people; *and* you can feel like hurting other people." But an active encouragement of that in saying, "That's okay, it's fine"—permission and validation for the experience, not the action. Under that valuing in the present, details about the abuse did emerge. Astoroth told me some things that had been done to him—and, of course, to her—and that acknowledgment was part of that validation. Acknowledgment about what happened, and acknowledgment of his or her feelings and rage; anger gone out of relationship with self turned up as rage.

So if you have no room for anger—anger is devalued, invalidated, dissociated, disowned—it shows up every once in a while as rage in what is most of the time the sweetest, nicest person. I had a client who was nicknamed "Sunshine" when she was growing up. She was being massively abused, but she was always nicknamed Sunshine and she smiled. And even as an adult when she got mad at someone, she was one of those people who would smile at you while she was mad, so you didn't really get the full impact of her anger. She would tell you that she was angry, but you didn't really get a sense of it. It would even be hard for her to tell you that she was angry. And then every once in a while, she would be in a rage with her kids or her husband over a seemingly little thing. So when something goes out of your narrative or out of relationship with your experiential self, and you don't include it in your self-identity, then I think that it starts to develop a life of its own.

Hoyt: What we might call "in the shadow."

O'Hanlon: And it's not only shadow stuff, too, because sometimes you get people who do multiple personality that have wonderful musical abilities or artistic abilities. They are not just shadow stuff.

Hoyt: Not all evil or bad.

---

and motivations, the therapist can more easily win the trust and cooperation of the secondary personalities. . . . Because the client's presentation of having multiple personalities is not viewed as a psychopathology, the therapist can approach all personalities with a more positive view." Also see Schwarz (1998) for further discussion of the collaborative treatment of dissociative disorders.

O'Hanlon: That's right. It's all out of relationship with self because it seems to have a mind of its own. Artists often have that experience. That brings up the question of how do you explain repression or forgotten memories in this narrative model? I think that there is a hint of this in Judith Herman's [1992] really nice book, *Trauma and Recovery*, that people have this whole narrative of who they are and where their life has been and where they are going; and that there are these pieces that are "unmetabolized," if you will, that aren't included in the narrative; and so if they never get in the narrative, they're not remembered very well. Why are more and more people experiencing and remembering sexual abuse and coming to terms with it more recently? Because our narratives aren't only individual narratives; they're influenced by cultural and social narratives. Many feminists and many theorists of trauma have pried open a space and said, "Oh, let's include in her story posttraumatic stuff, rape, and domestic violence, violence against women, sexual abuse against children," and that's become a lot more accepted and acknowledged. So we have the movie stars that come out and say they were sexually abused, they talk about it a lot more; the movie-of-the-week has a lot more of this stuff. There's many more books about it, a lot of books about multiple personalities. So we're going to see a lot more multiple personalities in the next 20 years, because the kind of problems that we see in therapy do not occur in isolation; they occur in cultural context as well. And when there's no room for a multiple personality in the cultural narrative, it shows up never or very rarely, as it has from the 1800s to the 1960s. It showed up so rarely it was not in the general therapeutic narrative.

Hoyt: What's the cultural milieu that's allowing us to recognize "multiple personalities" and allowing them to "come out," so to speak?

O'Hanlon: Or be *constructed* much more. As I said at the very beginning—and I want to emphasize this—I think *personality* is constructed, and I think *multiple personalities* are constructed, so they are the same degree of "real" as far as I'm concerned. I experience myself as a personality, even though I think that's clearly a construct, and I think most people would agree that it's a theoretical construct; they can't do an autopsy and find a personality inside me. I think it's really a function of some people being very persuasive at selling the narrative called "multiple personality." As more and more people get convinced of it, they become teachers and writers, and they convince other people, and that's how diagnoses get popular. I think that "borderline personality" having the stock that it does, being so popular, is a lot a function of some very articulate theorists. Kernberg [e.g., 1975] and Masterson [e.g., 1976] and other people who have done a lot of work became fascinated with them, became convinced that this was true—not that it was a good idea, but that it was true. It may or may not be a good idea, but very few other theorists have this idea that it is constructed; they think they discovered a new truth, and then they put it out there, and they become so persuasive and have conferences on it, and then they convince other people and it becomes "true" in our culture. Where were all the "codependents" 25 years ago? We didn't have them. It doesn't mean that that doesn't really explain a lot; it does explain a lot, and it's helped a lot of people. Is it "true"? Who knows? All we can say is we can't get rid of it now.

Hoyt: Do you think there's an external reality? I know that sounds like back in college, Descartes and Locke and Hume, or maybe Carlos Castaneda [1968] saying, "But, Don Juan, did I *really* fly?"

O'Hanlon: I know what you're talking about. Yes, I think there's a sensory-based reality. It's the interpretation of that reality that is variable. And, also, I don't think we can just make any construction. You can't just make any construction and sell it, because there are two constraints on it. One is that physical reality, sensory-based reality.

Hoyt: Gravity and the sharp edges will keep you honest.

O'Hanlon: Right. You'll knock into them no matter how you make up reality. If you're on LSD and you don't see them, you'll still get knocked over and you'll cut your leg, although you may not be aware of it. If you walk out into the middle of the freeway and the cars are going fast, no matter what your state of subjective reality, physical reality will run you over. That kind of physical reality is one of the constraints to what kind of narratives can be made up.

Hoyt: "My karma just ran over your dogma!"

O'Hanlon: *[laughter]* That's right. So the second constraint is, I think, there are cultural traditions and explanations—what Heidegger [1962] calls the "throwness."[12] You're not born as a blank slate. You're born into a culture that already shapes you by language and by practice, by interactions. So I don't know how Heidegger meant it, but I think of "throwness" like the clay being thrown on the wheel, the potter's wheel. And it's already shaped; there's a certain throwness to it. You're thrown in the middle of it, and you're not just bringing any possibility to it; the pot already has a shape before you get there. So there's only so much leeway there, because of the physical reality and because of the cultural social practices and traditions.

---

[12]James Hillman (1996, p. 55) elaborates: "Heidegger or Camus, for instance, places the human being into the situation of 'throwness.' We are merely thrown into being here (*Dasein*). The German word for 'thrown' (*Wurf*) combines senses of the throw of the dice, a projection, and a litter of pups or piglets cast by a bitch or a sow."

Hoyt: Not *tabula rasa.*

O'Hanlon: No, not that kind of radical constructionism. Because if that were the case, I'm really good at creating therapeutic realities, and all my clients would be cured in one session. They're not. They bring their own traditions and their own narratives, and then we have to be co-narrative.

Hoyt: That really speaks to the question of why can't people just change their mind or look at it differently or reframe it or say, "Oh, that was me then but this is me now"? Why do we sometimes get stuck in a persistent negative narrative?

O'Hanlon: I have no idea, and I'm not very interested in that question. I think that's a psychologist's question, to tell you the truth. I think that a therapist's question is, "How do we change that?"

Hoyt: I agree. Why build between us a narrative that will not get us to a better answer?

O'Hanlon: Right. Asking change-oriented questions is much more interesting to me than asking explanation-oriented questions—although some explanation-oriented questions get you to change.

Hoyt: How do people free themselves when they've been stuck? How does it happen that they get unstuck? By owning the parts that have been devalued, disowned, and . . .

O'Hanlon: . . . Valuing it, owning, associating to and taking actions to change the current situation to their goal. The other thing is changing their stories or their narrative so that there are possibilities for actions and possibilities for a future that will be more of what they want. So changing the doing and changing the viewing. And the prerequisite for that is, I think, valuing and validating experience before that, or along with that.

Hoyt: What else?

O'Hanlon: I think one more element. I say this is a present and future-oriented approach; how is it future-oriented? There are exceptional survivors—people that seem to belie the rule that this stuff messes you up for life and holds you back and keeps you stuck. There are some people who clearly have been massively abused or devalued, and that somehow do pretty well in the present and the future. How come that is? Some become presidents of the United States, and some really deteriorate and go into the psych hospital. What's the difference? Why, given similar kinds of backgrounds, and how do we encourage more people to live those better futures?

I think one of the places I learned that was from Viktor Frankl at the second Evolution of Psychotherapy Conference [Zeig, 1992]. He came and gave a keynote address and told the story about how he was in the Nazi death camp, several Nazi death camps, being marched through the field in the middle of Poland; and he fell down in a fit of coughing and couldn't get up. He's being beaten by a guard who said, "Get up and keep marching to this work detail or you're going to die." He just thinks, "Okay, that's it. I thought I was going to survive, but I'm not going to. I just don't have the physical wherewithal to get up and keep moving." All of a sudden, he's no longer in a field in Poland, he's standing at a lectern in postwar Vienna, giving a lecture which he had been working on all the time he'd been in the death camp, on the psychology of death camps [see Frankl, 1963]. He's giving this brilliant lecture to this imagined audience of about 200 people who are listening in rapt attention as he explains how people can dehumanize people so much to put them in death camps and treat them so terribly, and also how some people psychologically and spiritually and emotionally survive. He came up with the "will to meaning," and having found some purpose and meaning, those people seem to survive better than those people who didn't have any purpose and meaning and gave up hope. So he's talking in his imagined lecture about the day he almost died in the death camp, outside the death camp in Poland. The day he was walking through the snowy field with not enough clothes on, and he was ill in the middle of winter in Poland, and he said, "And I thought I was going to die there, and then I found myself getting up surprisingly and walking; I don't know how I did it, but I did it." Meanwhile, his body is still in Poland and it stands up, and he walks to the work detail, does the work, and comes home. All the time, he's just doing the work automatically by his body, not really experientially there any more, still giving his lecture when he gets back to the death camp; he collapses in the bed, and he survives another day. At the end of his imagined lecture in postwar Vienna, he got a standing ovation. In 1990, many, many years later in Anaheim, California, he got a standing ovation from 7,000 people.

Hoyt: I was in that audience.

O'Hanlon: Frankl did something different from what most of us do who are traumatized. He didn't stay stuck in the past and keep repeating it again and again in flashbacks, with the disowned and dissociated and devalued parts kind of coming and haunting him. He projected into a future where things worked out; it had meaning and had purpose. A future in which this terrible experience had contributed to him getting to that future, and he imagined back from the future to the present; he oriented himself to a future with possibilities, and let that future pull him out of the terrible present. Many sexual abuse survivors, victims, come in saying, "Nothing is right. I'm terrible. I'll never survive this. There's no reason to be alive." And I always think and somehow ask, "What are you doing in my office? Some part of you, some aspect of you, has a vision of a future where things work out, or you wouldn't be here. Why would you bother getting out of bed?"

Hoyt: They were hanging on until the time when it would pass and they would be survivors.

O'Hanlon: And they sometimes have, if you can help them articulate it, a very clear Viktor Frankl-like vision of a future where things work out.

Hoyt: In a way, a crystal-ball-type thing [Erickson, 1954].

O'Hanlon: Yes, very much like the crystal ball.

Hoyt: Looking to a time when the problem is no longer a problem.

O'Hanlon: Erickson would have people project into a future and tell him how they worked out the problem, and then he would bring them out of a trance with amnesia for that fantasized future, and then he would often tell them to do the things that they told him that they would do in that imagined future. Most of us have the notion that the present determines the present and the future, but what if the future determined the present? Think about it, if you knew you would win the Lotto tonight, would you be here interviewing me? Perhaps, but maybe not.

Hoyt: So if you have a different image of your future, you will conduct your life differently in the present.

O'Hanlon: That's right. It becomes a self-fulfilling prophecy sometimes. It definitely becomes presently oriented.

Hoyt: So it's not really the future; it's our image. There's only the present, but when we think of the future, that's expectation, and our expectation will lead us to do certain things.[13]

O'Hanlon: Right. So what I want to do as a therapist is open up a future with possibilities, instead of having the future be a repeat of the past. I think people come in "frozen in time" [see O'Hanlon, 1993b; O'Hanlon & Bertolino, 1998]. That is, they froze their sense of themselves or some aspect of themselves at that moment in time when they were abused. They froze and they keep doing the same experience over and over again through flashbacks, muscle behavior, interactions. They keep doing the

---

[13]St. Augustine observed in his *Confessions*: "What is by now evident and clear is that neither future nor past exists, and it is inexact language to speak of three times—past, present, and future. Perhaps it would be exact to say: there are three times, a present of things past, a present of things present, a present of things to come. In the soul there are these three aspects of time, and I do not see them anywhere else. The present considering the past is the memory, the present considering the future is expectation" (quoted in Boscolo & Bertrando, 1993, p. 34).

same damn thing over and over again, as John Weakland calls it, instead of one damn thing after another, which is what life usually is. It's not a flow, it's a repetition. It's frozen in time. Under the thawing of the therapist valuing and going through the door of the presenting complaint and focusing on a future with possibilities, it becomes less frozen in time and thaws out and starts to flow.

Hoyt: So it's the warmth of validation, and then they can begin to see a future and move into it.

O'Hanlon: Right. I think they already have a sense of that future, and under the warmth of the validation of their experience of who they are, of the disowned and devalued and dissociated parts, and under the questioning of the therapist and the focus of the therapist on that future, they become a lot more articulate about that future. And it becomes more available to them, and they become a lot more committed to it.

Hoyt: Some therapy theories have the idea that people have a script or an unconscious plan, a vision of the future, and a drive toward health or wholeness, but something can block it. Fear of pain, something I can't bear to experience, so I can't get to the future because it's too painful to walk across what I have to go through first. But if I can have the promise of getting there, I'll do almost anything to get there. But I don't want to just take the pain to be in pain; I'd rather be numb.

O'Hanlon: Right. It's like having some pain in labor that you know is going to produce a child is much different from just having abdominal pain that's extreme and thinking, "What's happening here? It's terrible. Am I going to die?" or whatever. It's a different sense and it's still the same kind of sensations, but a different sense of anticipation.

Hoyt: As a general idea, people when they are depressed foreshorten the future; they don't have a future. They don't see it.[14]

O'Hanlon: I think many people who come into therapy with the aftereffects of abuse are depressed.

Hoyt: In Zen they say, "Burn clean and leave no ashes." Metabolize the experience completely, like the saying, "Time flies when you're having fun"—living in the now, the endless now.

O'Hanlon: That's nice. And I think for people who are stuck with the aftereffects of abuse, it's the endless repetition of the past. It's showing up in the present and a foreshortened sense of the future.

Hoyt: It's not "burning clean," it's "frozen in time."

O'Hanlon: It's frozen in time. That's right.

---

[14]For discussions of therapy and the temporal structuring of experience, see Boscolo and Bertrando (1993), Hoyt (1990), Melges (1982), and Ricoeur (1983).

Hoyt: What do we learn from people who are not permanently victimized by sexual abuse?

O'Hanlon: I think this whole vocabulary of "victim" and "survivor" and all that stuff is difficult. Some people say they should acknowledge the pain and the victimization of it, make sure the people who were abused don't get blamed. Some people call them "survivors," to emphasize the fact that they survived. I would say let people call themselves what they will and give them the options and possibilities. I would rather call them "people who have been sexually abused," rather than "survivors" or "victims," because I think you're right: Some people come out of it not seeming to be in that victim stance or victim experience. So I think what I learned from some of the people that have survived it a little better or thrived, even though they have been abused and victimized—what I've learned from those people as adults (I mostly treat adults, who have gone through sexual abuse experiences when they were younger) is that the ones that seem to have done better seem to have four things happen for them, or some combination or some parts of these four. If they have all four, they seem to survive it a lot better. One is that somehow, somewhere, they acknowledged the abuse to themselves and/or to somebody else. They didn't not know about it.

Hoyt: So it's owned.

O'Hanlon: It's acknowledged. It's a little different from owned. Acknowledged: it happened.

Hoyt: If it's interpersonal, then it's even more acknowledged.

O'Hanlon: That's right. It's out there in the public dialogue world; even if they only tell one person, it's out of their bag of bones into external reality. So if they *acknowledge* it to themselves and/or to somebody else, they seem to suffer less. The quicker they do that, the sooner they do that, they seem to suffer less of the lasting effects. Second thing is, once they acknowledged it or if it's been acknowledged, do they get *validated* or do they get invalidated or blamed? Because sometimes people will go to a parent or somebody, and they won't be believed, so they will be invalidated: "You're making that up. It never happened. That couldn't have happened." Or they'll be blamed: "You should have stopped him. You're walking around here in those skimpy clothes. You made it happen," or "If you weren't a bad girl, this wouldn't have happened to you." Did they get blamed or invalidated for the experience during the experience, and/or if they ever acknowledged it, did they get blamed or invalidated?

Third thing is, once they acknowledged the abuse, once they went public with it, did they get *protected* ? Did it stop? Sometimes it's acknowledged and they are validated, but not protected: "Yes, honey, I know. The same thing happened to me when I was younger, and it's not your fault, but I can't meet your stepdad's needs and you're going to have to meet his needs," or "I can't stop him; he's beating me, too. Sorry" or "We need the money. We need to keep him around. I'll try to keep him from you, but I can't guarantee it," and they don't. Or they are put in foster care and abused there. Or the other person [the abuser] is brought back into the home, and the abused person doesn't feel safe or there's no protection. So, was and is the person protected?

Fourth one is, did someone ever give them the *message that they were worthwhile and lovable*, and did they get that experientially—not just have somebody mouth the words, but did they really get that from somebody somewhere along the line before the abuse? I think it's an inoculation; after the abuse, it's somewhat reparative and healing. I was teaching with Patrick Carnes, who is a sexual addiction therapist, and he was talking about the abuse that he went through as a kid, and his escape was in books. He found a librarian at school who took a great interest in him, and through her eyes, he starting seeing himself as a valuable, worthwhile person. She'd save out special books for him. When he showed up at the library she'd say, "Patrick, I held this one for you because I know you like this kind of book; it just came in." He developed a relationship with her, and through that relationship, he started to see himself as a worthwhile person. What did he do? He grew up and got a Ph.D. and wrote books [Carnes, 1983, 1989].

Hoyt: He developed the primary self-narrative that he's a worthwhile person, validated, respected, who had bad things happen to him—not that he's a bad person. He organized his identity.

O'Hanlon: That's right. Or at least he had an alternate story available. If you talked to him, I suspect he would say his primary narrative was he was bad and evil and had all the shadow stuff to deal with. His alternate model, though—which was an alternate voice, if you will, an alternate vision—said "I think you're okay." And that's the spiritual aspect of him. That's the librarian message to him. So, because that alternate was available, the one that said, "You're bad; you're devalued; you're terrible; you'll never do anything with your life," wasn't the only narrative. So there were alternative narratives available, and he would switch back and forth. In recent years, I think he would say that the librarian/spiritual/lovable narrative became his primary identification. And the other stuff was "Yes, and this happened to me and it's a part of my identity now, but it's not all of who I am and it doesn't define who I am and it doesn't define my worth." So, did anybody ever give them the sense of worth?[15]

---

[15]See O'Hanlon (1992) for a case study of helping a woman who had been sexually abused reclaim her own identity: "We worked together to cocreate a new view and expe-

Hoyt: What is the role of diagnosis and assessment in possibility therapy? What do you look for?

O'Hanlon: Well, first of all, I want to say I think there are labels and diagnoses that open up possibilities, and there are ones that close down. There are labels that respect people and validate people, and there are labels that invalidate people, I think. Some years ago, I did therapy in the prehistoric days that I call "BBB." This was "before borderlines and bulimics." There were no bulimics when I first started therapy. And "borderline" was an existent category, but it was rarely used; it was an obscure analytic concept that basically meant the border between psychosis and neurosis. Very rare. I saw a person who did bulimia, but was diagnosed as having anorexia based on *DSM-II*; there was no diagnosis for bulimia for that time. It was seen as a subset or part of anorexia—a phase or one of the symptoms of anorexia, that people would sometimes binge or purge—and it was called bulimia. But it wasn't a special diagnosis. I saw a woman who did bulimia, and I helped her stop bingeing and vomiting; she did stop bingeing and vomiting.

Some time later, I read an article [Boskind-Lodahl & Sirlin, 1977; see also Boskind-White & White, 1983] . . . and they were talking about how 11% of the females they saw in college did bulimia. "Eleven percent?" I thought. "That's a lot." I lived right next to a college, I was in a community mental health center. I was fascinated with this. I read everything I could about it. I put an ad in the college newspaper saying, "Do you binge and vomit or take laxatives or diuretics? If you do, there's a treatment or support group starting at Tri-City Mental Health Center. Call Bill O'Hanlon." I got one of my colleagues to do it with me; we did the group together. Over the next three days I got perhaps 50 phone calls, lots of phone calls. What was striking about those phone calls was that the people, all young women, said one or two or all three of these variations on the theme. One is "I never knew there was a name for what I did." They often cried on the phone, just out of relief of someone to talk to about this and get help from: "I never knew there was a name for it. I never knew that anybody did it. I always thought I was weird and strange and

---

rience for S. She had been living a life that was in many ways determined by her history, by what someone who had abused her had done to her in the distant past. She was living *his* story. We collaboratively opened the possibility for her to start to live *her* story, to take back her life and to create new chapters in the future" (p. 147). An analysis of how to use an externalization approach to separate the problem from the personal identity of the patient is presented in O'Hanlon (1994). For other discussions of constructive approaches to treating the aftereffects of sexual abuse, see Dolan (1991, 1994), Durrant and White (1990), and Meichenbaum (1994).

nobody else did this. And I never knew there was any help for it. Thank you." And, you know, sometimes that was what they needed to do, just tell me and acknowledge and that was it.

About 20 people ultimately came into the group out of that group of 50. And when they got to the group, about five people had stopped bingeing and vomiting—it took a month to get the group together. I'd read the literature and this wasn't to be expected. Bulimia is considered an intractable problem. I asked them, "What's that about?" Some of them said, "Just to know that there was a name for it and there was help for me helped me stop." Now, that's a label that empowers. Some of them said, "I was too embarrassed to tell anybody that I did this, so I determined that I would stop it before I came in here so I wouldn't have to tell you all I was still doing this. I was so embarrassed about it." And some people said, "It just helped me get a handle on it, and I knew I was coming here, and it helped me just get over the edge." So, that's a label that empowered, like going to an AA meeting and saying, "I'm Bill and I'm alcoholic." That can free me, save my life. Now, if I say to you, "You're Michael and you're alcoholic. Go get some help for your drinking"—if you don't believe it and you resist it, then it becomes a label that doesn't empower. It becomes a political matter between the two of us, a way for me to blame you or push you in a direction you don't want to go. It doesn't have that same empowering effect as if you went to an AA meeting and really chose it and said, "I'm Michael and I'm an alcoholic."

Hoyt: The politics of experience [Laing, 1967].

O'Hanlon: Yeah, the politics of experience and the politics of diagnosis. There are some labels that don't seem to empower. Some are mixed, like if you go to a codependency group and realize that, "Gee, after all these years I realize I'm codependent, and that's really great. I don't feel so weird." So that's one of the values of a label—it can validate or normalize your experience: "Other people feel this, other people experience this and I'm not so different or strange or bad or weird because of it." I think that sometimes, though, what goes on with this is "Once an alcoholic, always an alcoholic; once a bulimic, always a bulimic," and you never recover. You'll never really be able to drop this identity label: "You'll always be bulimic whether you do bulimia or not. You'll always be alcoholic whether you drink alcohol or not. And you'll always be codependent whether you're doing codependent behaviors or not." And I think that way sometimes closes down possibilities.

Hoyt: I have just written an article called "Is Being 'In Recovery' Self-Limiting?" [Hoyt, 1994b/1995]. I see many people in recovery and it's helpful, but I almost never see anybody say, "I am recovered." If you have to admit that you are weak and will always have this problem, then it becomes this self-limiting kind of thing.[16]

O'Hanlon: Yes, and there are some people who in their private moments will tell you, "I haven't had the urge for a drink for years, and I'm never going to drink again." They are truly not alcoholic any more, but the narrative in that subculture says that if you ever say that, that's a sign of trouble, so they are not going to say it out loud. That's a way that kind of story or that kind of diagnosis invalidates that person's experience. I think also when I said "BBB"—"before borderlines and bulimics"—sometimes one suspects that the label "borderline" is overly applied, sometimes because of therapist errors that create troubling situations or in which it is then applied to people who are just considered a pain in the butt. They call us a lot, or get too needy or dependent on us, or threaten suicide a fair amount in response to whatever we do, or maybe they were going to do that anyway. But that label doesn't typically empower and help people move on. It may help the therapist figure out what's going on and find some maneuvers, and if it does, that's a little better. But if you have the label for one of your clients as "borderline" and your colleagues commiserate and say, "Don't get too many in treatment and don't expect much," then it's not such a great label.

Hoyt: Do you know where the word *diagnosis* comes from? *Diagnosis* is *via gnosis*; it means "way or path of knowledge," or in modern parlance, information [Hoyt, 1989/1995]. A good diagnosis should be information that points a path or way to being helpful; it's not simply pejorative or pathologizing.

O'Hanlon: Or just good explanation. Bateson [1972] used to make fun of that in the "dormative principle" that came from the Moliere play in which this sort of shoot-the-breeze kind of BS'ing medical resident is asked by the learned doctors what is it in morphine that makes people go to sleep, and he says, "It's the dormative principle." That's just Latin for "It makes him go to sleep." The learned doctors all nod their heads, saying, "Yes, that's it." So if it's an explanation that doesn't give you anything to do, I think that's not so good. The other thing is sometimes the label that validates one person invalidates or blames another.

Hoyt: "ACA"—"adult child of alcoholic"—can be very useful: "I've had an experience other people have had; I picked up certain tendencies or

---

[16]As Kaminer (1992, p. 26) has commented: "It is an odd program in self-esteem that rewards people for calling themselves helpless, childish, addicted and diseased and punishes them for claiming to be healthy. Admit that you're sick and you're welcomed into the recovering persons fold; dispute it and you're 'in denial.' Thus the search for identity is perversely resolved: all your bad behaviors and unwanted feelings become conditions of your being."

made decisions." But sometimes people come in and say, "I can never be relaxed or enjoy spontaneity . . . "

O'Hanlon: " . . . because my parents did it to me."

Hoyt: It's disempowering, rather than it giving me a handle that I can work this better.

O'Hanlon: Yeah, that's right. Or it blames somebody else and external-izes your power. So I think there are some problems with diagnoses. Do they validate and capture people's experience in such a way that they say "Yes" with that nod of recognition, and it keeps the possibilities open and doesn't blame or invalidate the person getting the label or the other people around them? That's the role of *diagnosis* in therapy. The role of *assessment* is to figure out what they're complaining about and what they want. That's the quick version of the role of assessment. I think assessment is different from diagnosis. Assessment is assessing what is going on, not necessarily what the diagnosis is.

Hoyt: Not putting a word or a label on it.

O'Hanlon: That is diagnosis, and that's necessary to get insurance reim-bursement, so that's a very helpful thing. Sometimes it's necessary to help us organize our thinking about the case, and also to communicate in code words to our colleagues so we don't have to explain in detail all the time.

Hoyt: What about "false memory syndrome"?

O'Hanlon: There's a lot of debate even about that term, whether there's such a syndrome or not. I think that that's a little bit of a nitpicking thing. People in the sexual abuse field, of course, are concerned that if we get into this false memory syndrome idea that we might undo a lot of the cultural work that's been done to open up the narrative to recognizing knowledge that kids have been abused, and how much progress we've made in getting the society to recognize that. So they are concerned that people will get continually invalidated or more invalidated, or denial or minimization will take place. I think that's a good concern. I've seen many, many people who said they've been abused, and generally I don't lead people in that direction, I don't think. Because I'm briefly oriented and very problem-focused, I don't typically introduce the topic of abuse, and still I've heard from people that they've been abused; years ago, even before it was a popular thing, I heard it. I think people have been abused and a fair amount of people have been sexually abused—many more than we imagined, I think, in the years past.

I also think that not everyone who says they were abused was abused. Partly, I am really disturbed by this notion of "believe the children." Hav-ing four children of my own, I can tell you very clearly that if you get rid of the violent rhetoric on either side and you raise a child, you'll know that a child does not always tell the strict reality truth about things. A child can fabricate things; a child mixes stories together. Adults mix stories together; I mix stories together. What the heck, we do make some mistakes, or reshuffle our narratives and our memories, so I think that you can't always "believe the children." You'd better err on the side of caution in believing the children; I think that's a good idea. Adults remembering childhood events, I think, are a little shakier, and I think that we need to distinguish between a couple of things. One is, most of us who are doing clinical work are not forensic investigators. It's never going to be our role; we're not going to have the resources to do it; we don't have the expertise to do it. We're not trained in forensic psychology or psychiatry. If we are, we probably can't do clinical work with the same person, because you have to have a different stance to do forensic investigations. When you do clinical work you're advocating for them, you usually try for them. In forensic work you have to be a little more objective, a little less sided, I think, and you're also using different methods for investigation. So I think people who investigate factual truth are different from people who are investigating narrative truth. That is, "This shows up in your experience, and I'm not going to say it didn't happen, that you made it all up. And I'm also not going to say I'm a psychological forensic investigator, and the way you present your symptoms shows me clearly you have been sexually abused."

Hoyt: What do you do when the client says, "My experience is, my memory is, my recall is, this happened to me. Do you believe me?" Do you say, "I believe you experienced it that way"?

O'Hanlon: "Seems like it happened to me, and I don't know for sure; I wasn't there and I'll never know for sure." I'm not going to get into "Yes, I believe that," or "No, I don't."

Hoyt: And if they say, "You have to believe me"?

O'Hanlon: I say, "Look, it seems to me like it happened from the way you say it. It doesn't seem like you made it up to me, and I don't know." I have a client who I mentioned before, the Astoroth person, who went through an extended and, in part, regressive therapy. She "remembered" being abused by a cult; family members were involved in this cult activity. Treatment is over, has been over for some time, the multiplicity is resolved. The therapy went well. Recently there came a situation in which the person was confronted with the possibility of going public, the invitation to go public, with the story. And she said, "You know, I don't know whether this strictly happened or not." It wasn't the same as during treatment, when she said, "I must be making this up. I must be making this up," which she said quite a bit, and I said, "I don't know. It sounds like you're experiencing something and I don't know where it's coming from, but it's pretty heavy-duty stuff." She just said, "I think it happened; I'm pretty sure it happened. I'm not positive." Now, some people would say treatment is incomplete. The treatment issues that she came in for are resolved, the multiplicity is resolved, and she's still not sure it's true reality.

Hoyt: But she's functioning well. She got her therapy.

O'Hanlon: She's a very sophisticated person and is saying this with a very informed judgment. She knows a lot about the field of abuse herself and doesn't say it lightly.

Hoyt: There are also forensic issues, if I understand, that once someone has used hypnosis it may qualify or disqualify the possibility of her testimony.

O'Hanlon: My brother is a district court judge in West Virginia, and he had a case in which a man was accused of rape by two women. This was one of the first cases of DNA testing, where they were trying to use it to establish identity because they had DNA samples from him and from the sperm from both women. These two women became convinced that this guy was the rapist. In part it appears they became convinced because they were hypnotized, and in the hypnosis they remembered the details of it in much more detail, and they became convinced that the guy who was now arrested and accused of it was the guy. And when it was reported in court that the DNA ruled out the possibility that it could be the guy, my brother had to rule whether that could be allowed in because it was controversial new evidence, and the women were still convinced it was the guy, even in the face of this. Then it was discovered that they had been hypnotized. They didn't throw out all the testimony, but they disqualified all the testimony that was reported after the hypnosis. Now, in some jurisdictions, they throw out all the testimony. So, yes, one has to be careful.

Martin Orne [1979] and other people have done experiments that they say show that when one is hypnotized, that what one remembers isn't necessarily strict reality memory, but narratively influenced by the therapist's expectations, by the client's current conditions. And more than that, the client becomes more convinced because it happens experientially, and things that happen experientially seem to be much more potent for people, so they become more convinced even though it's not necessarily true memories. What the advocates of trauma work often say is that "We think experimental evidence is different than what we see in our clinical offices—that we think that traumatic memories may get encapsulated in a special way, so they are not influenced." As I was saying, "frozen in time." Perhaps that's true. Not influenced so much by current narrative, by current conditions. So they are sort of intact memories. But, of course, as soon as one started to remember them, they'd be influenced by current contexts.[17] How come the average number of personalities discovered in multiple personality was several, two to three, until the '70s and '80s, where now it's 36? Those were people who initially were investigating multiple personality who believed in multiplicity, but they didn't discover or know so many multiple personalities. Were there really more personalities? Were there not? I don't know. I just know that it's inextricably bound up with current ideas and current narratives, and you can't separate those things. It's the same as sexual abuse memories. They are inextricably bound up with current narratives as soon as you start to speak about them and bring them into an interactional setting.

In regard to the so-called "false memory syndrome," yes, I think some overzealous therapists can lead clients in the direction of believing that they were sexually abused when they weren't. Do I think it happens a lot? I don't know how much it happens. I think most people you talk to about sexual abuse were sexually abused. And I think what will come out of this polarized debate, which I'm sorry is so polarized, will be some better things for most of us who are in the middle ground. We will be more cautious about introducing those ideas and inadvertently or advertently influencing people, and we'll be more cautious about invalidating people. The people who take a polarized position are saying, "Oh, all this stuff is a bunch of hogwash and it never happened, and you've just been reading too many books or you've read *The Courage to Heal* [Bass & Davis, 1994], so therefore all your memories are invalid." Or, on the other extreme, "Believe the children; this false memory stuff is a conspiracy perpetrated by women-haters and perpetrators." I think that there will be a nice middle ground that will be reached by most of us, and the extremists will fight it out for years. Because they are true believers.

Hoyt: What's next, Bill? What's your current interest?

O'Hanlon: I think this sexual abuse stuff is very interesting, because it seems to me that, like hypnosis, the field of posttraumatic stress—and especially the aftereffects of sexual abuse—really is a proving ground or an experimental ground or learning ground that can shed light on the rest of therapy. This is a particularly difficult situation, the aftereffects of sexual abuse. I think I have learned so much from doing this work that then goes back and applies to general therapy work. I also think it's a very good way to get across to people who typically wouldn't approach anything called "brief therapy" or "solution-oriented therapy." I think it's a really good way to smuggle in some of these ideas about respectful and effective treatment that I've been trying to smuggle into psychotherapy

---

[17]For further discussion of the "true and false memories" controversy, see Courtois (1988, 1992), Loftus (1980; Loftus & Ketcham, 1991), Terr (1990, 1994), and Yapko (1994).

for a long time, through the rubric of treating the aftereffects of sexual abuse. Because I think you can show how respectful and effective these approaches can be, and therapists are desperate for anything that can help the clients that are really hurting so much and are often in physical danger through self-abuse and mutilation and suicidal tendencies and impulses. That's really exciting.

Hoyt: What's the message from your work?

O'Hanlon: Businesses are big on mission statements. Because I read a lot of business books, I decided to sit down and write my mission statement a while ago. I was shocked that it didn't have anything to do with Ericksonian approaches or brief therapy or solution-oriented or even possibility therapy.[18] I really want to transform the field of psychotherapy, change it. I want to oppose and stand against ideas and practices that are disrespectful or harmful and discourage people. I want us to be even better. There are people still hurting out there in the world that we haven't found ways to help. Various theorists and practitioners are coming up with promising ideas that if they really work, some of them are going to revolutionize our work—make it more brief, make it more effective, and really contribute to people, and so I'm really excited about that. I think it's important to stay flexible and stay interested, not just develop your narrow view of things. I have interest in any ideas that I think are respectful and encouraging, and also effective. I'm sure that the approaches that I use aren't as effective as they could be. I want to learn some more over the years, and I have learned more over the years. My contribution to the field of treating the aftereffects of sexual abuse is one of my ways of trying to make the field more diverse and effective, allowing different ideas and combining those ideas with people in ways that work, hopefully.

References

Bandler, R., & Grinder, J. (1975). *The Structure of Magic*. Palo Alto, CA: Science & Behavior Books.
Bandler, R., & Grinder, J. (1982). *Reframing*. Moab, UT: Real People Press.
Bass, E., & Davis, L. (1994). *The Courage to Heal* (3rd ed.). New York: HarperCollins.
Bateson, G. (1972). *Steps to an Ecology of Mind*. New York: Ballantine.

---

[18]In another interview (Bubebzer & West, 1993, pp. 370-371), O'Hanlon commented: "Mainly, what I read for pleasure or interest are business books. Therapy books are usually so pathologically oriented and although I occasionally find a good one, most of them are fairly boring to me. Business books are really good because I learn about creating results, quality, and customer relationships. They talk about getting close to the customer and finding out what the customer's perception is, what the customer's ideas are about, where they want to be, and what constitutes good results."

Bertolino, B., & Caldwell, K. (1999). Through the doorway: Experiences of psychotherapists in an intensive week of training. *Journal of Systemic Therapies, 18*(4), 42–57.

Bertolino, B., & O'Hanlon, W. H. (1999). *Invitation to Possibility-Land: An Intensive Teaching Seminar with Bill O'Hanlon.* Philadelphia: Brunner/Mazel.

Boscolo, L., & Bertrando, P. (1993). *The Times of Time.* New York: Norton.

Boskind-Lodahl, M., & Sirlin, J. (1977, February). The gorging-purging syndrome. *Psychology Today*, pp. 50–56.

Boskind-White, M., & White, W. C. (1983). *Bulimarexia: The Binge-Purge Cycle.* New York: Norton.

Bubenzer, D. L., & West, J. D. (1993). Interview with William Hudson O'Hanlon: On seeking possibilities and solutions in therapy. *The Family Journal: Counseling and Therapy for Couples and Families, 1*(4), 365–379.

Cade, B., & O'Hanlon, W. H. (1993). *A Brief Guide to Brief Therapy.* New York: Norton.

Carnes, P. (1983). *Out of the Shadows: Understanding Sexual Addiction.* Minneapolis: CompCare.

Carnes, P. (1989). *Contrary to Love: Helping the Sexual Addict.* Minneapolis: CompCare.

Castaneda, C. (1968). *The Teachings of Don Juan: A Yaqui Way of Knowledge.* New York: Ballantine.

Courtois, C. (1988). *Healing the Incest Wound: Adult Survivors in Therapy.* New York: Norton.

Courtois, C. (1992) The memory retrieval process in incest survivor therapy. *Journal of Child Sexual Abuse, 1,* 15–32.

Cummings, N. A. (1990). Brief intermittent therapy throughout the life cycle. In J. K. Zeig & S. G. Gilligan (Eds.), *Brief Therapy: Myths, Methods, and Metaphors* (pp 169–184). New York: Brunner/Mazel.

Dolan, Y. M. (1991). *Resolving Sexual Abuse: Solution-Focused Therapy and Ericksonian Hypnosis for Adult Survivors.* New York: Norton.

Dolan, Y. M. (1994). Solution-focused therapy with a case of severe abuse. In M. F. Hoyt (Ed.), *Constructive Therapies* (pp. 276–294). New York: Guilford Press.

Durrant, M., & White, C. (Eds.) (1990). *Ideas for Therapy with Sexual Abuse.* Adelaide, Australia: Dulwich Centre Publications.

Erickson, M. H. (1954). Pseudo-orientation in time as a hypnotic procedure. *Journal of Clinical and Experimental Hypnosis, 6,* 183–207.

Erickson, M. H., Rossi, E., & Rossi, S. (1976). *Hypnotic Realities.* New York: Irvington.

Frankl, V. E. (1963). *Man's Search for Meaning: An Introduction to Logotherapy.* New York: Washington Square Press.

Freud, S. (1958). Remembering, repeating and working-through. In J. Strachey (Ed. and Trans.), *The Standard Edition of the Complete Psychological Works of Sigmund Freud* (Vol. 12, pp. 145–156). London: Hogarth Press. (original work published 1914)

Gale, J., & Newfield, N. (1992). A conversation analysis of a solution-focused marital therapy session. *Journal of Marital and Family Therapy, 18,* 153–165.

Groddeck, G. (1976). *The Book of the It.* New York: International Universities Press. (original work published 1923).

Grove, D.R. (1993). Ericksonian therapy with multiple personality clients. *Journal of Family Psychotherapy, 4*(2), 13–18.

Grove, D.R., & Haley, J. (1993). *Conversations on Therapy: Popular Problems and Uncommon Solutions.* New York: Norton.

Heidegger, M. (1962). *Being and Time.* New York: Harper and Row.

Herman, J. L. (1992). *Trauma and Recovery.* New York: Basic Books.

Hillman, J. (1996). *The Soul's Code: In Search of Character and Calling.* New York: Random House.

Horowitz, M. J. (1986). *Stress Response Syndromes* (rev. ed.). Northvale, NJ: Jason Aronson.

Hoyt, M. F. (1989). Psychodiagnosis of personality disorders. *Transactional Analysis Journal, 19,* 101–113. Reprinted in M. F. Hoyt, *Brief Therapy and Managed Care: Readings for Contemporary Practice* (pp. 257–279). San Francisco: Jossey-Bass, 1995.

Hoyt, M. F. (1990). On time in brief therapy. In R. A. Wells & V. J. Giannetti (Eds.), *Handbook of the Brief Psychotherapies* (pp. 115–143). New York: Plenum Press. Reprinted in M. F. Hoyt, *Brief Therapy and Managed Care: Readings for Contemporary Practice* (pp. 69–104). San Francisco: Jossey-Bass, 1995.

Hoyt, M. F. (1994a). On the importance of keeping it simple and taking the patient seriously: A conversation with Steve de Shazer and John Weakland. In M. F. Hoyt (Ed.), *Constructive Therapies* (pp. 11–40). New York: Guilford Press.

Hoyt, M. F. (1994b). Is being "in recovery" self-limiting? *Transactional Analysis Journal, 24,* 222–223. Reprinted in M. F. Hoyt, *Brief Therapy and Managed Care: Readings for Contemporary Practice* (pp. 213–215). San Francisco: Jossey-Bass, 1995.

Hubble, M., & O'Hanlon, W. H. (1992). Theory countertransference. *Dulwich Centre Newsletter, 1,* 25–30.

Hudson, P. O., & O'Hanlon, W. H. (1992). *Rewriting Love Stories: Brief Marital Therapy.* New York: Norton.

Kaminer, W. (1992). *I'm Dysfunctional, You're Dysfunctional: The Recovery Movement and Other Self-Help Fashions.* New York: Vintage.

Kernberg, O. (1975). *Borderline Conditions and Pathological Narcissism.* New York: Jason Aronson.

Laing, R. D. (1967). *The Politics of Experience.* New York: Pantheon.

Lipchik, E. (1994). The rush to be brief. *Family Therapy Networker, 18,* 34–39.

Loftus, E. (1980). *Memory.* Reading, MA: Addison-Wesley.

Loftus, E., & Ketcham, K. (1991). *Witness for the Defense.* New York: St. Martin's Press.

Masterson, J. F. (1976). *Psychotherapy of the Borderline Adult: A Developmental Approach.* New York: Brunner/Mazel.

Meichenbaum, D. (1994). *A Clinical Handbook/Practical Therapist Manual for Treating PTSD.* Waterloo, Ontario, Canada: Institute Press, University of Waterloo.

Melges, F. T. (1982). *Time and the Inner Future: A Temporal Approach to Psychiatric Disorders.* New York: Wiley.

Miller, G., & de Shazer, S. (1998). Have you heard the latest about . . . ? Solution-focused therapy as a rumor. *Family Process, 37,* 363–378.

Miller, G., & de Shazer, S. (2000). Emotions in solution-focused therapy: A re-examination. *Family Process, 39*(1), 5–23.

O'Hanlon, W. H. (1987). *Taproots: Underlying Principles of Milton Erickson's Therapy and Hypnosis.* New York: Norton.

O'Hanlon, W. H. (1991). Not strategic, not systemic: Still clueless after all these years. *Journal of Strategic and Systemic Therapies, 10,* 105–109. Reprinted in S. O'Hanlon & B. Bertolino (Eds.), *Evolving Possibilities: Selected Papers of Bill O'Hanlon* (pp. 45–49). Philadelphia: Brunner/Mazel, 1999.

O'Hanlon, W. H. (1992). History becomes her story: Collaborative solution-oriented therapy of the after-effects of sexual abuse. In S. McNamee & K. J. Gergen (Eds.), *Therapy as Social Construction* (pp. 136–148). Newbury Park, CA: Sage. Reprinted in S. O'Hanlon & B. Bertolino (Eds.), *Evolving Possibilities: Selected Papers of Bill O'Hanlon* (pp. 109–121). Philadelphia: Brunner/Mazel, 1999.

O'Hanlon, W. H. (1993a). *Escape from DepressoLand: Brief Therapy of Depression.* [Professional training videotape]. Omaha, NE: Possibilities.

O'Hanlon, W.H. (1993b). Frozen in time: Possibility therapy with adults who were sexually abused as children. In L. VandeCreek, S. Knapp & T.L. Jackson (Eds.), *Innovations in Clinical Practice.* Sarasota, FL: Professional Resource Exchange. Reprinted in S. O'Hanlon & B. Bertolino (Eds.), *Evolving Possibilities: Selected Papers of Bill O'Hanlon* (pp. 169–184). Philadelphia: Brunner/Mazel, 1999.

O'Hanlon, W. H. (1994) The third wave. *Family Therapy Networker, 18*(6),18–26, 28–29. Reprinted as "What's the story? Narrative therapy and the third wave in psychotherapy" in S. O'Hanlon & B. Bertolino (Eds.), *Evolving Possibilities: Selected Papers of Bill O'Hanlon* (pp. 205–220). Philadelphia: Brunner/Mazel, 1999.

O'Hanlon, W. H. (1998). Possibility therapy: An inclusive, collaborative, solution-based model of psychotherapy. In M. F. Hoyt (Ed.), *The Handbook of Constructive Therapies* (pp. 137–158). San Francisco: Jossey-Bass.

O'Hanlon, W. H. (1999). *Do One Thing Different: And Other Uncommonly Sensible Solutions to Life's Persistent Problems*. New York: William Morrow.

O'Hanlon, W. H., & Beadle, S. (1994). *A Field Guide to PossibilityLand: Possibility Therapy Methods*. Omaha, NE: Center Press.

O'Hanlon, W. H., & Bertolino, B. (1998). *Even from a Broken Web: Brief, Respectful Solution-Oriented Therapy for Sexual Abuse and Trauma*. New York: Wiley.

O'Hanlon, W. H., & Hexum, A. L. (1990). *An Uncommon Casebook: The Complete Clinical Work of Milton H. Erickson, M.D.* New York: Norton.

O'Hanlon, W. H., & Hudson, P. O. (1994). Coauthoring a love story: Solution-oriented marital therapy. In M. F. Hoyt (Ed.), *Constructive Therapies* (pp. 160–188). New York: Guilford Press.

O'Hanlon, W. H., & Hudson, P. O. (1995). *Love Is a Verb*. New York: Norton.

O'Hanlon, W. H., & Martin, M. (1992). *Solution-Oriented Hypnosis: An Ericksonian Approach*. New York: Norton.

O'Hanlon, W. H., & Schultheis, G. (1993). *Brief Therapy Coach*. [Computer program, Macintosh or IBM-compatible]. Omaha, NE: Possibilities.

O'Hanlon, W. H., & Weiner-Davis, M. (1989). *In Search of Solutions: A New Direction in Psychotherapy*. New York: Norton.

O'Hanlon, W. H., & Wilk, J. (1987). *Shifting Contexts: The Generation of Effective Psychotherapy*. New York: Guilford Press.

Orne, M. (1979). The use and misuse of hypnosis in court. *International Journal of Clinical Hypnosis, 27,* 311–341.

Perls, F. S. (1969). *Gestalt Therapy Verbatim*. Lafayette, CA: Real People Press.

Ricoeur, P. (1983). *Time and Narrative*. Chicago: University of Chicago Press.

Rogers, C. (1951). *Client-Centered Therapy*. Boston: Houghton Mifflin.

Rogers, C. (1961). *On Becoming a Person*. Boston: Houghton Mifflin.

Rowan, T., & O'Hanlon, W. H. (1998). *Solution-oriented therapy for chronic and severe mental illness*. New York: Wiley.

Satir, V. (1967). *Conjoint Family Therapy* (rev. ed.). Palo Alto, CA: Science & Behavior Books.

Schwarz, R.A. (1998). From "either-or" to "both-and": Treating dissociative disorders collaboratively. In M. F. Hoyt (Ed.), *The Handbook of Constructive Therapies* (pp. 428–448). San Francisco: Jossey-Bass.

Terr, L. (1990). *Too Scared to Cry: Psychic Trauma in Childhood*. New York: Harper & Row.

Terr, L. (1994). *Unchained Memories: True Stories of Traumatic Memories, Lost and Found*. New York: Basic Books.

Whitman, W. (1993). *Leaves of Grass* (rev. ed.). New York: Random House/Modern Library. (original work published 1892)

Yapko, M. D. (1994). *Suggestions of Abuse: True and False Memories of Childhood Sexual Trauma*. New York: Simon & Schuster.

Zeig, J. K. (Ed.) (1992). *The Evolution of Psychotherapy: The Second Conference*. New York: Brunner/Mazel.

On Ethics and the Spiritualities of the Surface: A Conversation With Michael White and Gene Combs

Known for the great originality, scope, and humanism of his many contributions, Michael White is the prime enunciator and a key developer of such narrative therapy practices as "externalizing the problem," "deconstructive questioning," and the "reauthoring of lives." The Codirector of the Dulwich Centre in Adelaide, South Australia, his books include his *Selected Papers* (1989), *Re-Authoring Lives: Interviews and Essays* (1995), *Narratives of Therapists' Lives* (1997), and *Reflections on Narrative Practice* (2000) as well as (with his good friend, David Epston) *Experience, Contradiction, Narrative and Imagination* (Epston & White, 1992) and the widely noted *Narrative Means to Therapeutic Ends* (White & Epston, 1990).

Joining us for this interview was Gene Combs, another faculty member. Combs is the Codirector of the Evanston Family Therapy Center and (with his wife, Jill Freedman) is coauthor of *Symbol, Story and Ceremony: Using Metaphor in Individual and Family Therapy* (Combs & Freedman, 1990) and *Narrative Therapy: The Social Construction of Preferred Realities* (Freedman & Combs, 1996), as well as other works on narrative therapy (e.g., Combs & Freedman, 1994; Freedman & Combs, 1993),

The following conversation took place on July 16, 1994, at the Thera-

Originally appeared, with changes, in M. F. Hoyt (Ed.) (1996), *Constructive Therapies, Volume 2* (pp. 33–59). New York: Guilford Press. Used with permission.

peutic Conversations 2 conference held in Reston, Virginia (near Washington, D.C.), where White was serving as a core faculty member. An hour before our meeting, White had presented an excellent workshop on "Consulting Our Consultants." Sitting down to talk, we began by focusing on the heart and soul of his work.

Hoyt: I was very moved by the eloquence of your presentation this afternoon. I thought it was *practical love*. That's what came to my mind: *love in practice*.

White: I can relate to descriptions like this, and believe that we need to be reclaiming these sorts of terms in the interpretation of what we are doing—*love, passion, compassion, reverence, respect, commitment,* and so on. Not because love and passion are enough, but because these terms are emblematic of certain popular discourses; because they are associated with discursive fields that are constituted of alternative rules about what counts as legitimate knowledge, about who is authorized to speak of these knowledges, about how these knowledges might be expressed (including the very manner of speaking of them), about in which contexts these knowledges might be expressed, and so on. And these discursive fields are also constituted of different technologies for the expression of, or for the performance of, these knowledges—different techniques of the self, and different practices of relationship. So what I am saying is that terms of description like *love* and *passion* are emblematic of discourses that can provide a point of entry to alternative modes of life, to specific ways of being and thinking—which will have different real effects on the shape of the therapeutic interaction, different real effects on the lives of the people who consult us, and different real effects on our lives as well.

The rise of the "therapeutic disciplines" has been associated with extraordinary development in the discourses of science, and, of course, in the modern technologies of relationship. So notions of love and of passion haven't been considered relevant to what we might do in the name of therapy. Because we have become alienated from terms of description such as these, the popular discourses that they are emblematic of have not been all that constitutive of our work; these discourses have not had a significant effect on the shape of mainstream therapeutic practices in recent history.

Hoyt: Watching you work, I had the thought that in India people put their hands together and they say, *"Namaste"*—"I salute the divine in you"—meaning "Whatever the story on the surface is, I see something holy or special." If you're a Christian you'd say, "It's the Christ in you"—although I'm not particularly Christian. Watching you work, I keep seeing over and over in the tapes and the discussion with the audience how you hear the positive. I just want to ask you, how do you keep doing that? This has been a very congenial audience, but sometimes the patients are unpleasant, they are challenging, they've done miserable things, they've hurt people, abused people, and yet you're able to meet them with this respect—to kind of separate them from the culture that's been imposed on them. Where does that come from? How can I, how can other people, do more of that? Is there sort of a key or clue that would help us look at people more that way?

White: These are important questions. You have asked two questions. The first was about the spiritual piece, is that right?

Hoyt: Yes. What I'm getting at is not necessarily that we have to be "spiritual" or "religious," but it's looking at people and seeing something in them that's more than the story they're presenting, being able to see the positive underneath all this misery and stuff, seeing there's something good there.

White: The notion of spirituality does interest me. In the histories of the world's cultures, there have been many different notions of spirituality. I won't attempt to provide an account of these, as I've not had the opportunity to study them, and I don't believe that I have even established an adequate grasp of the dominant notions of spirituality in the recent history of my own culture—or, for that matter, in the history of my experience. But I am aware of the extent to which spirituality, in this Western culture, has been cast in *immanent forms*, in *ascendant forms*, and in *immanent-ascendant forms*.

Ascendant forms of spirituality are achieved on planes that are imagined at an altitude above everyday life. It is when people succeed in rising to these altitudes that they experience God's blessing, whomever that God might be. It is on these planes that an understanding of what would approximate a direct correspondence between God's word and one's life is attainable; it is on this plane that it becomes possible to achieve a relatively unmediated expression of God's word.

Immanent forms of spirituality are achieved not by locating oneself at some altitude above one's life, but by descending the caverns that are imagined deep below the surface of one's life. This is a spirituality that is achieved by "being truly and wholly who one really is," "by being in touch with one's true nature," by being faithful to the god of self. Much of popular psychology is premised on a version of this notion of an immanent spirituality—to worship a self through being at one with one's "nature."

And then there are *immanent-ascendant forms* of spirituality, in which spirituality is achieved by being in touch with or having an experience of a soul or the divine that is deep within oneself and that is manifest through one's relationship with a god who is ascendant.

These and other novel contemporary notions of spirituality are of a nonmaterial form. They propose spiritualities that are relatively intangible; that are split apart from the material world, that manifest themselves on planes that are imagined above or below the surface of life as it is lived. Although I find many of the contemporary immanent-ascendant notions of spirituality to be quite beautiful, and the notion of the soul far more aesthetically pleasing than the notion of the psyche, and although I remain interested in exploring the proposals for life (or, if you like, the ethics) that are associated with these notions of spirituality, I am more interested in what might be called the material versions of spirituality. Perhaps we could call these the *spiritualities of the surface.*

The spiritualities of the surface have to do with material existence. These are the spiritualities that can be read in the shape of people's identity projects, in the steps that people take in the knowing formation of the self. This is a form of spirituality that concerns one's personal ethics; that concerns the modes of being and thought that one enters one's life into; that is reflected in the care that one takes to attain success in a style of living. This is a transformative spirituality, in that it so often has to do with becoming other than the received version of who one is. This is a form of spirituality that relates not to the nonmaterial, but to the tangible. And I believe that this is the sort of spirituality to which Foucault [1980] referred in his work on the ethics of the self.

So, to return to your question, when I talk of spirituality I am not appealing to the divine or the holy. And I am not saluting human nature, whatever that might be, if it does exist at all. The notion of spirituality that I am relating to is one that makes it possible for me to see and to appreciate the visible in people's lives, not the invisible. It is a notion of spirituality that makes it possible for us to appreciate those events of people's lives that just might be, or might provide for, the basis for a knowing formation of the self according to certain ethics. The notion of spirituality that I am relating to is one that assists us to attend to the material options for breaking from many of the received ways of life—to attend to those events of people's lives that provide the basis for the constitution of identities that are other than those which are given. And in this sense it is a spirituality that has to do with relating to one's material options in a way that one becomes more conscious of one's own knowing.

I hope that this answer to your question is not too obscure, but this provides some account of what spirituality is about for me.

Hoyt: No, your response is not obscure. I get the essence. It is about knowing self-formation.

White: Yes. For me a notion of spirituality would have to be about this. It is about the exploration of the options for living one's life in ways that are other in regard to the received modes of being. It is to do with the problematizing of the taken-for-granted, the questioning of the self-evident. At times it is about the refusal of certain forms of individuality; about the knowing transgression of the limits of the "necessary" ways of being in the world; about the exploration of alternative ways of being, and of the distinct habits of thought and of life associated with these ways of being. In many ways it is about seizing upon indeterminacy, and about the reinvention of who we are. And it is about prioritizing the struggle with the moral and ethical questions relating to all of this.

Combs: The thing I'm interested in is how people decide which of those possibilities to privilege, and I think that's one of the places where therapists, whether they want to or not, are given power. To become one who one has not been could go in an infinite number of directions.

White: It could, I agree.

Combs: What can you say about what your experience is, what you're guided by? Which of those directions to privilege?

White: In the work itself, this is achieved by consulting people about the particularities of those alternative ways of being. This is to be in ongoing consultation with people about the real effects of specific ways of being in their relationships with others and on the shape of their lives generally. I don't think the goal is to settle on some specific "other" way of being in the world, to "fix" one's life. This work engages people with others in ongoing revisions of their images about who they might be, and about how they might live their lives. And it engages people in an ongoing critique of notions of identity that are based on our culture's many naturalized ideas about this. In fact, this work opens options for people to divest their lives of many of these notions. And in so doing, it raises options for people to explore the possibilities for disengaging from the sort of modern practices of self-evaluation that have them locating their lives on the continuums of growth and development, of health and normality, of dependence and independence, and so on. These options can also constitute a refusal to engage in those modern acts of self-government that have us living out our lives under the canopy of the bell-shaped curve.

Hoyt: So we offer them, "You know, you don't have to be this way. You could continue in the path you're on, but there are alternatives. Would you like to look at those?" Is that . . .

White: Yes. Well, I guess so, in a fairly crude way of putting it. I think it is about actually joining with people in the knowing exploration of, and the performance of, options for ways of being in life that might be available to them. It is to engage with people in a choice making, about these options, that is based on expressions of their lived experience and on expressions of alternative knowledges of life.

Hoyt: When we use invitations or wondering or externalizing or any kind of deconstructing,[1] it seems to me we're still in some way highlighting certain options or suggesting, "You may want to consider this"—putting it crudely—and that gets into the power differential. Are we in some way subtly suggesting which alternatives they might take?

White: Of course we are influential, and of course there is a power differential. And it has often been claimed that because of this there can be no way of differentiating between different therapeutic practices on the basis of subjugation; that because of this fact of influence and because of this fact of power, one therapeutic practice cannot be distinguished from another; that there is a certain equity between all therapeutic practices in terms of their real effects. But this blurring of important distinctions around forms and degrees of influence within the therapeutic context is unfortunate. In fact, I believe the blurring of this distinction to be a profoundly conservative act that permits the perpetration of domination in the name of therapy, and excuses those actions that establish therapists as unquestioning accomplices of the status quo.

It has also been said that because we are of our culture's discourses and that we cannot think and act outside of them, that we are condemned to reproduce in therapy the very relations of power and experiences of self, or subjectivities, that it might be our intent to assist people to challenge. What an extraordinarily reductionist, unitary, global, and monolithic account of culture, of life, we are being encouraged to embrace by this account. What are the real effects of this sort of argument? How does it mask contestation and undermine struggle? In what ways does it contribute to the further marginalization of alternative knowledges of ways of being in the world, of alternative subjectivities?

In terms of practice, there is a very significant difference between, on the one hand, delivering interventions that are based on some external

---

[1] As White (1991/1993, p. 34) has written: "According to my rather loose definition, deconstruction has to do with procedures that subvert taken-for-granted realities and practices: those so-called 'truths' that are split off from the conditions and the context of their production; those disembodied ways of speaking that hide their biases and prejudices; and those familiar practices of self and of relationship that are subjugating of persons' lives. Many of the methods of deconstruction render strange these familiar and everyday taken-for-granted realities and practices by objectifying them." He goes on (1991/1993, pp. 35–36) to explain: "Deconstruction is premised on what is generally referred to as a 'critical constructivist,' or, as I would prefer, a 'constitutionalist' perspective of the world. From this perspective, it is proposed that persons' lives are shaped by the meaning that they ascribe to their experience, by their situation in social structures, and by the language practices and cultural practices of self and of relationship that these lives are recruited into. The narrative metaphor proposes that persons live their lives as stories—that these stories are shaping of life, and that they have real, not imagined, effects—and that these stories provide the structure of life."

formal analysis of a problem, or suggesting to people that they should work on their independence" or "growth" or whatever, and, on the other hand, encouraging people to attend to some events of their lives that just might be of a more sparkling nature—events that just might happen to contradict those plots of their lives that they find so unrewarding and dead-ended—and to ask them to reflect on what these events might say about other ways of living that might suit them and that might be available to them; to join with people in the exploration of the knowledges and practices of life that might be associated with these alternative plots; to contribute to their exploration of the alternative experiences of the self that might be associated with these knowledges and practices; and to encourage them to take stock of the proposals for action that might be associated with all of this. There is an important distinction to be drawn in regard to these two classes of response.

Aside from such distinctions, we can't pretend that we are not somehow contributing to the process. We can't pretend that we are not influential in the therapeutic interaction. There is no neutral position in which therapists can stand. I can embrace this fact by joining with people to address all of those things that they find traumatizing and limiting of their lives. I can respond to what people say about their experiences of subjugation, of discrimination, of marginalization, of exploitation, of abuse, of domination, of torture, of cruelty, and so on. I can join them in action to challenge the power relations and the structures of power that support all of this. And, because the impossibility of neutrality means that I cannot avoid being "for" something, I take the responsibility to distrust what I am for—that is, my ways of life and my ways of thought—and I can do this in many ways. For example, I can distrust what I am for with regard to the appropriateness of this to the lives of others. I can distrust what I am for in the sense that what I am for has the potential to reproduce the very things that I oppose in my relations with others. I can distrust what I am for to the extent that what I am for has a distinct location in the worlds of gender, class, race, culture, sexual preference, etc. And so on.

I can take responsibility in establishing the sort of structures that contribute to the performance of this distrust. As well, I can find ways of privileging questions in therapy that reflect this distrust over ways of asking questions that would propose my favored ways of living. I can make it my responsibility to deconstruct my notions of life, to situate these in structures of privilege, in regard to which I can engage in some actions to dismantle.

Hoyt: Let me read you a quotation, if I may:

> There is a power differential in the therapy context and it is one that cannot be erased regardless of how committed we are to egalitarian practices. Although there are many steps that we can take to render the therapeutic

interaction more egalitarian, if we believe that we can arrive at some point in which we can interact with those people who seek our help in a way that is totally outside of any power relation, then we're treading on dangerous ground. [White, quoted in McLean, 1994, p. 76]

In addition to reflecting on and asking them to reflect on, how else can we stay aware of the ethics of our influence?

White: I think through a significant confrontation with this fact—that there is a power imbalance. When I propose this confrontation, I am not suggesting that this fact be celebrated, and I am not suggesting that the acknowledgment of this fact is a justification for the use of power by the therapist. And in proposing this confrontation, I am not suggesting that distinctions can't be made in regard to different therapeutic interactions on the basis of the exercise of power and on the basis of subjugation. Instead, I am proposing a confrontation that opens possibilities for us to take steps to expose and to mitigate the toxic effects of this imbalance. I am proposing a confrontation that encourages us to explore the options that might be available to us to challenge the interactional practices and to dismantle the structures that support this power relation.

For example, we can set up the sort of "bottom-up" accountability structures that I have discussed elsewhere [see McLean, 1994]. We can talk with the people who consult us about the dangers and the possible limitations of that power imbalance, and we can engage them in the interpretation of our conduct with regard to this. But I have also made the point that it would be dangerous for us to believe that it is possible to establish a therapeutic context that is free of this power relation. This would be dangerous for many reasons. It would make it possible for us to avoid the responsibility of monitoring the real effects of our interactions with people who seek our help. It would make it possible for us to deny the moral and ethical responsibilities that we have to people who seek our help, and that they don't have to us. It would make it possible for us to avoid persisting in the exploration of options for the further dismantling of the structures and the relational practices that constitute this power imbalance.

Hoyt: It is through accountability structures that this can be achieved?

White: Well, this is part of accountability: doing whatever we can to render transparent some of the possible limitations and dangers of that power imbalance, and setting up structures that encourage people to monitor this. In this way we are able to more squarely face the moral and ethical responsibilities that we have in this work. And I would again emphasize that it would be perilous to attempt to obscure, to ourselves, the fact of this power imbalance. This would only make it possible for us to neglect the moral and ethical responsibilities that we have to the people who consult us.

Hoyt: At the beginning of the [Therapeutic Conversations 2] conference, we were asked how would we know by the end if we "got it." I've come during the conference more and more to think of therapy as "empowerment through conversation." I just want to ask you to reflect on that. How are you defining "therapy" these days? Or what's an alternative word?

White: First, I'd like to address your initial comment. This idea of being able to predict where we might be at the end of a process if all goes well is, I believe, a sad idea. It is my view that this is an idea that is informed by the dominant ethic of control of contemporary culture, although I do know that many would debate this point. I figure that conferences probably wouldn't be worth going to if we knew, in advance, where we would be at the end of them. There is a certain pleasure or joy available to us in the knowledge that we can't know where we'll be at the end; in the sense that we can't know beforehand what we will be thinking at the end; in the idea that we can't know what new possibilities for action in the world might be available to us at that time. It seems to me that to engage in prediction about where we might be at the end of a process if all goes well is to obscure, and to close down, options for being somewhere else. And why obscure the options for being somewhere else?

Hoyt: It could take away surprise and discovery, couldn't it?

White: If I planned to go to a conference, and if I knew beforehand what I would be thinking at the end, then I wouldn't go. *[laughter]* It is like that with this work. If I knew where we would be at the end of the session, I don't think I would do this work. And this is also true for the sort of reflecting teamwork[2] that is structured according to the narrative metaphor. If reflecting team members got together and prepared their reflections ahead of their reflections—if their reflection was in fact a performance of previously articulated reflections—then it is more likely that team members will be where they predicted they would be at the end of these reflections, and the more likely it will be that everyone will become quite bored and possibly even comatose—and I have witnessed this sort of outcome. On interviewing therapists about their experience of working in this fashion, I find that it is invariably constitutive of their working lives and relationships in ways that are experienced as undesirable.

However, if team members don't undertake these preparations—if they don't know what they will be thinking about and talking about by the time that they arrive at the end of their reflections, and if the teamwork is structured in a way that facilitates this sort of interaction—then it is more likely that their work together will contribute to the shaping of their own lives and relationships in preferred ways.

---

[2]See Anderson (1991), Friedman (1995), Cohen, Combs, DeLaurenti, DeLaurenti, Freedman, Larimer, and Shulman (1998), and White (1995, 2000).

Hoyt: In Zen, they might say you need to keep a "beginner's mind" [Suzuki, 1970]—a fresh look, not having things preconceived.

White: So that's my response to the first part of your question. I think we will experience a better outcome from conferences if they contribute to some steps towards building some foundation for some other possibilities that we might not have predicted beforehand. The second part of your question had to do with how I would define therapy. Well, I define it in different ways on different days.

Hoyt: What's today's date?

Combs: The 16th.

Hoyt: At this point in time, at this moment.

White: At this very moment, just for today, I think it has to do with joining with people around issues that are particularly relevant and pressing to them. It has to do with bringing whatever skills we have available to assist people in their quest to challenge or to break from whatever it is that they find pressing. It is our part to work with people to assist them to identify the extent to which they are knowledged in this quest. And it is to join with people in the exploration of how their knowledges might be expressed in addressing the predicaments that they find themselves in.

In this work, people experience being knowledged, but this is not the starting point. Experiencing this is the outcome of a process that is at once characterized by *resurrection* and *generation*. As therapists, we play a significant role in setting up the context for this. We assist people to gain access to some of these alternative knowledges of their lives by contributing to the elevation of the substories or subplots of their lives, by contributing to the resurrection of some of the knowledges of life that are associated with historical performances of these subplots. And we join with people in the generation of knowledges of life through the exploration of the ways of being and thinking that are associated with these subplots. I have shared my proposals for this process at some length in a number of publications, and will not reiterate them here. Perhaps it would be sufficient to say here that the subplots of people's lives provide a route to the exploration of alternative knowledges of life.

It is our part to assist in the identification of possibilities for action that are informed by these other knowledges of life. It is also our part to encourage people to evaluate the desirability of these other ways of being and thinking, through an investigation of the particularities of the proposals for action that are informed by them—through the exploration of the particularities of a life as it is lived through and constituted by these alternative knowledges.

I don't know if this answer to your question is a particularly good or appropriate answer. And if it's not a good answer, it's my answer for to-day at least. Perhaps if we do this interview again tomorrow, I just might be able to answer your question differently at that time. This is my hope.

Combs: I guess I just want to make sure I was tracking what you were saying. So, as a therapist, you're curious about and listening for what are at the moment lesser plots, subplots, counterplots, whatever, and kind of sorting through those and exploring some of those with the person, and asking them which of those might be interesting to them or useful to them?

White: Yes, I guess so. People are explicitly consulted about these sub-plots of their life. If the therapist's position on these subplots is privi-leged—if the therapist's position is primary—then imposition will be the outcome, and collaboration will be not be achieved. To avoid this imposi-tion, and to establish collaboration, before proceeding we need to know how people judge those developments that might provide a gateway to the identification and exploration of these subplots: Do they see them as positive or negative developments, or both positive and negative, or nei-ther positive nor negative? And we need to engage people in the naming of these subplots of their lives. Apart from this, it is also important that we have some understanding of why it is that people so judge these de-velopments and these subplots of their lives. How do these developments fit with their preferred accounts of their purposes and values and so on?

But this is not the whole story. It is never just a matter of determining what developments might be interesting or useful to people. This is not predominantly a cognitive thing. In this work, these subplots of people's lives are actually experienced by those who consult us. In the course of the work itself, people live these subplots. Or, if you like, people's lives are embraced by these subplots. These subplots are not stories about life; they are not maps of the territory of life; they are not reflections of life as it is lived. These subplots are structures of life, and in fact become more constitutive of life.

And one further point about what is at work here. There is much that remains to be said about the language of this work, about how it evokes the images of people's lives that it does. Many of the questions that we ask about the developments of people's lives are powerfully evocative of other images of who these people might be, and other versions of their identities. These images reach back into the history of people's lived ex-perience, privileging certain memories, and facilitate the interpretation of many previously neglected aspects of experience. So the language of the work, of the very questions that we ask, is evocative of images which trigger the reliving of experience, and this contributes very significantly to the generation of alternative story lines.

Combs: So the expertise you bring . . .

Hoyt: Well, Michael made a very good distinction, I thought, in the last presentation between *expert knowledge*, meaning "I am the expert here," versus an *expert's skills*, as I took it, meaning knowing how to ask questions in a way that will let the clients experience *their* local expertise, their local knowledge [see Wood, 1991]. I think that is very different from the dominant voice.

Combs: So the knowledge you bring is knowledge about how to evoke in an experiential way these alternative images.

White: Yes. I have often been misrepresented on this point. I have never denied the knowledgeableness of the therapist. And I have never denied the fact of therapist skillfulness. I have, however, challenged the privileging of the therapist's knowledgeableness above the knowledgeableness of people who consult therapists. And I have critiqued the "expert knowledges." I have critiqued expert knowledge claims, including those that make possible the imposition of global and unitary accounts of life and the development of formal systems of analysis. I have critiqued the power relations by which these expert knowledges are installed, including those that are essential to the normalizing judgment of the subject, that are so effective in the government of people's lives. Throughout this critique, I have supported what is generally referred to as, after Clifford Geertz [1983], the "interpretive turn."

Hoyt: I had the idea that in looking for the "sparkling moments," looking for the "unique outcomes," looking for the "exceptions," in a way what we're trying to do is help the person build a past to support a better future [see White, 1993]—create some kind of structure under them, "thickening," I think you were using as a phrase, kind of fleshing it out or filling it in. Do I have that idea right?

White: I'm really interested in the conditions under which people might "take a leaf out of their alternative books," rather than defining a goal and determining what steps might be necessary to reach that goal. When people get to the point of experiencing the unfolding of preferred developments in the recent history of their lives, they have some sense of where their next step might be placed. Such steps are informed by a developing appreciation of a preferred story line.

Hoyt: We're making it up as we go along?

White: Yes, to an extent, yes. I say "to an extent" because, although there might be certain circumstances under which we might witness what we assume to be clear breaks from the "known," it is rather difficult to think outside of what we specifically know, and, more generally, rather impossible to think outside of knowledge systems.

In regard to the knowing formation of our lives, it seems that we are, to an extent, dependent upon developing an account of how some of our recent steps fit together with classes of steps that can be read as unfolding in sequences through time according to some theme or perhaps plot. Even upon stepping into unfamiliar territories of identity, coherence appears to be a guiding criterion. And because of this, so is culture and its knowledges of ways of being and thinking in the world.

Hoyt: As somewhat of an alternative to the idea of evolution being a continuous process, I think we're getting now into the idea of evolution not being continuous but being discontinuous, punctuated evolution.[3] Stephen Jay Gould [1980], for example, talks about how things are steady-state, and something extraordinary comes along—like meteorites strike the earth, stirring up dust which kills the plant-eating dinosaurs, then that wipes out the meat eaters, and that opens the niche for mammals. There can be a sudden shift or something can be discontinuous. I relate this to page 6 of *Narrative Means to Therapeutic Ends* [White & Epston, 1990], in that table where you talk about "before and after," "betwixt and be-tween," the whole "rites of passage" idea.[4] Sometimes we see people who feel prisoners of the path they have been on it so long, and how can they leap off it? So there are these submerged paths, I take from what you're saying, that remind them of other routes.

White: Yes, there are these sudden shifts, these apparent discontinuities. And at these junctures we can feel quite lost. Perhaps it is useful to think of this experience as a liminal or betwixt-and-between phase, one that is understandably confusing and disorienting. There is always a distance between the point of separation and the point of reincorporation. But the question remains: Is it possible to break with something without stepping into other ways of being and thinking that are not in some way continu-ous with something else? Is it possible to step apart from familiar modes of life and of thought and to step into some cultural vacuum, one that is free of contexts of intelligibility? Historical reflection suggests that there

---

[3]See Rosenbaum, Hoyt and Talmon (1990).

[4]Building on the work of van Gennep (1960) and Turner (1969), White and Epston (1990; also see Epston & White, 1995) suggest that rather than attempting to return a patient in crisis to a "good enough" status quo, if one thinks of the crisis in terms of a "rite of pas-sage," then a different construction of the problem is invited; different questions may be asked; and progressive movement is fostered in a different direction. By locating the crisis in relation to a *separation phase*, a liminal or *betwixt-and-between phase*, and a *reincorporation phase*, the person can determine (1)what the crisis might be telling him or her about sepa-rating from what was not viable for him or her, (2)what clues the crisis gives about the new status and roles that might become available, and (3)how and under what circum-stances the new roles and status might be realized.

are very few sites of radical discontinuity. But there are always margins of possibility.

Hoyt: I see what you are saying. We take something up as well as separate from something.

White: Yes. We step into other modes of life and of thought that go before us. But I believe that there are opportunities for us to contribute to the "drift" of these modes of life and of thought, as we live them, through processes that relate to the negotiation of the different subjectivities or experiences of the self that are associated with these, through interpretation, and through the management of indeterminacy.

Perhaps we could say that within continuity there is discontinuity. And this consideration takes us back to the discussion that preceded these comments. I have a problem with the idea of converting metaphors that come from the nonliving world, and from biology for that matter, into the realm of human life, which is the realm of practice and of meaning, and a realm of achievement. I don't believe that this is ever a realm of how things just happen to be. For example, the achievement aspects of this realm can be witnessed in the work that people put into attributing meaning to a whole range of experiences, and the extent to which many of their actions are prefigured on this.

Hoyt: Rather than mechanizing or animalizing or taking us to where we're not.

White: Exactly. And I can't think of one metaphor from the nonliving world that I think is appropriate to human life and human organization— to people who live in culture, who live in language, who participate in making meanings that are constitutive of their lives together. But I don't know if this is relevant to this interview or not.

Hoyt: It is now. *[laughter]*

White: Can I just come back to a point that was made earlier? Gene, around the time that we were talking about the image, you asked me about the nature of this work. What was the question again?

Combs: I was trying to imagine how it is that you conceptualize what it is that you do, what it is that you bring to the therapy situation, and I was also just trying to experience as much as I could for myself what it would be like to be you being a therapist. What am I thinking I should do next? To what am I listening?

Hoyt: What is going on in Michael's head when he is working?

Combs: Yeah.

White: "To what am I listening?" is a good question. And I would say that my listening is informed by some of my preferred metaphors for this work. I particularly relate to poetics. I could read you a piece on poetics by David Malouf, because it fits so well with my conception of this work, and because he says it so much better than I could.

Hoyt: Please.

White: *[searches in his bag and pulls out a typewritten page]* This is a piece from a book called *The Great World* [Malouf, 1991]. This book is substantially about men's experience of Australian men's culture. In it David Malouf talks about how poetry speaks:

> How it spoke up, not always in the plainest terms, since that wasn't always possible, but in precise ones just the same, for what is deeply felt and might otherwise go unrecorded: all of those unique and repeatable events, the little sacraments of daily existence, movements of the heart and intimations of the close but inexpressible grandeur and terror of things, that is our *other* history, the one that goes on, in a quiet way, under the noise and chatter of events and is the major part of what happens each day in the life of the planet, and has been from the very beginning. To find words for *that*; to make glow with significance what is usually unseen, and unspoken to: that, when it occurs, is what binds us all, since it speaks immediately out of the centre of each one of us; giving shape to what we too have experienced and did not till then have words for, though as soon as they are spoken we know them as our own. [Malouf, 1991, pp. 283–284]

I so relate to this invocation of the "little sacraments of daily existence." The word *sacrament* invokes mystery. And it evokes a sense of the sacred significance of the little events of people's lives; those little events that lie in the shadows of the dominant plots of people's lives, those little events that are so often neglected, but that might come to be regarded with reverence, and at times with awe. These little sacraments are those events that have everything to do with the maintenance of a life, with the continuity of a life, often in the face of circumstances that would otherwise deny this.

These little sacraments of people's lives can be read for what they might tell us all about existence, about the particularities of how we exist. I don't believe that there is such a thing as "mere existence." Existing is something that we all do, and have obviously been doing now for many, many years. But it has, in so many ways, had such bad press in recent decades. Why is this the case? Why is it becoming so hard for us to read and to appreciate the little sacraments of daily life? Perhaps this is because these sacraments are on the other side of our culture's ethic of control. Perhaps it is because these little sacraments of daily life don't relate all that well to the accepted goals for life in this culture—like demonstrating "control over one's life." And perhaps it is because they don't fit with contemporary definitions of the sort of actions that count as responsible actions. I believe that through the metaphor of poetics it becomes possible for us to challenge the marginalizing of existence, and to all play some part in the honoring of those facts that Malouf refers to as the "little sacraments of daily existence."[5]

Combs: When you say "the little sacraments of daily existence" and you talk about finding the words, I find myself thinking about the close of Ken Gergen's [1994] talk this morning. I don't know that it in any way relates to this. He was talking about inchoate experience, that experience that's not yet quite language and yet that is just before. Does that in any way relate to what you're talking about, sort of the next step of making that—sitting with somebody and then bringing that in a language, bringing that into society?

White: What Malouf is saying about the little facts of daily life fits, I believe, with the notion of the "spiritualities of the surface" that we have been discussing. But I don't know whether or not what I am saying here has any relation to what Ken Gergen was saying. But it might, and I would like to understand more about what he is proposing before responding to your question.

Hoyt: It's the "poetics of experience" as well as the "politics of experience."

White: Yes, it is that as well.

Hoyt: I heard Robert Bly, the poet, read a long, beautiful, evocative poem, and someone stood up in an audience and said, "Robert, what did it mean?" Bly said, "If I knew what it meant I would have written an essay, not a poem!" *[laughter]* I thought what Gergen was getting at was that same special moment, the sacrament, I think some people call it the spirit of life, when it's *happening* rather than just . . . I'll have to ask him.

White: It will be interesting to hear what he says.[6]

Hoyt: I once asked Ronnie Laing what he thought of transference. I said, "What's your definition of it, or what do you think of it?" He said, "Oh, it's posthypnotic suggestion with amnesia." *[laughter]* Posthypnotic suggestion with amnesia, which I relate to the whole idea of *mystification* [Laing, 1967]—that we've been sort of programmed or given this suggestion of how to take things, and we don't even remember that we were given it, so we're kind of locked in. I just wanted to ask if that, from a

---

[5]Along related lines, Bruner (1986, p. 153) reminds us of James Joyce's phrase "epiphanies of the ordinary." Mary Catherine Bateson (1995, p. 56) comment is also cogent: "As a society, we have become so addicted to entertainment that we have buried the capacity for awed experience of the ordinary. Perhaps the sense of the sacred is more threatened by learned patterns of boredom than it is by blasphemies."

[6]See Chapter 8 (pp. 200–202) for Gergen's comments.

very different frame, is a way of talking about deconstructing? Does deconstruction get one to the consciousness where you recognize you've been, to use a modern word, programmed?

White: Yes. This is a take on the practices of deconstruction that I can relate to. And I would like here to pick up Laing's contribution to the deconstruction of what we are talking about when we are talking about the phenomenon of transference. The notion of "posthypnotic suggestion with amnesia" does bring forth the history of the interactional politics that are generative of this phenomenon, and this encourages us to think of the "technologies of transference" as technologies of power. And, needless to say, since transference is a phenomenon that is invariably psychologized, to bring forth the technologies of transference does serve to deconstruct this.

But these technologies of transference are not just the historical conditions for the constitution of the transference phenomenon. Transference can also be read as the "trace" of very present power relations. People experience what they call "transference" most strongly in hierarchical situations when they are in the junior or subject position, and, of course, ideally (although it does occur in less formal contexts), when they are supine and in a state of vulnerability in relation to another person who is sitting erect—one who is considered an established authority on life, and who denies the subject any information that would situate this authority in his or her lived experience, intentions, or purposes. Here I describe just a few of the conditions and technologies of transference.

Perhaps it would be more appropriate to say that the experience of transference is the trace of power relations that are relatively fixed and approaching a state of domination. So, a strong and ongoing experience of transference can cue people to the fact that they are in a subject position in an inflexible power relationship that could lead to domination. This reading of transference opens possibilities for action that can include a refusal of this power relation.

I don't want to be misrepresented on this point. I'm not saying that there is no such phenomenon as transference. And I do understand that there are those who would justify bringing forth this phenomenon with the idea that this establishes a context for working though issues of personal authority, and so on. But I do think that there is a politics associated with this phenomenon, and [I] would raise questions about the deliberate and not so deliberate reproduction of these politics in the therapeutic context. And I would also want to explore the sort of questions that could contribute to a dismantling of the therapeutic structures that reproduce this phenomenon.

Hoyt: How would you describe the ethic of your work?

White: To answer this question, we should talk about what is generally meant by *ethics*. As Foucault [1980] observed, mostly, these days, when people are talking about ethics they are referring to rules and codes, and no doubt these have a place. But it is unfortunate that, in this modern world, considerations of the rule and the code have mostly overshadowed and even replaced considerations of personal ethics. Something precious is lost when institutional codes and rules for the government of conduct supplant notions of personal ethics. It is in the professional disciplines that we see this taken to its limits, and it is done so in the name of assuring appropriate professional conduct.

Invariably, it is argued that the privileging of matters of rule and code is preventative of the exploitation of people who consult therapists. But I don't believe that the elevation of the rule or code has achieved this anywhere in the modern world. In fact, it can be argued that such a reliance on the sort of top-down systems of accountability that are associated with systems of rule and code provide fertile ground for the very perpetuation of such injustices, of such exploitation.

At other times, when people are referring to "ethics," they are formulating questions about their existence that are informed by what Foucault refers to as a "will to truth," and, in this modern world, there has been a fantastic incitement to this will to truth. This is a notion of ethics that gives primary consideration to whatever it might be that is understood to constitute expressions of the truth of "who we are." The notions of rule and code are central to this version of ethics as well, as whatever it is that constitutes an expression of the truth of who we are is what is informed by the rules of human nature—however nature might be constructed, and however these rules might be determined.

Modern versions of this center on notions on the rule of needs: "How might we keep faith with our deepest needs?" It is chilling to consider the sorts of actions that can be justified according to modern need discourses. It is not difficult to apprehend the extent to which this will to truth marginalizes considerations of personal ethics, and obscures matters of discourse in the constitution of peoples lives. And this will to truth is still about the rule of law, only in this case it is a "natural law."

Then there is another style of ethical consideration that has a long history in Western culture, one that is referred to at those times when clashes of interest become apparent between people. This is the sort of consideration that makes it possible for people to discern between actions that are informed by selfishness on the one hand, or by altruism on the other. According to this determination, if altruism can be discerned in the actions in question, then such actions are judged to be ethical. Sarah Hoagland [1988] observes that this style of ethical consideration is one that women have principally been subject to, and that it has played a central role in women's subordination. She powerfully deconstructs this consideration in her book, *Lesbian Ethics*.

And other times the criterion of ethical action is not altruism, but "responsible behavior": people can be considered to be behaving ethically when they are taking responsibility in and for their lives. So often, the version of responsibility that is referred to here is one that is informed by the ethic of control. According to this ethic, responsible action is that version of action that reflects independent and singular action on the world that succeeds in bringing about some goal in the relatively short term, and when these actions are referenced to some universal notion of the good, or some principle, like "justice" or "rights." To behave ethically is to take action that counts in the sense that it "measures up." This notion of responsible action that is informed by the ethic of control is the version that Sharon Welch [1990] deconstructs in her book, *A Feminist Ethic of Risk*.

Hoyt: So, what is your account of the ethic of the work we have been discussing?

White: In different places, including during this interview, I have endeavored to draw out the version of personal ethics that frames the work that I do. I have talked of the *knowing formation of the self*. I have talked of a version of *responsibility* which supports a commitment to identifying and addressing the real effects or the consequences of one's actions in the lives of others. And because this is not something that we can independently determine, either by our own interpretations of our immediate experience, or through recourse to some guiding principle, I have talked of the necessity of *accountability*. This is a specific notion of accountability—a bottom-up version, rather than a top-down version—and it is a version of accountability that is available in partnership with other people, or groups of people. It is an accountability that is in fact constitutive of our lives, one that brings many possibilities for us to become other than who we are.

I have also talked of the principle of *transparency*. This is a principle that is based on a commitment to the ongoing deconstruction of our own actions, of our taken-for-granted ways of being in this work, of our taken-for-granted ways of thinking about life. This is a principle that requires us to situate our opinions, motives and actions in contexts of our ethnicity, class, gender, race, sexual preference, purposes, commitments, and so on.

I have talked of ways of being in the world that have to do with working with others to establish what we could call the "foundations of possibility" for their lives and for ours. This is not about acting independently on the world to achieve some predicted goal in a proscribed time, but about *working collaboratively in the world* in taking steps to prepare the foundations for new possibilities in the time that it takes to do this.

And I have talked about many of the other aspects of this ethic, including the extent to which we can make it our business to develop an *attitude of reverence* for what Malouf calls "the little sacraments of daily existence," and the extent to which we can enter into a *commitment to challenge the practices and the structures of domination of our culture.*

Hoyt: So, this ethic suggests a course of action that is distinct from one that is informed by a traditional goal orientation.

White: Yes. It is on the other side of this. But there are important distinctions to be made here. Not all practices that invoke the notion of goal wittingly or unwittingly reproduce this culture's dominant ethic of control. I doubt that anyone would read the work of Steve de Shazer and Insoo Berg in this way.[7] And I also want to state that this is not an argument for a return to long-term therapy. To the contrary. While the ethic of control structures a context in which there are not many events that really count for all that much, this alternative ethic structures a context in which just so much that couldn't be acknowledged previously can be acknowledged. And, in so doing, it provides for an antidote to despair, for a sense of possibility in regard to one's life going forward, and for a broad range of options for further action.

Hoyt: Why do you do therapy? Why do you do this work?

White: This is not a new question. Way back in my social work training, which I began in 1967, we were required to address this question. This was in the heyday of structuralist thought. At that time, in response to such questions, only certain accounts of motive were considered acceptable. These were psychological accounts of motive. Accounts of motive that features notions of conscious purpose and commitment were not fashionable and were marginalized. Responses to this question that emphasized a wish to contribute to the lives of others in some way, or that were put in terms of a desire to play some part in addressing the injustices of the world, were considered expressions of naiveté. Attempts to stand by such expressions were read as examples of denial, lack of insight, bloody-mindedness, etc. On the other hand, to traffic in psychologized accounts of motive was to display insight, truth saying, a superior level of consciousness, of maturity, and so on. And invariably, the psychologizing of motive translated into the pathologizing of motive. "Which of all of one's neurotic needs was being met in stepping into this profession?" "How did this decision relate to unresolved issues in one's family of origin?" "Did this decision relate to one's attempts to work through an enmeshed relationship with one's mother?" "Or did this decision relate to one's attempt to work through a disengaged relationship with one's mother?" And so

---

[7]See Chang and Phillips (1993), de Shazer (1993), White and de Shazer (1996).

on. I'm sure that you are familiar with questions of this sort, and that we could easily put a list together.

I always believe that this privileging of psychological accounts of motive to be a profoundly conservative endeavor, one that is counter-inspiration, one that could only contribute significantly to therapist experiences of fatigue and burnout. For various reasons, I could never be persuaded to step into the pathologizing of my motives for my interest in joining this profession, and mostly managed to hold on to what were my favored notions of conscious purpose and commitment. I have no doubt that over the years that expressions of these notions have been a source of invigoration to me, and in recent years I have been encouraging therapists to join together in identifying, articulating, and elevating notions of conscious purpose and commitment.[8] To this end I have developed an exercise that you can include along with the publication of this transcript. Readers might be interested in meeting with their peers and working through this together. [The exercise immediately follows this interview.]

Hoyt: At the beginning of this conference, they showed a short tape that was made two weeks ago of John Weakland greeting the conference, and John invited us to consider what are the priorities in the field now. What is important and what isn't? I want to ask if you have a sense of where we're headed, what you think is important, what we need to be doing more of, what you want to privilege?

White: I never want to make a prediction.

Hoyt: Not a prediction of where we're going to wind up, but more a sense of . . .

White: What's important for us to be looking at?

Hoyt: Yes.

White: It is necessary for us to be taking more seriously what many have been saying about race, culture, gender, ethnicity, class, age, and so on. For too long we have operated with the idea that the people who seek our help have ethnicity and we don't. *[laughter]* Not only do we need to join with people in assisting them to locate their experiences in the politics of these contexts, but we are challenged to break from the sort of practices that obscure our own location, and to find ways of engaging with others in reflecting on how this location might be affecting how we interpret our experiences of other people's lives—and, of course, how it might be affecting our conduct.

Hoyt: I heard Joseph Campbell [1983], when someone asked him his

---

[8]See White (1995) and Hoyt and Nylund (1997).

definition of *mythology*, say it's "other people's religion," which we kind of dismiss as superstition.

White: Unlike ours. Yeah.

Hoyt: Let me read a quotation that gets to something I want to ask. In *Experience, Contradiction, Narrative and Imagination*—a wonderful title as I've come to understand it—you and David Epston comment:

> One of the aspects associated with this work that is of central importance to us is the spirit of adventure. We aim to preserve this spirit and know that if we accomplish this, our work will continue to evolve in ways that are enriching to our lives and to the lives of persons who seek our help. [Epston & White, 1992, p. 9]

My question is, what's next in your adventure? What's sparking your interest now? I know you began to speak earlier today about some social justice projects.

White: This is a difficult question for me. There are so many things that have my attention at the moment, and they are all things that I want to step more into. Yes, some of these activities do have to do with what we have often formally referred to as "social justice projects." But this is not a discontinuity. I've always refused the sort of distinctions that put what is commonly referred to as "clinical practice" in one realm, and "community development and social action" in another.[9] This is not a distinction that I can relate to. It is a distinction that makes it possible for therapists to treat the therapeutic context as if it is exempt from the relational politics of culture, and to disavow the fact that therapeutic interaction is about action in the world of culture.

Perhaps I can answer your question about "where to from here" in a different way. I recently saw a movie called *Schindler's List*, and then read a piece about the latter years of Schindler's life. At the time he was living in a bedsitter somewhere in southern Germany, I think in Munich. He would frequent the local bars, and on those occasions when he found himself in the company of people of his own generation, he would ask the simple question: "And what did you do?"—referring, of course, to the Holocaust. Now it was my understanding that this was a genuine question, not a claim to moral superiority. I don't know how many people he found who had answers to this question. I found myself reflecting on this question, and thought it relevant to my life. It is a question that could be

---

[9]In discussing White's (1991/1993) masterful paper "Deconstruction in Therapy," Tomm (1993) comments on what he calls White's "courage to protest," to speak out effectively against oppression and injustice. Tomm makes a point of noting that White not only deconstructs but also helps clients to *re*construct, and says about White, "as a therapist he is an applied deconstruction activist" (1993, p. 174).

asked of me in relation to the many abuses of power and privilege, in relation to the many injustices, that I witness in my immediate world. But if anyone approached to ask this question of me right now, I would request a moratorium on it. I would say, "Please don't ask me this question yet, it is too soon. I'll keep working on the answer, but please come back later in my life. I hope to have an answer, one that is to my satisfaction, at that time." And I don't think that it will have to be a big answer, or a grand answer.

Combs: I was just the other day at the Holocaust Museum in Washington, D.C. I don't know if you've been there yet, but at the end of the museum you come to a Hall of Remembrance. It's a large open space where there are no flash cameras or loud noises. And when I got there I sat and found myself making a pledge, to myself or God or whatever. It wasn't even in specific words, but it was a clear pledge or a promise.

Hoyt: I know what you mean.

White: It takes us back to this issue of elevating and honoring the spirit of love and passion and conscious commitment.

Hoyt: Michael, in Australia, what does *fair dinkum* mean?

White: It means something said that is absolutely true, deeply genuine.

Hoyt: Michael, Gene: Fair dinkum!

☐ Conscious Purpose and Commitment Exercise

Introduction: We have discussed the extent to which the privileging of psychological accounts of motive has marginalized statements of conscious purpose and commitment in this work. We have reviewed the extent to which such statements are pathologized in the culture of psychotherapy, as well as the implications of this in regard to the stories that we have about who we are as therapists. The following exercise will engage you in acts of resistance to this—acts that are associated with the elevation and reclamation of statements of conscious purpose and commitment. I suggest that you invite another person or two to join you in this exploration, for the purposes of sharing your responses to this exercise, or for the purposes of being interviewed about these responses.

1. Talk about any experiences that you have had that relate to the psychologizing and the pathologizing of your motives for choosing this work, or any reinterpretations of this choice that may have encouraged you to mistrust your statements of conscious purposes or your personal commitment to this work.

2. Review what you can assume to be some of the real effects or consequences, in your work and your life, of this psychologizing of your
motives, and of this pathologizing of your accounts of your conscious
purposes and commitments.

3. Identify and retrieve some of your very early statements of conscious
purpose that relate to your chosen work, however unsophisticated
these might have been, and reflect on what they suggest about what
you are committed to in this work.

4. Share some information about the significant experiences of your life
that have contributed to a further clarification of your conscious purposes and commitments in taking up this work—that have generated
realizations about the particular contribution that you have a determination to make during the course of your life.

5. Discuss the experiences that you are having in the course of this exercise: those experiences that are associated with engaging in giving testimony and in bearing witness to expressions of conscious purpose;
those experiences that are associated with the honoring of statements
of commitment.

6. Talk about how the elevation of your notions of conscious purpose
and the honoring of your statements of commitment could affect:

a. Your experience of yourself in relation to your work.

b. Your relationship to your own life.

c. Your relationship to your colleagues and to the people who seek
your help.

d. The shape of your work and of your life more generally.

☐ References

Andersen, T. (Ed.). (1991). *The Reflecting Team: Dialogues and Dialogues about the Dialogues.*
New York: Norton.

Bateson, M. C. (1994). *Peripheral Visions: Learning Along the Way.* New York: HarperCollins.

Bruner, J. (1986). *Actual Minds, Possible Worlds.* Cambridge, MA: Harvard University Press.

Campbell, J. (1983). *Myths to Live By.* New York: Penguin.

Chang, J., & Phillips, M. (1993). Michael White and Steve de Shazer: New directions in
family therapy. In S. G. Gilligan & R. Price (Eds.), *Therapeutic Conversations* (pp. 95–
111). New York: Norton.

Cohen, S. M., Combs, G., DeLaurenti, B., DeLaurenti, P., Freedman, J., Larimer, D., &
Shulman, D. (1998). Minimizing hierarchy in therapeutic relationships: A reflecting
team approach. In M.F. Hoyt (Ed.), *The Handbook of Constructive Therapies* (pp. 276–
292). San Francisco: Jossey-Bass.

Combs, G., & Freedman, J. (1990). *Symbol, Story, and Ceremony: Using Metaphor in Individual
and Family Therapy.* New York: Norton.

Combs, G., & Freedman, J. (1994). Narrative intentions. In M. F. Hoyt (Ed.), *Constructive
Therapies* (pp. 67–91). New York: Guilford Press.

de Shazer, S. (1993). Commentary: de Shazer and White: Vive la différence. In S. G. Gilligan & R. Price (Eds.), *Therapeutic Conversations* (pp. 112–120). New York: Norton.

Epston, D., & White, M. (1992). *Experience, Contradiction, Narrative and Imagination: Selected Papers of David Epston and Michael White, 1989–1991.* Adelaide: Dulwich Centre Publications.

Epston, D., & White, M. (1995). Termination as a rite of passage: Questioning strategies for a theory of inclusion. In R. A. Neimeyer & M. J. Mahoney (Eds.), *Constructivism in Psychotherapy* (pp. 339–354). Washington, DC: American Psychological Association.

Foucault, M. (1980). *Power/Knowledge: Selected Interviews and Other Writings 1972–1977.* New York: Pantheon.

Freedman, J., & Combs, G. (1993). Invitations to new stories: Using questions to suggest alternative possibilities. In S. G. Gilligan & R. Price (Eds.), *Therapeutic Conversations* (pp. 291–303). New York: Norton.

Freedman, J., & Combs, G. (1996). *Narrative Therapy: The Social Construction of Preferred Realities.* New York: Norton.

Friedman, S. (Ed.). (1995). *The Reflecting Team in Action: Collaborative Practice in Family Therapy.* New York: Guilford Press.

Geertz, C. (1983) *Local Knowledge.* New York: Basic Books.

Gergen, K. (1994). *Between Alienation and Deconstruction: Re-Visioning Therapeutic Communication.* Keynote address, Therapeutic Conversations 2 Conference. Weston, VA.

Gould, S. J. (1980). *The Panda's Thumb: More Reflections in Natural History.* New York: Norton.

Hoagland, S. (1988). *Lesbian Ethics.* Palo Alto, CA: Institute of Lesbian Studies.

Hoyt, M.F., & Nylund, D. (1997). The joy of narrative: An exercise for learning from our internalized clients. *Journal of Systemic Therapies, 16*(4), 361–366. Reprinted in M.F. Hoyt, *Some Stories are Better than Others: Doing What Works in Brief Therapy and Managed Care.* Philadelphia: Brunner/Mazel, 2000.

Laing, R. D. (1967). *The Politics of Experience.* New York: Pantheon.

Malouf, D. (1991) *The Great World.* Sydney: Pan Macmillan.

McLean, C. (1994) A conversation about accountability with Michael White. *Dulwich Centre Newsletter,* Nos. 2–3, 68–79.

Rosenbaum, R., Hoyt, M. F., & Talmon, M. (1990). The challenge of single-session therapies: Creating pivotal moments. In R. A. Wells & V. J. Giannetti (Eds.), *Handbook of the Brief Psychotherapies* (pp. 165–189). New York: Plenum Press. Reprinted in M. F. Hoyt, *Brief Therapy and Managed Care: Readings for Contemporary Practice* [pp. 105–139]. San Francisco: Jossey-Bass, 1995.

Suzuki, S. (1970). *Zen Mind, Beginner's Mind.* New York: Weatherhill.

Tomm, K. (1993). The courage to protest: A commentary on Michael White's work. In S. G. Gilligan & R. Price (Eds.), *Therapeutic Conversations* (pp. 62–80). New York: Norton.

Turner, V. (1969). *The Ritual Process.* Ithaca, NY: Cornell University Press.

van Gennep, A. (1960). *The Rites of Passage.* Chicago: University of Chicago Press.

Welch, S. (1990). *A Feminist Ethic of Risk.* Minneapolis, MN: Fortress Press.

White, M. (1989). *Selected Papers.* Adelaide: Dulwich Centre Publications.

White, M. (1993). Deconstruction and therapy. In S. G. Gilligan & R. Price (Eds.), *Therapeutic Conversations* (pp. 22–61). New York: Norton. (Original work published in the *Dulwich Centre Newsletter,* 1991, No. 3, 1–21. Also reprinted in D. Epston & M. White, *Experience, Contradiction, Narrative and Imagination* [pp. 109–152]. Adelaide: Dulwich Centre Publications, 1992.)

White, M. (1993). Commentary: The histories of the present. In S. G. Gilligan & R. Price (Eds.), *Therapeutic Conversations* (pp. 121–135). New York: Norton.

White, M. (1995). *The Re-Authoring of Lives: Interviews and Essays.* Adelaide: Dulwich Centre Publications.

White, M. (1997). *Narratives of Therapists' Lives*. Adelaide: Dulwich Centre Publications.

White, M. (2000). *Reflections on Narrative Practice: Essays and Interviews*. Adelaide: Dulwich Centre Publications.

White, M., & de Shazer, S. (1996, October 10–11). *Narrative Solutions/Solution Narratives*. Conference sponsored by Brief Family Therapy Center, Milwaukee.

White, M., & Epston, D. (1990). *Narrative Means to Therapeutic Ends*. New York: Norton.

Wood, A. (1991). Outside expert knowledge: An interview with Michael White. *Australian and New Zealand Journal of Family Therapy, 12*(4), 207–214. (Reprinted in M. White, *Re-Authoring Lives: Interviews and Essays*, pp. 60–81]. Adelaide: Dulwich Centre Publications, 1995.)

CHAPTER

Cognitive-Behavioral Treatment of Posttraumatic Stress Disorder from a Narrative Constructivist Perspective: A Conversation With Donald Meichenbaum

One of the founders of the "cognitive revolution" in psychotherapy and a major proponent of the constructivist perspective, Donald Meichenbaum is Distinguished Professor Emeritus at the University of Waterloo in Ontario, Canada; and Director of the Melissa Institute for Violence Prevention and Treatment of Victims of Violence in Miami, Florida. A prolific writer, researcher, and international lecturer, he is the author of the classic *Cognitive-Behavior Modification: An Integrative Approach* (1977). His other books include *Stress Reduction and Prevention* (Meichenbaum & Jaremko, 1983), *Pain and Behavioral Medicine: A Cognitive-Behavioral Perspective* (Turk, Meichenbaum, & Genest, 1983), *The Unconscious Reconsidered* (Bowers & Meichenbaum, 1984), *Stress Inoculation Training: A Clinical Guidebook* (1985), *Facilitating Treatment Adherence: A Practitioner's Guidebook* (Meichenbaum & Turk, 1987), and *Nurturing Independent Learners: Helping Students Take Charge of Their Learning* (Meichenbaum & Biemiller, 1998). In a survey reported in *American Psychologist*, clinicians voted him "one of the ten most influential psychotherapists of the [20th] century."

Originally appeared, with changes, in M. F. Hoyt (Ed.) (1996), *Constructive Therapies, Volume 2* (pp. 124–147). New York: Guilford Press. Used with permission.

The following conversation took place in San Francisco on May 4, 1994, where Meichenbaum was to present a two-day workshop on "Treating Patients with Posttraumatic Stress Disorder" for the Institute for Behavioral Healthcare. We had just been looking at the typescript of his then-forthcoming magnum opus, *A Clinical Handbook/Practical Therapist Manual for Treating PTSD* (1994)[1], an extraordinary compendium of information for clinicians and researchers working with persons suffering the effects of traumatic stress.

Hoyt: The first question I want to ask you, Don, is how did you come to think of treating PTSD [posttraumatic stress disorder] as a narrative constructive endeavor?

Meichenbaum: For a number of years, I have been involved in treating adults, adolescents, and children with behavioral and affective disorders who were depressed, anxious, angry, and impulsive. Based on my research and clinical experience with these populations, I was invited to present a number of training workshops. Then a very interesting set of invitations came my way when I was given the opportunity to consult and conduct research on a variety of different distressed populations. I was asked to consult on a treatment program within the U.S. military on spouse abuse. I also consulted with mental health workers who conducted debriefing of natural disasters, occupational accidents, and combat. I also consulted at residential treatment programs for children and adolescents, some 40% of whom met the *DSM* criteria for PTSD. In addition, I was supervising various mental health workers (psychiatrists, psychologists, social workers, family physicians) who were treating clients who had a history of victimization experiences—child sexual abuse, rape, domestic violence. As I became more and more involved with these populations and spent many hours listening to the therapy tapes, looking at the debriefing experiences, I became quite fascinated with the nature of the "stories" that people offered to describe their traumatizing experiences and how they coped—that is, the narratives and the accounts that they constructed.

Hoyt: What about the stories?

Meichenbaum: I became fascinated with how people describe their experience and how their accounts changed over time. While victimization experiences can affect individuals at various levels (e.g., physiologically, behaviorally, socially), given my cognitive-behavioral background and my interest in cognition and emotion, I became particularly interested in the nature of the "stories" that people tell themselves and others, and the

---

[1]An updated and revised edition of this 600-page manual is available directly from Donald Meichenbaum (University of Waterloo, Department of Psychology, Waterloo, Ontario N2L 3G1, Canada).

manner in which they offer accounts of their experience. When something bad happens to you, when some natural or man-made disaster occurs, when some form of victimization experience occurs to you or to your family, ordinary language and everyday vocabulary seem inadequate to describe your experience and reactions. In their own ways, these "victimized" individuals became "poets" of sorts, using metaphors to describe their experiences. They conveyed their experiences by using phrases such as "This is like . . . ," "I feel like a . . . ," and so forth. The victimized individual may describe herself as a "prisoner of the past," as a "doormat," a "whore," as a "time bomb ready to explode," and the like. Just imagine the impact on yourself and on others if you go about describing your experiences in such metaphoric terms.

As a result of these initial clinical impressions, I undertook the task of analyzing the nature of the metaphors and the narrative accounts that clients offered over the course of their therapeutic sessions. I also analyzed the literature on PTSD in order to discern what were the narrative features of individuals who did *not* suffer PTSD following exposure to traumatic events [Meichenbaum, 1994; Meichenbaum & Fitzpatrick, 1993]. Based upon both the clinical analysis and the literature review, I came to appreciate the heuristic value of a constructive narrative perspective, not only for PTSD, but for other clinical disorders as well. Obviously, I am not the first to propose such a constructive narrative perspective. Let me note that there are people like Harvey [Harvey, Weber, & Orbuch, 1990], Gergen [1991; McNamee & Gergen, 1992], Schafer [1992], White and Epston [1990], and O'Hanlon [O'Hanlon & Weiner-Davis, 1989] who have also advocated for a constructive narrative perspective.

Hoyt: Let me read you a quotation from an article you wrote with Geoffrey Fong [Meichenbaum & Fong, 1993, p. 489]. You said:

> The constructivist perspective is founded on the idea that humans actively construct their personal realities and create their own representational models of the world. There is a long tradition of philosophical and psychological authors who have argued that the paradigms, assumptive worlds, and schemas that individuals actively create, determine, and in some instances constrain how they perceive reality.[2]

---

[2]Meichenbaum and Fong (1993, p. 489) go on:

Common to each of these proponents is the tenet that the human mind is a product of constructive symbolic activities and that reality is a product of the personal meanings that individuals create. Individuals do not merely respond to events in and of themselves, but they respond to their interpretation of events and to their perceived implications of these events. . . . Constructivists assume that all mental images are creations of people, and thus, speak of "invented reality." How individuals construct such meanings and realities, how they create their world view is the subject of narrative psychology.

When someone becomes a victim, has a horrible trauma, how does that affect them? What changes, especially in terms of their world view?

Meichenbaum: The answer to what changes after you've been victimized depends on which piece of the puzzle you look at—sort of like the old metaphor of the elephant, whether you examine the tusk, the tail, or whatever. Clearly, there is increasing evidence that something changes physiologically [see van der Kolk, 1994]. This is especially true of chronic, prolonged exposure, or what are called *Type II stressors* (e.g., abuse, domestic violence, Holocaust victim). Such exposure leads to what are called "disorders of extreme stress" that affect one's sense of trust in family and beliefs about self and the world. To use Janoff-Bulman's [1985, 1990] model, traumatic events can "shatter" your basic assumptions about the world; traumatic events can violate and invalidate your core beliefs. Another thing that trauma does is overly sensitize you to trauma-related cues, and this hypervigilance feeds into, and is in turn affected by, the ruminations, flashbacks, and avoidance behaviors that characterize PTSD. Trauma biases the ways in which you selectively attend to events. There is a great deal of data that I review in the PTSD clinical handbook [Meichenbaum, 1994] that examines the impact of trauma from an information-processing and a constructive narrative perspective.

Hoyt: Is this primarily a protective mechanism: "I need to be on alert so it won't happen again"?

Meichenbaum: I think there are functional and adaptive values in such behavior. To become vigilant and to overrespond after exposure to a trauma can be adaptive initially. But what happens to the people who have difficulty recovering, who evidence maladjustment, is that they continue to behave in ways that may be no longer necessary. From my point of view, a central feature of individuals with PTSD can be characterized as a "stuckness" problem. That is, people get "stuck" using techniques such as dissociation that were at one time effective in order to deal with trauma such as incest, or dealing with the aftermath of rape, or dealing with combat. What happens is that some individuals continue to respond in the same fashion even when it is no longer needed. It is my task as a therapist to help clients understand and appreciate the adaptive value of how they responded. But I also help them appreciate what is the *impact*, what is the *toll*, what is the *price* to them and others of continuing to respond in this fashion when it is no longer needed. This approach helps clients reframe their reactions (their "symptoms") as adaptive strengths, rather than as signs of mental illness. In a collaborative fashion, this approach "inoculates" them, in some sense, to the impact of future stressors. We work together to help them not only change their behavior, but also to tell their "stories" differently.

Hoyt: In your writing about stress inoculation training (SIT), you describe three phases: namely, *education, skills acquisition and consolidation,* and *application training.* The first phase, of education, sounds like you are having clients work to better understand the impact of their . . . [3]

Meichenbaum: I even go beyond understanding, to nurturing the client's discovery process by using Socratic questioning. In the PTSD handbook [Meichenbaum, 1994], I have included the best Socratic questions you can ask in therapy. Moreover, I believe that I am at my "therapeutic best" when the client I am seeing is one step ahead of me, offering the advice that I would otherwise offer. I try to train clinicians how to emulate that fine inquirer of sorts—namely, Peter Falk playing the popular TV detective character, Columbo. I want clinicians, at times, to play "dumb." For some clinicians this is not a difficult nor challenging role. *[laughter]* I encourage clinicians to use strategically their bemusement, their befuddlement; I want them to be collaborators. The goal is to help the client in the initial phase of stress inoculation to better understand what they have been through; how are things now; how would they like them to be; and what can *we* do, working together, to help them achieve their goals? The educational phase of SIT lays the groundwork whereby the client can come to say, "You know, I'm stuck." A related objective of this initial phase is to help clients move from global metaphorical accounts of their experience and reactions to behaviorally prescriptive descriptions that lead to change, and to nurture a sense of hope to undertake this change.

Hoyt: In essence, I think you're saying that as clinicians we're trying to help clients reauthor their narratives, rather than us undertaking the role of correcting their accounts. We're there as sort of an amanuensis, as an

---

[3]Meichenbaum (1993, 1994; Meichenbaum & Fitzpatrick, 1993; Meichenbaum & Fong, 1993) describes key features of SIT as including the following:
a. Establishment of a nurturant, compassionate, nonjudgmental set of conditions in which distressed clients can tell their stories at their own pace.
b. Normalization of distressed individuals' reactions.
c. Reconceptualization of the distress process.
d. Breaking down or disaggregating global descriptions of clients' distress into specific, concrete, behaviorally prescriptive stressful situations.
e. Performance of personal experiments that produce experientially meaningful occurrences, in a gradual manner. These experiments should test the limits of how clients will respond to reentering the stressful situation, via imagery, via behavioral rehearsal, and eventually in real situations.
f. Encouragement of taking credit for positive outcomes of coping efforts.
g. Relapse prevention, including teaching ways to anticipate, accept, and cope with lapses so that they don't escalate into full-blown relapses.
[4]What's "right" is what works for the client. Again, to quote Meichenbaum and Fitzpatrick (1993, p. 698):
There are two important features to recognize about this reconceptualization or new

assistant, rather than simply to correct their narratives or to tell them they're looking at it wrong[4] [see Simon, 1988, p.72].

Meichenbaum: Correct. The metaphors that describe my therapeutic approach include "rescripting," "reauthoring," "helping clients generate a new narrative," and "being a coach." I don't just record the clients' accounts; rather, I help them alter their personal stories. Such change occurs as a result of my helping clients attend to and appreciate the strengths they possess, or what they have done to survive. A second way is to help them engage in "personal experiments" in the present that provide them with "data" that they can take as evidence to "unfreeze" the beliefs they hold about themselves and the world. The results of such ongoing experiments that occur both within and outside of the therapeutic setting provide the basis for the client to develop a new narrative. This co-constructive process is one that emerges out of experientially meaningful efforts by the client. In terms of strengths and coping efforts, I help people who have PTSD to appreciate that their intrusive thoughts, hypervigilance, denial, dissociation, dichotomous thinking, and moments of rage each represent coping efforts, and metaphorically reflect the "body's wisdom." For example, intrusive thoughts may reflect ways of making sense of what happened, as attempts to "finish the story," to answer "why" questions. Denial may be an attempt to "dose oneself," dealing with limited amounts of stress at a given time—a way to take a "time out." Hypervigilance may be seen as being on continual "sentry duty" when it is no longer needed.

In other words, it is not that people get anxious, angry, or depressed per se; those are natural human emotions. Rather, it is what people say to themselves about those conditions that is critical. The collaborative process of therapy is designed to help the client "say" different things to herself, as well as to others. A key element of cognitive-behavioral interventions is that an effective way of having people talk to themselves differently is to have them *behave* differently. Thus, a critical feature of cognitive-behavioral interventions such as stress inoculation training, is to encourage and even challenge clients to perform personal experiments *in vivo*, so, as I mentioned, they can collect data that will "unfreeze" their beliefs about themselves and about the world. Cognitive-behavioral therapy is *not* just a "talking cure." It is a proactive, enabling form of intervention that fits an "evidential" theory of behavior change (see Meichenbaum, 1977, 1994).

But such change is *not* enough. It is critical for clients to take credit for

---

narrative reconstruction process. First, the scientific validity of the specific healing theory that is developed is less important than is its plausibility or credibility to the client. Secondly, this entire "narrative repair" effort is conducted in a collaborative inductive fashion and not imposed upon, nor didactically taught, to distressed individuals. The distressed client must come to develop and accept a reconceptualization of the distress that he or she has helped co-create.

the changes that they have brought about. There is a need for the therapist to ensure that the clients take data resulting from personal experiments as evidence, and thus assume a greater sense of responsibility for the changes that they have brought about. This process of "ownership" is evident in the new narratives that clients relate. I listen carefully to the clients' stories. I listen for their spontaneous use of metacognitive self-regulatory verbs as part of their new accounts. Improvement is evident when clients use such verbs as "I noticed . . . caught myself . . . interrupted . . . used my plan . . . felt I had options . . . patted myself on the back . . . became my own coach . . . anticipated high risk-situations . . . tried my other options." When clients incorporate these expressions into their narratives, then they have become their own therapists, and truly have taken (appropriated) the clinician's "voice" with them.

Hoyt: This is the power of new *experience*—not just explanation of what's wrong, but disconfirming the expectations with a new experience.[5]

Meichenbaum: But for meaningful change to occur, it has to be "affectively charged." I am referring to the time-honored concept of "corrective emotional experience" [Alexander & French, 1946]. People can readily dismiss, discount, dissuade themselves of the "data." They don't really accept data as "evidence," and it is critical therapeutically to work with clients in order to ensure that they take the data they have collected as evidence to unfreeze their beliefs—to get into the nature of the clients' belief system and to nurture an internal dialogue that they would find most adaptive, as compared to being "stuck" in maladaptive patterns of thinking and behaving.[6]

---

[5]Carl Whitaker (1983, p. 40): "Learning only brings recognition; experience produces change." As discussed in *The First Session in Brief Therapy* (Budman, Hoyt & Friedman, 1992), the introduction of *novelty* is a key element across different therapeutic approaches. As the adage has it, "If we don't change directions, we'll wind up where we are heading!" (Hoyt, 1990, p. 128).

[6]Some of the ways people who have experienced traumas get "stuck" are catalogued by Meichenbaum and Fitzpatrick (1993, p. 697). These include the following:

   a. making unfavorable comparisons between life as it is and as it might have been had the distressing event not occurred;
   b. engaging in comparisons between aspects of life after the stressful event versus how it was before, and also continually pining for what was lost;
   c. seeing themselves as "victims" with little expectation or hope that things will change or improve;
   d. engaging in "undoing" counterfactual thinking of "only if"; "If I only had"; "I should have"; and continually trying to answer "Why" questions for which there are no satisfactory answers;
   e. failing to find any meaning or significance in the stressful event;
   f. dwelling on the negative implications of the stressful event;
   g. seeing themselves as continually at risk or vulnerable to future stressful events;
   h. feeling unable to control the symptoms of distress (i.e., viewing intrusive images, nightmares, ruminations, psychic numbing, avoidant behaviors, hyperarousal, and exaggerated startle reactions as being uncontrollable and unpredictable);
   i. remaining vigilant to threats and obstacles.

Hoyt: Watching you work, I'm always impressed by how much caring and effort goes into developing a therapeutic alliance and a collaborative relationship with the client. It appears to be the vehicle that carries the rest of your work.

Meichenbaum: I agree. I think the therapeutic relationship is the glue that makes the various therapeutic procedures work. Some of the things that I try to highlight for a clinical audience watching my videotapes is how often I "pluck" and reflect the client's key words, use Socratic questioning, and often over the course of the session, I let the client finish my sentences. The most valuable tool that a clinician has is the art of questioning. As Tomm [1987a, 1987b, 1988) has highlighted, the questions we ask clients have presuppositions, and as a result the clinician can use questions effectively and strategically to move clients towards self-generated solutions.

Let me also highlight, however, that in this movement toward solutions, a major clinical concern which is critical is that of timing. If the clinician only focuses on the positive, if you have clients move toward solutions too quickly, then the clients may *not* feel you have heard their emotional pain, nor appreciated the seriousness of their situations. You need to encourage clients to tell their stories, at their own pace, and to be in charge. But out of the telling of their stories, out of the narrative sharing—and there's a lot of therapeutic value in sharing one's story—new stories emerge that also reveal strengths and resources. As the radio commentator Paul Harvey highlights, there is a need to hear "the rest of the story." Clients come in and tell us their stories. Their stories are often filled with expressions of hopelessness and helplessness. They often convey a tale of having been victimized by individuals, by events, by their feelings and thoughts. It is my job, as the therapist, to not only hear their stories and empathize with them, but also to help them appreciate what they have done to survive and to cope with their feelings—namely, help them attend to "the rest of the story." For "the rest of the story" is often the tale of remarkable strengths.

Keep in mind that the story of how people cope with stressful events such as incest, rape, the Holocaust, war experiences, urban and domestic violence, [and] man-made and natural disasters is inherently the story of resilience and courage of human beings. That is, if you look at the impact of disasters, most people are going to "make it" and *not* evidence long-term debilitating effects. So even in the worst scenarios, people evidence remarkable strengths. As a therapist, I need clients to attend to that part of their stories. There are a number of clinical techniques designed to accomplish this goal and to incorporate these features into their personal narratives. Thus, the "bad things" that happened to people are only one chapter in their life stories. And, as Judith Herman [1992] indicates, it is *not* the most interesting chapter of their autobiographies.

Hoyt: Oftentimes brief therapists (and others) rush past the painful material, trying to reframe or restructure so quickly that the person doesn't feel heard or validated. Do you think there's also—maybe following from Aristotle—a need for catharsis and abreaction? Is that part of the cure, or is it . . .

Meichenbaum: That is a challenging question. I can offer my clinical impressions, given the limited database that exists [see Meichenbaum, 1994]. The question about differential forms of treatment is complex. How one should proceed therapeutically is dependent upon which target group you are looking at. If you are treating people who have experienced traumas that are brief, sudden, yet life-threatening, such as automobile accidents, robberies, rape, and sudden disasters, or what have been characterized as "Type I stressors" [Terr, 1994] . . .

Hoyt: You mean relatively discrete, sudden-onset stressors.

Meichenbaum: Yes. The data suggest that having clients go through reexperiencing procedures as a means of "coming to terms" with what happened is therapeutic and beneficial. Indeed, there are a variety of very creative clinical techniques, including direct therapy exposure, guided imagery procedures, graded *in vivo* procedures, and the like, that are helpful. They fit your Aristotelian catharsis model and provide a means of "working through" that can prove valuable.

Hoyt: What about people with more prolonged trauma?

Meichenbaum: When, however, you are treating a different traumatized clinical group, where the PTSD is chronic and the traumatic events occurred many years ago, the treatment decision to undertake "memory work" of having clients "go back" may *not* be the most effective treatment strategy. Having clients recount and reexperience traumatic events, even in the area of incest, may not be the most therapeutic approach. Because in the attempt to conduct so-called "memory work," there is the danger that the therapist can inadvertently, unwittingly, and perhaps even unknowingly, help clients co-create memories. With such prolonged traumas that have a number of secondary sequelae, it is important to address the secondary consequences such as depression, interpersonal distrust, sexual difficulties, addictive behaviors, and the like that may accompany PTSD. The full cognitive-behavioral therapeutic armamentarium needs to be employed to address these signs of comorbidity. A "here-and-now" therapeutic focus, as compared to a "there-and-then" approach, may prove most helpful. Research is needed to determine how to blend the need for "memory work" with a coping skills model. But keep in mind that from a constructive narrative perspective, even when clients are doing so-called "memory work," they are not relating nor "uncovering" history, but rather they are co-constructing history in a mood-congruent fashion. As Donald Spence [1982] observes, it is the "narrative truthfulness," not the "historical truthfulness," of clients' accounts that needs to be the focus of therapeutic interventions.[7]

Hoyt: You have worked clinically with many diverse groups, and you have taught and given workshops internationally. How do these guidelines vary across these diverse settings?

Meichenbaum: That question raises the important issue of how important it is to be culturally sensitive in formulating a treatment plan. Let me give you an example. As I review in the clinical handbook on PTSD [Meichenbaum, 1994], there are "testimony" procedures that are sometimes used in treating people who have been victims of torture. These procedures have individuals "go public" with what traumas they have experienced and what retribution should occur. For instance, one group of torture victims for whom this testimony procedure has been used came from Argentina, Chile, and other South American countries. Agger and Jensen [1990] have described how having these survivors write out testimonies, bear witness, go back and relive what happened, was highly therapeutic. On the other hand, there is another group of victims of torture who come from Southeast Asia—Cambodia and other countries—who have also received treatment. Therapists such as Mollica [1988] and Kinzie [1994] have indicated that a somewhat different therapeutic approach—one that is designed to deal with their "here-and-now" problems, their practical employment and living situations, rather than do "memory work"—is more effective. The torture victims' cultural orientation suggested that treatment should *not* encourage clients to go back and relive their victimization experiences per se.

Thus, being sensitive to cultural differences should influence the nature and form of the intervention. When I am in doubt, I spell out the treatment options and collaborate with the client in formulating, implementing, and evaluating the therapeutic options. This is especially important when the database for alternative treatments is so limited. For instance, Solomon and her colleagues [1992] reviewed some 255 studies on the treatment of PTSD. Out of those 255 studies, there were only 11 clinical trials that employed randomized control groups. Eleven! Five of these were in the area of psychopharmacology with PTSD clients. These five double-blind studies employed a total of 134 subjects, mostly combat

---

[7]For some additional discussions of the role of memory in therapeutic reconstruction, see Bonnano (1990), Bowers and Meichenbaum (1984), Rennie (1994), Russell and van den Broek (1992), Sarbin (1986), J.L. Singer (1990), and J.A. Singer and Salovey (1993).

veterans. There were only six well-controlled psychotherapy outcome studies. As you can see, we are at such a preliminary stage in the area of PTSD treatment that anyone who gets on a soapbox and says that "Memory work interventions are essential," or who claims that "This is the way to conduct intervention," should be received with a great deal of skepticism and caution, no matter what the therapeutic approach they advocate. It is critical for clinicians to appreciate the scope of our limited knowledge. I also think, however, that straightforward empiricism is *not* going to advance the field. We need a theoretical framework to explain therapeutic approaches. One such theoretical framework is that of a constructive narrative perspective.

Hoyt: How would you distinguish the constructive narrative perspective from the other wing of cognitive therapy that sometimes is called "rationalist"?

Meichenbaum: I really take issue with the so-called "rationalist" perspective. It is *not* that people distort reality, nor make cognitive errors, that contributes to their difficulties. Instead of one reality that is distorted, as some "rationalists" would advocate, I believe that there are multiple potential "realities." Instead, the focus of therapy is to help the client appreciate how he or she has constructed his or her realities, and what is the impact, the toll, the price, of such constructions. Most importantly, what are the alternative (more adaptive) constructions? I am not alone in highlighting the distinction between the "rationalist" and "constructive" perspectives. For instance, see the ongoing debate between Michael Mahoney and Albert Ellis, and others.[8]

Hoyt: How does this apply in the case of individuals who have been traumatized or victimized?

Meichenbaum: For instance, consider the client who has been victimized sexually. Envision the clinical impact of this individual characterizing herself as being "damaged goods" or as "soiled property." Such labels, such metaphors, may be culturally reinforced. Whatever the origins and influences of such labels, the consequences of such narrative constructions are likely to lead to dysphoric feelings and distressing behavior. In therapy, I would help the client share her story either in individual or group therapy; validate her feelings; but at the same time help the client appreciate the toll, impact, and price she pays if she goes around telling herself that she is "soiled goods," that she is "damaged property," that she

---

[8]Summaries can be found in Guidano and Liotto (1985), Lyddon (1990), Mahoney (1991), Mahoney and Lyddon (1988), and Meichenbaum (1992a). Controversies abound, and readers interested in watching some of the recent jousting may want, in addition to these references, to look at Ellis (1990, 1992, 1992b, 1993a, 1993b, 1998), Lyddon (1992), Meichenbaum (1992b), and Wessler (1992, 1993).

is "useless." In this way, she can come to also appreciate that she speaks to herself in the same manner that the perpetrator spoke to her. She may inadvertently reproduce the "voice" of the perpetrator, as in the case of the victims of domestic violence. She needs to develop her own voice. One goal of treatment is to no longer let the perpetrator continue to victimize her when he is no longer present. Instead, what is the best revenge?

Hoyt: Living well.

Meichenbaum: To live life well. In therapy, we need to explore with clients operationally what it means to live life well. Moreover, given the cognitive-behavioral approach, therapists also consider with clients what are the barriers, the obstacles, the potential reasons why clients may *not* do anything that they said they are going to do.[9] Thus, when clients say, "I need to live well," there is a need to help clients translate such general admonitions into behaviorally prescriptive statements such as "Between now and next time, how will that show up? What will you do differently?" There is also a need to build relapse prevention procedures into the treatment regimen—anticipating high-risk situations, as well as ways of handling possible setbacks, so lapses don't escalate into full-blown relapses.

Hoyt: Some clients will get stuck in what I call a "persistent negative narrative," and oftentimes I think that a horrible stress event confirms for them some underlying schema, some assumptive thoughts they have. To use the example you were just giving, she says, "I *am* soiled property, useless; I *am* a piece of dirt; and this just proves it." How do we then get the person to move out of that belief about herself? Do we go back through the earlier assumptions?

Meichenbaum: I don't know the answer to your question, and I don't think the field knows either, but let me offer a clinical strategy that I would be prone to use in such a situation. When the client responds with "I'm soiled property," or "I'm useless," or words to that effect, it's usually said with a great deal of emotion. What I would be prone to do as a therapist is to not only attend to the client's words, but to the affect in which it is said. So I would say, "Soiled property? Tell me about that." I would pluck the key words and put them back in the client's lap, and encourage her to elaborate. I would also attend to the feelings with which this was said. The feelings might convey a sense of being overwhelmed, or feelings of being depressed, and the like. I want to learn about the circumstances that led to such self-perceptions and accompanying feelings.

---

[9]See Meichenbaum and Turk (1987) for a discussion of various clinical procedures designed to facilitate treatment adherence, reduce noncompliance, and enhance client motivation.

Next, as part of my clinical approach, I "commend" the client for being depressed. After empathetically listening to their distress, I might say something like: "Given what you've been through (citing specific examples), if you were not depressed at times, if you did not feel at times like you were 'soiled property,' or at times as if you were 'useless,' then I think I would be really concerned and conclude that something was seriously wrong." In this fashion, I attempt to validate the client's experience. I am going to go beyond that and even compliment the client for the symptoms of being depressed. For instance, I might say to the client, "What does your being depressed say about what's going on? . . . Perhaps it conveys that you are in touch with your feelings, that you are reading your situation, that you're responsive to what you have experienced."

Hoyt: The first step is to join with, to validate, to recognize . . .

Meichenbaum: And also to commend the client because her depression and the resultant withdrawal, the labeling of being "soiled property," at one time may have been adaptive. I need to help the client see that when she calls herself "soiled property," that maybe that self-attribution was an impression management stance and her way of trying to control the situation. So even if she says, "You know, I was a zombie with no emotions," I try to have her appreciate that the dissociative responses that she used were adaptive. The critical step in helping her to alter her view of herself is whether I can help her appreciate that what she is continuing to do now, even in "safe" relationships, is no longer her only option. The problem is that she is stuck. It is not that she is "deficient" nor "sick." I am helping her move away from a so-called "deficit model" where she continually questions her self-worth and even her sanity—"Am I losing my mind?" Instead, I want her to appreciate, I want to help her cognitively reframe her experiences as a form of "survival skills." The problem is that she is continuing to do what "worked" in the past, but it may no longer be necessary.

In order to facilitate this transition, I encourage the client to consider the question: What is the impact, toll, price she is paying for being stuck? The answer to this question is *not* discussed in the abstract, but rather the client is encouraged to experientially feel, in the session, the costs of being stuck. Moreover, if the client is stuck, I then ask, in my best Columbo-like style: "What, if anything, can you do to change your situation?" *If* I have laid the groundwork well—by means of

1. plucking key metaphorical terms;
2. validating the client's experience and the accompanying feelings;
3. commending the client for her presenting symptoms;
4. helping her cognitively reframe these symptoms as a form of coping and as a set of survival skills;

5. examining collaboratively how such survival skills worked in the past, but how she continues to do so now, even in situations in which the client is no longer in danger; and
6. considering the devastating impact, the emotional toll, and the interpersonal price of her being stuck—

it is *then* not a big step for the client to offer suggestions about possible ways that she can get unstuck. Remember, my therapeutic goal is to have the client come up with solutions about how to change. If she can come up with possible solutions that could be tried, then she will feel enabled and empowered, and moreover, since she came up with the ideas, there is a greater likelihood that she will follow through. Can I give you another example?

Hoyt: Please.

Meichenbaum: In fact, I have two cases that come to mind. First, I wish to describe a challenging case of a woman who has experienced a disastrous accident. She was with her fiancé—the only man she had fallen in love with after several previous broken relationships. They were returning from a party and decided to take a shortcut and cross some train tracks. They were running along the train track to get to the other side where this woman lived, and a horrendous thing happened. As the train approached, she yelled out to her fiancé, "Let's beat it," and she darted in front of the oncoming train safely. Her fiancé tripped and did not make it. He was hit by the train and instantly killed. His body was severed.

Hoyt: Oh, my gosh.

Meichenbaum: It was horrendous. In a dissociative state, she picked up his body parts. It was one of the most horrific stories that I have ever heard. She is suffering from PTSD, depression, and suicidal ideation, as she feels responsible and guilty about his death. Her intrusive thoughts are overwhelming.

I have another case of a mother who had a 10-year-old daughter. They were at home alone. In the middle of the night, she woke up thinking that someone had broken into her home. Since she had experienced such a robbery in the past year, she became fearful. In a state of panic, she reached into her night table to grab hold of a recently obtained pistol that her husband had given her. With gun in hand, she was running into her daughter's room when her bedroom door slammed open and hit her hand, and the gun discharged.

Hoyt: Don't tell me.

Meichenbaum: Yes. It was her daughter. The mother shot her daughter and blew her daughter's brain away.

Hoyt: That is terrible!

Meichenbaum: Michael, what are you going to say or do in therapy with these clients? In each instance, I listened sympathetically to the tale of the horrendous events. And eventually asked the mother, "What did you see in your daughter that made your relationship with her so special? Please share with me the nature of the loss." In fact, I asked the bereaved mother to bring to therapy a picture album of her daughter and to review with me the special qualities of her daughter. The picture album permitted the client to tell the story of her relationship with her daughter in some developmental (time-line) context, and thus not delimit her memories to only the time of the shooting—which she played over and over again, with the accompanying narrative of "If only . . . ," "Why didn't I tell my husband I didn't want to own a gun?", "Why my daughter?", "Tell me it is only a dream," "How could I have?", and so forth. Moreover, the review of the picture album provided the opportunity to query further what she saw in her daughter, and, in turn, what did her daughter see in her. Following this exchange, I asked the client, "If your daughter, whom you described as being 'wise beyond her years,' were here now, what advice, if any, might she have to help you get through this difficult period?" Fortunately, with some guidance I was able to help the client generate some suggestions that her daughter might have offered.[10] I then noted, "I can now understand why you described your daughter as being 'wise beyond her years.' She does sound special."

Moreover, if the client followed through on her notion to commit suicide in order to stop the emotional pain, what would happen to the memory of her daughter? Did she feel that she owed her daughter more? Like many victims of traumatic events, this client found a mission in order to cope with her distress. She undertook the task of educating parents about the dangers of keeping guns in their homes.[11] She became an expert on the incidence of accidental homicides, and developed a foundation named after her daughter designed to decrease the likelihood that this could happen to other children. She felt that if she could save one other child, then her daughter would not have died in vain. Through her actions, she was writing a new script, fashioning a new more adaptive narrative. In therapy, we also addressed her feelings of guilt. I will have to refer you to my clinical manual on treating PTSD [Meichenbaum, 1994] to see the discussion of how such guilt reactions can be addressed therapeutically.

---

[10]Note that this line of "internalized other" questioning (White, 1988, 1989; Tomm, 1989; Nylund & Corsiglia, 1993; Hoyt & Nylund, 1997) evokes the daughter as an ally rather than as a source of remorse (Hoyt, 1980, 1983).

[11]Each year there are approximately 1,400 such deaths in North America (Meichenbaum, 1994).

Hoyt: I can see what you mean by arranging the conditions whereby clients come up with suggestions themselves, although you could have offered all of the advice that the daughter might have offered.

Meichenbaum: You're right, but there is a greater likelihood that clients will follow through if they come up with the ideas than if you, the therapist, give them the ideas. I use a phrase to caution therapists not to act as "surrogate frontal lobes" for their clients.

Hoyt: *[laughter]* I like that—"surrogate frontal lobes." It's better to support the client's own construction.[12] What did you do with the client whose fiancé died in the train accident?

Meichenbaum: I used a similar therapeutic strategy, but I had to alter it somewhat. As in the case of the grieving mother, I asked the client who lost her fiancé to help me appreciate what happened exactly, and more importantly—"To help me understand what you saw in your fiancé, Jimmy. What was life like with him? What did you see in him that attracted you to him? . . . What do you think he saw that attracted him to you? . . . If Jimmy were here now, what advice, if any, would he have for you in this difficult time? . . . What do you think would be the best legacy, the best way to remember Jimmy—not only for yourself, but for others who knew him?"

Whereas this strategy worked with the bereaved mother, it did *not* work with this client. When I asked her to come up with advice that Jimmy might offer, she drew a blank. The image of Jimmy's grotesque death was so vivid and current (even some six months after the accident) that she could not assume any distance psychologically, to consider ways to handle her distress. So, instead, I pursued a somewhat different line of questioning. Since the image of Jimmy, her fiancé, was too emotionally laden to elicit suggestions about potential coping procedures, I asked her when else she might have experienced a personal loss. She described the loss of her grandmother, whom she loved a great deal. I then asked her what did she see in her grandmother that made the relationship so special. "What do you think your grandmother saw in you? . . . If your wise grandmother were here now, what words of support, what advice, if any, do you think your grandmother might have for you?" (Interestingly, this grandmother sounded like a good cognitive-behavioral therapist!) I then conveyed that "Now I understand why your grandmother was so special."

From my perspective, the "name of the game" is to use the art of questioning to enable and empower clients to come up with possible coping strategies.

---

[12]Long ago, Blaise Pascal (1623-1662) advised: "People are generally better persuaded by the reasons which they have themselves discovered than by those which have come from the minds of others" (quoted in Duncan, Hubble, Miller & Coleman, 1998, p. 301).

Hoyt: Thibaut and Kelley [1986], the social psychologists, wrote about "*bubbe* psychology," the native good sense of a wise grandmother.

Meichenbaum: But note that in this instance I could have told this client every single thing that the grandmother would have offered, but it would not have been as helpful. It is not just a case of giving information. There is data we review in the Meichenbaum and Turk [1987] book on facilitating treatment adherence that if people come up with ideas themselves and the accompanying reasons for behaving in this fashion, then, as the therapist, you have a greater likelihood of clients' following through than if you, the therapist, offer such advice. Whatever merit there is to our discussion, the readers should take away the notion that they should not be a "surrogate frontal lobe" for their clients. They should *not* do the thinking for them, nor put the words in their mouths; they should be respectful, collaborative, and remember that most people evidence the potential for a great deal of resilience and courage.

Hoyt: What about the client who did not have the positive experience that they can draw from with the lost object? The person who says, "I've always had low self-esteem. I'm no good. I deserve what I got." It stimulates earlier relationships that were very negative; the family abused them. What would you have done if she had said, "My father told me I'd never be happy"?

Meichenbaum: In fact, that is what happened. Did you see the videotape of this case that I show in my workshop?

Hoyt: No, I haven't.

Meichenbaum: Because you are right on target. One of the things she says is that her father called her up and conveyed that she is a "total screw-up" because she went down to the tracks. Not only that, but this guy, Jimmy, wasn't that good anyway, so the accident is a "blessing in disguise." Not very sympathetic, to say the least. In fact, she goes on to report a whole series of troubled parental interactions. During the course of therapy, the client came to realize that part of the reason she is so depressed is that she is talking to herself, reproducing the same narrative that her father said. Part of the reason that she is suicidal and depressed is not only due to this horrendous event, but she is playing the same "CD" she heard during her entire childhood. For the client who lacks positive developmental experiences, the therapist can help the client appreciate that she is reproducing someone else's script, that she is playing their narrative. The challenge or question is whether she can develop a voice of her own to write her own narrative.[13] Does she have the courage to do

---

[13]See Carol Gilligan (1982; Gilligan, Roger & Tolman, 1991) for a discussion of the idea of claiming one's "voice," especially in the lives of women. The work of White and Epston

that? But a cognitive-behavioral approach goes further by ensuring that the client has the intra- and interpersonal skills to implement such a new script or construct a more adaptive narrative. Moreover, built into the treatment regimen are such therapeutic procedures as problem-solving training, cognitive restructuring techniques, "homework" assignments, relapse prevention, "personal experiments," and self-attributional procedures. It is *not* enough to have clients produce a new narrative, but this new narrative must be tied into behavioral acts that lead to "data" that is taken as "evidence" to alter the client's view of oneself and the world. While I advocate a constructive narrative perspective, it is important to appreciate that I also employ the full clinical array of cognitive-behavioral procedures that have been found to be so efficacious in treating clients with a number of psychiatric disorders.

Hoyt: In psychodynamic terms, they might say that you try to help her "extroject the pathologic introject" in order to get the "voice" of her father out of her head [Hoyt, 1994].

Meichenbaum: As you know, mental health workers have their own metaphors to describe therapeutic interventions. There are innumerable potential metaphors. The bottom line is that people come into therapy with a "story," and you, the therapist, try to help them change their "stories." Now, clinical theorists can impose their metaphors to describe this process—for example, "extroject the introject." Other theorists use metaphors derived from learning theory, such as "deconditioning" and "habituation," or from information-processing theory in terms of "assimilating/accommodating," "schemas," etc. As I note in the PTSD handbook [Meichenbaum, 1994], there are many alternatives. My own approach is to remain much more phenomonologically oriented, using the client's metaphors. From my perspective, it is better to "unpack" the client's metaphor rather than to impose the therapist's metaphors. By "unpack," I mean help the client to appreciate the adaptive features of how he or she has constructed reality in the past, but to also consider anew what is the impact, toll, and price of continuing to view the world in such a fashion—moreover, to consider in some detail what exactly can be done to change his or her "construction," as well as the ways he or she behaves. From this perspective, the client's altered narrative becomes the "final common

---

(1990) is pertinent; for further applications of the narrative therapeutic use of "voice" in the treatment of eating disorders, see Epston (1989) and Zimmerman and Dickerson (1994). Mary Goulding (1985; Goulding & Goulding, 1979) also asks, "Who's been living in your head? and describes many ways to take charge of those "voices." Related ideas of "voice" as internalized others include Firestone's (1988) "voice therapy," Minuchin's (1987) discussion of his family therapy teachers and mentors as "the voices in my head," and Gergen's (1994; also see Chapter 8, this volume) ideas about social construction and "polyvocalism."

pathway" to behavioral change. (It seems that we can't get away from using metaphors when describing our own, as well as others', behavior.)

Hoyt: Are you saying that it is better to find *their* central metaphor rather than having to first educate them to believing our system?[14]

Meichenbaum: Yes. You want to help "unpack" their metaphor, to have them appreciate the impact, the toll, the price of the stories they tell. Note that this joint exploration is *not* just something intellectual.[15] You need to have the client *feel* in therapy the impact, the toll, the price. And out of such discussions, you can then play your Columbo role. I'll give you an example. A client comes in and says that she "stuffs her feelings." I say, "Stuff feelings? Tell me about that." And we behaviorally and operationally define what "stuffed feelings" means. It's important to listen for such verbs as "stuffed."

Hoyt: That is where the action's at, literally and figuratively.

Meichenbaum: Right. I usually listen very attentively to how clients tell their stories. I especially listen for how clients use transitive verbs. When I hear such verbs being used such as "stuffed," or "noticed," "caught," "put myself down," etc., I pluck these from their narrative and reflect it back to them in an inquiring fashion: "Stuffed feelings?" I explore what she does. And then we consider what is the impact of such behavior. Once we do that, I say, "What could you do about it?" You don't have to be a rocket scientist for the client to then say, "Well, maybe I should not stuff the feelings." Then I say, "Not stuff the feelings. That's interesting. What did you have in mind?" Once again, I am laying the groundwork where the client is going to codefine the problem and collaboratively generate possible solutions. We are now collaborating in this constructive narrative process. Another example is when clients spontaneously offer an example of some strength, some successful coping effort, and I then use this "nugget" (as I perceive it) to ask: "Are you saying that *in spite of* all that you experienced (give specific examples), you were able to do (to

---

[14]Since "the map is not the territory" (Korzybski, 1933), we can understand virtually all communication to be metaphor. Using clients' metaphors is a way of joining. Moreover, it appreciates their experience and allows it to unfold as they know it. Recognizing the validity of their reality avoids "resistance." They don't have to fight or defend against the therapist's incursion. It moves forward. Aristotle said, "The greatest thing by far is to have command of metaphor." (See Barker, 1985; Combs & Freedman, 1990; Kopp, 1995; Hoyt, 2000.)

[15]This same point—the power of experience in relearning—was emphasized by Freud (1914/1958) in his essay "Remembering, Repeating and Working-Through," and, as discussed above, is also central in the concept of the "corrective emotional experience" (Alexander & French, 1946). Cutting across different theoretical approaches, the induction of novelty requires a shift in narrative and thus generates change (Budman, Friedman & Hoyt, 1992).

try, to achieve—give specific examples)? How did you come to the decision that X? How did you manage to do X? Where did this courage come from?"

The strategy I employ to help clients "restory" their lives is (1) to solicit from the clients an example of their strengths; (2) ask an "in spite of" question, and (3) ask a "how" question. In turn, we can explore how clients can employ these coping skills and take credit for the change they bring about.

This is *not* just a "repair" process, as Schafer [1992] describes. The metaphor of "repair" implies that an individual's narrative is broken, like a tire, and one has to fix it. It conveys that the narrative one is using was "wrong"; it was "broken" and needs to be "fixed." Thus, I try to stay away from the term "narrative repair," but rather, talk about the "constructive narrative process" that clients are now engaged in. The client's narrative may have been adaptive at one time. It wasn't broken; it doesn't need fixing. I don't have to "fix the client's head." Instead, I help clients to become better observers and become their own therapist. As Tomm [1989] suggests, I ask the client, "Do you ever find yourself, out there, asking yourself the kind of questions that we ask each other right here in therapy?"[16] I convey to clients that the treatment goal is to become your own therapist, your own coach. In this way, the clients can learn to take the therapist's voice with them[17] and appropriate, own, and internalize the suggested changes. They can now write their own stories. That is what the therapeutic process is all about.

Our research task now is to demonstrate that doing all this makes a difference. The PTSD manual that I have spent the last two years writing [Meichenbaum, 1994] is designed to operationalize these procedures, so that investigators will be able to empirically validate what I have been describing. I thank you for the opportunity to share these ideas.

☐ References

Agger, I., & Jensen, S. B. (1990). Testimony as ritual and evidence in psychotherapy for political refugees. *Journal of Traumatic Stress, 3*, 115–130.

Alexander, F., & French, T. M. (1946). *Psychoanalytic Therapy: Principles and Application.* New York: Ronald Press.

Barker, P. (1985). *Using Metaphors in Psychotherapy.* New York: Brunner/Mazel.

Bonanno, G. (1990). Remembering and psychotherapy. *Psychotherapy, 27*, 175–186.

---

[16]In *Nurturing Independent Learners*, Meichenbaum and Biemiller (1998) discuss many pedagogical strategies, with clear implications for therapists, for promoting acquisition, consolidation, and transfer of metacognitive development.

[17]"My voice will go with you" was an expression Milton Erickson would use to encourage continued benefit (Rosen, 1982).

Bowers, K., & Meichenbaum, D. (Eds.). (1984). *The Unconscious Reconsidered.* New York: Wiley.

Budman, S. H., Friedman, S., & Hoyt, M. F. (1992). Last words on first sessions. In S. H. Budman, M. F. Hoyt, & S. Friedman (Eds.), *The First Session in Brief Therapy* (pp. 345–358). New York: Guilford Press.

Budman, S. H., Hoyt, M. F., & Friedman, S. (Eds.). (1992). *The First Session in Brief Therapy.* New York: Guilford Press.

Combs, G., & Freedman, J. (1990). *Symbol, Story and Ceremony: Using Metaphor Individual and Family Therapy.* New York: Norton.

Duncan, B.L., Hubble, M.A., Miller, S.D., & Coleman, S.T. (1998) Escaping from the lost world of impossibility: Honoring clients' language, motivation, and theories of change. In M.F. Hoyt (Ed.), *The Handbook of Constructive Therapies* (pp. 293–313). San Francisco: Jossey-Bass.

Ellis, A. (1990). Is rational-emotive therapy (RET) "rationalist" or "constructivist"? In A. Ellis & W. Dryden (Eds.), *The Essential Albert Ellis* (pp. 114–141). New York: Springer.

Ellis, A. (1992a). Discussion. In J. K. Zeig (Ed.), *The Evolution of Psychotherapy: The Second Conference* (pp. 122–127). New York: Brunner/Mazel.

Ellis, A. (1992b). First-order and second-order change in rational-emotive therapy: A reply to Lyddon. *Journal of Counseling and Development, 70,* 449–451.

Ellis, A. (1993a). Constructivism and rational-emotive therapy: A critique of Richard Wessler's critique. *Psychotherapy, 30,* 531–532.

Ellis, A. (1993b). Another reply to Wessler's critique of rational-emotive therapy. *Psychotherapy, 30,* 535.

Ellis, A. (1998) How rational emotive behavior therapy belongs in the constructivist camp. In M.F. Hoyt (Ed.), *The Handbook of Constructive Therapies* (pp. 83–99). San Francisco: Jossey-Bass.

Epston, D. (1989). *Collected Papers.* Adelaide, Australia: Dulwich Centre Publications.

Firestone, R. W. (1988). *Voice Therapy: A Psychotherapeutic Approach to Self-Destructive Behavior.* New York: Human Sciences Press.

Freud, S. (1958). Remembering, repeating and working-through. In J. Strachey (Ed. and Trans.), *The Standard Edition of the Complete Psychological Works of Sigmund Freud* (Vol. 12, pp. 145–156). London: Hogarth Press. (Original work published 1914)

Gergen, K. J. (1991). *The Saturated Self.* New York: Basic Books.

Gergen, K.J. (1994). *Realities and Relationships: Soundings in Social Construction.* Cambridge, MA: Harvard University Press.

Gilligan, C. (1982). *In a Different Voice.* Cambridge, MA: Harvard University Press.

Gilligan, C., Roger, A., & Tolman, D. (1991). *Women, Girls, and Psychotherapy.* Cambridge, MA: Harvard University Press.

Goulding, M. M. (1985). *Who's Been Living in Your Head?* (rev. ed.). Watsonville, CA: Western Institute for Group and Family Therapy Press.

Goulding, M. M., & Goulding, R. L. (1979). *Changing Lives through Redecision Therapy.* New York: Brunner/Mazel.

Guidano, V. F., & Liotti, G. A. (1985). A constructivist foundation for cognitive therapy. In M. J. Mahoney & A. Freeman (Eds.), *Cognition and Psychotherapy* (pp. 101–142). New York: Plenum Press.

Harvey, J. H., Weber, A. L., & Orbuch, T. L. (1990). *Interpersonal Accounts: A Social Psychological Perspective.* Oxford, England: Blackwell.

Herman, J. (1992). *Trauma and Recovery.* New York: Basic Books.

Hoyt, M. F. (1980). Clinical notes regarding the experience of "presences" during mourning. *Omega: Journal of Death and Dying, 11,* 105–111.

Hoyt, M. F. (1983). Concerning remorse: With special attention to its defensive function. *Journal of the American Academy of Psychoanalysis, 11,* 435–444.

Hoyt, M. F. (1990). On time in brief therapy. In R. A. Wells & V. J. Giannetti (Eds.), *Handbook of the Brief Psychotherapies* (pp. 115–143). New York: Plenum Press. (Reprinted in M. F. Hoyt, *Brief Therapy and Managed Care: Readings for Contemporary Practice* [pp. 69–104]. San Francisco: Jossey-Bass, 1995.)

Hoyt, M. F. (1994). Single-session solutions. In M. F. Hoyt (Ed.), *Constructive Therapies* (pp. 140–159). New York: Guilford Press. (Reprinted in M. F. Hoyt, *Brief Therapy and Managed Care: Readings for Contemporary Practice* [pp. 141–162]. San Francisco: Jossey-Bass, 1995.)

Hoyt, M.F. (2000) *Some Stories Are Better than Others: Doing What Works in Brief Therapy and Managed Care.* Philadelphia: Brunner/Mazel.

Hoyt, M.F., & Nylund, D. (1997) The joy of narrative: An exercise for learning from our internalized clients. *Journal of Systemic Therapies, 16*(4), 361–366. (Reprinted in M.F. Hoyt, *Some Stories Are Better than Others: Doing What Works in Brief Therapy and Managed Care.* Philadelphia: Brunner/Mazel, 2000.)

Janoff-Bulman, R. (1985). The aftermath of victimization: Rebuilding shattered assumptions. In C. R. Figley (Ed.), *Trauma and Its Wake.* New York: Brunner/Mazel.

Janoff-Bulman, R. (1990). Understanding people in terms of their assumptive worlds. In D. J. Ozer, J. M. Healy, & A. J. Stewart (Eds.), *Perspectives in Personality: Self and Emotion.* Greenwich, CT: JAI Press.

Kinzie, J. D. (1994). Countertransference in the treatment of Southeast Asian refugees. In J. P. Wilson & J. D. Lindy (Eds.), *Countertransference in the Treatment of PTSD.* New York: Guilford Press.

Kopp, R. R. (1995). *Metaphor Therapy: Using Client-Generated Metaphors in Pyschotherapy.* New York: Brunner/Mazel.

Korzybski, A. (1933). *Science and Sanity* (4th ed.). Lakeville, CT: International Non-Aristotelian Library.

Lyddon, W. J. (1990). First- and second-order change: Implications for rationalist and constructivist cognitive therapies. *Journal of Counseling and Development, 69,* 122–127.

Lyddon, W. J. (1992). A rejoinder to Ellis: What is and is not RET? *Journal of Counseling and Development, 70,* 452–454.

Mahoney, M. J. (1991). *Human Change Processes: The Scientific Foundations of Psychotherapy.* New York: Basic Books.

Mahoney, M. J., & Lyddon, W. F. (1988). Recent developments in cognitive approaches to counseling and psychotherapy. *The Counseling Psychologist, 16,* 190–234.

McNamee, S., & Gergen, K. J. (Eds.). (1992). *Therapy as Social Construction.* Newbury Park, CA: Sage.

Meichenbaum, D. (1977). *Cognitive-Behavior Modification: An Integrative Approach.* New York: Plenum Press.

Meichenbaum, D. (1985). *Stress Inoculation Training: A Clinical Guidebook.* Elmsford, NY: Pergamon Press.

Meichenbaum, D. (1992a). Evolution of cognitive behavior therapy: Origins, tenets, and clinical examples. In J. K. Zeig (Ed.), *The Evolution of Psychotherapy: The Second Conference* (pp. 114–122). New York: Brunner/Mazel.

Meichenbaum, D. (1992b). Response: Dr. Meichenbaum. In J. K. Zeig (Ed.), *The Evolution of Psychotherapy: The Second Conference* (pp. 127–128). New York: Brunner/Mazel.

Meichenbaum, D. (1993). Stress inoculation training: A twenty-year update. In R. L. Woolfolk & P. M. Lehrer (Eds.), *Principles and Practice of Stress Management* (2nd ed., pp. 373–406). New York: Guilford Press.

Meichenbaum, D. (1994). *A Clinical Handbook/Practical Therapist Manual for Treating PTSD.* Waterloo, Ontario, Canada: Institute Press, University of Waterloo.

Meichenbaum, D., & Biemiller, A. (1998) *Nurturing Independent Learners: Helping Students Take Charge of Their Learning.* Cambridge, MA: Brookline Books.

Meichenbaum, D., & Fitzpatrick, D. (1993). A constructive narrative perspective on stress and coping: Stress inoculation applications. In L. Goldberger & S. Breznitz (Eds.), *Handbook of Stress* (pp. 695–710). New York: Free Press.

Meichenbaum, D., & Fong, D. T. (1993). How individuals control their own minds: A constructive narrative perspective. In D. M. Wegner & J. W. Pennebaker (Eds.), *Handbook of Mental Control* (pp. 473–490). New York: Prentice Hall.

Meichenbaum, D., & Jaremko, M. E. (Eds.). (1983). *Stress Reduction and Prevention.* New York: Plenum Press.

Meichenbaum, D., & Turk, D. (1987). *Facilitating Treatment Adherence: A Practitioner's Guidebook.* New York: Plenum Press.

Minuchin, S. (1987). My many voices. In J. K. Zeig (Ed.), *The Evolution of Psychotherapy* (pp. 5–14). New York: Brunner/Mazel.

Mollica, R. F. (1988). The trauma story: The psychiatric case of refugee survivors of violence and torture. In R. Ochberg (Ed.), *Post-Traumatic Therapy and Victims of Violence.* New York: Brunner/Mazel.

Nylund, D., & Corsiglia, V. (1993). Internalized other questioning with men who are violent. *Dulwich Centre Newsletter,* No. 2, 30–35. (Reprinted in M.F. Hoyt, Ed., *The Handbook of Constructive Therapies* [pp. 401–413]. San Francisco: Jossey-Bass, 1998.)

O'Hanlon, W. H., & Weiner-Davis, M. (1989). *In Search of Solutions: A New Direction in Psychotherapy.* New York: Norton.

Rennie, D. L. (1994). Storytelling in psychotherapy: The client's subjective experience. *Psychotherapy, 31,* 234–243.

Rosen, S. (1982). *My Voice Will Go with You: The Teaching Tales of Milton H. Erickson.* New York: Norton.

Russell, R. L., & van den Broek, P. (1992). Changing narrative schemas in psychotherapy. *Psychotherapy, 29,* 344–354.

Sarbin, T. (Ed.). (1986). *Narrative Psychology: The Storied Nature of Human Conduct.* New York: Praeger.

Schafer, R. (1992). *Retelling a Life.* New York: Basic Books.

Simon, R. (1988). Like a friendly editor: An interview with Lynn Hoffman. *Family Therapy Networker,* September/October. (Reprinted in L. Hoffman, *Exchanging Voices: A Collaborative Approach to Family Therapy* [pp. 69–79]. London: Karnac Books, 1993.)

Singer, J. A., & Salovey, P. (1993). *The Remembered Self: Emotion and Memory in Personality.* New York: Free Press/Macmillan.

Singer, J. L. (Ed.). (1990). *Repression and Dissociation.* Chicago: University of Chicago Press.

Solomon, S. D., Garrety, E. T., & Muff, A. M. (1992). Efficacy of treatments for posttraumatic stress disorder: An empirical review. *Journal of the American Medical Association, 268,* 633–638.

Spence, D. (1982). *Narrative Truth and Historical Truth: Meaning and Interpretation in Psychoanalysis.* New York: Norton.

Terr, L. C. (1994). *Unchained Memories: True Stories of Traumatic Memories, Lost and Found.* New York: Basic Books.

Thibaut, J. W., & Kelley, H. H. (1986). *The Social Psychology of Groups* (rev. ed.). New Brunswick, NJ: Transaction.

Tomm, K. (1987a). Interventive interviewing: Part I. Strategizing as a fourth guideline for the therapist. *Family Process, 26,* 3–13.

Tomm, K. (1987b). Interventive interviewing: Part II. Reflexive questioning as a means to enable self-healing. *Family Process, 26,* 167–183.

Tomm, K. (1988). Interventive interviewing: Part III. Intending to ask lineal, circular, strategic and reflexive questions. *Family Process, 27,* 1–16.

Tomm, K. (1989). Externalizing the problems and internalizing personal agency. *Journal of Strategic and Systemic Therapies, 8,* 54–59.

Turk, D., Meichenbaum, D., & Genest, M. (1983). *Pain and Behavioral Medicine: A Cognitive-Behavioral Perspective.* New York: Guilford Press.

van der Kolk, B. A. (1994). The body keeps the score: Memory and the evolving psychology of posttraumatic stress. *Harvard Review of Psychiatry, 1,* 253–265.

Wessler, R. L. (1992). Constructivism and rational-emotive therapy: A critique. *Psychotherapy, 29,* 620–625.

Wessler, R. L. (1993). A reply to Ellis's critique of Wessler's critique of rational-emotive therapy. *Psychotherapy, 30,* 533–534.

Whitaker, C.A. (1983) Comment. *Voices,* 19, 40.

White, M. (1988). Saying hello again: The incorporation of the lost relationship in the resolution of grief. *Dulwich Centre Newsletter,* No. 1. (Reprinted in M. White, *Selected Papers* [pp. 29–36]. Adelaide, Australia: Dulwich Centre Publications, 1989.)

White, M. (1989). *Selected Papers.* Adelaide, Australia: Dulwich Centre Publications.

White, M., & Epston, D. (1990). *Narrative Means to Therapeutic Ends.* New York: Norton.

Zimmerman, J. L., & Dickerson, V. C. (1994). Tales of the body thief: Externalizing and deconstructing eating problems. In M. F. Hoyt (Ed.), *Constructive Therapies* (pp. 295–318). New York: Guilford Press.

CHAPTER

Contact, Contract, Change, Encore: A Conversation About Redecision Therapy With Bob Goulding

When I first met Bob Goulding he was presenting some of his ideas about redecision therapy at the Evolution of Psychotherapy Conference in Phoenix in 1985. It was immediately clear that this man had something to say worth hearing: He was clear, incisive, practical, human, funny, and effective. After his lecture I went up and introduced myself and asked about possibilities for training in redecision therapy. He briefly told me about the training programs he and his wife, Mary Goulding, were then conducting at the Western Institute for Group and Family Therapy (WIGFT) on Mt. Madonna near Watsonville, California. I asked a few prefunctory questions, and then inquired: "What will happen and what will I experience if I come to a training?" With a twinkle in his eye, Bob laughed and answered, "Well, that will depend on what you choose to do!"

I was intrigued and knew something valuable was available. Rather than thinking about it, missing the opportunity and then kicking myself, I went home and a day or two later sent in my registration. In a few weeks I was at the Western Institute, participating in the first of several training programs. In addition to facilitating my own much-needed per-

Originally appeared, with changes, in *Transactional Analysis Journal*, 1995, 25(4), 300–311. Portions also appeared in M.F. Hoyt, "Foreword." In C.E. Lennox (Ed.), *Redecision Therapy: A Brief, Action-Oriented Approach* (pp. xiii–xix). Northvale, NJ: Jason Aronson, 1997. Used with permission.

sonal growth and making some friendships that endure to this day, I learned a very powerful method of therapy based on the principles of highlighting client autonomy and competency in the direction of achieving the client's realistically defined treatment goals. Bob and Mary had woven together some of the ideas and methods of Eric Berne and Fritz Perls, along with their own myriad innovations, to create a teachable theory and technology that rightly earned them world-wide recognition as master contributors. To borrow the titles of two of their books, they emphasized that when we recognize that *The Power is in the Patient* (1978) people can engage in *Changing Lives through Redecision Therapy* (1979).[1]

The Gouldings' redecision therapy model is based on a thinking structure that includes the following features (after Goulding, 1989; Goulding & Goulding, 1978, 1986):

1. *Contact*: forming an alliance with the client;
2. *Contract*: co-constructing with the client the focus or goal of treatment in a way that can be specified and achieved;
3. *Con*: emphasizing clients' power and responsibility by confronting their efforts to disown autonomy through various ways they attempt to fool ("con") themselves and therapists into believing that others control their thoughts, feelings, and behavior or with disingenuous claims of "trying" to make changes;
4. *Chief bad feelings, thinkings, behaviors, and psychosomatics*: identifying the painful or problematic counterproductive symptoms;
5. *Chronic games, belief systems, and fantasies*: clarifying the interpersonal and intrapsychic ways symptoms are maintained;
6. *Childhood early decisions*: bring to vivid awareness a reexperience of childhood feelings via the imaginal reliving of an early pathogenic scene, including recognition of the chief parental messages (injunctions and counterinjunctions), childhood script formation, and stroking (reinforcement) patterns;
7. *Impasse resolution*: including redecisions, ego state decontamination and reconstruction (involving the strengthening of distinctions between Parent, Adult, and Child functions), re-parenting, and other techniques. Two-chair Gestalt work is often used to help the client "extroject" a pathogenic parental introject and then, in powerful dialogue, reclaim a sense of autonomy and self-determination; and
8. *Maintaining the victory*: including anchoring the client's new and healthier

---

[1]Their other books include the co-authored *Not to Worry* (1989), Mary's *Who's Been Living in Your Head?* (1985), her poignant memoir of Bob, *Sweet Love Remembered* (1992), and her extraordinary account of grieving and going forward since Bob's death in 1992, *A Time to Say Good-Bye: Moving Beyond Loss* (1996).

ways of responding, making changes in stroking patterns, and forming plans for how to use the redecision in the future.

The essence of the Gouldings' approach is distilled in the brilliant sentence that they (and other redecision therapists) would often use to begin a session: *What are you willing to change today?* Spelled out, almost like a haiku for therapeutic effectiveness, we can see all of the key elements of brief (efficient or time-sensitive) therapy:

What (specificity, goal, target, focus)
are (active verb, present tense)
you (self as agent, personal functioning)
willing (choice, responsibility, initiative)
to change (alter or modify, not just "work on," "try," or "explore")
today (now, in the moment)
? (inquiry, open field, therapist inviting and respectfully receptive but not insistent)

Students of comparative psychotherapies will see various points of contact between redecision therapy and other approaches, and practitioners of different theoretical orientations may find productive ways to integrate redecision ideas into their clinical repertoire. Psychodynamically-minded therapists will appreciate the role of "insight," the redecision process involving the making conscious of something previously out of awareness (yielding a "cognitive restructuring" or "schema change," a cognitive-behaviorist might say). The primary mechanism is not interpretation of a transference, however, but is having a new experience ("redecision") via a re-enactment of an early scene guided by the therapist who serves as a kind of travel agent expert at facilitating routes to destinations (therapeutic goals) selected by client-travelers. There is an orientation toward new action. Explanation may lead to recognition, but experience leads to change. The client is seen as competent to resolve her or his own problem with skillful facilitation, rather than having to rely upon an outside expert to make sense of or reveal "the truth." "The power is in the patient," as the Gouldings say.

Readers acquainted with narrative therapy (White, 1995; White & Epston, 1990) may see the Gestalt two-chair part of the redecision process as an externalization of the problem with enhancement of the client's sense of personal autonomy, and may find it helpful to think of injunctions and scripts as narrative themes and of redecision as a form of re-authoring of the stories that shape and constitute lives. Solution-focused therapists (following de Shazer, 1985, 1988) may appreciate the redecision therapist stroking the Natural Child as the evocation amd amplification of exceptions to the problem pattern, and may see the use of anchoring, changes in stroke economy, and Adult planning as ways to further structure and support the emergence of a pro-solution worldview and storyline. I would place all of this under the rubric of constructive therapies (Hoyt, 1994, 1996, 1998, 2000), ones that draw from the social constructionist idea that reality is known through the knower and that we actively construct our notions of what is real and what matters within an interpersonal matrix. I agree with Mary Goulding's comment (1997, p. 87), "What is important is that the client recover from the past, real and imagined, and go on to a fulfilling life."

The following is the annotated transcript of excerpts from an extended conversation we had in September 1990, at his home and workplace two hours south of San Francisco. Despite the encroachments of age and advanced emphysema, his generosity, curiosity, enthusiasm, tenderness, toughness, incisive intelligence, wit, and present-centeredness all were available and apparent.

Hoyt: I thought what we would do today, Bob, is to spend some time talking about Bob Goulding—how you got into psychiatry and psychotherapy, how you became the therapist you are, and the person you are.

Goulding: Well, that sounds like a lot of ground to cover for one interview—it might make about a 12-hour collection.

Hoyt: Where do you want to start? Here, or on the other end?

Goulding: Well, right now we're here, in my house, our house, Mary's and my house. I'd like to start where we're at professionally, at this point. I'm nearing retirement. All I'm planning in the future at this moment are some one-weekend-a-month ongoing trainings and maybe a couple of one-week workshops, some lectures, but pretty much not doing much else. It's taken me 72 years to get to this point.

Hoyt: Well, this is September 1990. Next month you'll be 73.

Goulding: Yeah, October. It seemed to me and it seemed to you that it would be a good time to stop and do some reflecting on what I've done, where I've been, and how I got there.

Hoyt: How long have you and Mary been at the Western Institute?

Goulding: Well, we've been here, at this place, Mt. Madonna, 20 years the first of May this year. When Mary moved to Carmel in 1965 from another part of California [Castro Valley], she went to work for the Salinas and Monterey mental health clinics where I was the Director of Adult Services. We've been working together in one way or another ever since then. First I taught her about group therapy; then we worked as cotherapists with both the clinic groups and other groups in private practice in Carmel; then she started doing groups on her own as well as doing groups with me. Then we started much more of a training program over in Carmel and did some workshops up in San Jose at a farmhouse—our institute was then called the Carmel Institute for Transactional Analysis. We changed it from the Western Institute for Group Therapy to the Western Institute for Group and Family Therapy at Virginia Satir's request. I had been friends with Virginia for a good number of years, and she wanted to come along with us on this adventure. She did the first workshop with us in our new house, in June of 1970. So we've been here since 1970. Mary and I have been married for 20 years. In fact, our wedding anniversary is coming up on October 12th.

Hoyt: You were married where?

Goulding: Well, the first time we were married informally and without sanction of the law *[laughs]* in Cuernavaca, Mexico, at Satir's conference. I remember it was her first conference, what they called "The 100 Beautiful People Conference"! I remember we got off the plane at the airport and we heard this person barking, "100 beautiful people! 100 beautiful people!" *[laughs]* We had a wonderful wedding—David Steere and Irma Shepherd were our marriage facilitators. They said the magic words, and the whole group sat around hand-in-hand in a big circle. . . . and we had a wonderful wedding ceremony. Then we were married here legally the following April with our family and good friends, which was really a whole lot of fun.

Hoyt: Does *here* mean here?

Goulding: Here on Mt. Madonna, here in this house, under the big tree that was just chopped down because of the big earthquake. So, we've been together ever since.

Hoyt: In addition to friendship, what did you get from Virginia in terms of learning to be a therapist?

Goulding: Oh, how to do family therapy her way [see Satir, 1967]. I'm sure it changed a lot from the time we were together years ago and the way it was before she died—I didn't see a lot of her in the last three years. She was busy gadding about, we were busy gadding about, and we didn't always gad about in the same circles. I think the last time we saw her was at the Evolution of Psychotherapy Conference.

Hoyt: In 1985.

Goulding: That Jeff Zeig [1987] put on in 1985. I may have seen her a couple of times since then, but that's the last I remember. She and her group did their Quest for Peace outside the conference one evening.

Hoyt: I remember that. That's when I first met you.

Goulding: Is that right?

Hoyt: I remember, I came up after your talk and said something about how much I enjoyed it, and you said, "Well, come and do a workshop!"

And I said, "What would happen?" and you said *[imitates Bob's deep voice]*, "You'll find out. Come and do a workshop!"

Goulding: *[laughs]* Always hustling *[laughs]* I've been good at hustling. I'm using "hustling" as a fun word, to identify the fact that I've not sat back and let the world come to me. I went out and met the world, writing, teaching all over the world, people coming here from all over the world. It's been a very exciting time.

Hoyt: You've promoted yourself, in the best sense. You offered people something that they wanted to come for.

Goulding: That's right. Good psychotherapy. And our model, the redecision model, is a really different model than has been taught before. Even the word is our word—we couldn't find it in the dictionary. It fit. People were asked to make *new decisions*, different than the decisions they made in childhood, which in childhood were perfectly appropriate for that period of time in their life, the people around them, where they lived, and so on, but are no longer appropriate in terms of their healthy life today. And our original concept was that the way to get into people changing is to get them to decide differently while they're in their Child ego state. What TA calls the Child ego state, which at that moment is free and is not in any way reacting to internal or external parents. It's made purely from what people want to do—not either for or against parental messages, injunctions, or counterinjunctions.

Hoyt: It comes from the *person.*

Goulding: From the internal guts, wanting to do it differently.

Hoyt: Tell me how you came to understand that, to see the importance of working with the inner Child.

Goulding: Well, I'm sure that some of that started with my general psychiatric training; it encompassed that idea because it always talked about parents and how parents affected development, and so on. But, of course, there are three parts to us, today what we call the Parent ego state, the Adult ego state, and the Child ego state. The Child ego state is that part of us which once was a child and still does things at times as that child did. And some of the things that we call "aberrant behavior" or "mental illness" or whatever are based upon those kinds of early decisions. So it seemed kind of obvious that the way then to get people to change is to get them to change what they had once decided, which means helping them get into their Free Child ego state so they can make that decision.

Hoyt: This is such a shift, though, from how many psychotherapists work who are very rational and sort of explain to people what they should do and point out how they're not doing the right thing and how their thinking is distorted or they're not making right choices.

Goulding: All of those things may be appropriate to do, but that's only doing Adult-to-Adult work. What we're doing is saying you've got to bring the Child into the act. The Child is the one who made the decision in the first place, so if you don't bring that Child, that part of the person, into the crux of the change, that Child will screw up the works, will destroy the work, will not allow the change to take place. Because if he says or she says, "Hey, what about me? I was getting my goodies all these years doing it this way and now you say up there, Adult, that I can't do it this way? Ho-ho-ho." That Child will sabotage the work. So, no matter how much Adult explaining you get, the Child still runs the roost. So until that Child has agreed to change, you don't get a good change.

Hoyt: Do you remember when you went "Ah ha!," when you recognized the importance of that? Was there a case, a moment, a discussion?

Goulding: Michael, I think it just grew. I'm sure there was a time, but I don't remember a case. I just recognized more and more . . . well, part of it was that I was aware that the Adult work done by Eric [Berne]—which was great work in which people really understood—didn't change what they wanted to change. You know, we were in the same office building, Eric and I and Dave Kupfer. So I started looking for what could we do that would facilitate them changing more than just Adult awareness. I was doing a lot of marathons. Dave Kupfer and I did our first marathon in 1962 at Esalen—no, our first was in Marin [County] at the fellow's house [Michael Murphy] who now has Esalen, matter of fact.

Hoyt: When a therapist is working in his or her office, not doing a marathon, what are some of the technologies, some of the methods they can use to get people back into their Child more quickly?

Goulding: Oh boy, that's an important question! One of the things that is important is to not take a classical history—"When were you born? Where were you raised? and Who were your parents?"—all "were" questions. What we do to start is to make the questions, "What year are you born? Who's living with you? and Where are you living?" Hear the "are's" rather than the "were's"? Every time we ask an "are" question people begin to get more and more in the present tense, they bring the past into the present. Well, when you bring the past into the present and use it as if you're in the situation right now, you're drawing more and more on a Child ego state kind of work, with affect immediately. As soon as people start saying "are" instead of "were," they begin to increase their affect—they get more sorrowful or more angry or more anxious or more scared—because they're beginning to tap into the reservoir of feelings that have not yet been resolved in that Child ego state. So it starts right in the beginning with the ways in which we get people working. And then, when you start doing Gestalt work, two-chair work, you separate out:

You have people sitting in their own chair, where they started from, talking to a Parent in another chair, and you begin to get a division between the Parent out there and the Child happening over here. And you get people to be able to fight back to that part of them which they no longer want to listen to when they sit back in the original chair. That's the easy way.

Hoyt: What else?

Goulding: Humor. Humor is a wonderful way of getting people into the Child ego state. And I'm a very funny therapist and I use a lot of humor in my work, including jokes and including profanity when it's appropriate or sometimes when it's not appropriate. Whatever it is that I can see I can do to get a laugh will facilitate getting into Child ego state work. Or doing physical stuff, for instance, when we do desensitization of heights or water. Now we do it in fantasy, as we learned from the behavior therapists, but we also do it in reality. We'll have people sit in a chair in the barn or seminar room and look at a ladder across the way and fantasize themselves walking across the driveway and climbing up the ladder and stepping over onto the roof and walking over to the top of the roof and looking at the view. And we'll have them do all that in fantasy first, and then have them do it in reality. When they do it really they're taking their body into it now and their movement into it, and it becomes an entirely different process, where they anchor in their Child ego state the feeling, the real feeling of climbing that ladder.

Hoyt: It's the power of *experience*, rather than talking about history or what went wrong. It's living in a new way.

Goulding: That's right. A lot of our work is experience, exactly. We learned from the Gestaltists, from the psychodramatists, a lot of it we developed ourselves—that's what redecision therapy is all about.

Hoyt: Tell me about the evolution of your learning to use experience. Were you trained as a psychoanalyst, were you sitting back and passive?

Goulding: No, my basic training in psychiatry was after I had spent 15 years in general practice. I was a general practitioner in North Dakota for 10 or 11 or 12 years, and then I was in Carmel for a year as a general practitioner, and then went back and got my psychiatric training. That was a very interesting program, because I was at a Veterans' Administration [V.A.] hospital in Perry Point, Maryland, and there I had a number of teachers, clinicians who were differing kinds of therapists. I had a guy who did marital therapy, a psychoanalyst who did classical psychoanalytic psychotherapy. I worked with a family therapist in Baltimore who did his classical kind of family therapy. I worked with some practical, pragmatic people who did practical, pragmatic stuff. So I learned a whole flock of different kinds of therapy skills. Then I came back to Carmel and looked up Eric Berne because I had just read his book [Berne, 1961]. We had played poker together in the past. I told him I wanted to learn TA, and also I wanted to complete my analysis with him that I had started in Baltimore. I wanted to do both.

Hoyt: What did he say?

Goulding: *[laughs]* That's an old story—he said *[imitates Berne's voice]*, "Well, that would be kind of sticky!" So, I decided that I wanted to learn TA. So I learned TA from Eric, at 11 o'clock every Saturday morning for a couple of years.[2] Then Fritz Perls came to Esalen, and I was going to Esalen a lot in those days. I attended a workshop led by Fritz and Jim Simkin. Satir was in the workshop, and Irma Shepherd and Joan Fagan and Howie Fink, and a number of other people that I've kept friends with all these years. Marvelous workshop. I learned as much about Fritz's keenness and savvyness by being a friend of his as I did by being in his workshops. He was really a wonderful guy. He did some things that people didn't like, but I liked him.

Hoyt: When you talk about Fritz you get a twinkle in your eye.

Goulding: Oh, yeah, well Fritz had a few in his eye, too! *[laughs]* Yeah, he was a lot of fun. But, anyway, Eric gave me an awful lot of stuff. Got a lot from Fritz. And I've learned from the Polsters [1973], and from the people I've worked with over the years.

Hoyt: How are you different from knowing Fritz, different as a therapist?

Goulding: I learned Gestalt therapy from Fritz. I think I got a lot of Fritz's wit. Well, I used Fritz as a good springboard for my own wit, let's put it that way. I didn't get it from him; I would use wit in therapy. And also, I made a major change in my own life with Fritz and Jim in the workshop that I did. I always knew that I was smart and I was hardworking and I was good at whatever I did, but I didn't realize how powerful I was until I got in touch with my own power at that workshop with Fritz and Jim. So, in addition to everything else I may have learned in terms of working, I also learned how important power is, and how important *my* power was, and how powerful I was.

Hoyt: Would it be fair to say you made a redecision?

Goulding: Sure it would! I didn't make it in that kind of conscious way at the moment, but I can remember when I claimed my own power. It

---

[2]In another conversation Bob indicated to me that it was he who had originated the "OK" concept and the term "I'm OK, You're OK" during one of those morning tutorials with Berne.

was a wonderful piece of work. I was in the group and it was the second or third day of the workshop, and I was beginning to feel very turned on but with some tears, and Fritz noticed that I was tearing and said, "What's up, Bob?" And I said, "I'm just feeling so moved." And he said, "So *move!*" And so I started to move, and erupted, as it were, and I kept saying "I feel like a volcano, about to blow up, but . . . " *[loudly imitates Fritz]*, "Then blow up! Blow up!" So I became louder and more noisy and *[imitates Fritz again]* : "BECOMING A VOLCANO SWIRLING INTO THE ATMOSPHERE!!" It was wonderful! *[laughs]* Like we reclaimed my volcanic powers, as it were. *[pause]* It's very touching, as I think about it now. I'm moved again to tears. Great experience—it was a good workshop.

The two big turning points in my life were that workshop and meeting Mary. *[pause]* It was very exciting to be around Carmel at the time—there was Satir and Fritz and Simkin [1976] at Esalen and Berne in Carmel.[3] It was really a great place to be. We all kind of developed together, as it were. Separately, because we were all on our own mountains, but we were all developing our skills and our knowledge. And I've kept learning. You've almost got to—if you want to stay with the flow you just have to keep at it. To stay on top of the psychiatric psychotherapeutic world I have to keep changing, too.

Hoyt: What are you looking at nowadays? What's exciting you?

Goulding: This is exciting right now, doing this interview. Teaching is exciting me. I've long since gotten tired of treating sick people. I like to treat people who are not sick, who have things that are blocking their own process, their own growth. Therapists, particularly. I love to treat therapists, that's what I do: treat therapists, train therapists. The treatment is part of the training. What I like to do is to get people like you here that I can not only train in the techniques of therapy but also facilitate grabbing your own power and your own stuff and increasing your own abilities by helping you get rid of those things that may be getting in your way.[4]

Hoyt: Let's talk about supervision and training.

Goulding: All right.

Hoyt: Mary and you have traveled all over the world teaching. You've taught thousands of therapists, you're world renowned, you've been honored by different associations, you've been on the faculty of the Evolution of Psychotherapy conference, the Fielding Institute has recognized

---

[3]For some histories of those times, see Anderson (1983), Hatcher and Himelstein (1976/ 1983), Jorgensen and Jorgensen (1984), Perls (1969a, 1969b), and Shepherd (1975).

[4]See Hoyt and Goulding (1989) for a detailed report of a supervision session we did together.

you with an honorary degree. When you approach a situation for supervising, do you have a thinking framework, do you have an idea of what you're trying to accomplish?

Goulding: Sure. I've got a list of things that I use in my head when I'm doing therapy that's really a very simple list. It's literally a list—I've written it hundreds of times. [The list: contact; contract; con; chief bad feelings, thinkings, behaviors, and body; chronic games, belief systems, and fantasies; childhood early decisions (injunctions and counterinjunctions, scripts, stroking patterns); impasse resolution (redecisions, ego state decontamination and reconstruction, reparenting, etc.); and maintaining the victory (anchoring, changing stroke patterns, plans for using the redecision in the future).][5] Things I am listening for and looking for and watching for and feeling for, and I am training people to do the same way. A whole series of things, starting with something very simple, very basic, and that's the original contact that people make. How do you make your first contact?

Hoyt: You're establishing the relationship, the parameters, and you're also paying exquisite attention to language.

Goulding: That's right. Absolutely. Even when I'm on the phone with somebody I will often pick up things that they do, and say something back differently. Like I want to get somebody up here to lay some rugs, and the guy says, "I'll try and be up there," and I say, "No, I don't want you to *try* to get up here. I want you to *be* here. When will you be here?" So in that first contact I pick up words that are not clear and which are part of what I like to call a *con*. When people come here, the first contact they get is driving up my driveway, which is full of redwood trees and beautiful yards and pasture and cows and cattle and horses. And so, immediately upon coming into our property they recognize that it's a different kind of place. They come up our brick steps and they're not even the ordinary regular brick walk steps. They're longer and thinner, so you have to take more steps in order to get up to the house. When they try to open the door, the door is still jammed from our earthquake of last year so it's hard to get open. They have to make an effort to get in—that's kind of interesting. I tried to fix it but I figured, "That's part of the contact, what the hell." *[laughs]* They walk in the front room, the foyer, and there are some artifacts from all over the world, some flowers, growing plants—a clarinet sitting on a shelf—a different kind of place. It's all part of the contact. It's all part of people saying to themselves in some way, "Hey,

---

[5]See Allen and Allen (1998), M.M. Goulding (1990), R.L. Goulding (1983, 1989), Goulding and Goulding (1978, 1979), Hoyt (1995), Kadis (1985), Lennox (1997), McClendon and Kadis (1983).

here's a different kind of place. Here's somebody, somebodies." They may not even think it consciously, but this kind of contact has got to push some buttons about differences, about "This place is different." So, the contact is a very important part of the process, and I teach that to people. How the contact is made in the therapy room is important. What people say when you start to form a contract. Eye contact. Being aware of what people are doing, making contact through what they're doing very often. That's all an important part of the process. I'm interested in who this person is, and I want people to be interested in who I am.[6]

Hoyt: Then what?

Goulding: Then I'm interested in *contracts* in therapy. How people change—no, *what* they change. What they want to change. And in listening to the contract I'm also listening for ways in which they're going to screw it up, like the words they use that I call the *cons*. "Try" is one. "What I'd *like* to do" or "What my husband wants me to do" or "What my wife wants me to do." All the words that indicate they're not going to do what they've said they're going to do. And I confront them, and confront them, and confront them. So that the contract ends up being clearly stated, workable, and without much danger of being sabotaged by the Child. The patient has the power. *[Reaches to the shelf behind him, pulls off a copy of* The Power Is in the Patient, *and thumps it.]*

Hoyt: The title of your book [Goulding & Goulding, 1978].

Goulding: Right. All we have is this knowledge of how *you* can change. You're the one who's going to change—we keep that in the foreground all the time. Then we go through the process of the work that has to be done. And really, it doesn't make any difference what kind of therapy you do in terms of whether it's redecision therapy or something else—anybody with good skills in any kind of therapy they do is going to effect some change.[7] If you're a good therapist, you'll get that done. You'll make good contact, have a good contract, and then do the work that needs to

---

[6]Mary Goulding (1995a, p. 315) quotes a mini-lecture by Bob Goulding: "People can't make redecisions by Talking About. I don't care how many years they spend in a therapy group talking about their problems, they won't make redecisions. That's why I want the client to bring the early scene to THIS room at THIS time and create an I-THOU dialogue with the others in the scene, to resolve the impasse. Look, here is my definition of redecision [*writes on board*]:
    I-Thou
    Here and Now
    WOW!"

[7]This is borne out in *The First Session in Brief Therapy* (Budman, Hoyt & Friedman, 1992), in which leading practitioners of different therapeutic schools, across varying methods, all attended early on to issues of alliance, clear goals, and patient involvement.

be done and anchor the work so that two days from now, two weeks from now, two months from now when they get in the same kind of stress, they have a little button inside of them, the kind that goes "bzzzz" like a reminder. So, the *contact* and *contract*, the *middle ground* and *anchoring* are some of the very important issues. Incidentally, my speech at the Evolution of Psychotherapy conference down in Anaheim this year is that: "Contact, Contract, and Encore," I call it.[8] The main body of my speech is going to be on those three things, not so much on redecision therapy.[9]

Hoyt: So it's making the contact; helping the patients realize their responsibility, their role in their problem; and then helping them continue to access their power regarding how they're going to keep from turning back into being passive or being a victim of their problem.

Goulding: That's right, that's right. So when they start to get back into the game, or back into the script, or whatever it was, they can really recognize it, and if they've done some good therapeutic work they can anchor themselves or facilitate their anchoring themselves. So you asked me how I teach—that was the original question—I teach all of that to people. I teach them how to facilitate making the redecision, because that's what we do, but that's not so important to me as teaching them how to do good general therapy. Whether they do redecision therapy or TA or whatever is not as much my issue as teaching them to do good therapy.

Hoyt: Be effective.

Goulding: Be effective. All of the things it takes to be a good therapist.

Hoyt: As I've watched you teach therapists I see a parallel between what

---

[8]In her introductory "Letter from the Guest Editor" in the Robert L. Goulding, M.D. memorial issue of the *Transactional Analysis Journal* (in which this interview originally appeared), Mary Goulding (1995b, p. 299) wrote:

> Michael Hoyt's interview is beautiful. It reveals the aging, sick Bob as he looks back at his professional life. Bob and I used to argue a lot, and I would argue with him today over his suggestion that the contract and the anchoring process are more important than the redecision process. I think redecision can be accomplished without a contract and often does not need anchoring, although it is important to discuss with clients how they will use their redecisions in their current lives. I do wish Bob were here to read, to argue, to add new insights. I loved him as much as he loved me.

[9]Bob's failing health kept him from attending the Second Evolution of Psychotherapy conference, held in Anaheim, California, December 12–16, 1990 (see Zeig, 1992). I went, and had two long phone conversations with him during the conference. In addition to wanting details about Mary's presentations and the audience's responses, he was keenly interested in a number of topics, discussed them intensely, and was very frustrated not to be physically present at the meetings.

you do with the trainee-therapist and what you want the trainee-therapist to be doing with the client-patient [see Hoyt, 1991]. You make the contact with the trainee, you listen for where this trainee is stuck, what this trainee needs to get unstuck, you help the trainee empower herself or himself, then try to help them remember that so they won't fall back into being ineffective.

Goulding: That's right. And in doing that, of course, I have to have the experience of doing therapy in front of me, so the best training I do is this live supervision in the live group doing live work. Not notes and so on— God knows I've supervised enough people with notes over the years, and that's important to do, to get people supervision of their own clientele, their own people that they're seeing, because people see all different kinds of people. It's also important for me, to train, to do it live as well.

Hoyt: If you're supervising the therapy from notes, you're actually supervising what they *said* they did, not what they're doing.

Goulding: That's right! That's why I'd rather have tape than notes. And I do that, as you know, if you've got a stuck patient that you're having a hard time with, you bring me notes of your work with that tough patient and I can still help you with looking for new ways of dealing with it. And that's an important part of supervision, too, and I like to do that. Most people who have trained with me do bring in notes of their work and occasionally bring in tapes. That is an essential area of supervision because people do get stuck—including me.

Hoyt: As part of your supervision work, you'll work with the trainee-therapist helping them overcome their difficulties working with a particular patient. Do you see a boundary between supervision and personal psychotherapy?

Goulding: I'm not sure what you mean by "boundary." Certainly people do things that get in their own way because of their own script and their own games, and so on. A therapist who plays "Kick Me," for instance, is going to do something in the process of the work so that the patient wants to kick him or kick her. The therapist who is afraid of closeness and intimacy is not going to be reaching out as much and, therefore, will stay somewhat withdrawn from personal work compared to a therapist who is much more intimate and much more able to deal with closeness and enjoy closeness, and so on and so on and so on. Whatever people are stuck with gets into their therapy.

Hoyt: Are there times you'll say to a trainee, "I think this is more a personal therapy issue. We shouldn't call this supervision"?

Goulding: If somebody's sitting there in a chair and they've done something that I think can be worked through right then, I'll work it through right then. I very rarely say what you just said, that it's a therapeutic issue. I'll make a note in my head, and the next time we're still in the group and I have a chance I may go back and say, "By the way, when you were doing the therapy awhile ago, blah, blah, blah, blah—that's something to deal with."

Hoyt: If you find that you're not getting it worked through in the moment, that it's a recurring theme that this particular trainee comes up with case after case or session after session, then how will you handle that situation differently?

Goulding: I'm not sure that I would. I'd just keep coming back. What I don't want to do, you see, is have them feel like I'm looking over their shoulder in that kind of way while they're working. It's impossible to work with me in the room and not feel like I'm looking over their shoulder—because I am, obviously—but I don't want that to get in the way of their work. Now, when I experience that it is getting in the way of their work, and I know that they're better therapists than they're being in their work in front of me, I may look into what kinds of parental experiences they had, like "When you're a little kid, when did you get scared when your dad was watching you?" or "When you were a little kid, what happens in your house that you get scolded for?" There's all kinds of ways of asking those questions.

Hoyt: I certainly remember the first times I was presenting work to you as my supervisor, and in the back of my mind I was thinking, "Am I doing it right? Am I doing it right? What's he going to think? Oh-oh, it doesn't sound perfect!"

Goulding: *[laughs]* Right.

Hoyt: And I realized, "If it sounded perfect, I wouldn't need to be having supervision."

Goulding: It doesn't need to be "bad." You might learn something different and still be perfect. [Ever sharp, Bob picks up a "Be perfect" remnant—one doesn't need to be "trained" until some mythical (and unattainable) standard of "perfection" is achieved.]

Hoyt: Thank you.

Goulding: You're welcome. *[both laugh]*

Hoyt: Have you watched other therapists supervise—other than Mary, of course, with whom you work as a cosupervisor?

Goulding: Not very often. Some. I watched Satir a little bit, but not much. I watched Shepherd and Fagan because I visited them in Savannah, at Georgia State, when they were on the faculty [see Fagan & Shepherd, 1970]. Of course I've watched people supervise here when they're here for workshops. I teach supervision. We get a lot of people here who are advanced members of the International Transactional Analysis Association and who come to Mt. Madonna to get more time for their Teaching Member credentials. So I do a lot of good teaching with them.

Hoyt: Do you see patterns of errors or mistakes or places that supervisors get stuck?

Goulding: Michael, I'm not thinking of any at the moment. Do you have a hunch, the way you asked the question?

Hoyt: Well, I've sometimes seen the reciprocal of the trainee wanting to be kicked and supervisors who feel they need to be always right and they're looking for ways to make supervisees wrong. Or they're making the supervisee unnecessarily dependent on them. They're not willing to stroke much; they're much more interested in finding what's wrong and in always being "one up" [see Hawthorne, 1975; Kadushin, 1968].

Goulding: The one set pattern that I think is more prevalent than anything else is people not willing to tell them when they're wrong. Most supervisors who are getting training here give all the positive strokes. They may give the supervisee an option, but not many. They say, "I like this, I like that." But it's very rarely they say, "I would have done this, as another option." Or, "You were absolutely wrong not to pick up on that suicidal gesture that they made. You should have picked that up." Very rarely do I hear them do that. I don't know if I do or not. I think I do. I'd say, "You missed picking up on the suicide gesture."

Hoyt: I've heard you give that feedback to people, but do it in a way that didn't make them wrong. You didn't say, "*You* were wrong." Rather, you said something like, "This was an error," or "This is something that needs to be attended to, because it's so essential."

Goulding: Right.

Hoyt: I think that's a problem in our profession. People sometimes try to be so nice and kind.

Goulding: Yeah, that's what I was saying. Sometimes they are too nice and don't pick up on stuff that's important to pick up on. Although I must say that my supervisees are a higher class of people! *[said with a wink]*

Hoyt: Indeed! *[both laugh]* In my work supervising I've found real differences between relatively beginning therapists and more advanced, experienced therapists who come to learn something new or come because they're stuck on a particular problem. I think beginning therapists need a lot of help learning to understand how patients get stuck and just learning basic techniques: what can you do in these situations. They also have their own contributions to the problem.

Goulding: As I say, everybody's at their own level. At an intensive workshop there's a chance to get both at the same time. Doing supervision in a group for me is much more than just economically sound. It's a way in which those who are advanced can get good advanced stuff and can relearn some early stuff, while those who are getting early stuff may have a chance to get some advanced stuff they wouldn't get otherwise if they were just in a group with people of the same level.

Hoyt: Much like group therapy is.

Goulding: Yeah. That's right. [see Goulding, 1987]

Hoyt: You learn from others.

Goulding: *[pause]* Well, I'm just thinking about this book, how much stuff is in this book. We published *The Power Is in the Patient* [Goulding & Goulding, 1978] from a lot of articles that Mary and I had written prior to this book except for a couple that we wrote just for the book. One of them that Mary wrote is a wonderful, wonderful one-page article, "To My Clients" [M. Goulding, 1978, p. 15]. Ever read that?

Hoyt: I have.

Goulding: Isn't it beautiful?

Hoyt: Mary has a way sometimes of saying in a phrase or page or paragraph what other people with hundreds of pages have not said well. She gets right to the heart. She does it poetically and poignantly and right on, in a way that sticks.

Goulding: Yeah. She sure does.

At this point, Bob and I took a break for lunch. As we resumed the interview, Bob referred to the nasal canula and oxygen tank by his side, noting, "I need to be on oxygen most of the time, so I'm on it. It makes working a little harder, but I probably wouldn't be working much more anyway, so that's not particularly important. It's no fun, but that's how I'm surviving. Right now Bob Goulding is on oxygen, and will probably never get off it." We then went on to talk about how he got into medicine. Influenced by a family doctor and by an uncle who was a physician, he had firmly decided as a young child to become a physician.

Hoyt: When did you think to become a psychiatrist?

Goulding: Well, that's a different case. When I was in medical school— well, I'm not sure about that now. I was very interested in psychology, and when I went to college I had already read a lot of stuff that was written in those days. I read a lot of Freud and books about Freud. Now Freud didn't die until I was almost through college, so he was around during my growing up years. I can recall reading the book Adler wrote, *Understanding Human Nature* [1927/1946] when I was very young. So I had an interest in psychology. I don't remember thinking, "I'm going to be a psychotherapist someday." And then when I was in medical school I took all the time I could get working in the psych unit. When I was in general practice in North dakota from 1948 to 1957 I knew that I needed to know more about the treatment of mental illness because most of my practice was psychosomatic stuff. I decided during all of those years that I had to go back and get some more training in psychiatry. What happened was, I had left North Dakota and was in Pacific Grove in 1957 when I decided to become a psychiatrist. I had a little Metropolitan, and I drove it all over the country looking for a residency. I chose Perry Point V.A. Hospital in Maryland—just exactly what I was looking for, a broad spectrum of therapies rather than just psychoanalytic stuff, which most hospitals were in those days, and I liked the people who were there, so I stopped my search and stayed. I remember it well, and I've never regretted it. I've had a great time as a psychiatrist and psychotherapist. But I'm not a classical psychiatrist in terms of I don't ordinarily deal with very sick patients anymore. I use almost no medications. I never did use much in the way of medication even when I was in full-time private practice. I'd rather make my interventions social or verbal, rather than chemical.

We went on to discuss his family of origin. From his father, "who ended up as the vice president of a large advertising firm," he learned "work hard, succeed." From his mother "I probably got more of my social graces. She came from a fairly prominent North Philadelphia family. She told a lot of stories. She was very pretty, a good musician, good pianist, a redhead with a violent temper. They weren't abusive, though—I didn't get any more licks than anybody else got. . . . She was funny, loud, kind of hysterical sometimes, but always with a cultured edge. Loving . . . my family were not much in the way of touchers. I don't know where I got my touching from. You know, I touch a lot. My mother touched certainly more than my father, but I don't remember her being very touching, particularly. Touching wasn't done much in my family, either side."

Our conversation then winded lambently through a variety of topics: life and medical practice in North Dakota, baseball, music, hunting, fishing, fun with old friends. He spoke fondly of his old North Dakota friend, Don Stewart, who taught him to fish [see R. L. Goulding, 1978].

Goulding: Every psychotherapist should also be a fly fisherman, know when to put the bait out and when to pull it in. *[laughs]* It's important: when to strike. Half the process is striking at the right time. Give a confrontation to a con when the person is not ready to accept the confrontation of the con, and it's much harder to get his attention, just like a trout. If you don't lay that fly right where that trout is feeding, they'll never even see the fly. You've got to be able to lay it in the right place at the right time, when the trout is there. It's nothing different than good psychotherapy—you lay the fly down at the right place at the right time. *[laughs]* GOT IT?

Hoyt: Got it!

Our discussion of life back then continued.

Goulding: Those North Dakota days were really different days for a city boy. Going on a house call at dawn and the sun is just beginning to light up the sky, not even a view yet, and I'm driving along the road seeing birds flush out of the ditch alongside the road and maybe scare a couple of deer that are feeding in the ditch or in the field nearby. Wintertime hearing the tires crunch on the snow as I was going out on this house call—and there was almost always snow—and sometimes so cold it was unbelievable. And I remember one day, one night, I was out on a house call—it wasn't really a house call, it was a road call—it had been reported to us that a guy had a coronary in his car. So, whoever it was who found him called me and I called the sheriff and the ambulance company—the ambulance company was also the mortuary in little towns like that; the mortuary van doubled for the ambulance. We went out Highway 85 looking for this guy, and we found his car, but we couldn't find him. And it turned out later on that some forestry service guy went by and found him and took him to the hospital in Dickinson. It was so cold out. We got up to the little town called Amidon, north of Bowman, when we couldn't find this guy, and went into one of the bars to warm up and get a drink. There at the bar was a guy, whose name I won't mention here because he may still be around, who had been working very hard in AA [Alcoholics Anonymous] for a couple of years in North Dakota, and here he was sitting at the end of the bar just drunk as a skunk. He thought if he got that far away from Bowman he could get away with it. And he tells the story: "Jesus Christ! I'm peeking through the door in the bar and in comes Bob Goulding, the sheriff, and the undertaker!" *[laughs]* Caught! Caught!!

Hoyt: *[laughs]*

Goulding: I remember one time I had two deliveries at one time in the hospital. One woman was on the gurney and one woman was on the delivery table. I had to go back and forth between the two women in the delivery room. They were simultaneously delivering. I had to make sure that neither one of them was in a bad place, and I could kind of let the nurses help, which they were very good at. This time I delivered one with my right hand and one with my left hand, standing in between the two women—which is not the world's best antiseptic condition—but we got the babies delivered. I was very careful not to cross them over. It was quite a hospital.

Hoyt: You loved being involved in people's lives.

Goulding: In that kind of medicine, yeah. I really did love it. I'm glad now that I quit it and went into psychiatry, cause I've had a lot of fun doing psychiatry, too. But it was a very rewarding ten years in North

Dakota. I was really a part of the community in all kinds of ways. This practice here, of course, I'm not part of this community at all. I'm part of a different community, but it's a worldwide community rather than a local community. I hardly go to downtown Watsonville. If I went back to North Dakota now probably half the people in the street, adults, I delivered.

Hoyt: There's a carryover, though, the way you work with people here: the contact. They come to your small town and you get totally into their life.

Goulding: Oh, yeah. Sure. I've said many times that the best experience that a psychiatrist could have is to do some general practice first.

Bob then talked about his days in the 82nd Airborne, where he was a medical doctor who made 37 practice parachute jumps. Our conversation continued, touching on various family memories. It had been a long day, and Bob was visibly tired. Before we stopped, I asked:

Hoyt: Tell me about this Mary Goulding woman that you're seen with.

Goulding: The most important thing I ever did was meet Mary. Incredible woman. She's just an incredible woman. Loving, caring. I didn't realize how caring she was capable of being, because it hadn't really been her thing, until I've been sick. And she's just been incredibly wonderful. It's hard for me to do a lot of stuff, you know, and she's been here and on hand taking me places where I had to go and being supportive and not denying me anything. Wonderful. We've had a *great* 25 years of working together. Couldn't be a better cotherapist. She's unique, intuitive, smart, quick, loving, caring, confronting—everything a good therapist should be, she is. She's incredible. That one page [p. 15] in *The Power is in the Patient* says it all, the page "To My Clients." She says, don't tell me about your problems. Tell me about your health. What better thing could you say as a therapist than don't talk to me about your problems? You've got to know about them, of course, but don't keep repeating them as part of the catechism or the ritual. [Or the "story" or "narrative" one constructs about self and life—M.F.H.] How are you getting well? What are you doing that's good? What are you doing that helping and healing? That's the important thing. What are you doing differently? What's your redecision? How are you bringing it about? These are not her words, they're my words reflecting her point of view—and mine. I think one of the problems with a lot of therapists is they listen too much for pathology and not enough for health.

The "interview" was over. We had more conversations, but none taped. When I look back, I think I am a better person, a sharper therapist, and more alive for having known Bob Goulding. I learned about both the creation and the acceptance of one's reality. As I have written elsewhere (Hoyt, 1992), I remember his brilliant ability to listen and get right to the heart of the matter; his simply refusing to argue with me; his wonderful humor and irritable moods; his compliments about my wife (which I reciprocated); his insisting on paying me for some teaching I had done; his clueing me in that his famous fishing story (R. L. Goulding, 1978) had something to do with making money, too.

Bob Goulding died at home, attended by his wife and family, on February 13, 1992. A few days later, there was a memorial gathering at the Western Institute. We laid his ashes to rest, held hands as we sang "Amazing Grace," and spent hours in a large circle sharing Bob Goulding stories. I remember Bob's integrity, caring, power, and friendship. Some say that when a star dies you can still see its light for a thousand years.

☐ References

Adler, A. (1946). *Understanding Human Nature* (W. B. Wolfe, Trans.). New York: Greenberg Publishers. (original work published 1927)

Allen, J. R., & Allen, B. A. (1998). Redecision therapy: Through a narrative lens. In M. F. Hoyt (Ed.), *The Handbook of Constructive Therapies* (pp. 31–45). San Francisco: Jossey-Bass.

Anderson, W.T. (1983). *The Upstart Spring: Esalen and the American Awakening.* Reading, MA: Addison-Wesley.

Berne, E. (1961). *Transactional Analysis in Psychgotherapy: A Systematic Individual and Social Psychiatry.* New York: Grove Press.

Budman, S. H., Hoyt, M. F., & Friedman, S. (Eds.) (1992). *The First Session in Brief Therapy.* New York: Guilford Press.

Fagan, J., & Shepherd, I. L. (Eds.) (1970). *Gestalt Therapy Now: Theory, Techniques, and Applications.* Palo Alto, CA: Science and Behavior Books.

Goulding, M. M. (1978). To my clients. In R. L. Goulding & M. M. Goulding, *The Power is in the Patient: A TA/Gestalt Approach to Psychotherapy* (p. 15). (P. McCormick, Ed.). San Francisco: TA Press.

Goulding, M. M. (1985). *Who's Been Living in Your Head?* (rev. ed.) Watsonville, CA: Western Institute for Group and Family Press.

Goulding, M. M. (1990). Getting the important work done fast: Contract plus redecision. In J. K. Zeig & S. G. Gilligan (Eds.), *Brief Therapy: Myths, Methods, and Metaphors* (pp. 303–317). New York: Brunner/Mazel.

Goulding, M.. (1992). *Sweet Love Remembered: Bob Goulding and Redecision Therapy.* San Francisco: TA Press.

Goulding, M. M. (1995a). Mini-lectures by Bob Goulding. *Transactional Analysis Journal, 25*(4), 314–315.

Goulding, M. M. (1995b). Letter from the guest editor. *Transactional Analysis Journal, 25*(4), 298–299.

Goulding, M. M. (1997) Childhood scenes in redecision therapy. In C. E. Lennox (Ed.), *Redecision Therapy: A Brief, Action-Oriented Approach* (pp. 87–94). Northvale, NJ: Jason Aronson.

Goulding, M. M., & Goulding, R. L. (1979) *Changing Lives through Redecision Therapy.* New York: Brunner/Mazel.

Goulding, M. M., & Goulding, R. L. (1989) *Not to Worry! How to Free Yourself from Unnecessary Anxiety and Channel Your Worries into Positive Action.* New York: William Morrow.

Goulding, R. L. (1978). How to catch fish. In R. L. Goulding & M. M. Goulding, *The Power is in the Patient* (pp. 1–8). (P. McCormick, Ed.) San Francisco: TA Press.

Goulding, R. L. (1983). Gestalt therapy and transactional analysis. In C. Hatcher & P. Himelstein (Eds.), *The Handbook of Gestalt Therapy* (pp. 615–634). Northvale, NJ: Jason Aronson.

Goulding, R. L. (1987). Group therapy: Mainline or sideline? In J. K. Zeig (Ed.), *The Evolution of Psychotherapy* (pp. 300–311). New York: Brunner/Mazel.

Goulding, R. L. (1989). Teaching transactional analysis and redecision therapy. *Journal of Independent Social Work*, 3(4), 71–86.

Goulding, R. L., & Goulding, M. M. (1978). *The Power is in the Patient: A Gestalt/TA Approach to Psychotherapy*. (P. McCormick, Ed.) San Francisco: TA Press.

Hatcher, C., & Himelstein, P. (Eds.) (1983). *The Handbook of Gestalt Therapy*. Northvale, NJ: Jason Aronson.

Hawthorne, L. (1975). Games supervisors play. *Social Work*, 20(3), 179–183.

Hoyt, M. F. (1990). On time in brief therapy. In R. A. Wells & V. J. Giannetti (Eds.), *Handbook of the Brief Psychotherapies* (pp. 115–143). New York: Plenum. Reprinted in M.F. Hoyt, *Brief Therapy and Managed Care: Readings for Contemporary Practice* (pp. 69–104). San Francisco: Jossey-Bass, 1995.

Hoyt, M. F. (1991). Teaching and learning short-term psychotherapy within an HMO. In C. S. Austad & W. H. Berman (Eds.), *Psychotherapy in Managed Health Care: The Optimal Use of Time and Resources* (pp. 98–107). Washington, DC: American Psychological Association. Reprinted in M. F. Hoyt, *Brief Therapy and Managed Care: Readings for Contemporary Practice* (pp. 63–68). San Francisco: Jossey-Bass, 1995.

Hoyt, M. F. (1992). Personal and powerful. In C. L. Pelton & L. Myers-Pelton (Eds.), *Reflections of Robert L. Goulding* (pp. 179–182). Aberdeen, SD: Family Health Media.

Hoyt, M. F. (Ed.) (1994). *Constructive Therapies*. New York: Guilford Press.

Hoyt, M. F. (1995). *Brief Therapy and Managed Care: Readings for Contemporary Practice*. San Francisco: Jossey-Bass.

Hoyt, M. F. (Ed.) (1996). *Constructive Therapies, Volume 2*. New York: Guilford Press.

Hoyt, M. F. (Ed.) (1998). *The Handbook of Constructive Therapies*. San Francisco: Jossey-Bass.

Hoyt, M. F. (2000). *Some Stories are Better than Others: Doing What Works in Brief Therapy and Managed Care*. Philadelphia: Brunner/Mazel.

Hoyt, M. F., & Goulding, R. L. (1989). Resolution of a transference-countertransference impasse using Gestalt techniques in supervision. *Transactional Analysis Journal*, 19, 201–211. Reprinted in M.F. Hoyt, *Brief Therapy and Managed Care: Readings for Contemporary Practice* (pp. 237–256). San Francisco: Jossey-Bass, 1995.

Jorgensen, E. W., & Jorgensen, H. I. (1984). *Eric Berne: Master Gamesman*. New York: Grove Press.

Kadis, L. B. (Ed.) (1985). *Redecision Therapy: Expanded Perspectives*. Watsonville, CA: Western Institute for Group and Family Therapy Press.

Kadushin, A. (1968). Games people play in supervision. *Social Work*, 13(3), 23–32.

Lennox, C. E. (Ed.) (1997). *Redecision Therapy: A Brief, Action-Oriented Approach*. Northvale, NJ: Jason Aronson.

McClendon, R., & Kadis, L. B. (1983). *Chocolate Pudding and Other Approaches to Intensive Multiple-Family Therapy*. Palo Alto, CA: Science and Behavior Books.

Perls, F. S. (1969a). *In and Out the Garbage Pail*. Lafayette, CA: Real People Press.

Perls, F. S. (1969b). *Gestalt Therapy Verbatim* (compiled and edited by J. O. Stevens). Lafayette, CA: Real People Press.

Polster, E., & Polster, M. (1973). *Gestalt Therapy Integrated: Contours of Theory and Practice*. New York: Vintage.

Satir, V. (1967). *Conjoint Family Therapy* (rev. ed.). Palo Alto, CA: Science and Behavior Books.

Shepard, M. (1975). *Fritz: An Intimate Portrait of Fritz Perls and Gestalt Therapy*. New York: Bantam.
Simkin, J. S. (1976). *Gestalt Therapy Mini-Lectures*. Millbrae, CA: Celestial Arts.
Zeig, J. K. (Ed.) (1987). *The Evolution of Psychotherapy*. New York: Brunner/Mazel.
Zeig, J. K. (Ed.) (1992). *The Evolution of Psychotherapy: The Second Conference*. New York: Brunner/Mazel.

Constructing Therapeutic Realities: A Conversation With Paul Watzlawick

No one has done more to explicate the theory and practice of constructivist and interactionalist approaches in psychotherapy than Paul Watzlawick, Ph.D. Long affiliated with the Mental Research Institute in Palo Alto, California, during his distinguished career he has been the recipient of numerous awards for his many outstanding contributions. Among his honors, Watzlawick has been recognized as a senior faculty member at each of the four Evolution of Psychotherapy conferences (held in 1985, 1990, 1995, and 2000). A prolific and extraordinarily erudite writer and editor, his 18 books (of which there exist more than 70 foreign-language editions) include *Pragmatics of Human Communication* (Watzlawick, Beavin & Jackson, 1967), *Change: Principles of Problem Formation and Problem Resolution* (Watzlawick, Weakland & Fisch, 1974), *How Real is Real?* (1976), *The Interactional View* (Watzlawick & Weakland, 1977), *The Language of Change* (1978), *The Situation is Hopeless but Not Serious* (1983), *The Invented Reality* (1984a), and *Ultra-Solutions: How to Fail Most Successfully* (1988).

Despite numerous demands upon his schedule from various writing, speaking, and travel commitments, Dr. Watzlawick graciously responded to a series of written questions I put to him during the Summer of 1997:

Hoyt: At the Third Evolution of Psychotherapy Conference, you (1997a, p. 306) commented:

Reprinted, with changes, from M. F. Hoyt (Ed.), *The Handbook of Constructive Therapies* (pp. 183–197). San Francisco: Jossey-Bass, 1998. Used with permission.

It is a great honor for me to make a commentary on Dr. Szasz' presentation. His *Myth of Mental Illness* [Szasz, 1961] was one of the most powerful single factors in my own professional development. It has helped me to do that 180-degree turn from being a Jungian analyst—a training analyst even—to a totally new perspective.

When I began to work as a Jungian analyst, I knew almost everything about Siberian creation myths, but I didn't know what to do with a person who chewed his fingernails. That bothered me.

Above all, what Dr. Szasz' book helped me to understand was the fallacy of the belief that mentally normal people see the world as it "really" is, while so-called mental patients have a distorted view of it. This myth of a real reality has maintained itself almost exclusively in our field. But in a conversation with Heisenberg, back in 1926 in Copenhagen, Einstein already is supposed to have said, "It is wrong to assume that theories are based on observation. The opposite is the case. The theory determines what we can observe." And in philosophy since Kant and Schopenhauer, the same issues have been questioned.

This leads me to ask: Why do you think the "myth of a real reality" has hung on so tenaciously in the psychotherapy field? What will therapists have to give up, and what will they gain, if they embrace the construction that we construct?

Watzlawick: They would have to give up the dogmatic belief in the "definitive truth" discovered by the schools of thought (and of therapy) they belong to. For—let us say—a physicist, this is much simpler, since it does not involve the "meaning of life," etc., etc.[1]

Hoyt: In your own presentation at the Third Evolution Conference, "'Insight' May Cause Blindness," you (1997b) remarked:

> One of the most important events in my evolution as a therapist was my discovery of a book by the philosopher Hans Vaihinger called *The Philosophy of 'As If'* (1924). . . .

Please, explain:

Watzlawick: According to Vaihinger, we always work with "fictions," and yet can arrive at practical results, after which the fiction "drops out." One of the countless examples contained in his book is the "fiction of liberty," which the judge uses only to arrive at a sentence: "The judge concludes that every man is free, and, therefore, if he has sinned against the law, he must be punished. . . . But the premise whether man is really free, is not examined by the judge. . . . Without the possibility of punishing men, of punishing the criminal, no government would be possible.

---

[1]Although scientists sometimes struggle, as Horgan (1995) nicely documents in *The End of Science*, with accepting the second-order idea of researching within paradigms rather than uncovering underlying fundamental truths about the universe.

The theoretical fiction of freedom has been invented for this practical purpose."

And later: "We have repeatedly insisted above that the boundary between truth and error is not a rigid one, and we were able ultimately to demonstrate that what we generally call truth, namely a conceptual world coinciding with the external world, *is merely the most expedient error.*"

Hoyt: Was there a moment or incident that led you to see "reality" as *constructed*?

Watzlawick: No, there was not—it was the outcome of years of research and practice.

Hoyt: What else led you to identify as a radical constructivist, and how is this related to your shift from an intrapsychic (monadic) to an interactional (systemic) way of conceptualizing problems?

Watzlawick: I was fascinated with the publications of the Bateson group; their insistence on a circular (rather than linear) causality of specific human behaviors, and their study of interactional (rather than individual) behavior patterns.

Hoyt: At the "Unmuddying the Waters" conference we attended in Saratoga, California, during March 1995 (see Efron, 1995; Hoyt, 1997), some attention was given to the importance of acknowledging pioneers in the field. In addition to Szasz and Vaihinger, please comment on how each of the following has influenced you: *Gregory Bateson*:

Watzlawick: The famous anthropologist and one of the members of the outstanding Josiah Macy Conferences (which led to the development of cybernetics) opened my eyes to what nowadays is called the interactional view in our field. Unlike the analyst, the anthropologist does not ask "*Why* does this person behave in this pathological manner?" but rather, "In what system of human interaction does this behavior make sense?"— whereby, of course, "make sense" does not necessarily mean that this behavior has to be "sane," "positive," "logical," etc. in a rational sense.

Hoyt: *Milton Erickson*:

Watzlawick: I met Erickson personally only twice, but our colleagues (the collaborators of Bateson) John Weakland and Jay Haley went to Phoenix numerous times and brought back fascinating information of Erickson's use of hynotic principles also outside of trance states.[2] Of decisive impor-

---

[2]See Watzlawick 's (1982) paper, "Erickson's Contribution to the Interactional View of Psychotherapy," as well as Haley's (1985) three-volume *Conversations with Erickson*. Milton Erickson (1974) also wrote the Foreword to *Change*, in which he said (pp. ix–x): "Watzlawick, Weakland, and Fisch have, in this extremely important book, looked at this phenomenon [of change] and put it in a conceptual framework—illuminated by examples from a variety of areas—which opens up new pathways to the further understanding of how people be-

tance for me (as a linguist by academic training) was Erickson's rule: "Learn and speak the client's language." As I would put it nowadays, this enables us to enter the client's "second order reality," rather than (as I was taught in my training as analyst) to teach clients a new "language" (that of the analytic perspective), make them see the world in terms of this "scientific" language, and lead them to "insight."

Hoyt: *Don Jackson:*

Watzlawick: The founder and first director of the Mental Research Institute, he had already abandoned the dogma of having to look for the causes in the past in order to bring about "insight" before he met Gregory Bateson. He was already practicing what later became known as "family therapy" (or, to use the modern term, "systemic therapy"). He would see the clients (the "identified patients") together with their families and not rarely managed to make effective interventions already during the first ten minutes of the first session.

Hoyt: Who else?

Watzlawick: *Heinz von Foerster,* the famous bio-cybernetician.

Hoyt: How would we act and see if we understood von Foerster's (1981, 1984; also see Segal, 1986) dictum, "If you desire to see, learn how to act"?

Watzlawick: For me this is exactly the difference between the classical, dogmatic assumption that "insight" permits us to change our behavior, and the constructivist assumption that different, "new" behavior may (but need not) make us aware of possibilities that we were unaware of before.

Hoyt: In an earlier discussion (1997, p. 307) you quoted Gregory Bateson as having precisely said that "An instinct is an explanatory principle." Is *insight* a parallel explanatory principle? In addition, is there something that produces change as it comes into awareness? Is *insight* an epiphenomenon that follows change?

 Watzlawick: I would consider "insight" an explanatory principle in Bateson's sense, except that it is believed to have a magical effect—if applied in therapy.

In my view, the most frequent factor that brings about change in human lives is what Franz Alexander [Alexander & French, 1946] called a *corrective emotional experience,* i.e., a chance event that suddenly opens my eyes for a different way out of my problem.

---

come enmeshed in problems with each other, and new pathways to expediting the resolution of such human impasses. The relevance of this new framework extends far beyond the sphere of 'psychological' problems from which it grew. This work is fascinating. I think it is a noteworthy contribution—a damn good book—and a must for anyone seeking to understand the many aspects of group behavior."

"Insight" may very well (and often does) *follow* change—which makes it into a consequence and not a cause.

Hoyt: In *Change: Principles of Problem Formation and Problem Resolution* (Watzlawick et al., 1974, p. 26) you wrote:

> It is generally held that change comes about through insight into the past causes which are responsible for the present trouble. But, as the nine-dot problem exemplifies, there is no cogent reason for this excursion into the past; the genesis of the self-defeating assumption which precludes the solution is quite irrelevant, the problem is solved in the here and now by stepping outside the "box." There is increasing awareness among clinicians that while insight may provide very sophisticated *explanations* of a symptom, it does little if anything to change it for the better.
>
> This empirical fact raises an important epistemological issue. All theories have limitations which follow logically from their premises. In the case of psychiatric theories, these limitations are more often than not attributed to human nature. For instance, within the psychoanalytic framework, symptom removal without the solution of the underlying conflict responsible for the symptom *must* lead to symptom substitution. This is not because this complication lies in the nature of the human *mind*; it lies in the nature of the *theory*, i.e., in the conclusions that logically follow from its premises. The behavior therapists, on the other hand, base themselves on learning and extinction theories and therefore need not worry about the dreaded consequences of symptom removal.

And, in a similar vein, in that paper at the Third Evolution of Psychotherapy conference, you (1997b, p. 310) seemed to dismiss totally the therapeutic utility of *insight*:

> Different and often contradictory as the classical schools of therapy are among themselves, they have *one* assumption in common—that problems can be resolved only by the discovery of their causes. This dogma is based on the belief in a linear, unidirectional causality, running from the past to the present, which in turn generates the seemingly obvious need to gain insight into these causes before a change can take place. Permit me to make a somewhat heretical remark: Neither in my own life (in spite of 3 1/2 years of training analysis), nor in my subsequent work as Jungian analyst, nor in the lives of my clients have I ever come across this magical effect of insight.

Have you abandoned the idea of an *unconscious* ? What is your response to those who, as you (1997b, p. 317) have put it, assert that "the results of this treatment (if any) must be short-lived, superficial and cosmetic, because the deep, underlying causes have not been lifted into consciousness through insight. . . . "?

Watzlawick: I have not abandoned the *idea* of the *existence* of the unconscious, but I have totally abandoned the classical conclusion that only insight into the unconscious can bring about a change in the present. Once this conclusion is accepted as a scientific "fact," any approach *not* based on it must either be totally ineffective or—at best—be "short-lived. . . . " etc. (as stated in my second quotation above).

Hoyt: In your response to Dr. James Masterson's discussion of your presentation at the Third Evolution Conference, you commented (1997c, p. 320):

> Let me briefly mention something that I found very useful in my approach to abandon totally; namely, diagnostic terms.

Elsewhere you have argued that "therapy is what you say it is" (Watzlawick, 1990) and that "the construction of clinical 'realities' for the relief of suffering is the proper domain of therapy rather than the reification and imposition of putative and arbitrary concepts of 'normalcy'" (Watzlawick, 1992).

Please elaborate: What types of categories *do* you find useful for organizing your approach to patients?

Watzlawick: One of the basic principles of systems theory is that every system is its *own best* explanation.

I have stopped thinking: "This is a case F 39, therefore I have to do this and this . . . " What matters to me (exclusively) is the patient's specific problem; and what he has done so far to "solve it," i.e., the *attempted solution*, which in our perspective is the main factor that maintains and exacerbates the problem.

Additionally, following one of Milton Erickson's most important rules, I "try to learn and speak the patient's language."

Hoyt: In *Change,* you and your colleagues, following Ashby's cybernetic definition of the two kinds of change, wrote:

> There are, then, two important conclusions to be drawn from the postulates of the Theory of Logical Types: 1)logical levels must be kept strictly apart to prevent paradox and confusion; and 2)going from one level to the next higher (i.e., from member to class) entails a shift, a jump, a discontinuity or transformation—in a word, a change—of the greatest theoretical and. . . . practical importance, for it provides a way *out of* a system. (Watzlawick et al., 1974, pp. 9–10)

Later in the book, noting that it is often the attempted solution that produces (or continues) the problem, you commented:

> A system which may run through all its possible internal changes (no matter how many there are) without effecting a systemic change, i.e., second-order change, is said to be caught in a *Game Without End.* It cannot generate from within itself the conditions for its own change; it cannot produce the rules for the change of its own rules. (p. 22)

You also provided four principles for the use of second-order change:

a. Second-order change is applied to what in the first-order change perspective appears to be a solution, because in the second-order change perspective this "solution" reveals itelf as the keystone of the problem whose solution is attempted.

b. While first-order change always appears to be based on common sense (for instance, the "more of the same" recipe), second-order change usually appears weird, unexpected, and uncommonsensical; there is a puzzling, paradoxical element in the process of change.

c. Applying second-order change techniques to the "solution" means that the situation is dealt with in the here and now. These techniques deal with effects and not with their presumed causes; the crucial question is *what?* and not *why?*

d. The use of second-order change techniques lifts the situation out of the paradox-engendering trap created by the self-reflexiveness of the attempted solution and places it in a different frame. . . . (pp. 82–83)

So, my question: What are some of the modifications that have developed in your thinking about the MRI interactional approach since the basic principles were articulated in *Change* (Watzlawick et al., 1974) and *The Tactics of Change* (Fisch et al., 1982)? How has your understanding of *change* changed?

Watzlawick: It has not *changed* (in the sense of having become different), but I have constantly remained interested in the understanding of change, as it occurs normally and spontaneously in human lives, and its applicability to therapy.

Hoyt: In the discussion after your presentation on "The Construction of Clinical 'Realities'" at the Second Evolution of Psychotherapy Conference, you commented (1992, p. 65):

The system imposes a certain world view, for example, on a child. But the child, being a person in his or her own right, reacts in a certain way. So you cannot just look at pieces of the system. It is wrong to believe that systems theory denies the dignity of the individual and the depth of his or her soul. Rather, mutual influences need to be taken into account: The way one behaves influences the system; the reactions of the system influence that person. That in no way denies one's dignity as an individual, although this accusation frequently is made.

While reminding us of the importance of systemic (circular, non-linear) thinking, this statement would seem to acknowledge an external reality as part of the equation. Is there something outside our consciousness that therapists should be attentive to?

Watzlawick: Yes, everybody's second-order reality, that differs from mine, is an external reality of which I may be totally unaware (to avoid the term "unconscious").

Hoyt: Some theorists have been critical of constructivism and social constructionism on primarily philosophical grounds. Barbara Held (1995), for example, has argued for what she calls a "modest realism," a recognition that there is a *there* there, an external referent by which interventionists gauge their work. She writes (p. 173):

> Here I draw the reader's attention to what I consider to be a point of fundamental importance in understranding the confusion generated by the postmodern emphasis on the linguistic, and the postmodern linking of linguistic entities (including theories/propositions/stories/narratives/discourses) with antirealism. It is this: *All theories are constructions* [boldface in original]. . . . But then to say, as social constructionists/postmodernists say, that those constructed theories are the *only* reality we have—that is, that reality itself, or knowable reality itself, is *only* a "social construction" (because we supposedly have no direct, theoretically unmediated access or even an indirect, theoretically mediated access to any reality that is independent of the knower/knower's theory)—is to confuse two things: (a)the linguistic status of the theory itself with (b)the (extralinguistic or extratheoretic) reality that the theory is attempting to approximate indirectly.

How do you understand and respond to this line of criticism?

Watzlawick: As far as constructivism is concerned, only the *name* is modern. That our views of reality are *subjective* and by no means an objectively "true" view, has been postulated by philosophers (e.g., Vico, Kant, Schopenhauer, Jaspers), by physicists (e.g., Einstein, Heisenberg, Schrodinger) and even mathematicians.

Regarding the last two lines of the above-mentioned quotation by Held: Constructivism does not "confuse two things"—it makes a clear distinction between reality of the *first order* (as conveyed to us by our sensory organs in terms of perceptions), and reality of the *second order* (i.e., the meaning, significance and value that every one of us inevitably attributes to the first-order reality—which remain totally subjective, unprovable, and, therefore, the cause of human conflict and misunderstandings).

Hoyt: Something about the (non)essence of the discussion about the two levels of "reality" seemed to be captured in a theater production of *Robin Hood* I saw the other night. Two characters were wandering in Sherwood Forest:

First Character: Where are we on the map?
Second Character: We're not on the map; we're in the forest!

This would seem equally to apply to the "co-constructivist" position that

Speed (1984a, b) advocated in response to your book *How Real is Real* , as well as your reply (Watzlawick, 1984b) to her that "adequacy" and "usefulness" in a particular situation does not (indeed, *can* not) reveal a nonsubjective *truth* about "reality." Do you agree?

Watzlawick: Yes, this is still my point of view.

Hoyt: Other critics of constructivism (e.g., Pittman, 1992; Minuchin, 1992) have focused on the possibility of pernicious situations being dismissed as simply being "your opinion" or "the way you look at it." In a radical constructivist approach, what safeguards are there?

Watzlawick: I would never hold a client "responsible" for his reality construction. Since I am "speaking his language" (Erickson), my main questions may be, for instance, "How can we change things? or "How can we get out of this unbearable situation?"

Hoyt: How does that jibe with what you wrote in your Epilogue in *The Invented Reality* (1984a, p. 330):

> ("What reality is constructed by constuctivism itself?") is a fundamentally wrong question. But we also see that this mistake had to be committed in order to reveal itself as a mistake. Constructivism does not create or explain any reality "out there"; it shows that there is no inside and no outside, no objective world facing the subjective, rather, it shows that the subject-object split, that source of myriads of "realities," does not exist, that the apparent separation of the world into pairs of opposites is constructed by the subject, and that paradox opens the way into *autonomy*.

Help! I may need a paradox: I realize that I may be slipping into just the kind of dualistic thinking that you were writing about, but how does one reconcile the notion of *responsibility* with the ideas of both *mutual (systemic) influence* and *personal* autonomy?

Watzlawick: Please, let me make it clear that—as I see it—even though we may not hold the client responsible for his reality constructions, he is—of course—responsible for (or a victim of) the practical consequences of these constructions.

Hoyt: I've been puzzling regarding the relationship between *reframing* and what cognitive-behavioral therapists call *cognitive restructuring* or *schema change*. It seems that certain interactional patterns (and narratives) often persist, and that some kind of *working through* process (to use a term psychodynamicists favor) may be required for change to be maintained. What keeps clients from quickly and durably adopting different (and seemingly less painful or dysfunctional) constructions?

Watzlawick: The lessening or disappearance of their suffering.

Hoyt: Are you saying that clients will often only change just enough to reduce their suffering to tolerable (from intolerable) levels? Sometimes a small change seems to get the ball rolling (leading to larger changes), but othertimes, not. Put in a different way, why resistance?

Watzlawick: At least in my experience, people who come into therapy demand, in essence, to have their problems solved, but not at the price of giving up what in their second-order reality is correct, right, necessary, etc. So, in effect, they are demanding "change us, without changing us."

Hoyt: This might be a good time to ask, why the term *brief therapy*? Was there something more intended than the simple temporal distinction with *long-term* approaches?

Watzlawick: No—simply its difference from the long-term classical approaches (which I myself practiced for years . . .).

Hoyt: What do you see as the major pragmatic distinctions (and similarities) between the MRI approach (Watzlawick et al., 1974; Fisch et al., 1982) and de Shazer's (1985, 1988) solution-focused method?

Watzlawick: Without claiming that I have fully understood these distinctions, I believe that my orientation is more interactional and system-oriented. My "patient" is the relationship.

Hoyt: Weakland and Fisch (1992, p. 317; also see Shoham et al., 1995) summarized the difference this way:

> We focus primarily on attempted solutions that do not work and maintain the problem; de Shazer and his followers, in our view, have the inverse emphasis. The two are complementary.

And, in *Propagations: Thirty Years of Influence from the Mental Research Institute* (Weakland & Ray, 1995), de Shazer and Berg (1995, p. 252) affectionately opined:

> (Is this a difference that makes a difference?) Of course, on a different level, deliberately replicating an exception—doing what works instead of what does not work—is a way of doing something different. But that particular something different is already part of the clients' repertoire and therefore promoting clients' cooperation (and task compliance) is greatly enhanced. Simply, a solution is developed by doing more of what is already working.
>
> Thus the flaw we see in the MRI version of Brief Thrapy is that they actually take their philosophy seriously and, therefore, since their model ain't broke they do not try to fix it. Weakland, Watzlawick, and Fisch stubbornly continue to do more of the same since it works. We owe our development to this "flaw" and pushed beyond it; the ultimate tribute disciples can pay to their masters.

Comment?

Watzlawick: I am somewhat confused—surely, if something works, we all are likely to do more of the same. But our clients' attempted solutions rarely work—otherwise they would not ask for help—and in such a case, not only we humans typically do *more of the same.*

Hoyt: In *Change* (Watzlawick et al., 1974, p. xvi) you wrote:

> The problem, therefore, is not how influence and manipulation can be avoided, but how they can best be comprehended and used in the interest of the patient.

You amplified this view in *The Language of Change* (1978, pp. 10–11):

> All that heals can also be abused; just as, conversely, a poison can also cure. But especially today *any* form of influence, in particular anything that can be labeled as manipulation, is attacked and condemned as being unethical. These attacks are not merely directed at the abuses of manipulation—which, needless to say, are always possible—but to manipulation as such. . . . I shall merely summarize here: One cannot *not* influence. It is, therefore, absurd to ask how influence and manipulation can be avoided, and we are left with the inescapable responsibility of deciding for ourselves how this basic law of human communication may be obeyed in the most humane, ethical, and effective manner.

What guidelines can you suggest for strategic therapists to assure ethicality as well as effectiveness (or, do the ends justify the means)?

Watzlawick: Whenever I am being accused of "manipulation," I ask: "Can you describe to me *one* act of help that is not being manipulative? In saving a drowning man, you 'manipulate' him," etc. etc. Of course, everything that helps can also be abused—commercials and propaganda being prime examples. But what is new about that?

Hoyt: I concur that influence is inevitable and that our job is to use it for the client's good. In the passage I quoted from *The Language of Change*, you mention having "the inescapable responsibility of *deciding for ourselves*" (emphasis added). When do we involve clients in this decision making? Many people use the term *manipulation* and object when they feel the client's wishes are not paramount; this may be especially important within the sometimes subtle, deliberately meaning-changing realm of constructive therapies. I think this is some of the concern behind recent discussions about the importance of "respecting client autonomy," "therapist transparency," and "ethical postures" (Freedman & Combs, 1996; Tomm, 1991; White, 1995). From your frame, how do think about *informed consent*?

Watzlawick: My "informed consent" is the question: "The next time you find yourself in the problem situation, would you be willing to carry out an experiment, namely to . . . ?

Hoyt: In an interview with John Weakland and Steve de Shazer that was published in *Constructive Therapies* (Hoyt, 1994—see Chapter 1, this volume, p. 27), John was talking about European developments and re- marked: "Usually, all I hear is what I hear from Paul [Watzlawick], and mainly what Paul will say is, 'A great deal is going on that you should know about.'. . . . Then he says, 'But you don't read German.'" Pray tell?

Watzlawick: Our Institute is far better known overseas than in the U.S. There exist about 70 foreign language editions of my books, but what I consider more important is the fact that many approaches, similar but not necessarily identical to our's, are developed, taught and applied, and by no means only in German-speaking countries.

John's remark about my alleged remark regarding "not reading Ger- man" must have been one of his little jokes.

Hoyt: Why do you think reception has been better overseas? I've won- dered if it has to do with the proximity of so many languages and cul- tures, which quickly brings home the idea that "reality" is constructed, not given or revealed. What might help further promote the systemic/ interactional perspective in the U.S.?

Watzlawick: As you say, more exposure to other languages and cul- tures.

Hoyt: What do you think (or hope) will be your enduring contribution to the psychotherapy field?

Watzlawick: I do not believe in any "enduring contribution" to any field of science. For me, the task of scientific research is the development of methods and techniques that are useful for a specific purpose, but will certainly be replaced by more effective approaches within a few years.

Hoyt: Thank you.

☐ References

Alexander, F., & French, T. M. (1946). *Psychoanalytic Therapy: Principles and Applications.* New York: Ronald Press.

de Shazer, S. (1985). *Keys to Solution in Brief Therapy.* New York: Norton.

de Shazer, S. (1988). *Clues: Investigating Solutions in Brief Therapy.* New York: Norton.

de Shazer, S., & Berg, I. K. (1995). The Brief Therapy tradition. In J. H. Weakland & W. A. Ray (Eds.), *Propagations: Thirty Years of Influence from the Mental Research Institute* (pp. 249–252). New York: Haworth Press.

Efron, D. (1995). Conference review. *Journal of Systemic Therapies, 14*(3), 1–3.

Erickson, M. (1974) Foreword. In P. Watzlawick, J. Weakland, & R. Fisch, *Change: Principles of Problem Formation and Problem Resolution* (pp. ix–x). New York: Norton.

Fisch, R., Weakland, J. H., & Segal, L. (1982). *The Tactics of Change: Doing Therapy Briefly.* New York: Norton.

Freedman, J., & Combs, G. (1996). *Narrative Therapy: The Social Construction of Preferred Realities.* New York: Norton.

Haley, J. (Ed.) (1985). *Conversations with Milton H. Erickson, M.D., Volumes 1–3.* New York: Triangle Press/Norton.

Held, B. S. (1995). *Back to Reality: A Critique of Postmodern Theory in Psychotherapy.* New York: Norton.

Horgan, J. (1995). *The End of Science: Facing the Limits of Knowledge in the Twilight of the Scientific Age.* New York: Broadway Books.

Hoyt, M. F. (1994). On the importance of keeping it simple and taking the patient seriously: A conversation with Steve de Shazer and John Weakland. In M. F. Hoyt (Ed.), *Constructive Therapies* (pp. 11–40). New York: Guilford Press.

Hoyt, M. F. (1997). Unmuddying the waters: A "common ground" conference. *Journal of Systemic Therapies, 16*(3), 195–200. Reprinted in M. F. Hoyt, *Some Stories are Better than Others: Doing What Works in Brief Therapy and Managed Care.* Philadelphia: Brunner/Mazel, 2000.

Minuchin, S. (1992). The restoried history of family therapy. In J. K. Zeig (Ed.), *The Evolution of Psychotherapy: The Second Conference* (pp. 3–12). New York: Brunner/Mazel.

Pittman, F. (1992). It's not my fault. *Family Therapy Networker, 16*(1), 56–63.

Segal, L. (1986). *The Dream of Reality: Heinz von Foerster's Constructivism.* New York: Norton.

Shoham, V., Rohrbaugh, M., & Patterson, J. (1995). Problem- and solution-focused couple therapies: The MRI and Milwaukee models. In N. S. Jacobson & A. S. Gurman (Eds.), *Clinical Handbook of Couple Therapy* (pp. 142–163). New York: Guilford Press.

Speed, B. (1984a). How really real is real? *Family Process, 23,* 511–517.

Speed, B. (1984b). Rejoinder: Mountainous seas are also wet. *Family Process, 23,* 518–520.

Szasz, T. (1961). *The Myth of Mental Illness.* New York: Hoeber, Harper. (Revised edition published by Harper & Row, 1974.)

Tomm, K. (1991). The ethics of dual relationships. *The Calgary Participator,* 1(Winter), 11–15.

Vaihinger, H. (1924). *The Philosophy of 'As If.'* (C. K. Ogden, Trans.) New York: Harcourt Brace.

von Foerster. H. (1981). *Observing Systems.* Seaside, CA: Intersystems Publications.

von Foerster, H. (1984). On constructing a reality. In P. Watzlawick (Ed.), *The Invented Reality* (pp. 41–62). New York: Norton.

Watzlawick, P. (1976). *How Real is Real? Communication, Disinformation, Confusion.* New York: Vintage.

Watzlawick, P. (1978). *The Language of Change: Elements of Therapeutic Communication.* New York: Norton.

Watzlawick, P. (1982). Erickson's contribution to the interactional view of psychotherapy. In J. K. Zeig (Ed.), *Ericksonian Approaches to Hypnosis and Psychotherapy* (pp.147–154). New York: Brunner/Mazel.

Watzlawick, P. (1983). *The Situation is Hopeless but Not Serious.* New York: Norton.

Watzlawick, P. (Ed.) (1984a). *The Invented Reality: How Do We Know What We Believe We Know? (Contributions to Constructivism)* New York: Norton.

Watzlawick, P. (1984b). Commentary: But what about mountainous seas? *Family Process, 23,* 517–518.

Watzlawick, P. (1988). *Ultra-Solutions: How to Fail Most Successfully.* New York: Norton.

Watzlawick, P. (1990). Therapy is what you say it is. In J. K. Zeig & S. G. Gilligan (Eds.), *Brief Therapy: Myths, Methods, and Metaphors* (pp. 55–61). New York: Brunner/Mazel.

Watzlawick, P. (1992). The construction of clinical 'realities.' In J. K. Zeig (Ed.), *The Evolution of Psychotherapy: The Second Conference* (pp. 55–65). New York: Brunner/Mazel.

Watzlawick, P. (1997a). Discussion. In J. K. Zeig (Ed.), *The Evolution of Psychotherapy: The Third Conference* (pp. 306–308). New York: Brunner/Mazel.

Watzlawick, P. (1997b). "Insight" may cause blindness. In J. K. Zeig (Ed.), *The Evolution of Psychotherapy: The Third Conference* (pp.309–317). New York: Brunner/Mazel.

Watzlawick, P. (1997c). Response. In J. K. Zeig (Ed.), *The Evolution of Psychotherapy: The Third Conference* (pp. 320–321). New York: Brunner/Mazel.

Watzlawick, P., Beavin, J. B., & Jackson, D. D. (1967). *Pragmatics of Human Communication: A Study of Interactional Patterns, Pathologies, and Paradoxes.* New York: Norton.

Watzlawick, P., & Weakland, J. (Eds.) (1977). *The Interactional View: Studies at the Mental Research Institute, Palo Alto, 1965–74.* New York: Norton.

Watzlawick, P., Weakland, J. H., & Fisch, R. (1974). *Change: Principles of Problem Formation and Problem Resolution.* New York: Norton.

Weakland, J. H., & Fisch, R. (1992). Brief therapy—MRI style. In S. H. Budman, M. F. Hoyt & S. Friedman (Eds.), *The First Session in Brief Therapy* (pp. 306–323). New York: Guilford Press.

Weakland, J. H., & Ray, W. A. (Eds.) (1995). *Propagations: Thirty Years of Influence from the Mental Research Institute.* New York: Haworth Press.

White, M. (1995). *Re-Authoring Lives: Interviews and Essays.* Adelaide, Australia: Dulwich Centre Publications.

CHAPTER

7

Solution Building and Language Games: A Conversation with Steve de Shazer (and Some After Words With Insoo Kim Berg)

How language is used to construct useful realities, and how this can be facilitated purposefully in therapy, are central concerns in the work of Steve de Shazer. A longtime leader in the field of brief therapy, as noted in Chapter 1, de Shazer is Senior Research Associate at the Brief Family Therapy Center (BFTC) in Milwaukee, Wisconsin. His books have included *Patterns of Brief Family Therapy* (1982), *Keys to Solution in Brief Therapy* (1985), *Clues: Investigating Solutions in Brief Therapy* (1988), and *Putting Difference to Work* (1991). His quest for simplicity and minimalist elegance has increasingly led him to focus on the ideas of linguistic theorists (especially Ludwig Wittgenstein). The title of de Shazer's (1994) book, *Words Were Originally Magic*, borrows a phrase from Sigmund Freud to attest to his views regarding the power of language.

The following conversation took place on April 10, 1994, in de Shazer's BFTC office in Milwaukee.

Hoyt: The first thing I want to ask, Steve, is how has what you mean by

Originally appeared, with changes, from M. F. Hoyt (Ed.) (1996), *Constructive Therapies, Volume 2* (pp. 60–85). New York: Guilford Press. Used with permission.

brief therapy changed over the years? What are some of the things that you've given up or you've added, and why?

de Shazer: Well, I guess that when it first started, there was really no definition whatsoever, except "brief." I don't think "brief" was ever defined in any way at all. Then, doing what I was calling "brief therapy," I ran into John Weakland and his gang at MRI [the Mental Research Institute in Palo Alto, California] with their 10-session limit. I knew 10 was an arbitrary number. I also knew it didn't fit with my experience. So we started a research project: we tossed a coin and decided whether to have a 12-session or 6-session limit. And we found out that in the 12-session limit, they waited until session 10 to do anything.

Hoyt: Parkinson's law.[1]

de Shazer: With a 6-session limit, they only waited until session 5. And the outcomes were no different. So we added a third condition—which was we wouldn't say anything about a time limit. It turned out that the average number of sessions with no time limit was less than with either 6 or 12, and the outcomes were slightly better.[2] So I abandoned having a numbered session limit in 1973 or 1974 or something like that. That was the first change. For some years it's been that brief therapy means, among other things, "as few sessions as possible and not one more than necessary." Who knows how many that may actually be, over how many years? The average number of sessions dropped to about four about 10 years ago. It's been relatively stable at around four.[3] Of course, it switched from problem solving to solution building in the early '80s. That switch is in the books.[4] "You can look it up," as Casey Stengel used to say.

Hoyt: In reading the early books and following the progression, it seems there's been a shift away from strategy and power.

de Shazer: Certainly away from strategy. You don't need strategies, or you don't need "strategic maneuvers" *a la* Haley or Haley's interpretation of Erickson, or even the earlier MRI stuff. I found out that when we switched from problem solving to solution development, you just don't need to do that sort of thing. You don't need these fancy interventions.

---

[1]Applebaum (1975; also see Hoyt, 1990) has noted what he calls "Parkinson's Law in Psychotherapy," the idea that therapeutic work expands or contracts to fit the time allotted for it.

[2]This project was never written up or published. Similar results have been reported by Fisher (1980, 1984).

[3][de Shazer adds:] Actually, for the past two years [1992–1994] the average has dropped to three!

[4]In addition to those authored by de Shazer himself, other books especially aligned with the solution-focused model include those by Dolan (1991), Walter and Peller (1992), Berg and Miller (1992), and Berg (1994).

You don't need all this elaborate stuff. It's no more effective than the simple things we are doing, maybe even less effective. Certainly they are far more work than what we're doing now. We were pretty good at it in the '70s; the early books and papers illustrate that we became pretty damn good at that style of intervention. We still have to resist doing it now and then, because we know it's no better than finding something the client already is doing that they can do more of.

Hoyt: It's the temptation you write about as "Erickson-the-clever."[5]

de Shazer: Yeah, absolutely. We set out to emulate that. I don't mind being thought clever, it's just hard as hell to teach it.

Hoyt: Where does hypnotic induction fit in now in your work?

de Shazer: As far as anything formal, it doesn't fit at all.

Hoyt: Why have you moved away from it?

de Shazer: Solution-focused brief therapy is easier on the therapist; it's less work for the therapist; it actually takes fewer sessions; and it has at least as good results. The problem with hypnosis, no matter how "naturalistic," etc., etc., it might be, how unobtrusive it might be, the client thinks it's "hypnosis." My conversations with clients later on indicate that they blame the hypnosis (and/or the therapist) for the "success" or "failure," no matter how little hypnosis you actually do. It's the magic of hypnosis.

Hoyt: So it's disempowering.

de Shazer: Yeah.

Hoyt: "I didn't do it; I don't have any control."

de Shazer: Right. That's another reason I moved away from it, aside from the fact that this works better.

Hoyt: You said it's easier on the therapist as well as getting better results. I see it as also resulting in less burnout. We're not fighting the client; we're not having to work through a hard "resistance."

---

[5]In *Words Were Originally Magic* (1994), de Shazer describes different ways of relating to clients. He contrasts Erickson's "expert" stance with other, less hierarchical and more egalitarian positions, including "de Shazer-the-stupid." He goes on to add: "Actually, I should have seen all of this long ago, since the two major influences on my interviewing style have been John Weakland's persona 'Weakland-the-dense' and Insoo Kim Berg's persona 'Insoo-the-incredulous'" (p. 34). Later (p. 266), he adds: "Having spent most of the '70s and part of the '80s designing 'novel tasks in the Erickson style,' I still find it difficult at times to restrain myself from proposing such interventions to clients. However, these fancy tasks are very difficult to design; furthermore, teaching therapists to design such clever tasks is not an easy job. In the great majority of cases these clever tasks seem to be no more, perhaps even less, effective than simpler ones based principally on what the clients have already said they know how to do."

de Shazer: Yeah, we don't have to be clever. It takes a lot of work for most people to be clever.

Hoyt: What about reframing techniques that we've all used? Is that something else that you've given up or don't see as useful?

de Shazer: I certainly won't go through and do any kind of reframing like we used to do, where we would invent a new frame *a la* MRI or our early work. I think that the compliments and the way we do the interview—our "procedural interventions," as Dick Fisch calls them—will lead the clients to spontaneously reframe things for themselves. The only reframe that counts is if the client buys it. So the best ones are the ones they come up with.

Hoyt: I might express it as you're punctuating and they're changing the meaning.

de Shazer: Yeah, okay.

Hoyt: Underscoring certain experiences for them or getting them focused on certain experiences.

de Shazer: Yeah.

Hoyt: What about the use of paradox?

de Shazer: That went away a long time ago. By that I assume you were asking about paradoxical interventions?

Hoyt: Right. Can you recall an episode that told you, "Enough of this"?

de Shazer: Well, I remember we used to do paradoxical interventions or attempt to do them [see de Shazer & Nunnally, 1991]. But most of what I see people doing that they call "paradoxical interventions" are not. Most of them are reverse psychology; they are not paradoxical interventions.

Hoyt: What's the distinction?

de Shazer: Well, a paradoxical intervention has to be exactly counter to what it is you're going after. The reverse double-bind kind of thing. There has to be no escape. Most of the "paradoxical interventions" don't have that feature.

Hoyt: Where reverse psychology is just, "Keep doing it."

de Shazer: Yeah. So most of what people call "paradoxical interventions" are not paradoxical interventions. We used to do some, and we came to the conclusion that paradoxical interventions were unnecessary for several reasons, the main one being that we aren't trying to stop anything. Paradoxical interventions are designed to stop something, and we aren't trying to stop anything. What we are doing is trying to start something or increase the frequency of something. So there's no need for paradoxical interventions. If you do it right, they work if you want to stop something. Doing it right actually involves following the rules, and I think

Watzlawick, Beavin, and Jackson [1967] put down the rules quite nicely in *The Pragmatics of Human Communication*. That was the most evolved version of it, I think. I don't think there's been any refinements of it after that.

Hoyt: When you're trying to start something rather than stop something, will we still encounter what is sometimes called "resistance"? The client doesn't want to start?

de Shazer: Well, if I were to use the word *resistance*—I wouldn't, but if I were—it would translate in my vocabulary as *therapist's error*. That would mean to me that the therapist wasn't listening, and therefore he told the client to do something the client didn't want to do. That means he wasn't listening during the interview. Most of our stuff is based on the fact of something they told us about, that they did such and such and it worked in some situation, so it's just a matter of transferring that from situation A to situation B. So there's nothing new. Most of our interventions are nothing new for them.

Hoyt: It's, as the title of that Zen book has it, *Selling Water by the River* [Kennett, 1972].

de Shazer: Yes. Or selling water *to* the river.

Hoyt: It's selling them themselves, in a sense. Something that's felt good before, so why resist it?

de Shazer: So we don't have that kind of difficulty ("resistance") very often, but if we do we know why. It means we weren't listening. We may have gotten ourselves into an Erickson mode.

Hoyt: Where we were trying to maneuver them into something they weren't ready for or wanting.

de Shazer: Right.

Hoyt: Can you give an example that brought home to you "the death of resistance" [de Shazer, 1984], where it could have been done one way but you did it another way and then you had to deal with resistance—you created resistance?

de Shazer: I haven't thought about "resistance" in so many years, it's hard. I don't think I can come up with anything.

Hoyt: It's not a very solution-focused question.

de Shazer: I don't have any idea how to answer that question. I can't remember.

Hoyt: I think another advantage, then, to a solution-focused approach is that it doesn't stimulate noncompliance because there's nothing they have to noncomply with. It makes it more user-friendly for both the therapist and for the client. It's less likely to drive clients away.

de Shazer: Less likely. What I see sometimes is the amateurs, so to speak—the beginners, who somehow think more is better and, therefore, they give this endless stream of compliments and bore the client silly with them and, therefore, the client stops taking them seriously. That's one thing I see happen with beginners, in particular: There's just too damn many compliments, and that will drive the client away.

Hoyt: I think there's an ethical position that it's very respectful. I know we talked with John Weakland in that other interview [see Chapter 1] about the importance of taking the client seriously. The person feels heard, validated, appreciated for who they are. How do we separate the idea of "influence" from "brainwashing," to call it that? We're influencing but not imposing our values, manipulating them?

de Shazer: There's that line, all right. Clients hire us to influence them; that's why they come. The more you are using their stuff, the less danger you are in of moving into brainwashing. The more you are putting in your stuff, the closer you're getting to brainwashing. That's pretty clear to me. Those are the two ends of it, perhaps. I'm not sure if it is a continuum, but there certainly is a line in between. And, frankly, I see many, many of the psychotherapy models as being closer to brainwashing than to anything else.

Hoyt: I think the respectful ethic is that it's truly informed consent. We're identifying what their goals are and helping them meet their goals, rather than imposing our agenda.

de Shazer: Right. You know, we have a saying around here—there used to be a sign made by somebody on the team (probably Gale Miller): "If the therapist's goals and the client's goals are different, the therapist is wrong."

Hoyt: I don't know if you've seen it yet, but in the latest issue of the *Family Therapy Networker*, Eve Lipchik [1994] has an article called "The Rush to Be Brief." She makes the point that sometimes therapists trying to be brief go forward before they have validated and before they've heard or acknowledged the client.[6] They are not being respectful in that sense. It's much like giving too many compliments, leaping ahead.

---

[6]There are many ways to achieve alliance and connectedness. In *Words Were Originally Magic*, a man starts to "present" himself as a clinical "case," and de Shazer (1994, p. 241) nicely interrupts him by saying, "No, no, not about that. . . . Tell me something about you, who you are . . . what you enjoy doing." For more on the importance of acknowledgment and validation in strategic and solution-focused therapy, see the discussions by de Shazer and Weakland in Chapter 1 and O'Hanlon in Chapter 2, as well as articles by Aponte (1992), Duncan (1992), Held (1992), Kiser, Piercy, and Lipchik (1993), Nylund and Corsiglia (1994), Real (1990), and Solovey and Duncan (1992).

de Shazer: John Weakland's first law of brief therapy still applies. He promulgated it for many years and I have continued to. It's a two-word law: "Go Slow."

Hoyt: What's another of John's laws?

de Shazer: The first one is very clear: "Go slow." The second one is "If you don't know what to do, the best thing to do is nothing." You'll notice if you watch either his interviews or mine that the therapist is doing relatively nothing much of the time, including just sitting there and not saying anything. Weakland and I have talked about this many times—what I call "actively doing nothing." Weakland was trained, at least in part, as an anthropologist, then married a Chinese family. I don't know if he knew he was marrying the whole family, but that's what happens when you marry an Asian woman. You marry the whole family. Then you get a position in the family. I did the same thing, married a Korean woman [Insoo Kim Berg]. So you marry this whole family and you get a position in the family that is uniquely yours, particularly because you're not Asian. But nonetheless, you have a position in the family that is absolutely unique. Nobody can tell you what the rules are, because you're supposed to know these things. You're supposed to know them. Your position in that family starts from the moment you're born, and you're still there in that same position relative to the rest of the hierarchy. But coming in there as an adult, you're assumed to know all these rules. Therefore, the likelihood is very high that whatever you decide to do in any given situation is going to turn out wrong—this likelihood is very, very high, and you're going to pay for it for years. So, as I learned from John Weakland, the best thing to do in that situation is nothing. If you do it often enough and long enough, eventually you acquire the label of "wise"!

Hoyt: *[laughter]* In talking about treating people respectfully, I just recently finished reading Insoo's *Family-Based Services* [Berg, 1994]. If there's the book *Pragmatics of Human Communication* [Watzlawick et al., 1967], I think this book could be subtitled *Pragmatics of Therapeutic Communication*. I thought it was an extraordinarily fine book. I was struck over and over how in these very multiproblem, painful family situations, Insoo was able repeatedly to form alliances with the people and work *with* them, where many of us just would have attempted to protect the children from the parents, thinking, "These are bad people; there's something that they've done wrong." We would be in a judgmental frame. How do you work with such folks? What helps you form alliances in difficult situations?

de Shazer: Well, I guess that there's two parts to that. Since you framed it around Insoo, I'll start there. She was raised in a different culture, and I've been studying that culture for 20 years or whatever it is now. There are big differences between Asian and American families. Both of them in general produce reasonable, functional adults. The difference between the two can be sketched this way. In the United States, if a kid does something wrong, he is likely to be grounded. That is, he is imprisoned within the family. Therefore, being with the family is negative—it's a punishment. In Asia, this same kid for the same offense is likely to be expelled from the family in some way. So being with the family is a positive. And we wonder why our families are disintegrating. Why kids can't wait to get away. The Koreans wonder how they will ever get rid of their kids. It does seem to be exactly the opposite. They both work in the long run; they produce reasonable adults. That was the first clue that led us (as a group, 20 years ago) away from something like Minuchin's [1974] structural family therapy that postulates some kind of ideal family. There ain't no such critter, so we moved away from that very quickly; it made no sense to us. I was doing brief therapy before I heard about family therapy. When I heard about family therapy, one of the ones I looked at was Minuchin's because I knew from its reputation that it actually worked, but I couldn't hold to its value system.

Hoyt: I understand what you're saying about the difference between the Asian and the American family, but how does that connect to alliance?

de Shazer: It allows us to accept whatever people are doing as having the potential of working. Let's go back into sociology, and there one talks about personality as being situationally determined or constructed, as opposed to psychology, where it's intrapsychically determined. Sociology more likely talks about it being situationally determined. Therefore, "If I was in this client's shoes, saw things the way this client does, I would be doing the same thing he's doing." That's the central constructivist principle. We can accept it and, therefore, we can develop an alliance with it.

Hoyt: It's recognizing the difference in "state" versus "trait."

de Shazer: Yeah, sort of.

Hoyt: They are in a state where this is appropriate behavior.

de Shazer: They're doing what they think is the best thing to do, given their situation. We would probably do the same if we were in their shoes.

Hoyt: It's recognizing people as problem solvers rather than as evil— that they are trying to cope as best they can with what they've been taught and their resources and the options that they see available.

de Shazer: So, therefore, we can develop an alliance with anybody who wants to develop an alliance with us. And do it very quickly, because this is something we take for granted. We just act as if we have an alliance right from the moment one.

Hoyt: What indicates, then, a difficult case?

de Shazer: That's not in our vocabulary.

Hoyt: If there hasn't been some change by a certain number of sessions, are there strategies?

de Shazer: Usually the people who ask that question have something in mind—something that they think is a difficult case, like a flasher or something. What makes it a difficult case in that instance is that you're thinking it's a difficult case. We did this project a couple of years ago because people often asked this question. We sat down and tried to operationalize the concept "difficult case" in order to have an answer for this question. Since our average is around four sessions, we decided that a difficult case must be one in which they are not reporting a significant change at the third session. That seemed a reasonable point. So we decided that that would be a "difficult case" for the sake of this project. We decided that we would then scrupulously work with the team with the next 50 intakes, we'd videotape, make predictions, etc., etc. In the first session, what is it that gave us the idea this would or would not be a difficult case? At the end of this, we had our 50 cases, 50 intakes in a row, and we looked at them all. There wasn't a single case that didn't report significant change by the third session. Well, what the fuck, now what? We decided that we'd look at all the second sessions and see if there was something there. We found, I think there were four cases, all of them had turned around in session 3. What we found out was that these were the four cases where we did something different from the standard protocol during or at the end of the second session. Therefore, we went right back to rule 3: "If what you're doing isn't working, do something else."[7] One thing that happened is with one case the therapist reassembled the client group after the break in a different room than he'd done the therapy in. The intervention message was exactly the same kind of thing we usually do, no different. Case number 2, I saw just the mother and left the kids out of the room. Case number 3, the person who was doing the interview stood up delivering the intervention message rather than sitting down. And case number 4, someone else from the team went in and delivered the message.

Hoyt: "If it's not working, do something different."

---

[7]The basic rules of solution-focused therapy: (1)If it ain't broke, don't fix it. (2)Once you know what works, do more of it. (3)If it doesn't work, don't do it again; do something different. Following from these rules, some heuristic questions: *First session*—What do(es) the client(s) want? What can the client(s) do (toward what is wanted)? What needs to happen? *Later (second and subsequent) sessions*—What is better? What did the client(s) do (toward better)? What happened (to make it better)? What compliments and tasks can be given (staying within the client's expertise)? Is it "better" enough—when should therapy stop?

de Shazer: No matter how trivial—standing up, somebody else going in, sitting in a different chair. So if you're stuck, the first thing you want to do is ask, "What part of this do I have control over?" You have control over where you meet, when you meet, where you sit, where they sit. You have some control over whether you're standing or sitting, a different office. Just anything that you have control over, you can do something, and therefore you stand a chance of having an impact.

Hoyt: Change the context, break the set, punctuate it differently. More of the same does not make a change.

de Shazer: It's very simple, sometimes.

Hoyt: If we're required to do an evaluation, it's good then to move to another room or change seats, to give the sense of "Now we're going to do something different" rather than "It's going to be more pathology talk."

de Shazer: Right. Absolutely. That's what people always ask, "How do we do solution-focused when we gotta do all these God-damned forms for managed care or the hospital or whatever?" Well, the simplest thing is, you can change rooms like that. If you're a medical doctor in the hospital, wear your white coat for the diagnostic part; take it off when you start doing therapy. Or switch. If you have a partner you trust, have them do the first part and you do the second, and for their cases you reverse.

Hoyt: That's a switch from being a mental illness professional to a mental health professional.[8]

de Shazer: It's easy, by just taking off the white coat.

Hoyt: When would you bring in more people? If we're stuck, should we bring in other family members?

de Shazer: Almost never.

Hoyt: Would you bring in less family?

de Shazer: I would be more tempted to bring in less.

Hoyt: You said you saw her [the mother in case 2] without the kids.

de Shazer: Much more likely to go that direction.

Hoyt: Simplify rather than bringing in more complexity?

de Shazer: As I see it, the idea of bringing more people in is based on the idea that you're stuck because you don't have enough information. That's the premise behind it. My idea, following Wittgenstein, is "The problem is you have too *much* information already, but you just don't know how to organize it." Or, furthermore, from Wittgenstein again, "You're in this situation and you've got what you got and that's all there is. There ain't

---

[8]An allusion to de Shazer and Weakland's comments in Chapter 1.

no more."[9] All you got is a problem of organization. So get people out and talk to just one person at a time, and maybe you can simplify it enough to do something. I haven't invited—I can't remember when last I said, "Bring your husband," or something like that. [See de Shazer & Berg, 1985] I can't remember that happening.

Hoyt: What about the situation of the so-called "multiproblem family" when they are presenting a number of issues at once, competing informations? How do you organize that? Ask them what their first goal is?

de Shazer: Oh, God, no. Then you just have another argument. First of all, I think it is perfectly normal and reasonable for any family to have everybody disagreeing about what the rules are; I think that's perfectly reasonable. So I don't consider that a problem. We think about them as "multi*goal* families." So I guess basically what we do is something like his in that kind of situation. First of all, if you ask the miracle question[10] early enough in the session, you oftentimes avoid that difficulty—having all these multiple goals. Sometimes.

Hoyt: Who do you ask the miracle question of?

de Shazer: Everybody.

Hoyt: And if everyone gives a different answer?

de Shazer: That's reasonable.

Hoyt: Then you have competing goals.

de Shazer: That's normal and reasonable. Then you say, "Okay, 10 stands for this package—everything you've been talking about, those kinds of things. Whatever it will take for you guys to each individually and collectively to recognize that a miracle has happened, that's 10. Where are we today?" We get different estimates where each of them are. Then we sort of work on getting everybody's number on the scale and ignore, if you will, the fact that their version of 10 is probably different, because it's always going to be different with more than one person. And even with one person, he's going to have more than one goal, and they may conflict with each other anyway. So, what we do then—and again, remembering Wittgenstein, we say something like, "Well, you have a wish and you make that wish. Then at some point you're satisfied. There's no guarantee that your wish has been met, and there's no guarantee that if your wish had been met you'd be satisfied." As they move up the scale, we

---

[9]"Our mistake is to look for an explanation where we ought to look at what happens" (Wittgenstein, 1968, #654).

[10]"The Miracle Question: 'Suppose that one night, while you were asleep, there was a miracle and this problem was solved. How would you know? What would be different?'" (de Shazer, 1988, p. 5).

keep saying, "Is this good enough? Can we stop now?" Our studies indicate that most people—most families stop with 7 being good enough, and that 6 months later they will have frequently moved up to 8, but that is almost the outer limit. Very few people make 10. Those that do make 10 usually end up going into the teens as well—"overachievers."

Hoyt: Again, the therapist has to be careful that she or he doesn't impose their perfectionism with the idea, "They're only at 8. We've got to keep working."

de Shazer: Oh, yeah. I remember one case fairly recently where I asked the scaling question [Berg & de Shazer, 1993], and she said she was at 2. I just sat there and didn't respond; I didn't do anything. I can imagine the people behind the mirror saying, "Oh, Christ, she's only at 2." I was just sitting there. But I was just waiting for her to expand some on what "2" might mean, without having to ask her. Then after a short pause, she said, "You know, that's pretty damn good for me." I shook her hand. She thought it would be a God-damned miracle for her to ever reach 3 or 4. So, her 2 was halfway to her goal—she knew she would never get past 4. If she maintained that 4, she would be satisfied.

Hoyt: I think we get into a therapeutic Xeno's fallacy, having to get halfway there, and then half of that, then half of that, etc., so that you can never get there.

de Shazer: Yes. You can never get there.

Hoyt: "I'm good enough, I made it, this works for me. I'm satisfied."

de Shazer: That's usually around 7.

Hoyt: Some patients come in and say they have a personality problem: "There's something wrong with me." And some therapists talk about "Axis II" [American Psychiatric Association, 1994] or a "personality disorder" diagnosis. How do you react to that?

de Shazer: In what sense?

Hoyt: I've been at workshops presenting, and somebody says, "Well, what about brief therapy with Axis II? How does brief therapy address the underlying personality problem?"

de Shazer: It doesn't. I'll frequently say something like, "I have no idea what you're talking about. Give me a case example so I can understand what you're talking about."

Hoyt: Deconstruct the diagnosis into what it really is.

de Shazer: I have no idea what "Axis II" might mean, and I don't want to know.

Hoyt: I remember one time hearing [Jay] Haley say to someone at a conference, "I wouldn't let that be the problem."

de Shazer: Yeah. Absolutely.

Hoyt: Find a problem that can be solved rather than a hypothetical construct.

de Shazer: Years and years ago, I saw a lot of research about the unreliability of diagnostic categories.

Hoyt: Especially when they're highly hypothetical and based on somebody's theory.

de Shazer: So the answer is, "Tell me about a case and I'll tell you how I might work with that case."

Hoyt: Let me read you a quotation from *Words Were Originally Magic* [de Shazer, 1994, p. 267]:

> The miracle question was not designed to create or prompt miracles. All the miracle question is designed to do is to allow clients to describe what it is they want out of therapy without having to concern themselves with the problem and the traditional assumption that the solution is somehow connected with understanding and eliminating the problem.

How do you see the role of causation and determination?

de Shazer: Absolute idiocy. I think the concept of causation, given the kinds of things that we deal with, is absolute nonsense.

Hoyt: What if the client wants or feels they need an explanation: "I need to figure out where this came from, why I do this"?

de Shazer: Well, actually, that's more of a hypothetical than a real client. That's the kind of thing a therapist would suspect clients are going to say. I think that's happened to me twice in my career. And both times I said, "Will it be all right if we solve the problem and then come back to that, if you are still interested?" And they both agreed. That doesn't really happen, and I'm talking, oh, how many cases? Ten thousand cases plus. I think it's happened twice that I can recall.

Hoyt: Some patients I've encountered have been convinced by popular media or something that "I have to get to the root of it," or "Until I really understand where it came from, I'm not really going to solve it; it's just putting a Band-Aid on it." It's almost like an agricultural metaphor: "I want to dig it up by the root and pull it out completely."

de Shazer: Well, as I said, that doesn't seem to happen to me. I can't explain why it doesn't happen. But I suspect that part of the reason it doesn't happen is that I never ask them what the problem is. I say, "What brings you here?" and then I go into the miracle question and start dealing with where we're going. Sometimes I realize at the end of the therapy I never did find out what the problem was.

Hoyt: I sense that when most clients come in, they want to be happy; they want relief from pain. And if we can focus on that, they may have had the theory "I need to dig it out," but once the pain goes away it's irrelevant to kind of dig around in archeology.

de Shazer: Right, and I think that people become very interested in where they're going in the future. If you can do that, you avoid all this stuff about causation, etc. But there's no way we can get at what might have caused something. There's no way we can get at that. Even the ideas of linear or circular causation—neither of them apply within this domain.

Hoyt: How did Freud and Wittgenstein go in different directions? What was the question for which they got such different answers?

de Shazer: They were both trying to figure out what the hell was going on at a particularly difficult time during history—turn-of-the-century Vienna, where you had this regal empire that was going around spending a lot of money on masked balls and all the great things that the Viennese monarchy did, with a country that was disintegrating and a country with no common language.[11] The Austrian-Hungarian empire had many, many languages, so there was a question about what in the world is language. That's why the Austrians are the ones who developed philosophies of language. You had to look behind and beneath whatever the monarchy was doing to find out what the hell was going on. So I think it's just two alternatives to the same difficulty. One being less obvious than the other, I suppose.

Hoyt: The two alternatives?

de Shazer: One being Freud's idea that "Whatever is going on is a mask for what's really going on." And Wittgenstein's idea that "It's just a matter of we can't decipher it," which is different.[12]

Hoyt: "Shadows on the wall that mean something else," as opposed to "All you have is what you have," not looking for a meaning beyond it.

de Shazer: "It's all there, it's just that you can't put the pieces together"— that's Wittgenstein. You have this puzzle on the table that's upside down; you have the gray side. You may suspect at times that you don't have all the pieces. Freud would assume immediately that you don't have all the pieces, that there must be a reason why it's on its face, gray side up rather than picture side up.

---

[11]Primary sources for Wittgenstein's thought include *The Blue and Brown Books* (1958), *Philosophical Invesitgations* (1969), and *Culture and Value* (1980). To learn more about his life and times, interested readers may want to consult Bartley (1985), Duffy (1988), Janik and Towlmin (1974), and Monk (1990), among others.

[12]"There must not be anything hypothetical in our considerations. We must do away with all explanations and description alone must take its place" (Wittgenstein, 1968, #109).

Hoyt: In a practical sense there may be enough there to solve it, rather than saying, "What else? What's missing?"

de Shazer: There are people who can solve jigsaw puzzles gray side up.

Hoyt: Why not look at the doughnut rather than the hole? Even Lacan's [w]hole.[13]

de Shazer: Yes.

Hoyt: Let me read another quotation I want to ask your thoughts about. In the article "Doing Therapy: A Post-Structural Revision" that you and Insoo wrote together, you say, "The user only discovers the meaning of his words in the act of using them in a language game. A word is not *sent* but only *received* " [de Shazer & Berg, 1992, p. 79]. What do you mean by "language game," and then how do you mean we only discover the meanings of our words after using them?

de Shazer: We have a language game right now that is between you and me and whatever, defined as an interview that will form a chapter in a book. That's a language game; it defines everything we're doing in this hour. So if I were to hit you over the head with this unabridged dictionary here, you can only interpret that within the context of this being an interview for this book of yours.

Hoyt: It would be a "foul" in the language game! *[laughter]*

de Shazer: Yeah. Therefore, an observer might say I've suddenly gone berserk, violating the rules of the language game. You can only find out what the rules are by participating. So, whatever words I choose to describe what I'm talking about, I choose these words internally somehow. Then they come out of my mouth and you react to them one way or another, and that's how I discover whether they meant what I thought they were going to mean or they meant something else.

Hoyt: So you never know what question you truly ask until you see what answer you get.

de Shazer: Right.

Hoyt: You may think you asked a certain question, but it's how it's received, how it's taken.

de Shazer: Right.

Hoyt: So we're creating the meaning rather than it sort of being revealed or objectively . . .

---

[13]An allusion to de Shazer's discussion of language, structure, and meaning in *Words Were Originally Magic*, especially his Chapter 3 ("Lacan's [W]hole") and Chapter 4 ("Getting to the Surface of the Problem"). Also see White's discussion in Chapter 2 of this volume, "On Ethics and the Spiritualities of the Surface."

de Shazer: Right. Meanings evolve during the course of the activity. So you take a pair or some interlocking pairs of our conversation here and move it into a different context, it may make absolutely no sense whatsoever. Because there's no language game to define what's going on. I can refer you to that mask over there [*gestures toward a carving on the wall*], and if you look at that mask at the right angle, you'll see how much it looks like Lyndon Johnson.

Hoyt: Yes, I can see LBJ. It looks like a Korean LBJ.

de Shazer: Yes, it's a Korean mask. We have a link then to the language game of hanging around in our living room last night, looking at masks on the wall.[14] If you include this thing about the mask in the transcript and we don't include this next part, that looks like, "What?" But *you* knew exactly what it was.

Hoyt: Why suddenly we were talking about masks.

de Shazer: Yes.

Hoyt: If the reader can't see the mask, it sounds like you've hallucinated.

de Shazer: You didn't have any trouble with it, because you were part of that language game of the masks last night.[15]

Hoyt: Orville Wright once said, "If we all worked on the assumption of what is accepted as true is really true, there would be very little hope of advance."

de Shazer: If we think it's true, then we won't ask any questions.

Hoyt: So we need to recognize there's a language game rather than there's an absolute reality.

de Shazer: Oh, yeah. Then there's reality, and if I hit you on the knee with this, this is going to hurt you.

---

[14]Context: After a delicious home-cooked meal the night before, we had discussed some masks I had been admiring.

[15]de Shazer and Berg (1992, p. 75) explicate:

One way to begin conceptualizing, describing, and using a post-structural view of what is involved in doing therapy is to borrow a concept developed by Ludwig Wittgenstein and to look at doing therapy as an example of an activity involving a set of related, but distinct "language games" (Wittgenstein, 1958, 1968). For Wittgenstein (1968, #23), "the term 'language game' is meant to bring into prominence the fact that the speaking of language is part of an activity." A language game is an activity seen as a language complete in itself, a complete system of human communication: You've got what you've got and that's all there is. There is no need to look behind or beneath since everything you need is readily available and open to view. Nothing is hidden.

Hoyt: Like the Zen teacher who whacks you and says, "Is that real?"[16]

de Shazer: You better believe it's real. That's an entirely different domain. People who confuse the two are what we call "crazy, psychotic perhaps.

Hoyt: How then can we be respectful of the client's belief, language game, the way they construct reality, and at the same time suggest things may not be as they seem to be, kind of casting doubt on or opening them to other possibilities? We're deconstructing.

de Shazer: Basically by emphasizing parts they aren't emphasizing. But it's something they said, so you can go with that enough to respect the whole package. That's the easiest way to say it.

Hoyt: One of the problems I've had lately trying to read psychoanalytic writers is they usually seem very much to believe that they're *right*, that there's a reality there and they are uncovering it. I'm expecting to read a psychoanalytic article soon called "Postmodernism as a Defense against Reality."

de Shazer: *[laughter]* I'm sure there already is such an article.

Hoyt: If there isn't, I'm sure there will be. Rather than accepting the idea that it's a game, that it's being created. It can be a serious game that is being played, but it's being made rather than it's being revealed.

de Shazer: Any day now you'll see that article.

Hoyt: I also see a danger in constructivist or postmodern views, which is some people consider that we can define anything away: "The Holocaust didn't happen, child abuse didn't happen. It's just something that you think happened, or maybe for you it did, but it didn't really." How do we protect against dismissing such important events?

de Shazer: There's actually a book, I'm trying to find it *[searches and pulls it off the shelf]* Here.

Hoyt: It's called *Uncritical Theory: Post-Modernism, Intellectuals, and the Gulf War*, by Christopher Norris [1992]. What does it tell us about the dangers of pretending?

---

[16]The all-in-your-mind view has never really recovered from the kick it received from Dr. Samuel Johnson more than two centuries ago:

> After we came out of the church, we stood talking for some time together of Bishop Berkeley's ingenious sophistry to prove the non-existence of matter, and that everything in the universe is merely ideal. I observed, that though we are satisfied his doctrine is not true, it is impossible to refute it. I never shall forget the alacrity with which Johnson answered, striking his foot with mighty force against a large stone, till he rebounded from it, "I refute it *thus*!" (Boswell, 1791/1980, p. 333).

de Shazer: First, he's drawing a distinction between postmodernism and poststructuralism, which is similar to the distinction I draw. I perhaps got it from him. The difference being that the postmodern is an inversion of modern, and, therefore, it is really a good question. How, as he says, how can we tell the difference between these rockets shooting over Baghdad or a video game of rockets shooting over Baghdad? He goes a lot into that. I'm not sure he comes up with a good conclusion.

Hoyt: Because now there's the danger of "virtual reality," that they can make it seem so close: "Is it Memorex or is it real?"

de Shazer: I think it's exactly the same problem. If I hit you on the knee with this, it's going to hurt you. It's exactly the same problem. There are documents of the Holocaust, there are lots of documents, etc., etc., a preponderance of evidence. You can do an archeological study that these things actually did occur. What it may mean, of course, is open to negotiation; but the events happened, we do have the hard physical evidence. It's a really different domain.

Hoyt: I recently toured the U.S. Memorial Holocaust Museum in Washington, and it was very archival. I think some of the need for the archival quality was the documentation to counter the assertions that this didn't occur—a heavy emphasis on the physical evidence. The meaning, as you say, is still subject to debate.

de Shazer: Yeah, and it always has been. The meaning of anything has always been subject to debate. That's why we have always had both a "true church" and "heretics," whatever that might be. There's never been a time when there was only one religious sect; there's always been a division into other truth or truths.

Hoyt: History is now being rewritten around The Alamo in San Antonio, Texas.

de Shazer: Well, and I think it probably should be. History will always be rewritten in terms of who is writing it. History doesn't change; what you write about it changes.

Hoyt: The event that occurred doesn't change, but the meaning we give.

de Shazer: Right.

Hoyt: History is not the events; it's our recollection, report, and analysis.

de Shazer: History is very difficult unless there are archives, so to speak. You can't depend on asking somebody.

Hoyt: So in a narrative constructive approach, we're assisting clients to write a history that works for them.

de Shazer: Yeah, but that is a long way, I think. You don't need to do that. All you need to do is get it started, and then get the hell out of the way. There's no reason to hang around to correct their grammar. *[laughter]* And you can start that by pointing out the historical truth that on Tuesday he didn't pop any heroin into his arm. That's just as true as the fact that he did on Wednesday, Thursday, and Friday, but he didn't on Tuesday; that's historical truth for the guy. Let's build on that one.

The "anything goes" school—we're back to Wittgenstein, with the whole elaborate private-language argument that he engages in with his interlocutor. The premise is that there is no way you can depend on a private language. They're not valid. You can't depend on its stability. You may have this idea that the Holocaust didn't happen, but you're going to have a hell of a time when you start bringing that out . . .

Hoyt: As an external reality.

de Shazer: When you start talking to somebody else about it, the more you maintain the Holocaust is really a "lie," the more crazy that becomes. You can't develop it. A psychotic episode is what you're having, and actually both people probably feel like they're having it. So reality, as I see it, is created by two or more people. One person can't do it by himself; if he does, he is in danger of becoming psychotic. That's the private-language argument.

Hoyt: Why will some people get stuck in what I might call a "persistent negative narrative"? One person may say, "Something has happened; that's me; that's my identity. I was molested; I am ruined." Another person says, "I was molested. It was a bad thing, but it's not me; it's not my whole identity," and they go on. Some people will get locked in.

de Shazer: Yeah. I guess I would start with this idea. Probably the majority don't get locked in. We're talking about out there in the world. We have evidence now that's accumulating, for instance, that half of the people who quit drinking, quit using heroin, crack cocaine—half of the ones who quit do it spontaneously, with no treatment whatsoever.

Hoyt: Is this Fingarette [1988]?

de Shazer: There are a number of studies [see Berg & Miller, 1992; Sobell, Sobell, Toneatto, & Leo, 1993; Hartmann & Millea, 1996].

Hoyt: So half the so-called "addicts" stop . . .

de Shazer: No, no, the other way. Half of those who quit.

Hoyt: Okay, half of those who quit, quit without "treatment."

de Shazer: No treatment whatsoever, right. So, I suspect that we don't know how they do it. So, that's what they, the researchers, are trying to get at. How do they actually do it? Can we design treatment along that line? Is there some way to design therapy? I don't know. Our whole model is based on this. That the people come in, and if you ask them right, they will tell you about when the problem doesn't happen and, therefore, you can increase the frequency of its not happening. It's very simple. Now, don't get confused—simple does not mean easy. It's a very simple idea. Most people whose 9-year-old boy wets the bed don't treat it as a problem to go to therapy about, and it goes away at some point.

Hoyt: It's one of the dangers of locking people in with diagnosis. It doesn't just describe the present and the past, but it shapes the future.

de Shazer: Oh, yeah, Thomas Szasz has been talking about that for a hundred years or however long. The diagnosis is more *pre*scriptive than it is *de*scriptive. It prescribes both what the patient's going to do and how the people around him are going to react.

Hoyt: So once you have diagnosed them as "alcoholic," if they come in and say, "I stopped drinking," rather than seeing it as a solution, it gets seen as a denial.

de Shazer: Oh, yeah, I heard this from a client years ago, who had gone into an inpatient alcohol treatment program back in the "good old days"— the 28 days business. He was telling me about this. In order to really get the benefit from going to this program, he stopped drinking three weeks before he went in. *[laughter]* And so he told them about that . . .

Hoyt: The cure precedes the treatment.

de Shazer: He told them about that in the first meeting that they had in the hospital, and the response from the therapist was, "You are lying. You will tell us the truth one of these days." The guy said to himself, first, "I'm not lying." Then he said, "Fuck you!" He got up and left. He came to see me. Three years later he still wasn't drinking.

Hoyt: That's the opposite of shaking the person's hand, building an alliance, and complimenting them on their strengths and successes.

de Shazer: Most people do it on their own. Most people that we see just don't realize they've done it on their own. They don't think they've done a good enough job yet. Most people—according to this research, at least half—do it on their own, and feel that they've been successful doing it, so they don't need to get coaching somewhere. I would suspect that 50% is an underestimate. That's my hunch. I'd go up to two-thirds. That's a hunch based on the number of clients over the years who have told me about things that they have stopped doing without treatment. So I would guess that there's more out there than we know about. I don't know how you go about finding these people—advertising in the paper, I suppose.

Hoyt: Let me shift and ask another question. How do you think of applying solution-focused work in supervision, training, and teaching? How does the trainer work differently when being solution-focused?

de Shazer: Well, you have to assume the same things about these kinds of clients as you do about clinical clients: that whatever they are doing makes sense to them. They are obviously doing something that works. Therefore, the first thing you've got to do is find out what that is, so you can build on it. If I'm doing consultation interviews, the first thing I will do is ask the client on a scale from 0 to 10 (or –10 to 0, if we're in Germany), "You started off therapy here, and here is where you want to get. Where are you now?" I do that not only to give the client the idea that he is making progress, but to give the therapist the idea that he's doing something right. You've got to be able to get that much very quickly in a consultation interview. So that the therapist you're consulting for, here's where he's doing something right. Out of the client's mouth is best, because there is the assumption that the client's going to tell you the truth, of course. So that's the first thing. You have to look at it exactly the same way. You have to find out what they're doing that's working—what are they doing right. Then you have to somehow determine how you're going to know when to stop. When is supervision done, consultation done, training done? Generally, I suppose that has to be arbitrary; somehow they determine that.

Hoyt: It's establishing goals and augmenting strengths.

de Shazer: Yeah, it's basically the same procedure, except you haven't got a complaint, no problem to solve. So you don't have to start with that. You can just start with the miracle question without asking anything else, so to speak. There's no problem involved. So it's *not* therapy. You can't measure success in the same ways.[17]

Hoyt: What's next? Do you see solution-focused therapy being developed in a different direction? The last time I asked you that question about a project [Hoyt, 1994—see Chapter 1, p. 30], you said you were working on a book; you weren't sure until you were done what it would be. It turned out to be *Words Were Originally Magic.* Are you working on another one?

de Shazer: Oh, no! I have no idea where it might go. I have no idea. I see a lot of nonsense out there. And there's a lot of "solution- focused" nonsense as well as other kinds.

Hoyt: How would we recognize it?

de Shazer: Anybody who believes that the miracle question creates miracles is somewhere in the vicinity of talking complete nonsense. But there are therapists out there—and I didn't realize this, not being a very religious-type person—I didn't realize that there were people out there

---

[17]See Selekman and Todd (1995), Storm (1995), and Triantafillou (1997).

who believe in miracles. They actually either think the miracle question can or should create miracles. And there are others who ask, "What if a miracle doesn't happen?" That's also complete, utter nonsense. Miracles don't happen.

Hoyt: The miracle question may be a useful tool, but it's a problem if one believes in miracles.

de Shazer: There is other, more subtle nonsense. The piece of nonsense I ran into most recently that is the most startling, most appalling, came from a well-known and highly-thought-of presenter who opened his presentation with the following sentence: "There is no such thing as a bad idea." I spent the rest of the day cataloging all the bad ideas I could think of, like Nazism, fascism, political correctness, and so on. I have no idea what else he had to say.

Hoyt: An idea can be very dangerous, especially if you only have one.

de Shazer: Yeah. Or none in this case. *[laughter]* If there are no bad ideas, then there are no ideas, I'm afraid. He doesn't have any idea.

Hoyt: How shall we close?

de Shazer: Wittgenstein [1980, p. 77e] has some tremendous advice for all authors: "Anything your reader can do for himself, leave to him."

☐ After Words With Insoo Kim Berg

As we were getting ready to leave the office, Insoo Kim Berg joined us. de Shazer's colleague, partner, and wife, she is a major developer of solution-focused therapy and Director of the Brief Family Therapy Center. Intrigued by the clarity of her perspective (see Berg, 1994; Berg & Dolan, 2000; Berg & Kelly, 2000; Berg & Miller, 1992; Kean & Chang, 1994; Miller & Berg, 1995), in the course of our continuing discussion I turned the tape-recorder back on and asked:

Hoyt: In a brochure description of your training staff, it says, "A native of Korea, Insoo balances her Eastern heritage with her Western scientific training in her clinical practice and teaching." How do you see that?

Berg: To me there's a clear distinction between the Eastern and Western approach to life itself. We're talking about the whole attitude toward life, the view of life. They're very different, I think. What's different about it is the whole notion of being scientific means that you go after the underlying causes. I think the whole scientific stance has been very useful because it builds on understanding the causal relationship.

Hoyt: It's very Western that life is to be analyzed . . .

Berg: Analyzed and solved. I think that medicine is a good example of where that has been very terribly helpful. It has led to many, many wonderful discoveries and treatment approaches and so on. But I think that somehow when it comes to human relationships, problems of living, we tend to have the same mechanistic approach to life, the issue of life. I think that medicine sees the body as a machine-like entity. So we can take it apart, we study it and fix it, and then put it back together. I think that kind of influence, a positive scientific quality, spilled over into the psychotherapy field.

Hoyt: Michael White writes a lot about this in *Narrative Means to Therapeutic Ends* [White & Epston, 1990]. He has a Table of Analogies [p. 6] where he spells it out very clearly. He doesn't relate it to East-West, but he talks about the positivist scientific approach of analyze it, dissect it, cure it, cut it out, fix it. This could be opposed to one of more appreciating sort of the—I don't know if you want to call it the mystery of it, but the totality of what it is.

Berg: This is life, and I think the Eastern mindset is that we rarely ask, "Why does this happen?" We say, "This happens, that's how life is."

de Shazer: We know from acupuncture: You stick a needle up here, it may have an effect down there.

Berg: For the first time in my life, I started going to an acupuncturist. If I went to a medical doctor he would do all the X-rays and blood tests, and blah, blah, blah, and then he will tell me the diagnosis of what my problem is. I was very dissatisfied with this acupuncturist; he sort of looked at me and he listened to my complaints, and he started to pull out his needles and he started sticking them into me. He never tells me what's wrong with me. He just sort of proceeded, "Oh, okay, seems like this could be useful for you." I'm lying there and I'm thinking with my Western mind, "Am I wasting my money? Am I throwing my money away?" But you know, that's how he proceeds. So I think that that's the kind of very different way.

Hoyt: In doing therapy, do you think that carries over? With what the patient's brought in: "This is what it is."

Berg: This is what is.

Hoyt: And I can kind of take it for what it is, rather than having to pull it apart and analyze it.

de Shazer: There's no "the way it's supposed to be."

Hoyt: There's no way it's supposed to be; this is the way it is.

Berg: This is the way it is.

Hoyt: You don't have to be judgmental, you have to be . . .

Berg: There's no right way to be. That's just the way it is.

de Shazer: Or back to the previous stuff about nonsense. All the non-sense is built upon "This is the way it's supposed to be."

Hoyt: The medical model, that you should be 98.6°, you should be this shape, this way, there's a right way, and you're outside of that.[18]

de Shazer: It's just the way it is. Just the way it is. There's no "supposed to be" about it.

Hoyt: I think when some people get nervous, they want to replace imagination with precision.

Berg: That's right. Or the illusion of precision.

Hoyt: Control.

Berg: There's no precision in life, right?

Hoyt: In a Greek model, we might say they're Apollonian rather than Dionysian. They want to fit everything into neat structured categories.

de Shazer: I had a client who said that impossibility coupled with certainty equals confirmed nonsense. *[laughter]* It's a translation out of German, but nonetheless it's still the same thing.

Hoyt: So the Eastern attitude is more of taking it for what it is. Some people might call it being a Taoist.

Berg: That's how it's been given, and you work with it and do the best you can, and see what unfolds. Because I don't know what is going to unfold.

de Shazer: We know from lots of experimentation, we can't make those predictions, so we don't know what's going to unfold. We tried to predict but it didn't work.

Berg: Does that answer your question?

Hoyt: Now I know what my question was. We don't know the answer to the question until we hear the answer. Now I know what I asked today.

☐ References

American Psychiatric Association. (1994). *Diagnostic and Statistical Manual of Mental Disorders* (4th ed.). Washington, DC: Author.

Aponte, H. J. (1992) Training the person of the therapist in structural family therapy. *Journal of Marital and Family Therapy, 18,* 269–281.

Appelbaum, S. A. (1975). Parkinson's law in psychotherapy. *International Journal of Psychoanalytic Psychotherapy,* 4, 426–436.

Bartley, W. W., III. (1985). *Wittgenstein.* Chicago: Open Court.

[18]See Hoyt (1979, 1985).

Berg, I. K. (1994). *Family Based Services: A Solution-Focused Approach.* New York: Norton.

Berg, I. K., & de Shazer, S. (1993). Making numbers talk: Language in therapy. In S. Friedman (Ed.), *The New Language of Change: Constructive Collaboration in Psychotherapy* (pp. 5–24). New York: Guilford Press.

Berg, I. K., & Dolan, Y. M. (2000). *Tales of Solutions: A Collection of Hope-Inspiring Stories.* New York: Norton.

Berg, I. K., & Kelly, S. (2000). *Building Solutions in Child Protective Services.* New York: Norton.

Berg, I. K., & Miller, S. D. (1992). *Working with the Problem Drinker: A Solution-Focused Approach.* New York: Norton.

Boswell, J. (1980). *The Life of Samuel Johnson, LL.D.* (unabridged). Oxford: Oxford University Press/World's Classics. (Original work published 1791)

de Shazer, S. (1982). *Patterns of Brief Family Therapy.* New York: Guilford Press.

de Shazer, S. (1984). The death of resistance. *Family Process, 23,* 79–93.

de Shazer, S. (1985). *Keys to Solution in Brief Therapy.* New York: Norton.

de Shazer, S. (1988). *Clues: Investigating Solutions in Brief Therapy.* New York: Norton.

de Shazer, S. (1991). *Putting Difference to Work.* New York: Norton.

de Shazer, S. (1994). *Words Were Originally Magic.* New York: Norton.

de Shazer, S., & Berg, I.K. (1985) A part is not apart: Working with only one of the partners present. In A.S. Gurman (Ed.), *Casebook of Marital Therapy* (pp. 97–110). New York: Guilford Press.

de Shazer, S., & Berg, I. K. (1992). Doing therapy: A post-structural revision. *Journal of Marital and Family Therapy, 18,* 71–81.

de Shazer, S., & Nunnally, E. (1991). The mysterious affair of paradoxes and loops. In G. Weeks (Ed.), *Promoting Change through Paradoxical Techniques* (pp. 252–270). New York: Brunner/Mazel.

Dolan, Y. M. (1991). *Resolving Sexual Abuse: Solution-Focused Therapy and Ericksonian Hypnosis for Adult Survivors.* New York: Norton.

Duffy, B. (1988). *World as I Found It.* New York: Ticknor & Fields.

Duncan, B. L. (1992). Strategic therapy, eclecticism, and the therapeutic relationship. *Journal of Marital and Family Therapy, 18,* 17–24.

Fingarette, H. (1988). *Heavy Drinking: The Myth of Alcoholism as a Disease.* Los Angeles: University of California Press.

Fisher, S. G. (1980). The use of time limits in brief psychotherapy: A comparison of six-session, twelve-session, and unlimited treatment with families. *Family Process, 19,* 377–392.

Fisher, S. G. (1984). Time-limited brief therapy with families: A one-year follow-up study. *Family Process, 23,* 101–106.

Hartmann, B.R., & Millea, P.J. (1996) When belief systems collide: The rise and decline of the disease concept of alcoholism. *Journal of Systemic Therapies, 15*(2), 36–47.

Held, B. S. (1992). The problem of strategy within the systemic therapies. *Journal of Marital and Family Therapy, 18,* 25–34.

Hoyt, M. F. (1979). "Patient" or "client": What's in a name? *Psychotherapy, 16,* 46–47. (Reprinted in M. F. Hoyt, *Brief Therapy and Managed Care: Readings for Contemporary Practice* [pp. 205–207]. San Francisco: Jossey-Bass, 1995.)

Hoyt, M. F. (1985). "Shrink" or "expander": An issue on forming a therapeutic alliance. *Psychotherapy, 22,* 813–814. (Reprinted in M. F. Hoyt, *Brief Therapy and Managed Care: Readings for Contemporary Practice* [pp. 209–211]. San Francisco: Jossey-Bass, 1995.)

Hoyt, M. F. (1990). On time in brief therapy. In R. A. Wells & V. J. Giannetti (Eds.), *Handbook of the Brief Psychotherapies* (pp. 115–143). New York: Plenum Press. (Reprinted in M. F. Hoyt, *Brief Therapy and Managed Care: Readings for Contemporary Practice* [pp. 69–104]. San Francisco: Jossey-Bass, 1995.)

Hoyt, M. F. (1994). On the importance of keeping it simple and taking the patient seriously: A conversation with Steve de Shazer and John Weakland. In M. F. Hoyt (Ed.), *Constructive Therapies* (pp. 11–40). New York: Guilford Press.

Janik, A., & Towlmin, S. (1974). *Wittgenstein's Vienna*. New York: Simon & Schuster.

Kean, M., & Chang, J. (1994). Outlook is everything: An interview with Insoo Kim Berg. *Journal of Collaborative Therapies, 2*(2), 1–6.

Kennett, J. (1972). *Selling Water by the River: A Manual of Zen Training*. New York: Pantheon.

Kiser, D. J., Piercy, F. P., & Lipchik, E. (1993). The integration of emotion in solution-focused therapy. *Journal of Marital and Family Therapy, 19*, 233–242.

Lipchik, E. (1994). The rush to be brief. *Family Therapy Networker, 18*(2), 34–39.

Miller, S. D., & Berg, I. K. (1995). *The "Miracle" Method: A Radically New Approach to Problem Drinking*. New York: Norton.

Minuchin, S. (1974). *Families and Family Therapy*. Cambridge, MA: Harvard University Press.

Monk, R. (1990). *Ludwig Wittgenstein: The Duty of Genius*. New York: Viking/Penguin.

Norris, C. (1992). *Uncritical Theory: Post-Modernism, Intellectuals, and the Gulf War*. Amherst: University of Massachusetts Press.

Nylund, D., & Corsiglia, V. (1994). Becoming solution-focused forced in brief therapy: Something important we already knew. *Journal of Systemic Therapies, 13*, 1–8.

Real, T. (1990). The therapeutic use of self in constructionist/systemic therapy. *Family Process, 23*, 255–272.

Selekman, M. D., & Todd, T. C. (1995). Co-creating a context for change in the supervisory system: The solution-focused supervision model. *Journal of Systemic Therapies, 14*(3), 21–33.

Sobell, L. C., Sobell, M. B., Toneatto, T., & Leo, G. I. (1993). What triggers the resolution of alcohol problems without treatment? *Alcoholism: Clinical and Experimental Research, 17*(2), 217–224.

Solovey, A. D., & Duncan, B. L. (1992). Ethics and strategic therapy: A proposed ethical direction. *Journal of Marital and Family Therapy, 18*, 53–61.

Storm, C. L. (Ed.) (1995). Postmodern supervision. [Whole issue.] *Journal of Systemic Therapies, 14*(2), i–78.

Triantafillou, N. (1997). A solution-focused approach to mental health supervision. *Journal of Systemic Therapies, 16*(4), 305–328.

Walter, J. L., & Peller, J. E. (1992). *Becoming Solution-Focused in Brief Therapy*. New York: Norton.

Watzlawick, P., Beavin, J., & Jackson, D. D. (1967). *Pragmatics of Human Communication*. New York: Norton.

White, M., & Epston, D. (1990). *Narrative Means to Therapeutic Ends*. New York: Norton.

Wittgenstein, L. (1958). *The Blue and Brown Books*. New York: Harper.

Wittgenstein, L. (1968). *Philosophical Investigations* (3rd ed., G. E. M. Anscombe, Trans.). New York: Macmillan.

Wittgenstein, L. (1980). *Culture and Value* (P. Winch, Trans.). Chicago: University of Chicago Press.

8

Postmodernism, the Relational Self, Constructive Therapies, and Beyond: A Conversation With Kenneth Gergen

A long-time proponent of a social constructionist perspective, Kenneth Gergen is Professor of Psychology at Swarthmore College in Swarthmore, Pennsylvania. His wide-ranging interests, along with those of his colleague and wife, Mary Gergen, bridge intellectual traditions and popular culture. His edited volumes include *The Self in Social Interaction* (Gordon & Gergen, 1968), *Historical Social Psychology* (K. J. Gergen & Gergen, 1984), *The Social Construction of the Person* (Gergen & Davis, 1985), *Texts of Identity* (Shotter & Gergen, 1989), *Everyday Understanding: Social and Scientific Implications* (Semin & Gergen, 1990), *Therapy as Social Construction* (McNamee & Gergen, 1992), and *Historical Dimensions of Psychological Discourse* (Graumann & Gergen, 1993). His authored books include *Toward Transformation in Social Knowledge* (1985a), the much-acclaimed *The Saturated Self: Dilemmas of Identity in Contemporary Life* (1991), and *Realities and Relationships: Soundings in Social Construction* (1994a).

Perhaps especially apropos of the postmodern sensibility discussed herein, the following interview was not conducted in one time, place, or state of mind. Rather, questions were asked, answered, adumbrated, and amplified over many months, from airplanes, trains, offices, hotels, and homes. The conversation commenced in June 1994. When Gergen gra-

Originally appeared, with changes, in M. F. Hoyt (Ed.) (1996), *Constructive Therapies, Volume 2* (pp. 347–368). New York: Guilford Press. Used with permission.

ciously telephoned in response to my letter of invitation, I quickly asked, "Why did you call your *Networker* speech [Gergen, 1992] 'The Polymorphous *Per*versity of the Postmodern Era' rather than 'The Polymorphous *Di*versity'? I know the reference to Freud [1905/1953],[1] but 'perversity' implies a deviance from a 'normal' or 'right' way." Gergen responded, "Let's talk." Our conversation, constructed over time, follows.

Hoyt: How do you conceptualize the "self," and how does this change moving from a modern to a postmodern perspective?

Gergen: For purposes of contrast, let's start with the tradition we inherit in the West, one which posits some form of inner essence. Whether we are speaking of Christian religion and its belief in a soul; Romanticists of the past century, with their championing of passion, inspiration, or *élan vital*; recent existentialist thinkers and their emphasis on conscious choice; or the belief of modernists in reason or cognition—all begin with the assumption of an essential core of the self. It is this essence that constitutes one's being and without which one would be something less than human.

As a social constructionist, I view all these perspectives as culturally and historically situated. It is not that they are mistaken, somehow failing to see the self as it truly is. The mistake is perhaps in presuming that we can determine "what truly is." The words we use to describe our being are not simply pictures of what exists, not maps of a territory. Rather, they construct us as this or that, and in doing so serve as logics for action. I think it is this de-essentializing that is the major ingredient of the move from the modern to postmodern conception of self. Within the spectrum of postmodern thought, it is the social constructionist who will treat the self as a manifestation of human interchange.

Hoyt: If the self is socially constructed, is there something essential that may be shaped or influenced, but is not created *sui generis*? I'm thinking, for example, of Stern's [1985] studies of infant development and Margaret Mahler's [Mahler, Bergman, & Pine, 1975] ideas about the "psychological birth of the infant." Other writers, such as Singer and Salovey [1993], have suggested that one's sense of self is "remembered"—organized or influenced by cognitive-affective processes.

Gergen: Again, the challenge for the constructionist is to avoid pronouncements about what is essential. This is not to say that the constructionist doesn't participate in culture, and would not use words like *soul*, *intentional choice*, *cognition*, and the like. Rather, it is to recognize that when we use these utterances we are participating in a particular set of cultural traditions, and not pronouncing truth beyond culture and history. To say

---

[1]In *Three Essays on the Theory of Sexuality*, Freud (1905/1953) used the phrase "polymorphous perversity" to describe the undetermined potential pansexuality of children.

"I love you" is not then a description of a mental state; it is active participation in a deeply valued form of relationship.

To deal with your question more directly, I don't want to say either one way or the other that there is or is not something essential to be shaped or influenced. Rather, let's ask what hangs on the question for different social or cultural practices. What will follow if I take one route in a conversation as opposed to another? As I mentioned previously, we have a substantial tradition of essentialism, giving an affirmative answer to your question. So for me as a scholar, I scarcely succeed in pressing our ideas forward if I simply say, yet once again, "We are emotional beings," or "cognitive beings," or "intentional beings."

One of my central interests has been to generate a new sense of what it is to be a person, a sense of what I call a "relational self." The hope is to transform the meaning of what it is to be a self—to have an identity, emotion, memory, motivation, and the like—so that we can understand it as constituted within relationship. Vygotsky [1986] and Bakhtin [1981] are useful as first steps in this direction, as are Mead [1934] and Bruner [1986]. However, in each of these cases there remains a strong commitment to an individual subjectivity that precedes relatedness. My hope (and I must say that there are many scholars and therapists who are engaged in these dialogues) is to go beyond this work by positing relatedness as the essential matrix, out of which a conception of self (or identity, emotion, etc.) is born, objectified, and embedded within action. On this account, for example, emotion is a constructed category, and emotional performance is culturally prescribed. However, such performances are never cut away from a relational dance or scenario. We participate in the dance together, and without the dance there would be no occasion for the performance. In this sense, it is *we* who possess the emotion. Much of this is spelled out in my new book, *Realities and Relationships* [1994a].

Hoyt: This is very consistent with the interactionalist notion that "the basic unit of analysis is at least two people," as I recently heard Jay Haley [1995, personal communication] express it, as well as the idea that "the mind is not in the head" [Maturana & Varela, 1987]. In your view, where is the *unconscious*? Is the term useful? Is there a *self* outside (beyond, below) narrative?

Gergen: As you can see, whether we posit an unconscious mind is optional. There is nothing about whatever we are that makes this kind of description necessary. Our beliefs in the unconscious as a reality are also culturally and historically situated, growing most recently from the soil of

---

[2]See de Shazer's comments regarding Freud and Wittgenstein in Chapter 7 (this volume). For an extended discussion of the history of the idea of the unconscious, see Ellenberger (1970).

19th-century Romanticism.[2] However, whether the term is *useful* or not is a very interesting one. It is not useful if what we mean by the term is that the concept gives us an accurate description—"real" insight into human functioning. However, if what we mean by "useful" is viewed in terms of social functioning—where does it get us in our relations to speak of the unconscious?—then the answer would be very multifaceted.

Hoyt: How so?

Gergen: For example, the concept has been very useful in augmenting our tendency to place moral judgment on the deviant in society. Rather than simply placing moral blame on the rapist, child molester, or murderer—leading unequivocally to punishment—the concept of the unconscious adds to our cultural repertoire by enabling us to see the deviant as in some sense "ill." We think increasingly, then, about ways to restore the individual to full functioning (as opposed to forms of punishment that will virtually ensure their remaining deviant). There is much more that could be said on behalf of the concept of the unconscious. However, there is also a very strong down side, and I guess I find it more compelling than the positive account. Here I am speaking of the many critiques of the assumption of the unconscious, for example, for its reducing all problems to the intrapsychic level, its blindness to cultural and economic conditions, its championing of the authority of the all-knowing doctor (in contrast to the ignorant patient), its alliance with the medical model of illness, and its providing the individual excuses for all forms of brutishness.[3]

Hoyt: How do you define *therapy*? Is that the right word? What might be an alternative?

Gergen: I would prefer not to define it. Rather, let's say that we find ourselves at this time in cultural history engaged in a range of interrelated conversations in which the concept of therapy plays a very significant role. The precise meaning of the term is contested, and it should ideally remain so. To legislate in this case would be to stop the conversation, oppress the many voices, and arbitrarily and misleadingly freeze history.

Hoyt: How do you currently see the therapeutic endeavor?

Gergen: My preference in this conversation is to view therapy as a process of constructing meaning. To be sure, we exist in what we commonly call "real-world" conditions—"biological," "material," "economic," and the like. However, in the main what we take to be the successes and failures in our lives, the worthwhile and the worthless, the satisfying as opposed to the frustrating, are byproducts of human meaning. It is not so much "how things are" as how we interpret them that will typically bring us

---

[3]See also Michael White's discussion in Chapter 2 of how even altruistic acts can be destructively made suspect, pathologized, and invalidated.

into therapy. A physical touch may itself be unremarkable; however, in different frames of meaning it may spark a sense of friendly support, move one to ecstasy, or incite litigation for harassment. A blow to the chin will send a family member in search of a therapist, but will move a boxer to change his tactics. With this emphasis in place, we are invited to see effective therapy as a transformation in meaning. However, as you can see from the preceding remarks, I don't see this transformation principally as a cognitive event. Rather, it is an alteration in actions—relying importantly on language but not at all limited to language.

Hoyt: As therapy moves more into postmodern context, what are the continuities from past tradition and practice, and what "new directions" should we consider? It would be perhaps premature and too specific to propose a curriculum, but what do you see as the major issues and challenges?

Gergen: These are very complicated issues and we could talk at length. For now, however, let me focus on just one aspect of what many see as the postmodern condition, and its particular implications for therapeutic practice. As I tried to describe in *The Saturated Self* [1991], the communication technologies of this century bring us into confrontation with a vastly expanded range of others—both in terms of physical presence and vicarious figures of the media. Our otherwise parochial worlds become shattered by the intrusion of a multiplicity of opinions, values, attitudes, personalities, visions, and ways of life. At the same time, there has been an increasing tendency for various groups to generate common consciousness. Again, the technologies allow otherwise voiceless people to organize, develop common goals, consider entitlements, and so on.

Under these conditions of increasing pluralism, it is very difficult for any therapeutic school to claim—as was long the tendency—ubiquitous authority. To reduce all problems, for example, to early family conditions, conditioned responses, or deficits in self-regard not only seems excessively parochial, but in a certain sense tyrannical.

Hoyt: The death of an orthodoxy makes it difficult to organize a counterorthodoxy.

Gergen: How then does therapeutic practice respond to these conditions? Of course, the most common practice among therapists is simply to "go eclectic." Rather than continuing in the school favored in their training, they continue to explore, learn, adapt, and eventually develop multilayered approaches. In my view, a constructionist orientation favors just this kind of practice, but as well furnishes such practice with a needed sense of integration and purpose.

Hoyt: I prefer the term *multilayered* or *multitheoretical* rather than *eclectic*. Being multiply informed is important, but to me *eclectic* sometimes seems like a cross between *electric* and *chaotic*, a directionless hodgepodge of techniques.[4]

Gergen: We could also use the term *polyvocal*, which better fits the metaphor of conversation. In any case, the greater the range of "vocabularies" available to the therapist, the greater his or her efficacy within wideranging relationships. At the same time, the constructionist therapist is drawn to the use-value of these various vocabularies (words and actions) as they are developed in the therapeutic relationship, and extended to further relationships outside. How well do the vocabularies travel, and what do they do to and for people's lives as they are pressed into action?

Hoyt: Holy hermeneutics! If modernism gave us "ontological insecurity," postmodernism could produce a panic attack! As Sheila McNamee and you [1992, p. 2] have commented, "Little confidence now remains in the optimistic program of scientifically grounded progress toward identifying 'problems' and providing 'cures.'" With conventional standards of "what's right" no longer valid compasses, what suggestions do you have for therapists as we search for (and co-create) therapeutic realities with our clients? Any guides for the perplexed?

Gergen: At the outset, I think we must all remain humble and interdependent in the face of the problem. This is not the time to look to a new guru who can remove our perplexities; we must together work toward new visions. With this said, my own preference is for a therapeutic approach that appreciates the force of local realities, but within an expanded context of connection. By this, I mean that the therapist would not begin with a single set of criteria as to what constitutes an effective intervention or a cure. Rather, he or she would be maximally sensitive to how such matters are defined within the local communities. What are the standards for judging satisfaction or dissatisfaction within the most immediate relationships at hand? At the same time, the therapist must remain concerned with the fuller range of relationships in which the immediate case is embedded. Meaning within the local condition is ultimately dependent upon broader cultural context. Again, this won't lead to a single standard. But the point is to allow the mix of standards into the therapeutic conversation.

Hoyt: This gets at one of the challenges of a multicultural society, where different groups have different mores and standards. How do we steer

---

[4]Like Pirandello's *Six Characters in Search of an Author*, the practice of therapy has sometimes seemed like "100 Techniques in Search of a Theory." Surveying the psychotherapy field, Hoyt and Ordover (1998; also see Neimeyer & Freixas, 1990) called for a "unified field theory" to coordinate the various "strong forces" that theorists and practitioners have evolved. A constructionist perspective provides this meta-potential.

between the Scylla of a Balkanized, "anything goes" separatism and the Charybdis of a colonization by the dominant culture?

Gergen: It is in the mix of voices, it seems to me, that we find the answer—in the blending, appropriation, and paradox. Yet, a therapist could find a family in which a certain degree of incestual activity or physical abuse was tolerated—simply "not part of the problem" as they see it. In this sense, it wouldn't be the therapist's immediate task to deconstruct the family's system of beliefs (legal issues notwithstanding). However, given the ultimate interdependence of this family on the broader array of cultural meanings, in the longer run therapy might usefully be directed to coordinating family meanings (and actions) with those of the dominant society.

Hoyt: In the last chapter of *Therapy as Social Construction* [McNamee & Gergen, 1992], Efran and Clarfield [1992] review what they consider to be "sense and nonsense" in constructionist therapy. They evoke Coyne's [1982] term *"epistobabble"* and note, to use their words [p. 200], that some critics dismiss such therapies as "little more than recombinations of familiar 'reframing' and team observation techniques already in use. They question whether constructionist lingo will prove any more substantive or long-lived than a dozen earlier infatuations." What do you see as truly different and likely to endure?

Gergen: It's difficult to understand why Efran and Clarfield were so hostile—to almost everyone unfortunate enough to draw their gaze. I think disagreements can be useful and wonderful means toward new visions, but it seems primitive to me to abuse your colleagues in the ways they selected.

Hoyt: Beyond the mean-spiritedness of their critique, what is added?

Gergen: In my view, the importance of social constructionism to current therapeutic theory and practice is that it enables many practitioners to articulate emerging beliefs and practices in such a way that they can more clearly see (1)how they truly differ from the "modernist" tradition; (2) the similarities between what they are doing and what many others are doing in the field; and (3)how their orientation is related to a vast range of cultural changes, including major intellectual transformations in the academy and changes in societal life patterns. I don't see constructionism as offering just another model of therapy, another "silver bullet" cure, a specialized vocabulary, or a new set of "musts." Rather, I see constructionism as inherent in a vast array of conversations taking place around the world—conversations that bring people together over pressing issues of common concern. To be sure, there are a circumscribed array of topics in these conversations, and in this sense constructionist discussions cannot do everything one might wish. However, they do raise fundamental questions about long-cherished traditions in Western culture. Given the rapid changes taking place in meanings, values, and practices, and the enormous conflicts among meaning systems around the world, they are likely to remain focal for some time.

Hoyt: Raising consciousness via the question, as Watzlawick [1976—also see Chapter 6, this volume] put it, "How real is real?", recognizing that we are "constructive" [Hoyt, 1994a, 1996, 1998] and that reality is "invented" [Watzlawick, 1984], could have, if not a humbling effect, at least suggest some pause and respect. It could open dialogic space, one would hope. In this regard, let me note that in your Foreword [Gergen, 1993] to Friedman's *The New Language of Change*, you comment that this shift entails a "formidable change of seas" in which there is "the suspicion of all reality posits. . . . coupled with a related distrust of the authoritative voice" [p. x].[5] Given that we cannot stand outside the equation, how can we practice therapy without imposing our values or ethics?

Gergen: There is no therapy that stands outside values or ethics; even the most politically neutral therapist is acting for good or ill by some standard. Given this fact, many therapists are drawn to the conclusion that therapy should thereby operate as advocacy. If we are bound to be advocates in any case, it is reasoned, then why not be clear and open about what it is we stand for and what we are against, and use therapy to build a better society? In certain ways I am drawn to this kind of thinking; it is surely an improvement over the old modernist attempt to step outside the conversation by declaring value neutrality. However, I also worry about the implications of the advocacy orientation if it is fully extended. Can you imagine the results for the profession if we split into hundreds of political encampments—the gay, the gray, the lesbian, the black, the

---

[5]Gergen (1998) also wrote the Foreword to *The Handbook of Constructive Therapies* (Hoyt, 1998), in which he said:

> The present volume forms an implicit commentary on the waning of concepts pivotal to the age of modernism: truth, objectivity, rationality, and moral principle. All too often we have found that such concepts have functioned to impede the flow of cultural conversation. Too often they have been used to delimit the nature of our expressions, to separate those allowed to participate in determining our collective future from those who are silenced, and ultimately to create self-rationalizing hierarchies of privilege. . . . [W]e must recognize and grapple with intelligibilities of all forms and varieties, for it is in the to and fro of the ensuing interchange that our best hopes for the future may be located. Thus, with the waning of the modernist faith in a "single great ordering" we find here the emergence of an alternative vision, one emphasizing at once the value of diversity and the simultaneous need for coordinating forms of communication. Whether on the level of individual life, the family, the community, or global relationships, our hope lies in the "con-joint" construction of the real and the good.

Chicano, the Asian, and so on—each with suspicion or antipathy toward the other? This would be multi-culturalism gone mad. If we separate along moral-political lines, not only do we diminish the possibility for dialogue and communality, but we also generate a therapeutic world of all against all. Perhaps you can see again why I favor forms of therapy that enable people to speak in many voices, to comprehend the paradoxes in their own values, to appreciate the positive force of many local intelligibilities. The challenge here would not be to locate the one right position, ethic, or political ideal; nor would it be to suppress informed political action. Rather, it is to enable people to move with greater fluidity in the world, with a greater potential perhaps for coordinating the disparate as opposed to eradicating the opposition.[6]

Hoyt: You have written eloquently [Gergen, 1994b] about ways that the therapeutic professions have developed and disseminated a language of mental deficit—a language that creates hierarchies, dependencies, and endless ways of constructing the self as deficient. We now seem to have a flood of new self disorders, such as "multiple personality disorder," "narcissistic disorder," "borderline disorder," "codependency," and the like. How can we redress this situation? Can we reeducate the profession, the media, and the public?[7]

Gergen: I do think the therapeutic community has provided an invaluable resource to people over the years, and particularly as the traditional social bonds have eroded. As families, committed friendships, and communities disappear into the past, therapists continue to "be there" for

---

[6]"Being transparent," laying our cards on the table, can help reduce subtle or duplicitous manipulation; but we may also need to embrace, not erase, inevitable tensions. Writing within the context of race relations, West (1994, pp. 150-151) suggests jazz as a useful metaphor:

> I use the term "jazz" here not so much as a term for a musical art form, as for a mode of being in the world, an improvisational mode of protean, fluid, and flexible dispositions toward reality suspicious of "either/or" viewpoints, dogmatic pronouncements, or supremacist ideologies. . . . The interplay of individuality and unity is not one of uniformity and unanimity imposed from above but rather a conflict among diverse groupings that reach a dynamic consensus subject to questioning and criticism. As with a soloist in a jazz quartet, quintet, or band, individuality is promoted in order to sustain and increase the *creative* tension with the group—a tension that yields higher levels of performance to achieve the aim of the collective project.

[7]See the discussion by de Shazer and Weakland in Chapter 1 (this volume), "On the Importance of Keeping It Simple and Taking the Patient Seriously," including their discussion of whether one functions as a mental *health* professional or a mental *illness* professional; see also Gergen's (1994b) remarks, "On Taking *Ourselves* Seriously." Some commentators, such as Masson (1994), seem to have gone so far as to conclude that the whole idea of professional psychotherapy in inherently wrong, and have suggested that it be abandoned and replaced with self-help groups.

support, insight, renewal, and the like. And given our technologies of saturation, this trend is only likely to continue. However, if there is one marked failure of the therapeutic communities, it is not in terms of outcome evaluation. (Personally, I think outcome evaluations are no more than window dressing for a given school of therapy, and the entire concept is misleading.) Rather, there has been a profound disservice in generating an enormous set of concepts through which people can see themselves as deficient. Worse, these vocabularies are self-serving; when people come to believe they possess these "diseases" or "failings," a therapist is required for "cure."

Yes, to be sure, education can be an important means of redress. However, this first means a major change within the therapeutic community. That is, it is first necessary to get our own house in order. Family therapists have been in the vanguard of criticism of diagnosis; however, there is simultaneously a move within the family arena to develop an entirely new range of deficit categories—namely, relational diagnostics. And there are still the clinical psychology and psychiatric professions for whom these deficit categories are no less than maps of the real world.

Coupled with this self-critical effort, and perhaps more realistic, is the decoupling of diagnosis and third-party billing procedures.[8] So long as diagnostic categories are necessary for insurance payments, the professions will knuckle under. This procedure can and should be reversed. After all, we have learned to live with "no-fault" divorce processes. Why can the same logic not apply in the case of difficulties in living? The day is also soon coming when an activist ex-mental patient will bring lawsuits against therapists for such unjustifiable and injurious classification. Perhaps such litigation can speed the process of change.

Hoyt: Some cultures, such as the traditional Balinese (Suryani & Jensen, 1993], create or construct "selves" that in some ways resemble the condition we call "multiple personality disorder" [MPD]. Other writers, such as Glass [1993] in *Shattered Selves: Multiple Personality in a Postmodern World*, are very critical of postmodern conceptions of the self, arguing that true MPD[9] is a fragmentation of self resulting from horrible childhood abuse and that such individuals suffer greatly for having to live without a firm

---

[8]See Wylie's (1995) trenchant article, "Diagnosing for Dollars" in the *Family Therapy Networker* issue, "The Power of DSM-IV." See also Blum (1978), Tomm (1990), and Kirk and Kutchins (1992). Long ago Ambrose Bierce (1906/1957, p. 36) offered this definition from *The Devil's Dictionary* : "*Diagnosis*, n., A physician's forecast of disease by the patient's pulse and purse."

[9]MPD is now called "dissociative identity disorder" in the *DSM-IV* (American Psychiatric Association, 1994). A good pros and cons summary of issues is available in Spiegel and McHugh (1995).

identity. How do you see the relationship between a postmodern view of "self" and "multiple personality disorder"?

Gergen: First, the assumptions embraced by Glass—that there simply are "MPD" persons in the world, and that they chiefly suffer from the lack of a firm identity—are exactly the kind of mentality I view as detrimental to the culture. Such presumptions not only serve to objectify the "illness," and to suggest that others may also possess this particular infirmity, but as well imply that there is something privileged in a state of "unified and coherent" being. In a certain sense, then, this kind of analysis is part of the problem.

Now this is not to doubt that Glass confronts clients who are in deep pain, and that they can understand themselves in just the way he describes. But there are many other ways in which one's personality can be rendered meaningful—many alternative conceptions that can be generated of what he is authoritatively classifying as "MPD." And many of these alternatives would, in my view, be far more promising for the client (and society) as they move from therapeutic relations into daily life.[10]

There is also a certain genre of postmodern writing that provides just such a promise. If one feels split among selves, torn between competing tendencies, capable of multiple personalities, this literature suggests that such a condition may be the newly emerging cultural form. And it is not to be lamented—but explored for its potential riches. Contributions to this genre would include the work of Jim Wertsch [1985, 1991] in psychology, and Peggy Penn [1982, 1985; Penn & Frankfurt, 1994] in family therapy.

Hoyt: Reading through some of the chapters in *The Saturated Self* in the rapid way you recommend [Gergen, 1991, p. 49] did produce the existentially dizzying, almost disorienting "multiphrenic"[11] effect that, by parallel process, was the subject. The medium became the message, as Marshall McLuhan [1964] said. Writers such as Kegan [1994] have suggested that we're "in over our heads," that the complexity of (post)modern life exceeds our cognitive grasp. In "multiphrenia," what will provide a sense of stability/identity/self?[12]

---

[10]For discussion of some therapeutic alternatives, see Grove (1993), Grove and Haley (1993), Schwarz (1998), and O'Hanlon (Chapter 2, this volume).

[11]Gergen (1991, p. 16) describes

the fragmenting and populating of self-experience, a condition I call "multiphrenia." Critical to my argument is the proposal that social saturation brings with it a general loss of our assumption of true and knowable selves. As we absorb multiple voices, we find that each "truth" is relativized by our simultaneous consciousness of compelling alternatives. We come to be aware that each truth about ourselves is a construction of the moment true only for a given time and within certain relationhips.

[12]Tom Hanks, the actor who played the title role in the film *Forrest Gump*, described preparing for the part: "I went to a school for mentally challenged kids who are now adults.

Gergen: As you might guess from what I just said, we might ask, "What is necessarily wrong with 'instability' and 'fragmentation'?" These are, after all, negative labels for conditions that might also be described as "fascinating," "exciting," and "transformative," on the one hand, and "multifaceted" or "richly complex" on the other. The opposite of instability could be viewed as a boring and oppressive status quo, while the opposite of fragmentation might be seen as rigidity and narrow-mindedness.

This is not to say that I wish to abandon the quest for stability and simplicity. There are days and hours in which I long for it. But I can also understand these wishes in terms of my immersion in a cultural history in which these conditions are valued, and understand that these yearnings are not for something fundamental, deeply ingrained in nature. They are simply one of the facets or desires of self within the vast multiplicity. That idea in itself I find helpful.

Hoyt: What will *character* mean in a postmodern world? How do we understand *ethics* and *integrity* (acting consistent with one's values) if we are "saturated" and "polymorphous"?

Gergen: I do feel that postmodern writers have been unfairly criticized for their inability to support firm moral values and their exploration of relativism.[13] For who in this century, outside the highly parochial and fanatic, are willing to declare what is good and right for all people for all time? The postmodern writers are too frequently scapegoated for the incapacities of those who criticize.

I also feel that in their explorations of relativism, multiple selves, and constructed realities, postmodern writings open important new vistas in our comprehension of morality and for practices more fully suited to living together in a world of differences. They suggest, for one, that we should cease looking to a slate of ideals, ethical foundations, a code of justice, or canons of morality in order to create "good persons" or "the just society." High-sounding words and phrases themselves require nothing in the way of subsequent action, and may be interpreted in so many ways that even the most violent persecution can be justified on the basis of the most glowing ideals. I believe we should turn away from abstract justifications and look to *ourselves*, to our relationships. For it is out of these relation-

---

But Forrest wasn't quite like that. It was more like creating an alien. What are the rules of his world? It was like creating a whole new take on the universe" (Morrison, 1994, p. 49). His intellectual limitations and resultant literalism seemed to render Forrest a kind of "master of deconstruction." Is part of Forrest's wide appeal that he is today's Everyman (and Everywoman) looking for simple truths amidst the multiphrenia? Everyone is not as sweet and open-minded as Forrest, however. Might there be the peril that too much complexity, especially if coupled with economic hard times, could generate a backlash "escape from freedom" (Fromm, 1976) of reactionary fundamentalism?

[13]See the exchange between Gergen (1994c, also 1985b) and Smith (1994), plus Comment (1995), for their (and others') responses to the dialogue.

ships that we generate the hells for ourselves that we term *unjust, oppressive, immoral,* and so on.

Hoyt: I take what you're saying as suggesting a higher moral challenge. If we give up the notion of an "ultimate truth," then we have to take full responsibility for all of our constructions and actions, *and* realize that others are just as entitled to theirs.

Gergen: Almost. Faced now with ourselves, we may then *together* ask about the kinds of practices that bring about these conditions, and the ways in which these practices might be altered. This kind of thinking has also inspired some work I am doing with Sheila McNamee [McNamee & Gergen, 1995] on what we are calling "relational responsibility." Here we are raising criticisms with the traditional view of holding individuals morally responsible for problematic actions, and trying to develop some conversational resources that might enable people to explore the forms of relatedness in which the problematic action takes place.

Hoyt: I expect that this may be related to the experience you wrote about [Gergen, 1994e, pp. 76–77] in "The Limits of Pure Critique." Let me quote at length:

At the beginning of a three-day conference, the organizers arranged a confrontation pitting radical constructivism (as represented by Ernst von Glazerfeld) against social constructionism (which I was to profess). The subsequent critiques were unsparing, the defenses unyielding, and as the audience was drawn into the debate polarization rapidly took place. Voices became agitated, critique turned ad hominem, anger and alienation mounted. As the moderator called a halt to the proceedings, I began to see the three days before me as an eternity. . . . Here [Karl] Tomm asked if von Glazerfeld and I would be willing to be publicly interviewed. Most important, would we be willing to do so *as the other?* Uneasily, we agreed. . . . Our exposure to each other did allow each of us to absorb aspects of the other—intellectual views, attitudes, values—which we now carried with us as potentials. The initial question was whether we were willing and able to give these potentials credible voice. Through an extended series of questions, carefully and sensitively addressed, Tomm was able to elicit 'the other within.' Playing the other's identity, we discussed issues of theory, views of the other, self-doubts, fears, personal relationships, feelings about the conference and so on.

The results of the procedure were striking. As both we and the audience learned, we could communicate intelligibly and sympathetically from within the other's framework. Each could give voice to the rationality of the other. Further, the binary was successfully broken. Rather than a showdown between competing epistemologies, the debate could be understood within the context of a long interpersonal history, imbricated friendships, private aspirations and doubts, the demands of public debate and so on. A new level of discussion ensued. The conference was thereafter marked by its civility of interchange; there was expression without domination, careful listening and sensitive reply. No, this did not mean a resolution of differences; the lines of difference remained clear. However, it did allow the exploration to move forward, and with the resulting emergency of new complexities, the old yearnings for victory and defeat—heroes and villains—receded from view.

When I recently asked David Epston what he would like to ask you, he called my attention to this passage and said he would ask, "Where do you think you will take such developments both in the realm of ideas and everyday life from here?" Pray tell?

Gergen: On the theoretical side, you might imagine from my earlier comments that my major concern is with expanding consciousness of relatedness. I call this "relational theory," a project that begins with *Realities and Relationships* (Gergen, 1994a), but has since expanded in several directions. Given the quotation you just cited, you can imagine that such theorizing is directed toward more practical domains—including therapy, education, organizational management, and politics. The challenge is to bring about metaphors, stories, distinctions, images, and so on that don't so much reflect what is, but create what can be. I also work with various therapists, organizational consultants, global businesses, and the like to develop practices that embody a relational perspective. With some friends, we created The Taos Institute, an institute centered in New Mexico that brings theorists and practitioners together to work on cutting-edge issues in relational process. Perhaps the most wonderful thing about this kind of work is that you never feel you are alone—fully responsible for all the ideas, plans, practices, outcomes, and so on. The work becomes lighter, more joyous, and more optimistic. Also, I find the creative potential of dialogue is just enormous.

Hoyt: The work of Michel Foucault [e.g., 1975, 1978, 1980], especially his views on the relationship of power and knowledge, has influenced many therapists working within narrative constructive frameworks. Not everyone is so impressed, however. Camille Paglia [1992, p. 174] has written: "Foucault's biggest fans are not among the majority of philosophers, historians, and sociologists, who usually perceive his glaring inadequacies of knowledge and argument, but among well-meaning but foggy humanists, who virtually never have the intellectual and scholarly preparation to critique Foucault competently. The more you know, the less you are impressed by Foucault." What do you think of Foucault's contribution, and what do you think of Paglia's dismissal?

Gergen: To pick up on an earlier theme, I don't look to Foucault or any other writer now for "the truth," nor for a perfect and well-defended logic, new set of guides, ideals, or premises for a new life. Rather, from my constructionist background, I am inclined to ask whether a given piece of writing can offer resources for the kinds of conversations in which I now find myself. If I borrow from the words, the metaphors, the logics within the writing, what happens now to my various relationships? In this sense I have found certain Foucaultian concepts very useful—as have many others. They seem to help us do things in conversations that we could less easily or not possibly do before. No, I don't find all of Foucault so useful; by contemporary American standards the writing is often opaque, incoherent, and mystifying, and his major analyses of history unjustifiable. However, in his critiques of earlier views of power, and in his emphasis on the relationship of language to power and on the effect of various professional discourses on society, for example, he has been enormously useful.

Hoyt: How about Paglia?

Gergen: Along these same lines, I don't find Paglia so very helpful. If I put her discourse into action, I am more likely to find myself in a set of conflictual and aggressive relationships. To borrow her discourse too often leads to an argumentative form of relationship in which mutual annihilation is the implicit end. Do we need more of this in our current cultural condition?

Hoyt: In "The Social Construction of Narrative Accounts," you and Mary Gergen [M. M. Gergen & Gergen, 1984; see also K. J. Gergen & Gergen, 1986, 1988; M. M. Gergen & Gergen, 1993] discuss *progressive, stabilizing,* and *regressive* narratives. You also comment [1984, p. 177] that what might look "regressive" could be a part of a forward movement ("unless the crisis is viewed as a critical integer in a progressive narrative") or a larger homeostasis. As the French say, to make an omelette you have first to break the eggs. With multiphrenia and such a complexity of competing goals, how is primacy established? What dialectic, what values guide complex, competing choices?

Gergen: Perhaps I can answer this in a way that will clarify what I was trying to say regarding value positions. It seems to me that in the Western tradition we are supposed to possess some personal logic, set of values, or well-considered aim in life that should guide us through such complex situations. Yet, it is just such a view that social constructionism calls into question. From this perspective logic, values, aims, and the like are positions in language. As language they do not require any particular form of action; they are action in themselves. And if they occur privately (what we have traditionally considered "in the mind"), nothing necessarily follows in terms of "choices" (another term heavily weighted by our psychologistic and individualistic tradition).

Further, as I have tried to stress, we might usefully see intelligible action in terms of its place within a set of relationships. In this context, rather than trying to work out a fully developed set of priorities abstracted from concrete conditions of relationship, it seems more promising from the constructionist standpoint to immerse oneself more fully within ongoing relationships. This does not mean acting only within the present moment, for one is also a participant in numerous other relationships. These relationships, too, should ideally be made salient to the ongoing process. I rather like as an illustration the actions of the unmarried pregnant adolescents interviewed in [Carol] Gilligan's [1982] *In a Different Voice*. When confronted with the difficult question of abortion, they didn't resort to abstract principles, but primarily engaged in an array of conversations—with friends, parents, the potential father, and so on.[14] From the process of relating, decisions emerged—decisions which were presumably lodged within the array of existing coordinations.[15]

Hoyt: There seem to be two opposite trends occurring simultaneously. One involves the emergence of the "relational self," the other a tendency toward greater isolation and loneliness. Do you agree? How do you understand the "relational self" and what's happening?

Gergen: There are a number of ways to go with this question; let me try only one. There is a sense in which I want to argue that all selves are relational, and always have been. (This position is part of my own attempt to create a sense of the reality of relatedness.) Unless a feral child or severely cerebrally damaged, even the isolated individual (for example, the elderly shut-in or the derelict) is immersed in otherness. At the same time, I think you are absolutely correct in your surmise that people are more physically isolated than ever before. This is part of the irony of *The*

---

[14]In fairness to Camille Paglia, in light of the earlier discussion it should be noted that in an interview (Paglia, 1995, p. 58) she, too, advocated—without abandoning her in-your-face style—that recognition be given to the legitimacy of competing views in the abortion controversy:

> The people who are pro-abortion—I hate the cowardly euphemism of pro-choice—must face what they are opposing. The left constantly identifies the pro-life advocates as misogynists and fanatics, but that doesn't represent most of those people. They are deeply religious and they truly believe that taking a life is wrong. If the left were to show respect for that position and acknowledge the moral conundrum of unwanted pregnancy, the opposition to abortion would lessen. We must acknowledge that people should be a little troubled by abortion. Not to acknowledge that this is a difficult decision is wrong. . . . You have a stronger case if you give due respect to the other side.

[15]As the well-known business negotiator Chester Karrass (1992, p. 11) observes, "The children of tomorrow *must* be good negotiators. They must be prepared to resolve differences in a civilized way; to listen; to be responsible; and to be unafraid to adjust conflicting values. The alternative in an age of rising expectations is violence." He goes on (p. 215) to give some sage marital advice: "Love, honor, and negotiate."

Saturated Self. The very technologies that bring the teeming array of images, voices, dramas, logics, and so on into our lives (e.g., television, radio, mass print, telephone, VCRs, personal computers), are also the same
technologies that allow us to exist without others' physical presence. So
we are more multiply related but more physically alone. I worry a great
deal about this trend; the consequences for society are profound. A major
interest for me now is whether we might use some of these same technologies (and especially computer networks) to generate new forms of
community.

Hoyt: The information and networking possibilities are thrilling, but I
hope "virtual reality" and "cybersex" won't replace older forms! In *We've
Had a Hundred Years of Psychotherapy and the World's Getting Worse,* James
Hillman and Michael Ventura [1992] argue that the pendulum has swung
too far toward the individual self, producing a narcissistic preoccupation,
and call for a greater identification with society. Some religious and spiritual practices also advocate connection to humanity or nature as part of a
larger sense of self. How does this fit with your idea of the relational self?

Gergen: I entirely agree with the thesis that the pendulum has swung
too far toward the individual self. A narcissistic preoccupation is only one
of the problematic consequences. I'm less positive about a solution which
requires a greater identification with society, as it suggests that I exist
separate from society. In the same way I can resonate with some spiritual,
religious, and ecological movements which generate a sense of our greater
relatedness. A great deal of my recent work explores the ways in which
we are always already constituted by relationship. As I mentioned earlier,
I try to focus on various ways in which to be a self, to have an idea, to
possess an emotion is to be acting out of and into relatedness. And as in
the case of the work with McNamee [McNamee & Gergen, 1995], we try
to generate practices of relationship (as opposed to individual) responsibility. I am also working with therapists and organizational consultants to
bring these kinds of ideas into practice, and with an artist and a film-
maker in trying to give this consciousness a visual dimension.

Hoyt: In an earlier discussion with Michael White and Gene Combs [see
Chapter 3], I promised to ask you about your remarks at the end of your
keynote speech at the Therapeutic Conversations 2 conference in Washington, D.C., when you commented that "We don't live in narratives, we
live with them," and spoke of moving "beyond stories to relatedness itself."[16] It's hard to talk about what is beyond words. At the risk of asking

[16]Gergen's (1994f) words:

> So is it right that we live in narratives? Well, the communicational view, this rela-
> tional view that I'm trying to develop here would say, "No, we don't live in them,
> we live *with* them. They are what we *do* with people. . . . " Well, if that's the case—

an oxymoronic question, would you expound on the ineffable lightness of being?

Gergen: My major aim in that conclusion was to "put language in its place."[17] That is, as we move in this constructionist and narrational direction, we sometimes fix on the words as ends in themselves. We try as therapists to generate new sense of meaning, new narratives, new constructions, as if a new set of words would "do the trick." In fact, I tend to talk that way myself at times. However, this is to miss the ultimate concern, which is relatedness itself—out of which meanings are generated. In effect, relations precede meaning.

and this is the part that interests me—is it possible that we could imagine therapy or relationships themselves as moving to the point where pure relatedness is honored before the meaning? When you move, let's say, with a client not to the point where they've got a good or better story, but *beyond* stories to relatedness itself. I tried at one place to call this a kind of "relational sublime," beyond reason. A sublime state where one is simply in an inarticulable sense of relatedness with others, with the world—not like swimming in an ocean, but more like being in the ocean and moving with all the waves, not like having a direction but moving in synchrony. A kind of inarticulable state beyond meaning where one is simply *embedded with*: that intrigues me.

[17]As Gergen (1991, p. 157) explained in *The Saturated Self*:

The case is clarified by focusing on the languages of self-construction—the words and phrases one uses to characterize the self. . . . It is impossible to sustain the traditional view of language as an outer expression of an inner reality. If language truly served as the public expression of one's private world, there would be no means by which we could understand each other. Rather, language is inherently a form of relatedness. Sense is derived only from coordinated effort among persons. One's words remain nonsense (mere sounds or markings) until supplemented by another's assent (or appropriate action). And this assent, too, remains dumb until another (or others) lend it a sense of meaning. . . . In this way, meaning is born of interdependence. And because there is no self outside a system of meaning, it may be said that relations precede and are more fundamental than self. Without relationship there is no language with which to conceptualize the emotions, thoughts, or intentions of the self.

In his Foreword to *The Handbook of Constructive Therapies*, Gergen (1998, pp. xiv-xv) elaborates:

Central to the modernist tradition is the presumption of the individual mind as the fundamental atom of society. It is the individual's capacity for independent thought upon which our democratic institutions are based; it is on the basis of the individual's capacity to love that we trust our institutions of intimacy; and it is the individual's capacity for free agency that forms the foundation for our conceptions of moral responsibility. Yet as the dialogues on constructive therapy unfold, we find the presumption of independent self-contained individuals increasingly problematic. To construct an intelligible world essentially requires relationship; indeed, out of relationship emerges the very intelligibility of the individual self. In effect, the fundamental material out of which society emerges, from which institutions of democracy, intimacy, and moral responsibility derive, is that of relational process.

However, in trying to speak about moving "beyond stories to relatedness itself" I find myself resisting clarity, wanting rather to move by intimation. This is because in the struggle to articulate a state of relatedness out of which articulation springs, you rather place walls around that state; you construct it as "this as opposed to that."[18] And in doing so relations themselves are delimited. So I look to metaphors, ambiguous concepts, or parables. In the concept of a *relational sublime*, I borrowed heavily from the Romanticist idea of a mental condition which transcends the capacity of rational comprehension [Gergen, 1996]. The Romanticists often used the term to depict a condition in which one sensed the incomprehensible scope and power of nature (and by implication, God). I rather like these images, and feel that we might develop a sense of ourselves as fully immersed in relatedness—with all humanity, all that is given—and that we might conceive of this awesome sensibility of pure relatedness (itself born of relationship) as approaching what we might mean by the domain of the spiritual.

Hoyt: We're all in this together. Thank you.

☐ References

American Psychiatric Association (1994). *Diagnostic and Statistical Manual of Mental Disorders* (4th ed.). Washington, DC: Author.

Bakhtin, M. (1981). *The Dialogic Imagination*. Austin: University of Texas Press.

Bierce, A. (1957). *The Devil's Dictionary*. New York: Sagamore Press. (Original work published 1906)

Blum, J. D. (1978). On changes in psychiatric diagnosis over time. *American Psychologist, 33,* 1017–1031.

Bruner, J. (1989). *Actual Minds, Possible Worlds*. Cambridge, MA: Harvard University Press.

Comment (1995). *American Psychologist, 50*(5), 389–394.

Coyne, J. C. (1982). A brief introduction to epistobabble. *Family Therapy Networker, 6*(4), 27–28.

Efran, J. S., & Clarfield, L. E. (1992). Constructionist therapy: Sense and nonsense. In S. McNamee & K. J. Gergen (Eds.), *Therapy as Social Construction* (pp. 200–217). Newbury Park, CA: Sage.

Ellenberger, H. F. (1970). *The Discovery of the Unconscious*. New York: Basic Books.

Foucault, M. (1975). *The Birth of the Clinic*. New York: Vintage.

Foucault, M. (1977). *Discipline and Punish: The Birth of the Prison*. New York: Pantheon.

Foucault, M. (1980). *Power/Knowledge: Selected Interviews and Other Writings, 1972–1977*. New York: Pantheon.

Freud, S. (1953). Three essays on the theory of sexuality. In J. Strachey (Ed. and Trans.), *The Standard Edition of the Complete Psychological Works of Sigmund Freud* (Vol. 7, pp. 125–243). London: Hogarth Press. (Original work published 1905)

---

[18]For discussions about how we delimit ourselves by constructing what we will *not* include within our identities, see O'Hanlon (Chapter 2, this volume), S. Gilligan (1996), and Rosenbaum and Dyckman (1996).

Fromm, E. (1976). *Escape from Freedom*. New York: Avon.

Gergen, K. J. (1985a). *Toward Transformation in Social Knowledge* (2nd ed.). Beverly Hills, CA: Sage.

Gergen, K. J. (1985b). The social constructionist movement in modern psychology. *American Psychologist, 40*, 266–275.

Gergen, K. J. (1991). *The Saturated Self: Dilemmas of Identity in Contemporary Life*. New York: Basic Books.

Gergen, K. J. (1992, May). *The Polymorphous Perversity of the Postmodern Era*. Keynote speech, Family Therapy Networker Conference, Washington, DC.

Gergen, K. J. (1993). Foreword. In S. Friedman (Ed.), *The New Language of Change: Constructive Collaboration in Psychotherapy* (pp. ix–xi). New York: Guilford Press.

Gergen, K. J. (1994a). *Realities and Relationships: Soundings in Social Construction*. Cambridge, MA: Harvard University Press.

Gergen, K. J. (1994b). Therapeutic professions and the diffusion of deficit. In K. J. Gergen, *Realities and Relationships: Soundings in Social Construction*. Cambridge, MA: Harvard University Press. (An abbreviated version appeared in *Journal of Mind and Behavior*, 1990, 11, 353–368.)

Gergen, K. J. (1994c). On taking *ourselves* seriously. *Journal of Systemic Therapies, 13*(4), 10–12.

Gergen, K. J. (1994d). Exploring the postmodern: Perils or potentials? *American Psychologist, 49*, 412–416.

Gergen, K. J. (1994e). The limits of pure critique. In H. A. Simons & M. Billig (Eds.), *After Postmodernism: Reconstructing Ideology* (pp. 58–78). Newbury Park, CA: Sage.

Gergen, K. J. (1994f, July). *Between Alienation and Deconstruction: Re-Envisioning Therapeutic Communication*. Keynote speech, Therapeutic Conversations 2 Conference, Washington, DC.

Gergen, K. J. (1996). Technology and the self: From the essential to the sublime. In D. Grodin & T. Lindlof (Eds.), *Constructing the Self in a Mediated World: Inquiries in Social Construction*. Thousand Oaks, CA: Sage.

Gergen, K. J. (1998) Foreword. In M. F. Hoyt (Ed.), *The Handbook of Constructive Therapies* (pp. xi–xv). San Francisco: Jossey-Bass.

Gergen, K. J., & Davis, K. E. (Eds.). (1985). *The Social Construction of the Person*. New York: Springer-Verlag.

Gergen, K. J., & Gergen, M. M. (Eds.). (1984). *Historical Social Psychology*. Hillsdale, NJ: Erlbaum.

Gergen, K. J., & Gergen, M. M. (1986). Narrative form and the construction of psychological science. In T. R. Sarbin (Ed.), *Narrative Psychology: The Storied Nature of Human Conduct*. New York: Praeger.

Gergen, K. J., & Gergen, M. M. (1988). Narrative and the self as relationship. In L. Berkowitz (Ed.), *Advances in Experimental Social Psychology* (Vol. 21, pp. 17–56). New York: Academic Press.

Gergen, M. M., & Gergen, K. J. (1984). The social construction of narrative accounts. In K. J. Gergen & M. M. Gergen (Eds.), *Historical Social Psychology* (pp. 173–189). Hillsdale, NJ: Erlbaum.

Gergen, M. M., & Gergen, K. J. (1993). Narratives of the gendered body in popular autobiography. In R. Josselson & A. Lieblich (Eds.), *The Narrative Study of Lives* (pp. 191–218). Newbury Park, CA: Sage.

Gilligan, C. (1982). *In a Different Voice*. Cambridge, MA: Harvard University Press.

Gilligan, S.G. (1996) The relational self: The expanding of love beyond desire. In M.F. Hoyt (Ed.), *Constructive Therapies, Volume 2* (pp. 211–237). New York: Guilford Press.

Glass, J. M. (1993). *Shattered Selves: Multiple Personality in a Postmodern World*. Ithaca, NY: Cornell University Press.

Gordon, C. & Gergen, K. J. (Eds.). (1968). *The Self in Social Interaction*. New York: Wiley.

Graumann, C. F., & Gergen, K. J. (Eds.). (1993). *Historical Dimensions of Psychological Discourse*. New York: Cambridge University Press.

Grove, D. R. (1993). Ericksonian therapy with multiple personality clients. *Journal of Family Psychotherapy, 4*(2), 13–18.

Grove, D. R., & Haley, J. (1993). *Conversations on Therapy: Popular Problems and Uncommon Solutions*. New York: Norton.

Hillman, J., & Ventura, M. (1992). *We've Had a Hundred Years of Psychotherapy and the World's Getting Worse*. New York: HarperCollins.

Hoyt, M. F. (1994a). *Constructive Therapies*. New York: Guilford Press.

Hoyt, M. F. (1994b). On the importance of keeping it simple and taking the patient seriously: A conversation with Steve de Shazer and John Weakland. In M. F. Hoyt (Ed.), *Constructive Therapies* (pp. 11–40). New York: Guilford Press.

Hoyt, M.F. (Ed.) (1996) *Constructive Therapies, Volume 2*. New York: Guilford Press.

Hoyt, M. F. (Ed.) (1998) *The Handbook of Constructive Therapies*. San Francisco: Jossey-Bass.

Hoyt, M. F., & Ordover, J. (1988). Book review of J. K. Zeig (Ed.), *The Evolution of Psychotherapy. Imagination, Cognition, and Personality, 8*(2), 181–186.

Karrass, C. L. (1992). *The Negotiating Game* (rev. ed.). New York: HarperCollins.

Kegan, R. (1994). *In Over Our Heads: The Mental Demands of Modern Life*. Cambridge, MA: Harvard University Press.

Kirk, S.A., & Kutchins, H. (1992) *The Selling of DSM: The Rhetoric of Science in Psychiatry*. Hawthorne, NY: Aldine de Gruyter.

Mahler, M., Bergman, A., & Pine, F. (1975). *The Psychological Birth of the Human Infant*. New York: Basic Books.

Masson, J. M. (1994). *Against Therapy* (rev. ed.). Monroe, ME: Common Courage Press.

Maturana, H. R., & Varela, F. J. (1987). *The Tree of Knowledge*. Boston: New Science Library.

McLuhan, M. (1964). *Understanding Media: The Extension of Man*. New York: Signet.

McNamee, S., & Gergen, K. J. (Eds.). (1992). *Therapy as Social Construction*. Newbury Park, CA: Sage.

McNamee, S., & Gergen, K. E. (1995). *Relational Responsibility*. Unpublished manuscript, University of New Hampshire.

Mead, G. H. (1934). *Mind, Self and Society*. Chicago: University of Chicago Press.

Morrison, M. (1994, August). The evolution of Tom Hanks. *Us: The Entertainment Magazine*, pp. 46–52.

Neimeyer, R. A., & Freixas, G. (1990). Constructivist contributions to psychotherapy integration. *Journal of Integrative and Eclectic Psychotherapy, 9*, 4–20.

Paglia, C. (1992). Junk bonds and corporate raiders: Academe in the hour of the wolf. In C. Paglia, *Sex, Art, and American Culture: Essays* (pp. 170–248). New York: Vintage.

Paglia, C. (1995, May). Interview. *Playboy*, pp. 51–64.

Penn, P. (1982). Circular questioning. *Family Process, 21*(3), 267–280.

Penn, P. (1985). Feed-forward: Future questions, future maps. *Family Process, 24*(3), 299–310.

Penn, P., & Frankfurt, M. (1994). Creating a participant text: Writing, multiple voices, narrative multiplicity. *Family Process, 33*(3), 217–231.

Rosenbaum, R., & Dyckman, J. (1996) No self? No problem! Actualizing empty self in psychotherapy. In M. F. Hoyt (Ed.), *Constructive Therapies, Volume 2* (pp. 238–274). New York: Guilford Press.

Schwarz, R.A. (1998) From "either-or" to "both-and": Treating dissociative disorders collaboratively. In M. F. Hoyt (Ed.), *The Handbook of Constructive Therapies* (pp. 428–448). San Francisco: Jossey-Bass.

Semin, G., & Gergen, K. J. (Eds.). (1990). *Everyday Understanding: Social and Scientific Implications*. Newbury Park, CA: Sage.

Shotter, J., & Gergen, K. J. (Eds.). (1989). *Texts of Identity*. Newbury Park, CA: Sage.

Singer, J. A., & Salovey, P. (1993). *The Remembered Self: Emotion and Memory in Personality*. New York: Free Press.

Smith, M. B. (1994). Selfhood at risk: Postmodern perils and the perils of postmodernism. *American Psychologist, 49*, 405–411.

Spiegel, D., & McHugh, P. (1995). The pros and cons of dissociative identity (multiple personality) disorder. *Journal of Practical Psychiatry and Behavioral Health, 1*(13), 158–166.

Stern, D. N. (1985). *The Interpersonal World of the Infant*. New York: Basic Books.

Suryani, L. K., & Jensen, G. D. (1993). *Trance and Possession in Bali: A Window on Western Multiple Personality Disorder, Possession, and Suicide*. Oxford, England: Oxford University Press.

Tomm, K. (1990). A critique of the DSM. *Dulwich Centre Newsletter, 2*(3), 5–8.

Vygotsky, L. S. (1986). *Thought and Language* (rev. ed.). Cambridge, MA: MIT Press.

Watzlawick, P. (1976). *How Real Is Real?* New York: Random House.

Watzlawick, P. (Ed.). (1984). *The Invented Reality: How Do We Know What We Believe We Know?* New York: Norton.

Wertsch, J. V. (Ed.). (1985). *Vygotsky and the Social Formation of Mind*. Cambridge, MA: Harvard University Press.

Wertsch, J. V. (1991). *Voices of the Mind: A Sociocultural Approach to Mediated Action*. Cambridge, MA: Harvard University Press.

West, C. (1994). *Race Matters*. New York: Vintage.

Wylie, M. S. (1995). Diagnosing for dollars? *Family Therapy Networker, 19*(3), 22–33.

CHAPTER

About Constructivism (or, If Four Colleagues Talked in New York, Would Anyone Hear It?): A Conversation With Scott Miller, Barbara Held, and William Matthews

What you've got here, really, are two realities, one of immediate artistic appearance and one of underlying scientific explanation, and they don't match and they don't fit and they don't really have much of anything to do with one another. That's quite a situation. You might say there's a little problem here."
—Robert M. Pirsig, *Zen and the Art of Motorcycle Maintenance* (1974, p. 63)

At the August 1998 "Brief Therapy: Lasting Impressions" Conference in New York City sponsored by the Milton H. Erickson Foundation, Scott Miller and I were scheduled to have an hour-long public dialogue on "Constructivism." We invited Barbara Held and William Matthews, Jr., to join us, and also invited audience participation.

Scott Miller, a co-founder of the Institute for the Study of Therapeutic Change (based in Chicago, Illinois), is the co-author of *Working with the Problem-Drinker: A Solution-Focused Approach* (Berg & Miller, 1992), *The Miracle Method: A Radically New Approach to Problem Drinking* (Miller & Berg,

Reprinted, with changes, from the *Journal of Systemic Therapies*, 2000, 19(4), pp. 76–92. Used with permission.

1995), *Escape from Babel: Toward a Unifying Language of Psychotherapy Prac-tice* (Miller et al., 1997), *Psychotherapy with "Impossible" Cases: Efficient and Effective Treatment of Therapy Veterans* (Duncan et al., 1997), and *The Heroic Client: Doing Client-Directed, Outcome-Oriented Therapy* (Duncan & Miller, 2000), and the co-editor of *Handbook of Solution-Focused Brief Therapy* (Miller et al., 1996) and *The Heart and Soul of Change: What Works in Therapy* (Hubble et al., 1999). Barbara Held, an outspoken critic of narrative constructivist approaches and the author of *Back to Reality: A Critique of Postmodern Theory in Psychotherapy* (1995) as well as the tongue-in-cheek *Stop Smiling Start Kvetching: A 5-Step Guide to Creative Complaining* (1999), is the Barry N. Wish Professor of Psychology at Bowdoin College in Brunswick, Maine. Bill Matthews, long associated with Ericksonian approaches to psychotherapy and the co-editor of the *Current Thinking and Research in Brief Therapy* se-ries, is Professor and Director of the School Psychology and Counselor Education Program at the University of Massachusetts in Amherst.

Hoyt: We're going to construct the discussion as we go, I believe. We really invite people to join in. I wanted to start, just to throw something out to get us going, with two jokes or quips, if you will. You've probably all heard them before, but in the event somebody has not, please don't shout out the punch line. I think the issues that I want to focus on fall somewhere between these two. The first is the famous story about the three baseball umpires. They're disputing their acumen, who's the best umpire. The first umpire says, "Well, I call 'em the way I see 'em"—he's the honest, ethical fellow. The second one says, "That's good, but I call 'em the way they are"—he's the objectivist, the accurate, the realist. And the third umpire listens and finally he says, "They ain't nothin' until I call 'em!" He is in some ways the constructivist—by calling them they will somehow come into being. I have some problems with that even though I have quoted it in book chapters [see Hoyt, 1996a, p. 315]. The other is the famous joke about "Sorry, but my karma ran over your dogma." My path, my way ran over your belief system, if you will, your dogma. (Sorry if anyone's a dog lover—I am.) There was a very interesting discussion yesterday that Bill [Matthews, 1998] got into about realism and anti-realism. My understanding of constuctivism, the way I think about it, is that people are meaning makers and they are constructing their social reality. There *is* an external reality, there is an objective physical reality and there are social forces outside of us, but there's no knowing without the knower; in some way we're taking it in, we're processing it. So I've been concerned, as I've heard discussions about constructivism, that some people have had the idea that the constructivists think "it's all in your mind" or "it's just the way you look at it" or "it's just a language game." The people that I know who practice constructivist approaches are very concerned about the real effects that the stories have on peoples' lives; it's not just trying to change your mind or change your opinion. So I wanted to throw that out and just go from there.

Miller: My name is Scott Miller. I live and work in Chicago. My practice, which is done *pro bono*, is primarily oriented toward traditionally under-served clients: chronically mentally-ill folks, homeless people, and work-ing-class poor clients; and I have sort of this interest in constructivist *prac-tice* [see Miller, Duncan & Hubble, 1997]. I am the token intellectually challenged person on the panel today. When I listen to de Shazer speak on the one side about constructivist thought, I'm always amazed and struck by the depth of that thinking. Then when I listen to Barbara Held and read her fabulous, I think almost exposé, *Back to Reality* [Held, 1995] a couple years back, I was impressed by that. What ends up happening to me is I go back to my practice and I say, 'So what can I do different as a result of this thinking?' So, from a constructivist perspective what I've been interested in is listening and watching these people work—how do they speak *with* their clients? What is it that they *do* with their clients that may be different from me (who I think straddles the fence between a constructivist and an empiricist or reality-based practitioner)? And when it gets too far out there in the ozone, I typically glaze over, feel bad about my intellectual capabilities, and then go back to whatever it is that I nor-mally do in my clinical work. So I'm here to chat about all those things.

Held: I don't want to make a statement because I know in reality I'm capable of rambling on, being a college professor (at Bowdoin College on the coast of Maine, which makes me just a simple country psychologist). I've written at length about this stuff. So I guess my opening statement is I would like to know what people in the audience would like to know to get a discussion going, rather than just assume that whatever thoughts I have are of interest. So I'm going to leave my unprepared opening state-ment at that.

Matthews: I do want to hear what folks are thinking about, but Scott's a good example—everything he said is an empirically testable proposi-tion. He says, 'Well, I look at what de Shazer did, I observe what he does, and then I say that could effect the way I work, then I go and do what de Shazer did and that works for me or it doesn't.' It works for him because he gets change with a client or he doesn't get change with a client. And that is all empirically based. I guess my opening statement is that oftentimes within constructivism, people confuse the notion that scientific theories are constructed knowledge. No scientist would disagree with that notion. It's an absolutely true statement. However, it is constructed and constrained by reality, i.e., empirical observation. That's how science works. So, every day we see what looks to us like the sun rises and sets. Well, we know that it doesn't, and to say that some superstition says, 'Well, it does'—no one would accept that belief system. Some people just do not have the scientific basis for evaluating certain belief systems. And that's what I want to be about when we talk about this issue or when we talk about science: *How do we evaluate what we know?* If we take the position that knowledge is only constructed, with an absence of empirical verification, then there is no way to distinguish superstition from objective reality.

Hoyt: If we accept the notion that there is a *there* there—that there is an outside reality—what other criticism do you have of constructivism?

Matthews: That would be the key one for me, what I'm interested in. I'm a trained scientist and I am an active scientist. I do research. For 20 some-odd years I did clinical work—I don't do so much of that anymore. So my only issue, particularly as trained in Ericksonian work [see Matthews, 1990, 1997; Matthews, Lankton & Lankton, 1993] is you make a claim, how do you know that that claim is valid? How do you know what it is that you're saying is true? In other words, indirect suggestion is a better way in hypnosis supposedly to get clients to respond and make certain responses. So that's an empirically-testable proposition.

Hoyt: I think you conflated two terms together. You said that it's con-strained by *observation* and *reality*. I think those are separate. They're cer-tainly related, there is the reality, but then there's the lens through which we observe the reality. The constructivists are not saying there isn't a reality, but they're saying . . .

Matthews: . . . well, radical constructivists do. Gergen says that there's no reality, Michael White says there is no objective reality; then you have certain constructivists like von Glaserfeld [1984] that do talk about, 'Well, there is a reality but it's not knowable.' So ultimately they're in the same category of being anti-realists. And that begs the question of how can you know it's not knowable? It's an empirical question.

Miller: For me, I bring it back to the practical, what I actually do. I can tell you the constructivist thinkers have helped me in a very specific, measurable way. It's helped me pay attention to where our professional discourse has excluded certain populations of people in our clinical work. I feel very much informed by constructivist dialogue about work with people who have not been part of the empirical studies about psycho-therapy thus far. So under-privileged populations, their voice has not been included. It's when the idea is taken one step further that I stumble. Prac-tically speaking, I find constructivism very useful for opening my eyes, creating possibilities, but when it gets to the level of 'Is it real, is it not?' I sort of glaze over and lose touch with reality—whatever that is!

Held: I'd like to respond. I'm now going to contradict my opening state-ment and say some things. I want to respond to Michael. Having written a book about this stuff and having read more than I ever thought I would—

and I'm going to agree with Bill on this—I have not yet read anything in the constructivist /social constructionist/postmodernist (these are not identical but there's great overlap) camp that takes a realist position. Now, the position Michael takes, that there is a *there* there, has been taken in the constructivist literature. And I'm perfectly willing to admit that there may be something out there I haven't read because I don't have time to read it all and I'm not going to pretend I have. The book *[Back to Reality]* was written in '95 and I have continued to read since then. Bill alluded to what I call a *more radical* and a *less radical* anti-realism. The more radical anti-realism—and Ken Gergen does typify this—I find more in the social constructionist camp than the constructivist camp. Social constructionists argue that we socially and actively construct reality in language. They sometimes say that language itself is the only reality, there is no extra (that is, outside of language) reality to which our language refers: there is no *there* there. That I call the more radical form of anti-realism because you first have an epistemological anti-realism, meaning in terms of the knower and knowing, the knower can never have access to a reality independent of the knower's mind, language, or culture because it ain't there: it's *constituted* (that's their favorite word, *constituted*) in language by the knower. So we literally—and I think this is what Bill was also saying—make the reality that is known. We bring it into being as we speak in our discursive context. And nothing about anything out there constrains our discourse. This is not only an *epistemological* anti-realism (meaning the knower cannot know any mind-independent or knower-independent reality), it is also an *ontological* or *metaphysical* anti-realism (meaning there *is* nothing out there beyond the knower's constructions).

So you have two forms of anti-realism in the radical camp. The less radical, I think a more moderate, anti-realism is when Michael [Hoyt] says there is a reality out there but our lens gets between us and it. When I read radical social constructionists—and maybe Michael knows of some that I don't know of yet (and I'll concede that)—they say there isn't a mind-independent reality out there. But the less radical anti-realists say our knowing processes, our language, our theory, our context, our culture, our values, our discourses always stand between the knower and the independent reality to be known, so that the knower cannot have access to the thing in itself as it is independent of the knower—so there is always relativism, bias, or subjectivity built into the knowing process. Anti-realism basically means whether there is or is not an independent reality out there, whether you're in the more or less radical camp, you cannot get at the thing in itself, the objective reality, as it is independent of your knowing process, and I've just never seen anything in the constructivist writing that supports that you can to any extent.

Hoyt: I'll give you two references.

Held: Okay, good.

Hoyt: In *The Handbook of Constructive Therapies* that I edited, I would suggest you read the interview that I did with Paul Watzlawick when he responded [Watzlawick & Hoyt, 1998, pp. 189-190; see Chapter 6, p. 151 this volume] to a quotation from your book that I read.[1] That would be one. The second is in the book I edited, *Constructive Therapies, Volume 2* . I did an interview with Ken Gergen and in the last couple of pages [Hoyt, 1996, p. 365; see Chapter 8, pp. 201–202 this volume] Ken talks about *relational sublime* in the sense of going past knowing to having a sense of directly connecting with other people. What he seems to be recognizing is that there's a reality that's beyond language.

Held: Oh good.[2]

Matthews: Plus, he recognizes that in his daily life or else he wouldn't . . .

---

[1] As reported in Chapter 6, I had presented Watzlawick with the following quotation from Held (1995, p. 173): "Here I draw the reader's attention to what I consider a point of fundamental importance in understanding the confusion generated by the postmodern emphasis on the linguistic, and the postmodern linking of linguistic entities (including theories/ propositions/stories/narratives/discourses) with antirealism. It is this: *All theories are constructions* [emphasis in original]. . . . But then to say, as social constructionists/ postmodernists say, that those constructed theories are the *only* reality we have—that is, that reality itself, or knowable reality itself, is *only* a "social construction" (because we supposedly have no direct, theoretically unmediated access or even an indirect, theoretically mediated access to any reality that is independent of the knower/knower's theory)— is to confuse two things: (a)the linguistic status of the theory itself with (b)the (extralinguistic or extratheoretic) reality that the theory is attempting to approximate indirectly." Watzlawick's reply: "Regarding the last two lines of the previous quotation from Held: Constructivism does not 'confuse two things'—it makes a clear distinction between reality of the *first order* (as conveyed to us by our sense organs in terms of perceptions), and reality of the *second order* (that is, the meaning, significance, and value that every one of us inevitably attributes to the first-order reality—which remains totally subjective, unprovable, and therefore the cause of human conflict and misunderstandings)."

[2] [Held adds:] In earlier quotations that follow, Watzlawick appears to take the more radical antirealist position that there *is* no independent reality to be known (ontological antirealism) and thus we cannot *know* any independent reality (epistemological antirealism). The scare quotes around the words "thing" and "out there" are noteworthy: "On reflection it becomes obvious that anything is real only to the extent that it conforms to a *definition* of reality—and those definitions are legion. To employ a useful oversimplification: real *is* what a sufficiently large number of people have agreed to *call* real—except that this fact is usually forgotten; the agreed-upon definition is reified (that is, made into a 'thing' in its own right) and is eventually experienced as that objective reality 'out there'. . . . This process of first 'creating' a reality and then 'forgetting' that it is our own creation and experiencing it as totally independent from ourselves was already known to Kant and Schopenhauer" (Watzlawick, Weakland & Fisch, 1974, p. 96, emphasis in original); and "Language does not so much *reflect* reality as *create* it" (Watzlawick, 1978, p. 16). If, in the new quotation given by Hoyt, Watzlawick is saying that there *is* a mind-independent reality (the so-called "first order") but we don't *know* it as it exists, he is adopting a less radical form of antirealism. If, by contrast, he is saying that there is a mind-independent reality, and we know/ perceive it *as it is, before* we add to it our interpreations/meanings (the so-called "second order"), then he has indeed moved into a more radically realist position, in which case I rejoice.

Hoyt: . . . or he wouldn't get on any planes.

Matthews: Yeah, he wouldn't get on any planes, and I don't want to fly with a guy or a woman who's flying the plane who's socially constructing the data from the altimeter or those sorts of things.

Hoyt: But that's the difference between physical reality and social construction—a lot is opinion and thought and view. Where would you put things like imagination, self-fulfilling prophecy, vision, the idea that sometimes we'll bring some thought into mind and act on that thought, and then change the reality? I know the word *reality* is in there, Barbara.

Held: Good.

Hoyt: Maybe I should take the word *constructivism* out and put the word *psychology* in. I've used the term *constructivist* simply to mean *psychological,* if it's boiled down.

Matthews: That's not how the word is typically used by constructivist thinkers. So you're using it in an idiosyncratic way, which I understand and I appreciate, but that's not how constructivist thinkers use the term.

Hoyt: Well, some constructivist thinkers. But where would *imagination* and all those ideas go?

Matthews: Let me answer that or open that up in a minute, but one question that I wanted to throw out before we get to that is how do we come to think this way? How did this emerge? You look for certain times and contexts in human history. There was a time in the early '20s, when Einstein's work was just coming to be, it was on the heels of World War I which was an unbelievable devastation for Europe and a failure of science and technology to protect humankind from being devastated. So the pendulum starts to swing. The Enlightenment and science and developments in science in the 19th century had failed miserably and, as a result of World War I, then there's a context for certain thinkers to begin to emerge to question how is science a failure? Gross and Levitt [1994] make this point in their book, *Higher Superstition.* So a question for me is how did this thinking come to be at a given point and time. We look at the issue of technology and science now and it's under attack, and I think if you look at scientists and you look at post-modernists and you gave them personality inventories, my prediction would be that you would see the postmodernist thinkers would be more tender-minded, using that personality dimension, than the scientists.

Audience Member #1: That's a constructivist argument.

Matthews: No, it's a scientifically-based argument.

Audience Member #1: If I understand you correctly, there's something in the social contexts that points to why these ideas arise at certain points in time and that could be said to be a constructivist argument or at least that was what some of the constructivists argue, that social forces create a context that makes possible certain ideas.

Hoyt: Like paradigm shifts.

Audience Member #1: Yes, yes. So what confuses me in the debate is first that, I listened to you yesterday [Matthews, 1998] and thought that I liked the questions, but your answers bring me in the position where I feel very uncomfortable because I have to make a choice—either be a realist or something called an anti-realist. My clinical experience is that I always negotiate these different positions, and I sort of try to find a way of getting out of making the either/or choice, to sort of live in this tension. So you say that constructivists use realist arguments and yesterday also I felt you used constructivist arguments.

Matthews: Science is a constructed process, absolutely.

Audience Member #1: Yes, so to get further in the discussion, to me it would be good if I had not to make this choice. One problem that I think that we should look at, the people who are interested in constructivist ideas, is this idea that reality is constructed through language. One way of understanding post-modernism, as I understand it, is that they say you shouldn't have one start point. For instance, essence or . . . I don't know the English word for it.

Held: *Essentialism.*

Audience Member #1: Yes, and the problem for me with Ken Gergen is that he turns language into sort of an essentialism. The essential start point. So he ends up being what he criticizes. I think the interesting part, for instance, with deconstruction and Derrida, to me it seems that he is trying to find a way to live in this tension without ending up in this war. The reason I got interested in constructivism was for empirical reasons because I felt that empirical science couldn't help me in my practice. That was a practical empirical result I was experiencing. Now the pendulum has gone back. I think at least, we come from another country, I come from Norway and I see now that the pendulum is going towards empirical signs.

Audience Member #2: Can I add something to that since I'm also from Norway. I think that the idea, 'Is it right or is it wrong?'—I also went to your talk yesterday—some people can be engaged in that. That's okay. But see what a big influence it has on practice and how people relate to each other from this idea—and we see this in our milieu, from being more in the brief therapy field and now going into the family therapy field and maybe trying to bridge those two fields. (I think that to ask questions that have a much bigger meaning to me than this is to read the Bible in a constructive way.) But now, going back from that was when Maturana said that reality is made from enough people that have power.

The constructivist view has made it so much better and so much more challenging and so many more questions to ask in therapy. So I think it is a very central thing.

Hoyt: This goes back to the three umpires joke that I began this discussion with: the one that says "They ain't nothin' until I call it." I think there's a difference in my mind between discourse—how we talk about it, call it, bring it into language— versus reality. For a long time people did not talk about racism and child sexual abuse and all sorts of terrible things. That doesn't mean they didn't go on. They were submerged or unspeakable in some way, but I think we make a mistake if we take the idea that only language brings things into reality.

Held: I'd like to respond to that, too. I think, if I'm understanding you and you correctly, you're saying, 'You know, there's something in this thing that liberates my practice or helps me.' I tried to analyze that, in fact I organized my book *Back to Reality* around the question *why* because I've been saying for a long time—and I agree with Bill—all knowers construct knowledge claims in language or in other forms of symbolic activity. That's not postmodernist, that's modern science. No scientist would argue that they don't actively construct, and I think the active part is a big component of the word constructivism. I think the word *construct* is a culprit . . .

Miller: . . . right.

Held: . . . it has so many different meanings and I think it's never quite clear what meaning is used in any context. The question in terms of realism and anti-realism, and on this part I'll be brief, is do you think your constructed discourse gets at (to some extent) an extra-linguistic or mind-independent reality, or do you think you never have any access to it whatsoever? Let that pass for now. Why is the psychotherapy world so captivated by this? Well, he's right. Psychology is important, it is real, we have subjective processes—even to say that is an objective truth claim. I thoroughly agree with the constructivists/postmodernists that the way we think and talk determines the options we see and the actions we take. That's not postmodern.

Miller: No.

Held: Now why is this stuff going on? Here's my thesis [see Held, 1995, 1998, 1999]. I think a core problem of psychotherapy is how to get from *generality* to *particularity*. I think the scientific research has not done a good job of addressing the real realities clinicians face, which are always steeped in the particularities of every case. Particularities, I would add, that we must get hold of as realistically as possible. Even if your client's psychological experience is delusional, the clinician should try as hard as possible, in my opinion, to get the reality of that experience as objectively as possible without imposing his or her own stuff as much as possible—knowing we clinicians have psychology, too, and that we can never ever get it 100 percent right. But I think there's a moral imperative to try, and I worry that this anti-realist discourse gives lazy license not to strive to do that. That's my personal concern. I went through a whole bunch of cynical reasons for this stuff, like psychotherapy is a really trendy field and deconstruction is trendy, except it's now passé in lit-crit. There are cynical reasons, but I think there's a more substantive reason and that is how do you get from generality to particularity, and I think science has not done it for us as clinicians. So here comes a doctrine that says—and I'm not accusing all constructivists of saying this, although some radical feminist postmodernists have—'Hey, folks, science is just the patriarchal hegemonic discourse. There's no truth in it, it's a power move by the white patriarchy.' I think this goes to what you were saying, that who's in power gets to determine the discourse. If you say there is no truth, then it legitimates freeing the therapist from having to—and I'll use a constructivist term—*impose* on clients any particular predetermined theory or discourse, and then you can stay with the particularities of the patient, of the case in front of you. And I think there's some good that comes out of that, because there are two mistakes you can make. One is you can come with your theoretical baggage and impose on patients problems they didn't come in with and make them sicker . . .

Miller: . . . like psychoanalysis.

Held: . . . but also you can not have a knowledge base that might help you see things—so we're between a rock and a hard place on this. So, in my analysis, what I conclude when I read, is that there's all this realism/anti-realism emphasis when a goal, at least as I perceive it, is how to get at *particularity*. Now, of course, if you have no generality, you don't have a system you're working with. Yesterday, Bill [Matthews, 1998] put up on a slide my very crude three-part generic model (of therapy): descriptions of problems, theories about how you get them, theories with methods of how you resolve them. What I see going on in this camp is they're trying to eliminate all predetermined content. All predetermined descriptions and causes of problems—get rid of *DSM*, get rid of personality theory—and just have a method, that is, work with the narrative, that lets you help someone see their life differently so they can have new options. That means you work with a more minimalist or incomplete system of therapy. The question is, does that lead to better therapy?—and that is an empirical question.

But more to the point that I want to make, there is nothing in what I call an anti-systematic aspiration—that is, the aspiration not to impose predetermined systems of therapy—that necessitates anti-realism, which is the prevailing meaning of the term *constructivism* as at least I have found it . . .

Miller: . . . right.

Held: . . . in the literature. All it means is try not to come in with a predetermined idea of problems. I think this is impossible, by the way, but this is I think the goal. Try not to come in with predetermined theories of problem causation. But here's my claim: If you do that, you need more realism, not less, because then you have to pay even more careful attention to the unique realities of the patient's subjective experience and objective facts of their life than if you have some theory to guide you.

One other thing and then I'll try to shut up. I've thought long and hard about this. I wrote a paper about this in 1992 and I'm still not satisfied with my analysis, but it seems to me it's very hard to have a method of therapy that doesn't have at least implicit within it some predetermined idea of what the problem is and what are its causes, because even to say 'the method is deconstruct the patient's text or give them a new narrative' implies that you think the problem is in the way they're linguistically constructing their experience. It's a very general implicit notion, so there's lots of wiggle room for the particularities compared to traditional, conventional, complete systems of therapy, and I haven't completely worked that out yet.[3] Now I'll shut up.

---

[3] In her article, "How Brief Therapy Got Postmodern, or Where's the Brief?" Held (1999) begins (p. 135) by quoting Jay Haley's (1973, pp. 17-18) definition of *strategic therapy* ("Therapy can be called strategic if the clinician initiates what happens during therapy and designs a particular approach for each problem. . . . Strategic therapy is not a particular approach or theory but a name for those types of therapy where the therapist takes responsibility for directly influencing people") and then goes on (p. 136): "Champion of brief therapy Michael Hoyt, at the Fifth International Congress on Ericksonian Approaches to Hypnosis and Psychotherapy [see Chapter 1, this volume], asked brief strategic therapy giants John Weakland and Steve de Shazer, 'What do you think is the essence of being a brief therapist?'" She goes on (p. 136-137) to quote from their responses and then summarizes: "Following are the objectives that I found expressed by them in their own answers to Hoyt's questions:

1. Brief therapists see and treat each and every case as unique or particular (Haley, Weakland, de Shazer).
2. Brief therapists are careful observers (Weakland) who listen to (Weakland, de Shazer), are curious about (Weakland), and are acutely sensitive to their clients (Haley).
3. Brief therapists omit the general, predetermined theoretical constructs (i.e., those determined *prior* to any particular therapy case; hence the term "predetermined") that other therapists rely upon to guide their interventions—for instance, irrational thoughts in cognitive therapy, cross-generational coalitions in structural family therapy, weak defenses in psychoanalysis, poor self-concept in humanistic therapy. Brief therapists avoid such predetermined theory, which allows them to simplify therapy (Haley, Weakland, de Shazer).
4. Brief therapists are active; they directly influence the client (Haley).

Audience Member #3: So how do you create a method that's not applied, because we don't stand over here watching ourselves, how do you create a method that's not applied but practiced . . .

Held: You mean practiced in therapy?

Audience Member #3: In therapy, yes, so the approach is more cultural as opposed to scientific and by cultural I don't mean hippy-dippy or ignoring the substantial pain and profound . . .

Hoyt: . . . you mean person-made?

Audience Member #3: Yes, that's created by the people creating the therapy: the therapist and the client together, and it seems to me that that means giving up epistemology which doesn't mean that there's not a huge institution of knowing . . .

Matthews: You can't give up epistemology. As Gregory Bateson [1972, 1979] said, you have epistemology—either you're consciously aware of it or you're not. You cannot not have a way of knowing the world.

Audience Member #4: It seems that some ways of knowing appear to work out better than others.

Matthews: That's right.

Miller: We look around and it seems that some cultures are doing quite well. Now, by my standards, of course, I think the people are happy here, getting enough to eat, or whatever.

Matthews: They're doing well because they have evolutionary adaptability and, therefore, they're giving the genes to the next generation.

Audience Member #4: Right, if that's the point which we're assuming . . .

Matthews: . . . It's ultimately the point.

Audience Member #4: Well, we're assuming it's ultimately the point. I operate on the notion that, 'Yeah, I think that's ultimately the point' and I also don't know if that's ultimately the point. I find that operating on that notion seems to work out well for me.

Matthews: Yes, and there is a lot of scientific data. Science is not an absolute; that's reserved for religion. But the scientific approach is to say, 'Our data says to this point that . . . '

Audience Member #4: Yeah, and I think it's actually, '*My* data says . . . "

Notice that there is good agreement among our three leaders about the first three defining objectives of brief therapy. Objective 4 eventually split the brief therapy movement over the question of whether brief therapists should take a relational/collaborative/nonimpositional stance instead of the hierarchical/interventionist/directive/manipulative/strategic stance they started out with. . . . "

and if you agree, then it's, '*Our* data says . . . ' But it's not actually *our* data. I think it's *your* data, your assessment of your data comes out similar to my assessment of my data. The use of the word empirical . . .

Hoyt: You co-construct it.

Matthews: It's verifiable, testable observation. That's how we use it in science.

Audience Member #4: That's how *you* use it.

Matthews: That's how scientists use it.

Audience Member #4: No, that's how *you* use it as a scientist.

Matthews: That's the standard way scientists use it. You ask any scientist, whether they're a physicist or a psychologist, that's what they will say, that science involves refutability.

Audience Member #4: Have you done that experiment, where you've asked all scientists that question?

Matthews: Well, that's an empirical question, that's a good point.

Hoyt: That hasn't been done with all scientists, but you ought to take a look at the interesting book by John Horgen [1996] called *The End of Science,* where you've got lots of Nobel Prize winners and men and women of science and you see them struggling. Some of them get it that they're working within a paradigm, looking through lenses, and others think, 'No, we're working on the hard wiring of the universe—The Reality.' There's tension—it raises all the religious questions of what is meaning? what is reality? all those sorts of things.

Miller: Listening to the discussion, this is sort of where I start the glaze-out process. Ultimately, the meaning of an idea is in its use. So, at least what constructivist thinking does for me, once again, it seems to open up some possibilities that my original scientific training didn't do—to play with language in a way my clients do, to challenge me to use new perspectives. And, in that respect, I feel challenged by constructivist discourse. I challenge my own presuppositions that I thought were based on a good sampling of the data or my review of the data. In that respect, I think the scientists had it coming, that there's now something at the edge of science pushing and challenging us to clarify what our meanings are and to actually stand up and ask what do the data say. In that respect, as somebody who meets clients every day, I find that very useful. I think you can do that same thing scientifically. It's when it goes one step beyond that and we start talking about what really is or is not out there that I sort of lose touch with reality. I tend to align a little bit more with William James [1890], more with how an idea is used is what it means.

Hoyt: Didn't William James say the major discovery of the century is if a person changes his attitude it will change his life?

Miller: Yes.

Hoyt: To me that was constructivism, if you will, or whatever term we're using instead of it: *psychology, mediated subjectivity.*

Matthews: Attitude and beliefs are only indirectly measurable. And, by the way, we know from the literature that changing attitude does not necessarily change behavior.

Held: Do you think changing your life changes your attitude? That's the old chicken-and-egg question. Social psychologists have been working on this a long time. It's certainly in the psychotherapy literature, the debate between the behaviorists and psychoanalysts: Do you change someone's behavior first and then the way they think and feel changes, or do you change the thoughts, feelings, perceptions first and then the behavior?

Audience Member #3: I'm asking the question, do you think the person as a changer of his or her life—the changing of life-conditions, creating a new play, subjectivity, give it whatever terminology you want—do you think those changes help people to create new emotionality?

Hoyt: I think it's reflexive—we change what we do in our head, that changes our behavior and that changes the world and the world affects us and we effect the world.

Audience Member #3: So you don't think we change the world and that changes . . .

Held: Could you give an example of what you mean?

Audience Member #3: Yeah. So people come to me, I've been practicing for 20 years now. I practice a postmodern approach . . .

Matthews: How do you know it works or not?

Audience Member #3: Then we get into a whole dialogue about how do you decide what works or who says if it's empirically tested or not; but people say it does, they come back.

Matthews: So you have some empirical data.

Audience Member #3: They come back. So people come and they say, 'I'm terribly depressed . . . '

Hoyt: . . . may I interrupt a second? I want to hear your example, but Steve de Shazer [1998] yesterday talked about the importance of outcome, Michael White (whose work I'm somewhat familiar with) talks constantly about the real consequences in people's lives [see Chapters 3 and 12, this volume]. I don't recognize in this discussion the practice of any of the people that we're supposedly talking about. As clinicians, we're all interested in outcomes, not just spinning a yarn or getting a different thought.

Audience Member #3: So are our clients.

Matthews: Let her finish her example.

Audience Member #3: Yeah. People come in and they say they're terribly depressed and they have a deeply held belief that they have to change how they feel before they can change their practice, their activity, and there's a whole set of other beliefs that go with that, such as their feelings are located somewhere inside them and they have to get them out and so on and so forth. What if those feelings aren't located inside them and what if the depression is the activity that they're engaging in? And if they change their activity, they can produce, create, change, have new feelings? Instead of the other way around.

Matthews: Everything you're saying is always based on empirical observation. The person has shown depressed behavior and the person was saying (and this would happen with Erickson's work), 'I've got to figure out why I feel depressed, how I became depressed, and you've got to help me understand this before I can change.' Erickson would go 'Huh-huh' and then he would get them to say, 'We'll talk about that next week,' and he would say, 'But before next session, I want you to go do this, this, and this' and get them to do behaviors. And then the person would come in (at least as Erickson reported it) and show changed behavior and then end up reporting less feelings about depression. But the point is, either way, whether you believe feelings change behavior or behavior changes feelings, that it's an empirical question. By the way, there's a fair amount of research about that.

Held: There's 50 years of it. There's nothing postmodern about it.

Audience Member #3: Unless you give up the conception of behavior. Isn't *behavior* another term that's borrowed from the natural science paradigm?

Hoyt: This is sort of the Marx/Freud debate: Does existence determine consciousness or does consciousness determine existence? Which goes first? It seems like they interact, or perhaps are part of a larger unity.

Matthews: There's a confusion of if you have data, how that data is interpreted. Refutability is the essence of science, whether it's hard science or social science, but most social scientists are not trained in the notion of refutability. The scientific method is completely entrenched with hard scientists and although they fight and may want to kill each other, they accept the notion of refutability, but it is not in the social sciences. If you ask any hard scientist, they go, 'How do you guys do what you do?' Because there's so many variables I can't control them all. I know if I can get to see a star wobbling I'm going to infer the existence of a black hole and gravitational pull. I can't see the black hole, so I'm going to infer it indirectly. So there's nothing postmodern with anything that you said and no one will deny culture is the context.

Held: I want to respond to this. As I said at the outset, modernist therapies have always worked to co-construct a new way of understanding, a
new way of being, a new way of thinking, a new way of acting that will
have ramifications. The fact that there's some cultural context that drives
that doesn't require anti-realism in the postmodern or constructivist sense.
What I'm saying to you is that I agree with everything that you're saying.

I want to pose a question to you. So your client comes in and you're
thinking to yourself, 'You know, let's make a new life and see what happens to this depression.' Let's try to get them to be a different way in the
world and that different way of being will have ramifications for relationships and the way things go and, lo and behold, great! they come back
not depressed. I have no problem, I mean that's not inconsistent with
what I'm saying. Here's my question for you: What is the stuff that you
use to co-construct with the client the new way of thinking and being? I
think if you use a minimalist or incomplete system that tries not to impose a lot of predetermined stuff, you have to pay very close attention to
the realities of that patient's life, including the subjective realities, because you've got to work with those, and if you ignore that you're going
to lose the patient—and that's an objective truth claim that I'm happy to
make.

Matthews: Right.

Held: So, I think you wouldn't co-construct just any narrative. When I
look at the tapes of narrative therapists, it looks to me like traditional
insight therapy with some behavioral twist when they have the patient
go out and try something new, and it looks very reality-based, like they're
staying with both the subjective and objective realities of the patient's
life. You don't have to answer this, I'm sort of putting it out rhetorically.
But that's my question. On what is the narrative based? I have not found
a constructivist who's willing to say, 'Well, you know, you don't have to
pay attention to the realities of life.'

Miller: Actually, Harlene Anderson [e.g., 1997] is probably the closest to
someone who . . .

Held: . . . to someone who says that?

Miller: Well, who's work I can't figure out what it's about.

Held: Harry and I, Harry Goolishian [a long-time collaborator of
Anderson's, now deceased] and I used to fight about this all the time.

Miller: I love to watch her, but I can't figure out what the heck she's
doing.

Audience Member #2: Is it possible to make a comment around what I
see? I didn't know any of you before, so I am sitting and thinking that the
two of you [Held and Matthews] are from the reality position, the know-

ing position, and that you two [Hoyt and Miller] are sort of more of the constructivist position. What I see from the behavior, this must have an influence on the behavior because you two [Held and Matthews] are taking much more a knowing position also in relation to you [Miller and Hoyt]. You behave as experts. Even if you said 'I'm not an expert,' the behavior is otherwise. And you had the freedom also to define some of the things that I said. I can see there is a difference, and that's a very important difference for me in therapy—from being in a not-knowing position, absolutely, to being the one that can define what it is.

Matthews: No, no, no. It's an empirical question.

Audience Member #2: No. That is to ask a question without an answer to sort of delay a little bit, so let it stay up. That is what is for me, for me, a very meaningful contribution, that . . .

Matthews: . . . I agree, and nothing about that is . . .

Audience Member #3: . . . you don't get my point.

Matthews: I do. I think I get your point because what you're talking about . . .

Hoyt: . . . I think you're agreeing that she thinks you're wrong.

Matthews: Yeah . . . I guess. *[laughter]*

Audience Member #2: You're defining what I say before I even manage to talk it all over, and that is my point. This way of thinking has influence in a therapeutic relationship. And you asked her a question and you didn't even wait for her to answer the question. You said, 'I have some ideas about the answer.'

Held: What about my saying to her, 'Please give me an example, I'm not sure I understand'? Could you answer that?

Audience Member #2: No, I don't want to answer that question.

Held: Okay.

Audience Member #2: I'm trying to get my point through. My point is that the answer is not as important as the question. It's related to what I started to say. I got this feeling that it either has to be in *this* position or in *that* position, and by you saying, 'I understand you/I don't understand you' and 'It's right/It's wrong,' there is the uncomfortable in-the-knowing position and not the not-knowing position.

Held: Can you give me an example that I'm taking a knowing position? When I said to her, 'I'm not sure I understand what you're saying, could you give me an example'—was I taking a knowing position?

Audience Member #3: No, she was saying when you asked me a question and it was rhetorical . . .

Held: . . . oh, I see.

Audience Member #3: Yeah, and I think of the issue which comes up in our work all the time—are we creating an environment where there's a right and a wrong, or are we creating an environment where people can re-ignite their capacity to create their lives, to do things in advance of their development, that they don't already know how to do? Because if you're only able to do things you know how to do, you can't go beyond yourself, you can't qualitatively develop.

Hoyt: That was my question about *imagination*, to see something beyond the 'real.'

Miller: I had an experience. As I know this stuff, I think that both or either of these positions can be taken, whether it's from a constructivist camp or not. So I was in China doing a workshop about a year ago and I met with a gentlemen and his son and in the midst of this—again, for me I have to take it back to a practical level—I'm meeting with a man and his son and I'm doing very constructivist (in my mind) oriented questions, relational stuff, with Tom Andersen-style questions [see Andersen, 1991] basically back and forth, and all the translation I'm getting sounds very good through the two translators, but I just get this sense that something is askew in the session. So I stop the translator and I look at her and I say, 'What is wrong here?' and she says, 'Well, the father keeps telling me that you don't get it, that you just don't get it.' But I haven't heard any of this stuff because it wasn't being translated to me—they were trying to help me 'save face' in front of the 400 people who were watching me work who knew how inept I was in the therapy but weren't telling me, thank God, so I would leave the country feeling really great about myself, even though I had been a jerk. So I said, 'Thank you for telling me this. I need to know that,' and I sent the son out of the room and I talked with father. Essentially what the father told me is that in his country, in their culture, it's not appropriate for the therapist to have dialogues where the son and the father are equal. And I'd been committing this incredible cultural error in my therapy because I was applying my constructivist technique that actually was a cultural-bound technique based on what works here in America. Once I recognized this, then I took a very know-ing position with the father—'Here's what I needed to do, here's what he needed to do to solve the problem'—and then the session was on track.

Audience Member #4: Was it a real cultural *faux pas* you were commit-ting or just your linguistic conception of a *faux pas*?

Miller: I have no idea. All I know is that when I got a translation, the father said that I was making a *faux pas* in his culture, his family.

Hoyt: We are about to end. I want to thank everyone for coming and I want to thank my colleagues. I've felt that we've had a genuine dialogue and exchange. There are certainly different views and opinions, but we all had a chance to hear each other, and I appreciate that. Thanks very much.

☐ References

Andersen, T. (Ed.). (1991). *The Reflecting Team: Dialogues and Dialogues about the Dialogues*. New York: Norton.

Anderson, H. (1997). *Conversation, Language, and Possibilities: A Postmodern Approach to Therapy*. New York: Basic Books.

Bateson, G. (1972). *Steps to an Ecology of Mind*. New York: Ballantine.

Bateson, G. (1979). *Mind and Nature: A Necessary Unity*. New York: Dutton.

Berg, I. K., & Miller, S. D. (1992). *Working with the Problem Drinker: A Solution-Focused Approach*. New York: Norton.

de Shazer, S. (1998, August 27). *Getting to the Surface of the Problem*. Invited address at "Brief Therapy: Lasting Impressions" Conference. New York: Milton H. Erickson Foundation.

Duncan, B. L., Hubble, M. A., & Miller, S. D. (1997). *Psychotherapy with "Impossible" Cases: The Efficient Treatment of Therapy Veterans*. New York: Norton.

Duncan, B. L., & Miller, S. D. (2000). *The Heroic Client: Doing Client-Directed, Outcome-Oriented Therapy*. San Francisco: Jossey-Bass.

Gross, P. R., & Levitt, N. (1994). *Higher Superstition: The Academic Left and Its Quarrels with Science*. Baltimore, MD: Johns Hopkins University Press.

Haley, J. (1973). *Uncommon Therapy: The Psychiatric Techniques of Milton H. Erickson, M.D.* New York: Norton.

Held, B. S. (1992). The problem of strategy within the systemic therapies. *Journal of Marital and Family Therapy, 18*, 25–34.

Held, B. S. (1995). *Back to Reality: A Critique of Postmodern Theory in Psychotherapy*. New York: Norton.

Held, B. S. (1999). *Stop Smiling Start Kvetching: A 5-Step Guide to Creative Complaining*. Brunswick, ME: Audenreed Press/Biddle Publishing Company.

Held, B. S. (1998). The antisystemic impact of postmodern philosophy. *Clinical Psychology: Science and Practice, 5*, 264–273.

Held, B. S. (1999). How brief therapy got postmodern, or where's the brief? In W. J. Matthews & J. H. Edgette (Eds.), *Current Thinking and Research in Brief Therapy: Solutions, Strategies, Narratives* (Volume 3, pp. 135–164). Philadelphia: Brunner/Mazel.

Horgan, J. (1996). *The End of Science: Facing the Limits of Knowledge in the Twilight of the Scientific Age*. Reading, MA: Addison-Wesley.

Hoyt, M. F. (1996a). A golfer's guide to brief therapy (with footnotes for baseball fans). In M. F. Hoyt (Ed.), *Constructive Therapies, Volume 2* (pp. 306–318). New York: Guilford Press. Reprinted in M. F. Hoyt, *Some Stories are Better than Others: Doing What Works in Brief Therapy and Managed Care*. Philadelphia: Brunner/Mazel, 2000.

Hoyt, M. F. (1996b). Postmodernism, the relational self, constructive therapies, and beyond: A conversation with Kenneth Gergen. In M. F. Hoyt (Ed.), *Constructive Therapies, Volume 2* (pp. 347–368). New York: Guilford.

Hubble, M. A., Duncan, B. L., & Miller, S. D. (Eds.). (1999). *The Heart and Soul of Change: What Works in Therapy*. Washington, DC: American Psychological Association.

James, W. (1890). *Principles of Psychology*. New York: Henry Holt.

Matthews, W. J. (1990). More than a doorway, a shift in epistemology. *Ericksonian Mongraphs*, 7, 15–21.

Matthews, W. J. (1997). Constructing meaning and action in therapy: Confessions of an early pragmatist. *Journal of Systemic Therapies*, 16(2), 134–144.

Matthews, W. J. (1998, August 27). *Post-Modernism and Brief Therapy: A Critique*. Invited address at "Brief Therapy: Lasting Impressions" Conference. New York: Milton H. Erickson Foundation.

Matthews, W. J., Lankton, S., & Lankton, C. (1993). Ericksonian approaches to hypnotherapy. In J. Rhue, I. Kirsch, & S. Weeks (Eds.), *Handbook of Clinical Hypnosis* (pp. 187–215). Washington, DC: American Psychological Association.

Miller, S. D., & Berg, I. K. (1995). *The Miracle Method: A Radically New Approach to Problem Drinking*. New York: Norton.

Miller, S. D., Duncan, B. L., & Hubble, M. A. (1997). *Escape from Babel: Toward a Unifying Language for Psychotherapy Practice*. New York: Norton.

Miller, S. D., Hubble, M. A., & Duncan, B. L. (Eds.). (1996). *Handbook of Solution-Focused Brief Therapy*. San Francisco: Jossey-Bass.

Pirsig, R.M. (1974). *Zen and the Art of Motorcycle Maintenance: An Inquiry into Values*. New York: Random House.

von Glaserfeld, E. (1984). An introduction to radical constructivism. In P. Watzlawick (Ed.), *The Invented Reality* (pp. 17–40). New York: Norton.

Watzlawick, P. (1978). *The Language of Change*. New York: Basic Books.

Watzlawick, P., & Hoyt, M. F. (1998). Constructing therapeutic realities: A conversation with Paul Watzlawick. In M. F. Hoyt (Ed.), *The Handbook of Constructive Therapies* (pp. 183–197). San Francisco: Jossey-Bass.

Watzlawick, P., Weakland, J. H., & Fisch, R. (1974). *Change: Principles of Problem Formation and Problem Resolution*. New York: Norton.

CHAPTER

Brief Therapy and Managed Care: A Conversation With Michael Hoyt and Jon Matthew Carlson

I want to be seen here in my simple, natural, ordinary fashion, without straining or artifice; for it is myself that I portray.
—Michel Eyquem de Montaigne (1580) (*Essays*, Book 1, "To the Reader")

The following interview took place in November 1995 over the kitchen table at my home in Mill Valley, California. We discussed issues regarding brief therapy, some of the promises and problems of managed care, and several likely future trends and their implications for marital and family therapists and counselors.

Carlson: It is evident today that psychotherapy in the 1990s and beyond will be increasingly influenced by financial forces. The shift seems to be moving from the traditional fee-for-service model to health maintenance organizations (HMOs) and managed care. What trends do you see from working with a large HMO?

Hoyt: I think we are going to see more and more a push toward efficiency and accountability. Because there are limited resources, we need to find out what works and do more of what works. Why are you doing

Note: Reprinted, with changes, from J. M. Carlson (1997), "Interview: Michael F. Hoyt," *The Family Journal: Counseling and Therapy for Couples and Families*, 5(2), 172–181. Used by permission of the publisher.

what you are doing? Is it helping clients or patients achieve their goals? Is it the most direct route?

Managed care, generically speaking, can be defined as various arrangements to regulate the costs, site, and utilization of services, with treatment decisions partially determined by parties other than therapist and client/patient. Whatever one's particular theoretical orientation and health care delivery system, there seem to be eight characteristics of therapy under managed care:

1. specific problem solving
2. rapid response and early intervention
3. clear definition of therapist and patient responsibilities
4. time used flexibly and creatively
5. interdisciplinary cooperation
6. multiple treatment formats and modalities
7. intermittent treatment or a "family practitioner" model
8. results orientation and accountability.

There is going to be lots more emphasis on time-sensitive or time-effective therapy, which sometimes is called "brief therapy." Actually, I do not particularly like the term "brief," although it has been used in the title of some books I have been involved with, because "brief" suggests rapid or quick. I prefer the idea of time sensitivity or making the most of each session. "Efficient therapy" might be the best term.

Carlson: It seems that the next psychotherapy "wave" or shift is being pushed by financial forces.

Hoyt: We had the third Evolution of Psychotherapy conference in mid-December 1995. Although I was not on the faculty at the conference, I have been thinking a lot about the field. To have evolution, we need to have two factors. One is genetic variability, and the other is environmental pressures. The financial part is certainly an environmental pressure. We also have multiculturalism and postmodern conceptions suggesting there are different ways of looking at problems and at looking at solutions. We are also in the information processing era, and so there is much more thinking about things in terms of information processing and cognitive therapy; similarly, there are cybernetics and systems thinking motifs in both environmental ecology and family therapy. In another era, Freud's time, we were looking at things through the hydraulic model. There is a lot of interaction between the culture and models of psychotherapy.

Carlson: So, therapists are not necessarily being pushed by finances, but they are being influenced by what works and also by what society is telling them.

Hoyt: Well, I think the financial forces are paramount. Managed care initially was about cost containment. It has not really been managed *care*; it has been mostly managed *cost*. I think some of the better companies are now recognizing the importance of emphasizing quality of care rather than just trying to hold down costs.

Carlson: Managed care systems often work on an individual diagnostic model. How do you think they accommodate families?

Hoyt: That is a very complicated and important question. Of course, we should recognize that there is no one entity called "managed care." Different companies approach it in different ways. Generally, however, there was a movement toward it being very individualistic, and marital or family therapy was often not a covered benefit. Some of the more enlightened companies have now come to realize the importance of family and couples therapy. Oftentimes, however, they still insist that at least one of the family members have an Axis I *DSM-IV* diagnosis, a diagnosable psychiatric condition, for which conjoint or family therapy is seen as the treatment of choice. This, then, raises questions about the identified patient versus a more systems or interactional perspective.

Again, it depends on the particular service delivery system you are involved in. Some will say whoever is willing to come to therapy can be treated, and they will not require a psychiatric diagnosis, at least not if the problem can be resolved relatively quickly. Sometimes there is an apparent psychiatric diagnosis, but then we enter into a double-speak, where we may tell the patients that we need to put one person's name down on the form to get treatment authorized, although it involves all of them equally. So, we wind up having to explain unilateral versus systemic thinking. We also get into double-speak if insurance requires pathology-based diagnoses and we think therapeutically more in terms of learning or growth.

Carlson: One of the keys to doing therapy in a managed care organization seems to be planned or best use of available resources within the facility, within the therapist, and within the patients themselves.

Hoyt: I think we are seeing a shift toward what I have been calling *constructive therapies*, those that are collaborative and competency based. This very much keeps with the HMO idea of *health* maintenance—looking for health, resources, and strengths, not just pathology, defects, and weaknesses. I think there are some real good advantages. One is that it is much more user-friendly. Patients or clients like to be seen as whole people, not just as diagnoses or defects. It is also, I think, more user-friendly for therapists. It helps reduce the problems of burnout, when you are not just looking for problems but rather looking at the entire person or family. There has not been enough systematic research yet on the newer forms of brief therapy, but we have already seen that many of the solution-focused, solution-oriented, narrative, and other competency-based therapies get good results.

Carlson: What attracts you to solution-focused therapy?

Hoyt: It's simple, optimistic, respectful, versatile, and effective. It appreciates clients' own resources and worldviews. I am interested in helping clients to achieve their goals, so I like to use whatever works. This is not an "either/or" situation; it is a "both/and" situation. I find a lot of value in other approaches as well, particularly those that can be termed *constructive* —including narrative, strategic, Ericksonian, and others yet to be determined.

Carlson: Do the brief therapies have common characteristics?

Hoyt: In their own ways, and to varying degrees, they all seem to emphasize certain features:

1. rapid and positive alliance
2. focus on specific achievable goals
3. clear definition of patient and therapist responsibilties, often with tasks or assignments to be carried out between sessions
4. emphasis on strengths and competencies, with an expectation of change
5. novelty and assisting the client toward new perceptions and behaviors
6. here-and-now (and next) orientation
7. time sensitivity.

Carlson: In *Brief Therapy and Managed Care* (Hoyt, 1995a), you discuss ways that time can be seen more as an attitude than just as the number of sessions you are going to have. How do you look at time?

Hoyt: I think we are coming to realize that there is only now. If we talk about history or memory, we are still in the present remembering or looking backward. If we talk about the future, we are looking forward; it is expectation. But there really is no time but the present. So, I think of time as a perspective or medium in which we work. To give a very specific and practical example, we can think about the length and spacing of sessions. Traditionally, we have oftentimes seen patients for 50 minutes week after week after week. That may sometimes be the best model. Other times it may be better to see patients maybe twice in the first week and once or twice in the second week, and then they have some skills and some support and there are some things they need to do before we see them again.

Carlson: Structuring time concentrates the focus.

Hoyt: Right. There is also Parkinson's Law in psychotherapy (Appelbaum, 1975), which says that work expands or contracts to fit the time allotted. Sometimes if we tell people that they have 20 sessions, they will start to get down to it on the 18th. You tell them they have 5, and they will begin to focus on the 2nd or 3rd or 4th. Most of us studied the night before the exam.

We may also not want always to have every session be 50 minutes. Particularly with a family or couple, it may be useful to have a 75- or 90-minute session. We could say, "Let's roll up our sleeves and talk until you have some ideas about what you need to do next. And then after you've done it, call me." Notice the language. It's not that "We're going to talk until we solve all of this" but rather "until you have some ideas of what you need to do next." I think of this as an empowerment model in the sense that we are helping people find their power and assuming they can make some changes without having to be in weekly contact with the therapist.

Carlson: This is a new approach to therapy.

Hoyt: For some people, yes. I think Nicholas Cummings (1990; Cummings & Sayama, 1995) was one of the first to talk about intermittent therapy or therapy throughout the life cycle, where people will come when there is a particular problem for a period of time, but then they may not be seen for long periods of time.

Carlson: Therapy is used at certain times, much like you use a family practitioner.

Hoyt: Oftentimes people will come in around developmental crises, during passages or life-cycle transition points. For example, when people get married, it may raise issues that were not salient until then; or when a child is born; or the so-called "empty-nest" syndrome; or if there is a divorce or a bereavement. Thinking this way, we can also sometimes normalize some of the problems that bring people to therapy as developmental challenges, noting that they may already know some of the skills but that they may also need to learn some new skills in order to deal with a particular problem. It is very different from the traditional cure model, where we are going to find a problem, get to the root of it, work it out, and be rid of it once and for all.

Carlson: So, treatment may be more focused and specific?

Hoyt: Well, some research evidence has been coming out lately. For example, Jacobson's (1995) article that was in *The Family Therapy Networker* suggested that therapy may be helpful at the time, but we should not always assume that it has permanent long-term enduring effects. So, I think what we try to do is help clients get unstuck or back on track and do not necessarily expect that we will solve this problem for all time. It is like the family practitioner model, where when I'm ill, I go and see my doctor. I have not seen her in a couple of years, but I will have episodes of care when there is a particular problem. The fact that I go back to see her does not mean that we did not do a good job. Quite the opposite. I go back when the time is right for more therapy.

Carlson: In the meantime, the problem may have changed a bit, so you can adapt and change your approach.

Hoyt: Therapy is very powerful, but I think we have overestimated the power of therapy. There are many other factors that help people make changes—friendships, spirituality and religion, life circumstances, maturation, or the psychotherapy of everyday life. Salvador Minuchin, in his fine book, *Family Healing* (Minuchin & Nichols, 1993), says therapy may take place in the office, "but change takes place at home" (p. 84). It is interesting to ask clients later what was most helpful in their therapy and hear what they report. Sometimes it is not what the therapist felt was most important. And sometimes it can be a humbling experience to find out that it was something not so clearly related to our "brilliant" interventions.

Carlson: This also seems to be a shift in therapy, decreasing the authority of the therapist and making the relationship between the therapist and the client more equal. Therapists become more like guides and less directive.

Hoyt: Well, this is a controversial area. I think we are seeing a general shift toward being egalitarian or co-equal rather than hierarchical or authoritarian. It is not "I'm an expert and I'm going to fix you." However, I do think that we have certain expertises or skills that we need to call on. I was involved in a conference at one time when a very well-known therapist who is an M.D.—a psychiatrist—worked with a family, and later I asked him why he had not suggested medication, and he said that because the patients had not brought it up themselves, he did not want to impose on them. I thought it might have been wise for him to suggest medication, not to insist on it perhaps, but at least to use his expertise and say, "This is a resource I know that might be helpful. Are you interested in it?" So, I think we have to be careful that in the move toward not taking over patients' lives, we do not let it swing too far and forget that we do have certain training and expertise they may not know about.

Carlson: After all, there is a reason why the client is seeing you in the first place.

Hoyt: Yes, although I think part of our real expertise is also knowing how to ask questions in a way that will help the patient realize his or her own competency or expertness. A number of people have written about the importance of asking good questions. Socrates recognized how important it is to ask questions that help people see what they have got.

Carlson: So, the purpose of the question, in this respect, would be to lead, not simply to elicit information?

Hoyt: Well, all questions are leading questions. If I asked you how old you are, or your marital status, or what you do for an occupation, or how many times you have been in the hospital, or how often you feel depressed, all those questions are leading your consciousness, your attention, in one direction rather than another. So, I think there is this balance where we have to ask questions that are going to lead—or perhaps "invite" would be a better word, as Freedman and Combs (1993) have used it—to help people to consider alternatives or possibilities. We are not insisting, but we are inviting them. This also ties in with some of the interesting work being done with reflecting teams. Friedman (1995) has just edited a new book on reflecting teams in family therapy that beautifully illustrates ways wherein by hearing the reflections of the therapeutic team, clients are in a position to choose different options, different constructions of reality that may suit them. We should not be manipulative in the sneaky, self-serving sense of the word, but we do inevitably influence. It is our job as therapists to promote change.

Carlson: So, it goes back to the basic skills of listening, reflecting, and good questioning.

Hoyt: While Carl Rogers talked about "reflecting and clarifying," he of course did more than simply reflect and clarify. He chose what we would reflect and clarify, what he would pay and call attention to. An image that I have become fond of lately is the image of the compassionate Buddha. In Buddhist iconography, the compassionate Buddha is holding his hand up; it is called a *mudra*, which is a hand position that depicts an overall attitude toward life. And the idea is that the compassionate Buddha is just reflecting back what is given. However, I think that therapists, when we hold a hand up, so to speak, the hand is a convex and concave mirror on a swivel, and we can turn it and open or close certain parts of the story. So, for example, when patients tells us that they have been having problems for 10 years but the last couple of weeks have gone well, we have to choose: do we talk about the last couple of weeks that have gone well or the 10 years of the history of the problem? Perhaps both, but we may want to open part of the story and shrink part of the story. Oftentimes when we talk about taking history, I think it would be better to realize that we are making history. As Michael White (1993a) has put it, there are many histories of the present. It would be interesting, I think, for therapists to not just take a history of the present complaint but rather take a history of the present recovery.

Carlson: You are talking about what is happening with the client right now. Constructivist approaches are also based on the idea that people create their own meaning. Lerner (1995) has spoken about how we are currently in a crisis of meaning. In the face of this crisis, why are these approaches so popular with therapists and clients?

Hoyt: First, let me say that I do not know. It is an interesting question. Why now does something come up in the culture? Is there some collective unconscious or need that is being filled? There does seem to be a breakdown in meaning, at least in terms of one overarching worldview that provides organization and purpose. Some of the impetus is the information saturation that Gergen (1991) has written about so well. Everything seems relative nowadays. I am worried that there is a kind of alienation or anomie or breakdown in basic values. The recent O.J. Simpson trial got an enormous amount of attention. Whatever you think of the verdict, the whole thing did not seem to reduce anybody's cynicism. We also see right now a reactionary right-wing movement that is going under the banner of family values. The issues are complicated, although sometimes their values seem as oxymoronic as the idea that one can "kill for Christ."

Carlson: How about in the therapy realm?

Hoyt: Many therapists, like Alfred Adler and Viktor Frankl, have long talked about how we build our understanding and search for meaning. The philosophical idea—traceable through Epictetus and Marcus Aurelius, through Vico and Kant, through Husserl and Merleau-Ponty, amongst others—that we are putting together our sense of reality rather than just knowing an objective "truth" is central to constructivism. This, I think, is also manifesting itself in a positive way in the idea that there are many different schools of therapy now, that there is not an orthodoxy anymore, be it psychoanalysis or cognitive-behavioral or a certain form of family therapy. This is one of the overarching messages in *Constructive Therapies, Volumes 1 and 2* (Hoyt, 1994a, 1996a; see also Hoyt, 1998). We are recognizing that there are many different ways to look at reality. I think we and our clients have to find ways of looking and making meaning that have the basic values that we believe in, values of justice and cooperation—values that hold up human beings as being most important. In that wonderful movie, *Smoke*, I love the line when, in ambiguous circumstances, the female character says, "It's your call, Augie."

Carlson: What is another overarching message from the *Constructive Therapies* volumes?

Hoyt: Responsibility. Our perceptions and practices have consequences. One implication is that, because all approaches are not equally effective, therapists need to find out and do what works best—with all the attendant problems of who defines "best."

Carlson: In constructive therapy, you are finding what is meaningful for the client. What do you think is meaningful for therapists themselves?

Hoyt: I think most therapists have gone into this field for very positive reasons. In *Constructive Therapies, Volume 2* (see Chapter 3, this volume), Michael White speaks very eloquently about efforts that have sometimes been made to undermine or pathologize therapists' own motivations for becoming helping professionals. We are sometimes questioned if there are some unresolved issues in our families, if we are working on some problems with our mothers or our fathers, if we are codependent, if we are on some kind of power trip, and so on. I do not think that is why most therapists go into this field. I think we have gone into this field because we have basic values—wanting to see the world be a better place, wanting to make things right, trying to help people. We have to resist being undermined in our commitment and our motivation. Having said that, I do think sometimes therapists are enticed by a certain kind of process. There is a certain kind of intimacy, there are certain status and financial payoffs for being a therapist, and there is a need to be needed sometimes, and I think we have to be honest with ourselves about what our motivations are to make sure we are serving the best reasons rather than others.

Carlson: As therapists continue to search for meaning in their work, there has been some debate about where therapists and therapy will fit in managed care. Is it still going to be good therapy? Being someone who works in an HMO and writes about managed care, how do you address those critics?

Hoyt: I think therapists working in HMOs generally see it as a positive experience. They enjoy the stimulation and the challenge. They enjoy the idea of trying to be effective with a wide range of patients, although the work is hard and the caseload volumes are not easy. They value efficacy and efficiency in getting the job done. Those therapists who are primarily long-term process-oriented, however, may find it too frustrating, and most therapists, working in HMOs and in private practice, are feeling financially pinched nowadays. So, if those are the primary motivations, they may be dissatisfied.

Carlson: Some people who have been highly critical of managed care have not seen it having positive values.

Hoyt: Bennett (1988) wrote an interesting article called "The Greening of the HMO" where he talked about how when HMOs were formed initially, they were seen as almost revolutionary; the therapists who went to work for them and the patients who enrolled in them had a social mission of wanting good treatment for the masses. Recently, some of the HMO ideas have been taken over by the rest of managed care and there has been "greening" or monetarization. Some of the initial pro-social values have been lost, and it is just being seen as another business enterprise. For me, the positives of managed care and HMOs are accountability, availabililty, and an emphasis on quality of care. The negatives have to do with greed. And sometimes we hear stories—unfortunately, sometimes they are true—that are shocking about patients being denied care that they truly needed. This should not be tolerated. But it raises another issue, which is who is going to pay for all of this? It has been very easy for therapists to take the high moral ground and say we are not involved in a business, we are involved in a special human service calling. The fact is there is also a financial aspect. Somebody has to pay for all of it. Everyone wants more care to be provided, but very few people want to raise their taxes enough to pay for it. In California, voters recently [1995] rejected Proposition 186, a single-payer health care reform initiative. Some of the other countries that have been held up as models—Canada, Great Britain, and Japan—when I have consulted with people in those countries, they have told me they are not so satisfied with their health care delivery systems, there are oftentimes long waiting lists, and therapists are not accustomed to being paid and having the standard of living that we have in the United States. There seems to be no free lunch. Somebody is going to pay for it.

Carlson: It is also very interesting reading where therapists are being held accountable for some of their work, maybe where they have not been in the past.

Hoyt: There are ethical and medical-legal abuses by some companies, to be sure, but some therapists and clients also contributed to the current situation by submitting billing for a lot of dubious "treatment." We are going through a "correction" right now, and I expect the pendulum will swing back toward meeting a broader range of true clinical needs. I certainly hope so, for the sake of our patients and our professions. We all have heard stories about "mangled care." I'm not an apologist or even entirely a supporter, but I do not see managed care as the "Evil Empire" either.

Carlson: When people voice their concerns, their problem with managed care can be viewed in terms of profit versus people or money versus service. Yet, it seems that what is lost is the idea that there is some very good work being done, very effective work being done.

Hoyt: Everything can not be cost-effective or pay for itself. I do think there is some good work being done. There are some good innovations questioning some of the very basic ideas of how therapy should be delivered. Is it best that it be one-on-one, week after week? Would it be better to have more group therapy? Would it be better to have more focus on natural systems such as families or work groups? Sometimes innovations will only come when there is a pressure requiring an innovation. At the same time, I am concernd that there is a great temptation toward greed, particularly if the managers of the managed care company are only interested in the next quarter—the next 3 months—if their attitude is to show that they have held down costs for 3 months so that they can get promoted and move up to headquarters and they do not have an interest in the long-term relationship and the long-term outcomes for patients. Then we are going to have a problem.

Carlson: In *Brief Therapy and Managed Care*, you wrote two chapters on single-session therapy, one coauthored with Robert Rosenbaum and Moshe Talmon. How do therapists create pivotal moments in single sessions?

Hoyt: I think one way we create a pivotal moment is by listening for the moment in the therapy where the client brings up a past success—the ideas that Steve de Shazer and Bill O'Hanlon have written about as "exceptions" and "solutions" and that Michael White and David Epston have written about as "unique outcomes" and "sparkling moments"—and trying to amplify the positives. That is one way. Another is to help the client get "unstuck" by introducing humor. One time I was obsessing about something and one of my mentors, Carl Whitaker, remarked, "Don't worry. Whatever you decide, you'll regret it!" Pop! That was Carl! We can also look for strengths in the patient's complaint. The patient comes in and is unhappy about something, but we can hear the positive intention. For example, not long ago I saw somebody who had made a suicide attempt in an effort to get a life insurance payment to help his family members, who were suffering financial hardship. As he told me about it, I said to him, "You know, in some ways you're a hero." He said, "What do you mean, a hero?" I said, "Well, you're a hero." And he said, "I heard you, doctor, but what do you mean? Why do you say I'm a hero? I couldn't even do that right." And I said, "Well, have you ever heard the term 'deadbeat dad'? Many men in your situation would have run away, but you were even willing to consider giving up your life to try to feed your children and keep a roof over your family. Your technique, the way you went about it, I don't think was particularly good, but I think it sounds like your heart is in the right place." He and I were both very touched by this recognition. We went on to talk about some other ways he could help his family and also talked about what he was going to need to do to cope until he could find a job again. So, looking for the strength, even in the problem or even in the complaint, I think is very helpful. Most patients are doing the best they can. The father who is very domineering or passive, or the mother who is very domineering or passive, their technique might not be good, but they are trying as best they know how, and I think we have to recognize that if we are going to respect people and get them to engage in therapy, we have to hear what they are trying to accomplish and give honor to that and then offer them some other ways of going about doing it.

Carlson: So, it seems that the basic skill is listening but also knowing what to listen for. In addition, you are looking to reframe the past experience and create an optimistic idea that things are possible.

Hoyt: When my wife and I went to see *La Bamba*, the movie about the singer Richie Valens, while we were walking out of the theater we started to talk about his brother, who I thought had been quite destructive in Valen's life. And my wife said, "He had such heart and such passion; too bad he couldn't find a positive way to use it." My wife often sees the light while I'm still cursing the darkness.

Carlson: Single-sesison therapy certainly fits well with the current tendency toward shorter and shorter treatments.

Hoyt: Sometimes it can be done in one session. If therapy requires more than one session, however, it does not mean that it was a failure; it just means it took more than one session. Our finding that some patients could in one session make a useful, constructive shift and did not require more therapy has sometimes been misquoted or misused. It has been held up to say that therapy *should* take only one session. That was not our intention at all. Our intention was to say that some patients can get enough in one session, that they can get unstuck, empowered, and go on. If patients need more therapy, I think they should have more therapy.

Carlson: One of the keys to the constructive approaches is looking for positives, looking for the light in the person, maybe in the past or maybe in his or her story.

Hoyt: Sometimes we "see" the other person and we make a healthy connection, which may be both a corrective experience in itself and the start of bringing something good forward. It sure makes therapy more enjoyable. In an interview we did together (Hoyt, 1994c; see Chapter 1, this volume), John Weakland and Steve de Shazer said that most clinicians are not mental health professionals; rather, they are mental illness professionals. We spend a great deal of time being trained to look for illness, pathology, and so on. I think patients will respond much more positively if they see we are looking for their strengths. If we keep focusing on what the patients feel badly about, we tend to move more and more to a shame-based therapy. That is not to say we should ignore problems or pretend they are not there, but I think many patients expect therapy to be getting dragged through the mud or being reminded of all their failures and flaws rather than a more balanced view.

Carlson: So, what you are doing is acknowledging the past but at the same time looking toward the future so there is someplace that the patient wants to go to.

Hoyt: Yes. Otherwise, we do not have a message of hope. By taking too much terrible history and focusing too much on the past, we can give patients the message, "You've got this enormous bag of problems you're carrying around. How could you ever be different?" I think the real question is not how far back the problem goes but rather how much farther forward the patient is going to carry it. And the idea of hope is that something could be different. We have a saying, "If you don't change directions, you're going to wind up where you're heading." More of the same does not make a change. We are trying to help patients change something in their "viewing and doing," to use O'Hanlon's excellent phrase. Sometimes we can do this by reframing, by giving different meanings to things that have happened. Other times we can also do this by helping patients begin to construct a different idea of their futures that will give a different meaning to what they are going through in the present.

Carlson: Looking back at the past, you are not eliminating it or glossing it over. You are just looking at it in a different way. In *Brief Therapy and Managed Care*, you highlight the distinction between being a "shrink" versus an "expander."

Hoyt: Right. Oftentimes I think people are so stuck in one view of the past that we need to help them get some degrees of freedom to look at themselves differently. The brief therapy principles of co-creating achievable goals, focusing on strengths and exceptions to the problem, and looking forward can be especially useful with people who have had terrible pasts. So-called chronic and persistently and severely mentally ill patients can be very discouraged and discouraging if the therapist does not help them focus on the possible.

Carlson: In constructing the future, constructing an individual's life, how do people deal with problems outside of the self, problems of society, and social problems that they're facing? How do those filter in?

Hoyt: Well, I think it's very important that people recognize that some of the problems they experience personally are larger social problems such as ageism, racism, sexism, homophobia, and economic displacement. Sometimes we can help patients recognize how they may have internalized certain beliefs—how they were indoctrinated or "recruited," to use the narrative therapy term, into certain self-limiting or self-defeating beliefs. Sometimes this happens very subtly, and people do not even recognize that they have been in a trance or politically oppressed. A lot of the good work done in feminist therapy, for example, gets patients to recognize how some of their oppression is not originally intrapsychic but rather politically based. We need to help people see what their roles in their problems may be and what options they may have, but we also need to recognize that many people live in a pernicious world. Some problems need to be addressed on a political or socioeconomic level.

Carlson: How does a family conflict, let us say, create or prefigure their reality, their future?

Hoyt: One time I asked R.D. Laing what he thought about transference, and his response was "It is posthypnotic suggestion with amnesia." I think we get programmed to see things a certain way, and we do not even know where the program came from. So, in that sense, we are truly doing consciousness raising in therapy. We are helping people become conscious of some unconscious scripts or trances that they have been put into.

Carlson: What trends do you see with psychotherapy and managed care?

Hoyt: There are 12 likely trends, as outlined in *Brief Therapy and Managed Care* (Hoyt, 1995):

1. more outcomes measurement
2. more treatment planning
3. greater involvement of mental health services in primary care
4. increasingly organized and integrated systems of care
5. fewer and larger managed care companies
6. more group practices and fewer solo practitioners
7. more care provided by masters-level clinicians, psychiatric nurses, and various certified counselors
8. more group therapy
9. much less inpatient care
10. greater reliance on computer technology, with information processing and research advantages as well as "Big Brother" risks to confidentiality
11. less utilization review, especially in the outpatient arena, as education, certification, and credentialing of efficient preferred providers move forward
12. more emphasis on constructive therapies, ones that are collaborative, future oriented, and based on patients' competencies and resources.

I'm concerned, however, that managed care may prematurely foreclose some of the creativity in the field. Some of the companies, wanting therapy to be as efficient as possible, have begun to authorize certain treatments and not other treatments. This may be premature. I do not think it has all been worked out. People are much too complex. We cannot have a simplistic formula—here's the diagnosis, and here's the treatment. There has to be room for individual differences, therapist autonomy, and new innovations. I am also very concerned about those patients who truly need longer or ongoing therapy and support. Managed care has not managed to care for these people. Intensive and continuous care arrangements will have to be made, at considerable expense, if we are really going to reform health care.

Carlson: What do you think therapists can do right now to address these needs or these concerns?

Hoyt: I think there are several things. Who pays the piper calls the tune, so I think it is very important that we spend a lot of effort, both as individuals and through our various professional societies and associations, educating the purchasers of health care about good health care, including psychotherapy, so that they do not just buy the cheapest and later find out that it was not adequate. I think therapists also need to pay more attention to the purpose of therapy and be able to document that they are achieving successful outcomes with patients so that we can demonstrate that what we are doing has value (Carlson, Hinkle, & Sperry, 1993). We know as clinicians that what we are doing adds quality, meaning, purpose, and beauty to life. The purchasers of health care, more and more, are interested in symptom resolution, patient satisfaction, reduced absenteeism, and so-called bottom-line ideas, and I think we are going to have to pay more attention to that. If we do not, the risk will be that companies will only insure so-called catastrophic illness. They will say that this other kind of therapy, although nice, is not clinically or medically necessary. They will say people can pay for it if they want it but that it should not be insured.

Carlson: Do you see therapy with families falling into this category?

Hoyt: I hope not. I think family therapy needs to be held up as one of the more valuable approaches. But again I think we are going to have to ask, "What is the problem that is being treated? Why are they in family therapy?" Otherwise, the risk is that it will be seen as enrichment or personal growth, which companies will say is laudatory but not something they should insure. They are trying to define what insurance is going to cover very narrowly in terms of clinical or medical necessity.

Carlson: What do family therapists working within HMOs need to do?

Hoyt: Well, I think one of the problems has been that most of the diagnoses that managed care organizations and insurance companies have agreed to pay for are individual psychopathology diagnoses. Family distress, family dysfunction, and parent-child conflict oftentimes have been excused as a "V" code or "problems in living" and are not seen as things legitimately needing intervention, therapy, treatment, or whatever you want to call it. So, I think we need to advocate that these are human interactional problems that are as important as anxiety disorders or depression. Patients often request "marriage counseling," so this can be a selling point for market-oriented companies. HMOs also need increasingly to recognize that unless treated, family problems will often eventuate in expensive medical and psychiatric cases. This is the idea of the "medical utilization offset phenomenon," the well-documented finding that mental health services reduce the need for medical care. Family therapy needs to be seen as an integral part of the overall health enterprise.

Carlson: Do you think it is important for therapists to be more open, to break down some of their walls around their theoretical orientation and look at others?

Hoyt: When a new school is forming, it is important to highlight differences to sharpen thinking, to distinguish it from other schools, but eventually I think we discover that most good schools of therapy have certain things in common. We need to look for the common factors and draw from whatever works for a particular patient rather than saying "I'm only going to do narrative or solution," "I'm only going to do Bowenian or Ericksonian," "I always use hypnosis," or "I always make psychodynamic interpretations." I like to ask myself, what would be the best treatment for this patient with this therapist in this situation at this time? I try to be what I call multitheoretical, drawing from different theories and different approaches. I think we need to have some kind of overall thinking structure of what we are trying to accomplish so that we do not simply throw techniques at people willy-nilly or helter-skelter, but I think it is important that we be technically heterodox instead of orthodox and draw from whatever seems most likely to work. There is also an increased need to take a serious look at what does work best for certain problems and not just say "anything goes." What treatments are most likely to give good results given certain kinds of problems? Everything does not work equally well.

Carlson: Where do you see us heading?

Hoyt: It is very hard to predict where the field is going. There are so many different things going on. There are the economic pressures, and there is managed care. There are a lot of new theoretical approaches being developed. There is multiculturalism. As Jay Haley [see Hoyt, 2000, p. 198] has commented, much of therapy as most of us understand it was developed on a white European population. Now we are facing new waves of immigrants from other places. There may be important differences in how people go about understanding problems and solving problems if they or their ancestors have come from Asia or South America or from Africa or Europe, so I think the field is open now. It is a very exciting time. There is an old curse: May you live in an interesting time. And I think this is both an opportunity in a positive sense and a very challenging time. We have to be careful we do not look for a simple answer just to reduce the complexity.

Last week I had someone come to my office who had certain conflicts or problems about family members living with her, and she was Hawaiian. The solutions that made sense to her in her cultural milieu were somewhat different, I think, than those for someone who might have had a European background or perhaps a background from another continent. I also saw another patient who came from the Philippines and approached the therapy, the doctor, and the sense of self somewhat differently than someone from another ethnic group might. I think this is going to be an interesting challenge, for us to recognize while we are working with lots of different people that we all have ethnicity. What I would be concerned about would be if we decided we can only work with people of our own group. I would hate to see African Americans only treated by African Americans, Jewish Americans only treated by Jewish Americans, Hawaiians only treated by Hawaiians, Hispanics only treated by Hispanics, and so on. So, I think we are going to have to learn from one another much more.

Carlson: Where are your professional interests right now?

Hoyt: I have got several things going that I am very, very excited about. I am involved in teaching workshops on brief therapy and managed care, and there has been a lot of response to that, so that is continuing. In 1995, I had a wonderful opportunity to go to Japan with some colleagues and do some presentations there, and I have also spent a couple of weeks in Austria, Hungary, and England doing some teaching on brief therapy. Having contact with colleagues in other countries and seeing both how their health care systems work and how they conceptualize psychological processes differently has really brought home to me more and more the idea of how much of what we do is constructed. Particularly being in Asia, I became aware of how much of what we normally would take for granted—ideas such as the self, family, love, authority, and emotion—how much of that is constructed, and we need to deconstruct it or at least see it in its cultural context.

I am pleased with the publication of the two volumes of *Constructive Therapies* [and with *The Handbook of Constructive Therapies*, 1998]. I was the editor and, although I made certain contributions, major kudos go to the authors. I think they are incredibly exciting books in terms of the ideas that they present about different ways of working with narrative, solution-focused, or possibility therapies and so on. I expect that professional audiences will find the books very, very helpful. I certainly have.

My job at Kaiser is a constantly stimulating challenge. I am also working on several other endeavors including a couple of new workshops, some conference presentations, more teaching abroad, and a number of writing and editing projects.

Carlson: You sound busy.

Hoyt: There is a lot to do.

Carlson: In the book *Constructive Therapies, Volume 2* (Hoyt, 1996a) you have a chapter that draws on your passion for golf and baseball.

Hoyt: In addition to writing an introductory chapter and doing some interviews with a number of colleague, I wrote a chapter entitled "A Golfer's Guide to Brief Therapy (With Footnotes for Baseball Fans." It contains my favorite explanation of constructivism, which is not a theoretical disquisition but rather a joke that many people may already have heard. But let me repeat it. It is about the three baseball umpires who are disputing their acumen. The first umpire says, "Well, I call 'em the way I see 'em"; he's the honest, ethical ump. The second ump says, "Well, that's not bad, but I call 'em the way they are"; he's the objective, accurate guy. And finally, the third ump says, "You know, they ain't nothin' until I call 'em!"; he's the narrative constructivist. I think what we need to do as therapists is to recognize that we have to help patients "call 'em" in a way that will be constructive and productive and will allow them to move into healthier ways of being that they want.

Carlson: Thanks for the interview.

Hoyt: I am honored to be asked.

☐ References

Appelbaum, S. A. (1975). Parkinson's Law in psychotherapy. *International Journal of Psychoanalytic Psychotherapy, 4,* 426–436.

Bennett, M. J. (1988). The greening of the HMO: Implications for prepaid psychiatry. *American Journal of Psychiatry, 145,* 1544–1549.

Budman, S. H., Hoyt, M. F., & Friedman, S. (Eds.). (1992). *The First Session in Brief Therapy.* New York: Guilford Press.

Carlson, J., Hinkle, J. S., & Sperry, L. (1993). Using diagnosis and DSM-III and IV in marriage and family counseling and therapy: Increasing treatment outcomes without losing heart and soul. *The Family Journal, 1,* 308–312.

Cummings, N. A., & Sayama, M. (1995). *Focused Psychotherapy: A Casebook of Brief, Intermittent Psychotherapy Throughout the Life Cycle.* New York: Brunner/Mazel.

Freedman, J., & Combs, G. (1993). Invitations to new stories: Using questions to explore alternative possibilities. In S. G. Gilligan & R. Price (Eds.), *Therapeutic Conversations* (pp. 291–303). New York: Norton.

Friedman, S. (Ed.). (1995). *The Reflecting Team in Action: Collaborative Practice in Family Therapy.* New York: Guilford Press.

Gergen, K. J. (1991). *The Saturated Self: Dilemmas of Identity in Contemporary Life.* New York: Basic Books.

Hoyt, M. F. (Ed.). (1994). *Constructive Therapies*. New York: Guilford Press.

Hoyt, M. F. (1995). *Brief Therapy and Managed Care: Readings for Contemporary Practice*. San Francisco: Jossey-Bass.

Hoyt, M. F. (Ed.). (1996). *Constructive Therapies, Volume 2*. New York: Guilford Press.

Hoyt, M. F. (Ed.). (1998). *The Handbook of Constructive Therapies*. San Francisco: Jossey-Bass.

Hoyt, M. F. (2000). Unmuddying the waters: A "common ground" conference. In M. F. Hoyt, *Some stories are better than others* (pp. 195–200). Philadelphia: Brunner/Mazel.

Jacobson, N. (1995). The overselling of therapy. *Family Therapy Networker, 19*(2), 40–47.

Lerner, M. (1995). The assault on psychotherapy. *Family Therapy Networker, 19*(5), 44–48, 51–52.

Consumer Reports (1995, November). Does therapy help? 734–739.

Minuchin, S., & Nichols, M. P. (1993). *Family Healing: Strategies for Hope and Understanding*. New York: Simon & Schuster.

Seligman, M. E. P. (1995). The effectiveness of psychotherapy: The *Consumer Reports* study. *American Psychologist, 50*, 965–974.

White, M. (1993). Commentary: Histories of the present. In S. G. Gilligan & R. Price (Eds.), *Therapeutic Conversations* (pp. 121–135). New York: Norton.

Honoring Our Internalized Others and the Ethics of Caring: A Conversation With Karl Tomm and Stephen Madigan

Joy is the energy that allows a person to see with their own eyes. Consciousness moves from the level of imitation to imagination. . . . The joy of seeing oneself with new eyes after being released from unfocussed fear, anger, and sadness allows a spirit to sing.

—Winnie Tomm (1995, p. 31)

Karl Tomm has for many years been a Professor of Psychiatry and Director of the Family Therapy Program at The University of Calgary Faculty of Medicine in Alberta, Canada. He is known both as an original thinker and as an integrator and explicator of key developments in the adjoining fields of family therapy and social constructionist theory. Through various publications (cited throughout the following pages) and worldwide workshops, he has shown special sensitivity to interactional processes in the roles of the family therapist, the ethics of therapeutic discourses and practices, and the social/systemic construction of the self.

We had planned to join together at the 1996 Therapeutic Conversations 3 conference in Denver, where we were all participating as faculty members, to do a public interview focused on Karl's ideas and the devel-

Reprinted, with changes, from M. F. Hoyt (Ed.), *The Handbook of Constructive Therapies* (pp. 198–218). San Francisco: Jossey-Bass, 1998. Used with permission.

opment of his work. Stephen, the Director of the Yaletown Family Therapy group based in Vancouver and Toronto, Canada, is the coeditor of *Praxis: Situating Discourse, Feminism and Politics in Narrative Therapies* (Madigan & Law, 1998) and the author of a number of valuable papers (e.g., Madigan, 1992, 1993, 1996a,b; Madigan & Epston, 1995; Madigan & Goldner, 1998). He had known Karl for many years, while I had met Karl only once before. We got (re-)acquainted over lunch a couple of days before the scheduled interview, and the three of us agreed that we would like to have a more interactional conversation rather than a formally structured interview.

The actual conversation took place on Sunday morning, June 30, 1996. We were surprised when an audience of approximately 200 people arrived for the 8:15 a.m. session. The room became extraordinarily still and focused almost as soon as we began; there was a kind of supportive attentiveness that contributed to what unfolded. As the following (slightly condensed) transcript may suggest, some of the qualities of Karl's work—thoughtfulness and intelligence, soul-searching and ethics, a focus on the systemic construction of the self—were in the air.

Karl: One of the things we decided we would like to do is have more of a discussion rather than just a one-way process of me being interviewed, because I'm interested in you guys as well. One thing I'm particularly interested in, that's relevant this morning, is your interest in me. I guess I'm interested in knowing more about the 'distributed Karl' because I see myself as not only located within myself but among others who know me and, in a sense, if I can get to know the 'distributed Karl' in you, I can come home to myself in a new way.[1] So I'm curious about your interest and experience of me.

Michael: Well, I'd heard of Karl Tomm for a number of years and then I read the innovative interviewing papers [Tomm, 1987a,b; 1988] and found them very well organized, very intelligent, very clear. I also read some earlier work [Tomm, 1980; Tomm & Wright, 1979] that was very organized and very clear, particularly in approaching the issues of being an executive or more directive therapist. In myself, I've been struggling with how to let go of that perspective and how to shift to more of an egalitarian position, how to allow more space and not be so in control; so I was interested to hear how you were making that evolution so that, while

---

[1]Tomm (1992, 1994; also see Epston, 1993; Nylund & Corsiglia, 1993; Hoyt & Nylund, 1996) has developed the idea that the "self" is made up of a person's internalized community of significant others. From this idea comes the useful therapeutic practice of "internalized other questioning," in which one can "step into" the experience of the other by being addressed as the other person and asked a series of questions. This can be used in various creative ways to both enhance one's sense of empathy as well as to achieve a greater awareness of how one may have taken into one's self another's views.

maybe not walking in just the same path, I might be able to get some ideas.

Karl: See, I'm curious where that question is coming from, like why you're interested in that, why that particular aspect of my work appealed to you. What is it about you as a professional, as someone who is interested in this field, that led you to getting connected with me? There's some resonance here, right?

Michael: Yes. Partly the clarity. I respond very well to organization, and when I've read things of yours I find them very organized and that attracted me. Then we also had that conversation on the bus at the last Therapeutic Conversations conference [June 1994 in Reston, VA], and I thought "What a warm, wonderful person," and I wanted to make a further personal contact. I think that was some of it.

Karl: OK. What about you, Stephen?

Stephen: Well, in 1982 it was 30 below out at Woods Homes and I remember walking up a half-mile hill to your program where you were giving lunch-bag seminars at Foothills Hospital. Myself and my colleagues at that time were following whoever Karl was bringing to town. I was thinking of telling you the other day [at lunch] that when you brought the Milan team in that was fine [see Tomm, 1984a,b] but when you brought [Humberto] Maturana in I had to form a support group in order to get a sense of Maturana! It was through you that I first met Michael White in October of 1986 [see Madigan, 1992; Tomm, 1993a]. So there's that stream—I feel that you've always had a really good nose for what's current and to embrace new ideas, so that's one way that I've come to be interested in you. It's more of an academic, theoretical, practice way.

Karl: You're bringing people in [for narrative therapy conferences] now, right?

Stephen: Yes.

Karl: To Vancouver. So, in a way, you and I are together in that.

Stephen: Yes.

Karl: Like you're younger and more energetic than I am now. *[laughter]*

Stephen: I don't know about energetic, but I think I'm younger.

Karl: You stayed up until two o'clock last night!

Stephen: That was my distributed self! *[pause]* I also wanted to speak to other places that I became very interested, and continue to be interested, in you. You appear to me to be a man to never duck the pain and never duck a fight. You stand up no matter what happens, no matter how many people are there that may disagree, you will voice your opinion. I think that you have taken some very difficult positions for a lot of us, but you always seem to be the front person out there, and I really respect that in you. And there was a time, and I'll say this publicly, when you began coming to Vancouver in the early 90s and I began to get to know you personally—and it is a very odd feeling for me sometimes to be around you, and you were the only person in the world that I would ever do this with, it was quite embarrassing—but I found that when I was around you, and I've spoken about this to you, I sort of have to move away because I tear up. I still have no idea why this is, but I think it comes from the enormous amounts of respect I have for you as a person. So there's you as a person in terms of your ethics and integrity, there's you as a rebel that will speak to very difficult issues, and there's you the man with the very good nose that seems to have brought a tremendous amount of theory and talent to North America. This is a long-winded answer. But that's part of the reason why I'm interested in you.

Karl: Thank you. I appreciate that. I haven't had a lot of respect for myself, in a way, and so if I can internalize some of the respect you have for me that could help in a way.

Stephen: Do you have a sense of the respect that you carry in this therapeutic world we travel in?

Karl: Well, I have a sense that I carry much more authority than I deserve, and it frightens me a bit . . . because sometimes when I say things, I realize afterwards that I've affected a lot of people, sometimes in ways I didn't intend, you know, even offending people.

Stephen: Do you have a sense of the many ways that you affect people, at various levels across various ideas, not only to do with theory and practice but the way in which you affect, say, someone like me, that really respects your ability to wade through the pain and stay with the pain?

Karl: Well, I felt really connected to you because I felt your interest over the years and your enthusiasm for some of the things that I was also enthusiastic about. Like I felt we could come together in that enthusiasm, and seeing you doing some of the things you're doing now in Vancouver gives me a lot of excitement and pleasure. I guess it's because I see you doing what I used to do and I enjoy that, but I don't have to do the work anymore, I can just go and attend the meeting! *[laughter]*

Stephen: We have you doing a lot of work [at the upcoming Narrative Ideas conference] next year! *[smiles]* Do you see yourself as being influential in any way, or shaping what's going on in Vancouver? Do you have a sense of that?

Karl: Shaping Vancouver? *[asked jokingly]*

Stephen: As a city, yes. *[responding in kind]*

Karl: Well, I was born there, you know.

Stephen: Yes.

Karl: That's hard for me to imagine, actually.

Michael: How does *our* internalized Karl Tomm fit with *your* internalized Karl Tomm? We're giving you this information, how you're 'distributed,' what you've meant to us in different ways (and I think we can speak for a lot of people), and yet I'm wondering if you're taking it in or if you're kind of saying, "Naaaah, that's what they think but they didn't really get me."

Karl: Well, my reaction is that you guys respect me too much. You don't know enough about me. I guess I feel like I've made a lot of mistakes in my life, in a lot of ways, and so I'm still learning from old mistakes. So I feel like, I don't want to be humiliated, that's not a good place to be, but I want to remain humble. So I'm cautious with respect to becoming too confident or too complacent with respect to what I've done and so forth. I'd like to be respected and feel some respect for myself.

Michael: I experience this as frustrating. It doesn't feel like a healthy interpersonal process[2] that we're doing. It feels to me like—in a subtle way, you may not intend it—but you're discounting my feedback to you. I'm saying "You've meant a lot to me" and you're saying, "Well, if you really knew, you wouldn't think that."[3]

Karl: I appreciate you saying that, because I don't want to disqualify your appreciaton of me. I want to be able to receive your gift. Maybe I could do that more easily if I could tell you about some of my mistakes. *[laughter]*

Stephen: I think so, that would make sense.

Karl: Yeah, because then if you hear them and still feel appreciative, that might be good.

Michael: Pray tell.

---

[2]An allusion to Tomm's (1991a) "HIPs and PIPs" contrast of Healthy Interpersonal Patterns (virtuous cycles that open space and support growth and wellness) versus Pathologizing Interpersonal Patterns (vicious cycles that close down space and promote defensiveness and cut off healing and relatedness). Tomm (1996) had presented a conference workshop on "Bringing Forth Healthy Interpersonal Patterns to Replace Pathologizing Interpersonal Patterns" the afternoon before this conversation.

[3]Karl's hesitance to wholeheartedly accept the admiration and respect being offered by Michael and Stephen appears to have been experienced by Michael as a form of rejection. A transient pathologizing interpersonal pattern (PIP) of disqualification coupled with protest emerges in the interview. Karl's effort to escape this PIP entails an initiative towards more self disclosure, which was accepted. The resultant pattern of increased openness and vulnerability coupled with acceptance and appreciation led to a deepening of intimacy during the interview that surprised all of us.

Karl: First of all, I think I was raised to be extremely privileged: being male, being white, being socialized into a profession that had a lot of status, a psychiatrist. And I think that without realizing it I took advantage of these privileges, and I ended up inadvertently diminishing others, a lot of other people, crowding their space in various ways. I regret that very much. And also in terms of the whole gender dialogue and so forth, I realize that during my marriage I also closed space for my wife with respect to her emerging as a full person. I like to think of Winnie and I having between six and eight marriages. We began with a lot of passionate excitement and mutual discovery and so forth, which was great. Then when we started having children there was sort of a sudden increase in depth of commitment. I remember a critical moment of me making a decision to not go on a third expedition I was planning. I used to climb: I was a mountaineer: I went to the Himalayas and the Andes. When we had our first daughter, I said "This is crazy. I mean, why should I risk my life when I've got a child and a spouse to take care of and so forth?" So that was a shift into a different kind of marriage where I took my responsibility as a provider very, very seriously. But in the process, I drifted into taking Winnie for granted, and I remember at one moment, this happened many years later, I realized that toilets weren't self-cleaning! *[laughter]* I thought these things just remained clean automatically, and I had no idea what an incredible amount of work was going into sustaining me and maintaining my activities and my career. Of course, Winnie found that increasingly difficult to cope with and became rather depressed and rejecting of me, not of me so much, but of the practices I engaged in of taking her for granted. So that led to a more difficult time in our lives where she began a protest and so forth and had to become a very strong feminist to cope with a guy like me who is pretty persuasive and powerful.[4]

Stephen: So what kept you open to that, to the six or eight marriages and to a different position on gender? What's kept you open to that?

Karl: I think it was my commitment to the relationship, partly for the wrong reasons, you could say, and you could say it was for the right reasons, in a different sense. Because my mother died when I was eight, I had this issue of loss all my life to cope with, so I didn't want to lose the relationshp with Winnie. So I think I was hanging on to it more than I otherwise would have and we may well have parted company during

---

[4][Karl adds:] It is inappropriate for me to take any credit for Winnie becoming a strong feminist. In would be more accurate to say that my sexist behavior gave Winnie plenty of reason to be angry with me and that she found support in feminist theory and knowledge to maintain a concerted protest of my domineering practices at the time.

those early years. It took me a long time to see what I needed to see in terms of the injustices that were going on. I remember a very critical moment when things started to shift for me and I became aware and started to make some of the changes you're referring to. I refer to this as "Winnie and I and the apple pie." We had this traditional arrangement where I'd bring home the bacon and she'd fry it. *[laughter]* I came home from work one day and we had a wonderful dinner. She had cooked this apple pie and we had the pie for dessert. It was just wonderful. I love apple pie, especially her apple pie. So I asked for a second piece and she said, "Well, help yourself." *[laughter]* I said, "No. I want you to serve me another piece." She said, "No." She just sat there, and I couldn't believe it. *[laughter]* How can this be? I felt totally powerless and I couldn't do anything about it. I started yelling and screaming; fortunately it didn't become physical; but I felt indignant. How could this be that I didn't have the power and authority to get her to submit? I remember what Maturana said about "Power is the effect, submission is the cause."[5] My power rules through her submission, and when she didn't submit I didn't have that power.[6] So for me, that was a very significant turning point in terms of realizing the injustices and imbalance of power I had just taken for granted at that point. Of course, she became very scholarly; she went to learn how to think by studying philosophy, getting her Ph.D., so she could maintain her position vis-a-vis me. We actually got to a point where I was intimidated by her knowledge. It was incredible! So I learned a lot from her.[7]

Michael: What keeps you from accepting our feedback?[8]

---

[5]In a related vein, Ritterman (1994) has observed that abuse requires three roles: the destructive process cannot continue if the *hater* stops perpetrating, the *victim* stops submitting, or the *witness* stops standing by passively.

[6][Karl adds:] I realize that placing responsibility for stopping any abuse on the victim or on bystanders (such as children) is inappropriate and dangerous. As pointed out by Phyllis Frank and others (Frank & Houghton, 1987), the abuser must take full responsibility for his abuse. Women and children are sometimes killed when they try to stop the abuse. In this situation, Winnie took an enormous risk in defying my bullying. It is hard for me to respect myself in having resorted to such unfair intimidation practices. Indeed, I now support my internalized Winnie, who maintains a healthy protest within me. What I can respect in myself is my ability to acknowledge the sexist assumptions of male dominance and control I have enacted and my current efforts to escape those assumptions and practices. Needless to say, my growing awareness of these gender dynamics has profoundly influenced my patterns of clinical practice.

[7]For a sample of her scholarly work, see *The Effects of Feminist Approaches on Research Methodologies* (W. Tomm, 1989), *Gender Biases in Scholarship: The Pervasive Prejudice* (W. Tomm & Hamilton, 1988), and *Bodied Mindfulness: Women's Spirits, Bodies and Places* (W. Tomm, 1995).

[8]Michael still seems to be struggling with the pathologizing pattern of disqualification coupled with protest.

Karl: Well, I wouldn't say I'm not accepting it. I'm just being cautious about it, I guess. What would you like me to accept that you feel I'm not?

Michael: You said a few minutes ago—these are my words—'If you knew the other side you wouldn't be so generous toward me. And if you knew some of the negatives, I could be more accepting.'

Karl: Yeah. Well, there's more to this, of course. I ended up being so invested in my career which, in a sense, you've been the beneficiary of, right, in terms of what contributions I have made. But I didn't participate in raising our children to the extent that I could have. I left that all to Winnie. *[chokes up]* So I guess they paid a big part of the price for my so-called success.

Michael: Is this self-imposed? I've recently gone through something myself. About 10 weeks ago my older brother died. He'd been ill for some time. And when he died, while I miss him in some ways, I've experienced an enormous relief. He was quite emotionally abusive of me at times. And oftentimes when I would have a success, I wouldn't let myself fully experience the success because I'd hear his voice, so to speak—he's an internalized other. And he'd be critical: "Well, it's good, but not good enough" or "Well, that's good, but you didn't do this other thing," and so on. If I'd do something in error, make a mistake, I would really hear his voice. So I've struggled with this, too.[9] As I'm listening to you I've been kind of thinking, "How can *I* let myself feel good, how can I take my credits?", if you will. I oftentimes will say, "Yes, but . . . " I recently published a book [Hoyt, 1996a], someone came up and congratulated me, and I told them the three typographical errors I've found in the book so far. *[laughter]* There's always a little flaw, it's not good enough, there's something wrong. I think as I'm hearing you, while I'm interested in your story, what resonates to me is that it's also bringing up for me my story of "Yeah, I do that, too." I think maybe that's sort of a deeper level of attraction.[10]

Karl: I guess maybe what I'd like is for you to . . . *[chokes up]* . . . to appreciate and respect my family for their support. *[weeps]*

Stephen: And what they've given us through you?

Karl: That's right. I suppose I should share with the group, some people

---

[9][Michael adds:] In fairness, he was also a beneficial influence, encouraging and teaching me (Michael) a lot. On balance, the legacy is positive, but mixed. As I said in his eulogy, "I am sure Bill and I will be having more conversations before we're done."

[10][Michael adds:] As the interview unfolds, I join Karl with increasing self disclosure. This continued afterwards in a washroom conversation with him, as well, where I acknowledged my penchant for interviewing "famous" therapists as (in part) a way to obtain some of the appreciation and respect that I longed for from my older brother.

will know, that Winnie died last November . . . *[chokes up]* . . . It's hard...I think this [interview] is turning out to be a little different than I anticipated. *[laughter]* . . . I think my family of origin, too, needs a lot of credit because they created conditions for me to be able to invest myself in my career instead of having to take a lot of responsibility in the family. *[chokes up]*

Stephen: It sounds like you stand on many people's shoulders to be with us. I just have a question: Do you have a sense of Winnie's respect of you now that you continue to be in the world?

Karl: I guess I should finish the sequence of marriages. [Eventually Winnie] got into establishing herself and her career. She had to actually do so in another city because it was hard for her to do that in my shadow, as it were, so she got a position at the University of Alberta in Edmonton, which is three hours north of Calgary. So we lived apart during the week for six years. During that time, she really did come into her own, and that was really good for her and I supported that very strongly. Then we could really renegotiate as equals, which was a wonderful experience. It was a pleasure to be able to have that kind of egalitarian relationship. I felt really good about that and I think she did as well. Then the last part when she got ill and allowed me to take care of her, and I think she appreciated that a great deal[11] . . . *[chokes up]* . . . I don't want to stay on this too long *[laughter]* . . . I think there's a lot of other people I need to acknowledge in terms of my colleagues, my students, the client families I worked with. So, if you can appreciate and respect all of them, then it's easier for me to accept your respect for me.

Michael: This may be presumptive of me to say it this way, but I think you honor their memory by accepting our appreciation, with us knowing that we're honoring them as well. It's not just you, but it's all the people that have influenced you. I think it's a better way of honoring them, if you will, than saying 'Well, I really didn't do that much.' I think you did it, with a lot of help.

Karl: Yeah, I agree.

Michael: This isn't the interview I expected, either, but in another way, it is.

Karl: Ask me a good intellectual question. *[laughter]*

Michael: 'Well, in your 1988 formulation . . . ' *[laughter]*

Stephen: . . . What other areas are you beginning to get opened up to and why and what's influencing that?

Karl: Well, one of the other big areas for me is racism. I always thought of myself as non-racist or even anti-racist. In Canada, we don't have a lot

---

[11]For an extraordinary report of her coping with her illness, see W. Tomm (1996).

of minorities, or haven't until pretty recently. I didn't realize I was a racist until I realized that I had some discomfort with the thought of my daughters possibly marrying someone of a different race. I was curious about where that came from. When I looked at it, I could see that it was clearly a function of the way I think and feel about people of color or other ethnic backgrounds and origins. What's really interesting, my father and my whole family actually, but especially my father, was very opposed to Winnie and I getting married because my background is German and Winnie's background was English. The English and the Germans were at war, and there was no way I was going to marry someone who is part of the enemy, as it were. So that was quite a trauma for the family because prior to that my older brother and older sister married good German partners, and I was supposed to do the same [. . . .]

I always protested those kinds of demands or specifications, but when it came to my own views about myself and my privilege, I wasn't in touch with my white privilege at all until fairly recently, I guess. It wasn't until the last eight or nine years, I would say, that I really got in touch with this, and it was through that thought about my daughters, who they would marry. I remember actually at a workshop in London when this really came home to me. I had already done some thinking about it, but I was doing a demonstration interview in front of a group there and I was interviewing a white woman who had returned from Africa where she had lived for many years and she was now in England and she was being accused of being racist, and she just couldn't understand this. So I was asking her some questions, demonstrating reflexive questioning[12], and there were some black social workers in the audience who were just jumping up and down in their chairs because of her blindness to her privilege of whiteness moving in front of her and she couldn't see that. I felt I had to do something about this because the process was so intense and the only way I could see myself doing anything about it was just to openly acknowledge *my* racism in front of that group, which is the first time I had ever did something like that. Then I started addressing the issue with them and particularly with one of the very militant black social workers

---

[12]Definition: "Reflexive questions are questions asked with the intent to facilitate self-healing in an individual or family by activating the reflexivity among meanings within pre-existing belief systems that enable family members to generate or generalize constructive patterns of cognition and behavior on their own" (Tomm, 1987b, p. 172; also see Tomm, 1987a, 1988; plus, for case reports, MacCormack & Tomm, 1998; Tomm, 1993b; Tomm, Cynthia, Andrew, & Vanessa, 1992). There are many types of reflexive questions "that seem to fall into natural groups: future-oriented questions, observer-perspective questions, unexpected context-change questions, embedded-suggestion questions, normative-comparison questions, distinction-clarifying questions, questions introducing hypotheses, and process-interruption questions" (Tomm, 1987b, p. 172).

that was involved. Of course, since then I've learned a lot through Kiwi [Tamesese, of the New Zealand 'Just Therapy' group] and other colleagues, Ken Hardy, and so forth. I have taken up what I can in that cause. [. . . .]

Stephen: How is opening up to culture and white privilege and gender shaping your practice at this time?

Karl: *[pause]* Well, those who know my work realize that I take the position of assuming that the mind is a social phenomenon first and foremost, and secondarily becomes psychological. So I see these dynamics of interaction that convey injustice as arising in interaction between persons and communities and so forth, which we then internalize. I see that I've internalized these things as someone who's been born into a culture that's been going for a long time already. It helps me, I think, to recognize possibilities for change because if one can re-externalize previously internalized dynamics, one can do something with them, work on them. These dynamics have an incredible history.[13]

Another area that I maybe should comment on is the fact of me being German and the Germans being involved in the Holocaust. Like I had an experience of existential guilt, if you like, when I was a kid, and I had no idea where this was coming from, but I felt this for years and it wasn't until I went to Yad Vashem, the museum in Israel, that I realized suddenly that I could have been an SS officer who sent people to their death. If I was born in a different time, in a different place I could very easily have done that and been part of that atrocity. When I realized that, I just trembled. I was just shaking inside because, of course, I don't want to. But I had to realize that it was a possibility for me. I didn't want to think that I could ever do something like that. I'd like to think that I would have the courage to say "No" and sacrifice my own life rather than doing that. But I had to be honest with myself and recognize that I'm so much a part of my culture that I could have ended up in that, given the anti-

---

[13]The injustices of sexism, heterosexism, racism, ethnocentrism, classism, etc. are epidemic and deeply embedded in our dominant cultural patterns. They continue to produce widespread human pain and suffering and are continuously being reproduced unless we take a proactive stance to alter the pattern. We do not arrive as *'tabulas rasas'* but, rather, are prefigured by the situation in which we find ourselves. As Bill O'Hanlon (in Hoyt, 1996b; see Chapter 1, p. 53, this volume) has said in a conversation on related themes: "[Another] constraint is, I think, there are cultural traditions and explanations—what Heidegger [1962] calls the 'throwness.' You're not born as a blank slate. You're born into a culture that already shapes you by language and by practice, by interactions." James Hillman (1996, p. 55) elaborates some of the existential implications: "Heidegger or Camus, for instance, places the human being into the situation of 'throwness.' We are merely thrown into being here (*Dasein*). The German word for "thrown" (*Wurf*) combines senses of the throw of the dice, a projection, and a litter of pups or piglets cast by a bitch or a sow. Life is your project; there is nothing to tell you what it's all about. . . . It's all up to you, each individual alone, since there is no cosmic guarantee that anything makes sense."

Semitism that was prevalent during that time. If I had been born 15 or 20 years earlier, you know, and been born in Germany rather than being born in Vancouver, then I could have been there. And that was a very shaking experience for me.

One of the things that I guess I'm trying to do is my own personal process of becoming, as it were. Sometimes I think of myself as evolving from being a psychiatrist, to becoming a family therapist, to becoming just a therapist, then becoming a human being, but then that's . . . *[laughter]*

Michael: *[interrupting]* . . . That seems to be the usual progression! *[laughter]*

Karl: . . . [Believing that you're a human being] can mean 'You've Arrived,' too—so I want to be a 'human becoming.' I want to keep on evolving as far as I'm able to until I do die. So I want to acknowledge in myself all of my possibilities or potentials, including those of being murderous, being suicidal, being psychotic, being delusional—and if I can get in touch with those possibilities myself I feel that I can work more effectively with whoever I'm working with. If I deny them and see that, "Oh, *you've* got that problem," . . .

Stephen: . . . they become more aberrant and *Them vs. Us.*

Karl: Right . . . they become more objectified. It's harder for me to honestly connect with them in creating this platform of *therapeutic loving* which I see as so important.

Michael: May I read you a quotation? This is something you said at the last Therapeutic Conversations conference, in 1994. Talking about preparing yourself to do therapeutic work, you said:

> One of the things I do is I try to focus on my own emotional disposition to be in a relationship. I came to this through the work that I did on examining different ethical postures[14] that we as therapists can adopt in relation to our clients. I realized that probably the emotion of mutual caring and respect or *love*, I'd like maybe to use that term, is the most appropriate emotional dynamic to ground our therapeutic work in. I use the word *love* in the way that Maturana [Maturana & Varela, 1987] does, to talk about opening space for the existence of the other" [Tomm, Dolan & Furman, 1994].[15]

---

[14]Tomm has described therapists' ethical postures in terms of how they combine the dimensions of *shared vs. secret knowledge* and *increased vs. decreased options*, with four possibilities resulting: the therapist can primarily engage in *succorance, empowerment, confrontation,* or *manipulation* (see Bernstein, 1990; Freedman and Combs,1996, pp. 269-272; also Tomm, 1991b).

[15]See also Michael White's discussion (in Hoyt & Combs, 1996; see Chapter 3, p. 72, this volume) about the importance of "reclaiming these sorts of terms in the interpretation of what we are doing—*love, passion, compassion, reverence, respect, commitment,* and so on. . . . what I am saying is that terms of description like *love* and *passion* are emblematic of discourses

When we were having lunch the other day, we were discussing some of the problems of the *DSM* [*Diagnostic and Statistical Manual*: APA, 1994] and managed care and the objectification of people,[16] and I asked, "What do you think the solution is, or how are we going to move this in a healthy way?" I was really struck when you said, "We need more love." I wanted to ask you if you would reflect on that.

Karl: I know the term *love* is problematic in some respects because it means so many different things to different people. Yet at the same time, it is a term that captures people's interest because I think people can resonate with it. If we could find a way to open space for more loving to emerge in our culture generally, I think it would go a long way to countering some of the entrepreneurial values and the dollar-being-God ethos that is a part of our way of organizing ourselves in relation to each other. We give so much priority to "the bottom line," namely, the dollar. And I have a problem with this, too. This is something that's unresolved for me—I was raised in a context where I didn't have a lot of money[. . . .] Anyway, the money issue is such a big issue in our culture, and I think it's becoming a bigger issue; so how are we going to counter that? I think we need to find a way to open space for people to give priority to the richness of being in relationship.

I would like to introduce a slightly different sense of love. Rather than just opening space for the existence of the other, to say, opening space for the *enlivened* existence of the other. Just material existence is important, you know, but in American culture by and large we can handle that, but we need to enlarge that existence to add life to our lives and each other's lives. Certainly I get more excitement out of seeing other people being excited and responding, and it adds to my life. If people give me the gift of

---

that can provide a point of entry to alternative modes of life, to specific ways of being and thinking—which will have different real effects on the shape of the therapeutic interaction, different real effects on the lives of the people who consult us, and different real effects on our lives as well."

[16]Tomm (1990) has written passionately about the "spiritual psychosis" that results from the "DSM syndrome" of compulsively objectifying people. Tomm's (1991, p. 28) "HIPs and PIPs" concepts are directly relevant: "The process of clinicians assessing mental problems is, in itself, a culturally determined pattern of interaction which could have either pathologizing or healing effects. As already noted, when the process becomes one of sticking psychiatric labels on to persons, it can be pathologizing. Our alternative is for clinicians to distinguish, assess, diagnose, and label selected interpersonal patterns as pathological rather than the individuals involved in those patterns. This implies a fundamental shift from the personal to the interpersonal. . . . In other words, labeling PIPs pathologizes the pathology, not the person. A further effect of labeling an interaction pattern is that doing so leaves space for the persons involved to disassociate themselves from the pattern [i.e., externalizes the problem but not the persons' autonomy—see Tomm, 1989] which could be the beginning of healing." For additional discussion of dilemmas of postmodern practice within the context of managed care, also see Hoyt and Friedman (1998).

opening space for me to be a therapist, to have that joy of responding to them and opening space for them, that's fantastic. I get high on that.

Michael: Stephen and I both have small children and we're very involved in nurturing and parenting. It's not enough to let them be there, to just say, "I'm going to open this space." Children thrive when they get welcoming and warming and nurturing, when we say "I'm going to open it and I'm going to enrich it, I'm going to take delight in your coming forward." Is that what you're referring to?

Karl: Yes. I think there's another dimension to this, though, in terms of the dangers of opening too much space. It's more than just being warm that I'm referring to. I think we need to sometimes look at the condition of the other and the situation the other is in and be prepared to do some work, some hard work—a labor of love—in terms of trying to do something that is going to, indeed, open possibilities. But even then, I think the possibilities sometimes need some structure to be optimal because if one opens too much space, one can give people the rope to hang themselves, and that can be risky. One can open the space for chaos or confusion.

I had an experience only a couple of years ago where I participated in creating the space for a women to commit suicide. A young woman did take her life, and I feel partly responsible for that . . . I don't know if you want me to tell you about this?

Stephen: Sure. Go ahead.

Karl: It was a young woman of about 29 or 30, who had been involved in various kinds of therapy activities for 10, 12, 15 years, something like that, since she was an adolescent. It's a long, complex story, but I got involved at a point where she was in a hospital and had been in the hospital for many months and a psychiatric colleague asked me to consult because they were having increasing difficulty with her in terms of escalating patterns of control and suicidality. For instance, she'd want to go out on a pass, and they'd say, "Well, you have to sign a statement not to hurt yourself or else we can't give you the pass," and she'd refuse; then she'd try to run out; then they'd take her clothes away and so on, put her in a hospital gown. It was just this kind of escalating thing. The family, of course, were trying hard to get her to not entertain suicide either. The more they imposed their wishes upon her, the more she felt compelled to assert her own independence or autonomy by wanting to kill herself. So, seeing this pattern, I began working with her and I recognized that she had a habit of disqualifying the good intentions of the hospital staff or the family or even me as a therapist. So I tried to externalize this disqualifying habit, but then I realized that she was experiencing my externalizing conversation as disqualifying her having this habit. So I realized, "I can't do that, that's contributing to more difficulty here." So I thought, "Well, the only way to honestly get out of this is to give her the space to kill herself if she chooses to—with the hope that she might choose not to." I asked her whether she wanted me to do this with her. I had a separate meeting with her. I asked if she would want me to orient my work with the staff and the psychiatrist in charge in that direction. She said, "Yes," that is what she would appreciate. So I embarked on that process with the staff and with her family. Her family could see the pattern because they had been in it for so many years, and so they recognized how they were caught in it, and they gradually accepted this. I invited them to meet with her individually to talk about the possibility of her death, to accept that as a possibility. But, of course, I opened space for them to feel entitled to have their preference for her staying alive and so forth; but I tried to help them stay at the level of preference rather than an imposition. She started to improve, started getting better, going out, and being responsible. Then there was the issue of discharge, and we invited her to participate in that decision-making and that eventually went well. So things gradually improved over a period of a few months, but there were some momentary slips. She used to be in conflict with the family, in struggles, and those dissipated and disappeared, but she had these inner conflicts that were still going on which were harder to get at because she had internalized so many of these dynamics. There were lots of patriarchal issues going on with an older brother and the family business, and he was privileged in terms of the business. We tried to address all these issues in so far as we were able to.

Then there was a very trivial event which was a trigger that led to her suicide. Her father was looking at a book and the television was on. She came into the room—she was living at home at this time—and she picked up the channel changer and switched the channel. He looked around and said, "I was watching that," and she threw down the channel changer and ran off and they didn't know what this was all about. But his disqualification brought forth a whole series of prior life experiences with him which she just couldn't cope with, as it were. She spent that night in the office on the computer writing letters to various people. Fortunately, I had an appointment scheduled with her after this incident, and she mentioned it to me. So I was trying to help her recover from this and she was talking about leaving town and going to visit some friends in Vancouver. This seemed like a reasonable plan but I felt uncomfortable. It didn't seem right to me. So I asked her if we could have another family meeting before she left and she said to me, "Well, you promised me that you wouldn't force me to go back in the hospital." I said, "Yes, I did. I agree." And I said, "I realize that you don't want to have another meeting, but I would appreciate it if you would do it for my sake, because I'm having difficulty at this point." So she did—she called her family and, amazingly, later that day everybody showed up: both parents, all her siblings and their partners, and the psychiatrist from the hospital. I managed to get my team together, a reflecting team,[17] and we had our last meeting with the family. She said, "No, I don't want to go back in the hospital. No, I don't want to try another medication. I've tried that many, many years, and this and that and everything, and so forth. I just want to go away and think and I want to have some time for myself." Then the whole family went out and had pizza together and she drove into the mountains, which she loved. And three days later, she in fact did kill herself.

It was, in a sense, fascinating. I mean, she wrote letters to everybody in the family which were very healing letters. They weren't negative, hostile letters. She sent me a card thanking me for giving her the choice and so forth. But I always felt that I should have done more. While I realize that may be an unfair position to take, I allow myself to take that position because it helps me to stretch myself, so I want to honor that. At the same time I want to accept her decision. What I found that was amazing is that the respect for her in the family took an incredible leap following her suicide. The respect she commanded for having the courage to do what she did, and especially in her father and her older brother, because up to that point, they tended to demean her and diminish her, not deliberately or consciously, but it was part of their way of being together. They had been socialized in these patterns. My feeling was, "If only we had more time." I don't know if time would have made a difference. It seemed to me it would have.

I made some other mistakes in my work with her which I found very interesting. It makes me worry sometimes about the ethical posture of *empowerment*, the limits of that. One of the things she would say to me was, "It's too late. You know, I really appreciate what you're doing, but it's too late. If I had met you two years ago, maybe we could have done something." She would say, "I'm not entering into relationships with anybody," and then I would say that "But my experience is that you're opening up to me, that you're sharing a lot with me." That was a mistake because I was disqualifying her when she was saying she wasn't. After every interview she wouldn't commit to another interview. I'd offer another appointment and she'd say, "Well, I don't know whether I'll be back or not." But she kept coming back so there was a relationship and it was evolving. But I had the idea that if I made it conscious that it would help her. Part of my idea in terms of ethical postures is inviting people to be consciously aware of their resources. In this case, that was a mistake

---

[17]See Andersen (1991), Friedman (1995), and Madigan (1993) for more on the uses of reflecting teams.

because I think it invited her to experience being disqualified. So I think it would have been better to work with her more in the domain of *suc-corance.*

Michael: May I interject a process comment? We've all sooner or later had a horrible case and we're not sure if we did the right thing. What comes across to me the most in what you're describing now is your honesty, your clarity of thought, and your personal soul-searching. Instead of just dismissing it, what comes across the most to me is how hard you've worked with yourself to stretch yourself. There's a lot of content in the case, but the degree of intelligence and integrity, of honesty with yourself, is remarkable to me.

Stephen: Yes.

Michael: And especially to be willing to do that in a public forum.

Stephen: Which brings me to a question then. Looking back on this hour-long interview, do you now get a taste of the love and the respect that we might have for you *[laughter]*, given who you are and how you are with us in this domain of therapy?

Karl: Of course, and I appreciate it. There's no question. Just this happening itself is a reflection of that, and your way of being with me has certainly conveyed that. So, thank you very much.

Michael: When you take that in, how will that help you reauthor the internalized Karl Tomm?[18]

Karl: Well, I want to take it in as some self-respect and appreciation of self as I feel appreciated by you, but I guess I want to be a bit careful with it. I don't want to go too far and get arrogant. So I want to be careful about that.

Stephen: Should we commit to you now to keep on talking about that with you?[19]

Karl: Actually, if you could, I would really appreciate that. One of the things that I value the most from colleagues is offering feedback, constructive feedback, even if it seems negative or painful and hurts a bit.

---

[18][Michael adds:] This question was inspired by a similar question asked of me the day before by my colleague, David Nylund, as we reviewed the feedback from a workshop (Hoyt & Nylund, 1996) we had just presented. The workshop, interestingly, featured an application of Tomm's internalized other questioning technique to help therapists learn from their internalized clients. I can also detect a more distant echo from a supervisor-mentor, Robert Goulding, who emphasized the importance of not letting a discount or self-disempowerment pass as well as the value of deliberately connecting psychological work back to the person's initial goal (see Hoyt, 1995—Chapter 5, this volume; Hoyt & Goulding, 1989).

[19]See Madigan (1996a, 1996b; Madigan & Epston, 1995; Madigan & Goldner, 1998) regarding the supportive value of "communities of concern."

Like when it's offered in the spirit of honesty and integrity, that's where I learn the most. When people simply say, "That's great, that's great," that's nice and I appreciate that, too, and I should be more open to receive those gifts, but I find those less enabling because, I guess, I'm afraid I have a propensity to arrogance or something. I need to keep countering that.

Stephen: That's interesting. Arrogance is something I see that isolates and I think in this domain what we're attempting to do is offer connection and not isolation.

Michael: I want to thank you, Karl. I don't know what I was looking for in terms of the content of the interview, but I got it.

Karl: Thank you.

☐ References

American Psychiatric Association. (1994). *Diagnostic and Statistical Manual of Psychiatric Disorders, Fourth Edition*. Washington, DC: Author.

Andersen, T. (1991). (Ed.) *The Reflecting Team: Dialogues and Dialogues about the Dialogues*. New York: Norton.

Bernstein, A. (1990). Ethical postures that orient one's clinical decision making. *AFTA Newsletter*, 41, 13-15.

Epston, D. (1993). Internalized other questioning with couples: The New Zealand version. In S. Gilligan & R. Price (Eds.), *Therapeutic Conversations* (pp. 183–189; with commentary by M. White, pp. 190–196). New York: Norton.

Frank, P. B., & Houghton, B. D. (1987). *Confronting the Batterer: A Guide to Creating the Spouse Abuse Educational Workshop*. New York: Volunteer Counseling Service (VCS).

Freedman, J., & Combs, G. (1995). *Narrative Therapy: The Social Construction of Preferred Realities*. New York: Norton.

Friedman, S. (1995). (Ed.) *The Reflecting Team in Action: Collaborative Practice in Family Therapy*. New York: Guilford Press.

Heidegger. M. (1962). *Being and Time*. New York: Harper & Row.

Hillman, J. (1996). *The Soul's Code: In Search of Character and Calling*. New York: Random House.

Hoyt, M. F. (1995). Contact, contract, change, encore: A conversation with Bob Goulding. *Transactional Analysis Journal*, 25(4), 300–311.

Hoyt, M. F. (1996a). (Ed.) *Constructive Therapies, Volume 2*. New York: Guilford Press.

Hoyt, M. F. (1996b). Welcome to Possibilityland: A conversation with Bill O'Hanlon. In M. F. Hoyt (Ed.), *Constructive Therapies, Volume 2* (pp. 87–123). New York: Guilford Press.

Hoyt, M. F., & Combs, G. (1996). On ethics and the spiritualities of the surface: A conversation with Michael White. In M.F. Hoyt (Ed.), *Constructive Therapies, Volume 2* (pp. 33–59). New York: Guilford Press.

Hoyt, M. F., & Friedman, S. (1998). Dilemmas of postmodern practice under managed care and some pragmatics for increasing the likelihood of treatment authorization. *Journal of Systemic Therapies*, 17(3), 23–33. Reprinted in M. F. Hoyt, *Some Stories are Better than Others: Doing What Works in Brief Therapy and Managed Care*. Philadelphia: Brunner/Mazel, 2000.

Hoyt, M. F., & Goulding, R. L. (1989). Resolution of a transference-countertransference impasse using Gestalt techniques in supervision. *Transactional Analysis Journal*, 19, 201–

211. Reprinted in M. F. Hoyt, *Brief Therapy and Managed Care: Readings for Contemporary Practice* (pp. 237–256). San Francisco: Jossey-Bass, 1995.

Hoyt, M. F., & Nylund, D. (1996). *The Joy of Narrative: An Exercise for Learning from Our Internalized Clients.* Workshop, Therapeutic Conversations 3 conference, Denver. A version appeared in *Journal of Systemic Therapies*, 1997, 16(4), 361–366. Reprinted in M. F. Hoyt, *Some Stories are Better than Others: Doing What Works in Brief Therapy and Managed Care.* Philadelphia: Brunner/Mazel, 2000.

MacCormack, T., & Tomm, K. (1998). Social constructionist/narrative couple therapy. In F. M. Dattilio (Ed.), *Case Studies in Couple and Family Therapy: Systemic and Cognitive Perspectives* (pp. 303–330). New York: Guilford Press.

Madigan, S. P. (1992). The application of Michel Foucault's philosophy in the problem externalizing discourse of Michael White. *Journal of Family Therapy, 14,* 265–279.

Madigan, S. P. (1993). Questions about questions: Situating the therapist's curiosity in front of the family. In S. Gilligan & R. Price (Eds.), *Therapeutic Conversations* (pp. 219–230; with commentary by D. Epston, pp. 231–236). New York: Norton.

Madigan, S. P. (1996a). The politics of identity: Considering community discourse in the internalizing of internalized problem conversations. *Journal of Systemic Therapies, 15*(1), 47–62.

Madigan, S. P. (1996b). *Narrative Therapy, Eating Disorders and the Hospital Ward.* Workshop, Therapeutic Conversations 3 Conference, Denver.

Madigan, S. P., & Epston, D. (1995). From "spy-chiatric gaze" to communities of concern: From professional monologue to dialogue. In S. Friedman (Ed.), *The Reflecting Team in Action: Collaborative Practice in Family Therapy* (pp. 257–276). New York: Guilford Press.

Madigan, S. P., & Goldner, E. M. (1998). A narrative approach to anorexia: Discourse, reflexivity, and questions. In M. F. Hoyt (Ed.), *The Handbook of Constructive Therapies* (pp. 380–400). San Francisco: Jossey-Bass.

Madigan, S., & Law, I. (Eds.) (1998). *Praxis: Situating Discourse, Feminism and Politics in Narrative Therapies.* Vancouver, Canada: Yaletown Family Therapy.

Maturana, H. R., & Varela, F. J. (1987). *The Tree of Knowledge.* Boston: Shambala.

Nylund, D., & Corsiglia, V. (1993). Internalized other questioning with men who are violent. *Dulwich Centre Newsletter, 4,* 29–34. Reprinted in M. F. Hoyt (Ed.), *The Handbook of Constructive Therapies* (pp. 401–413). San Francisco: Jossey-Bass, 1998.

Ritterman, M. K. (1994). A five-part poetic induction in favor of human decency (countering the hate movements). In J. K. Zeig (Ed.), *Ericksonian Methods: The Essence of the Story* (pp. 465–481). New York: Brunner/Mazel.

Tomm, K. (1980). Towards a cybernetic systems approach to family therapy at the University of Calgary. In D. S. Freeman (Ed.), *Perspectives on Family Therapy* (pp. 3–18). Vancouver, BC, Canada: Butterworth.

Tomm, K. (1984a). One perspective on the Milan systemic approach: Part I. Overview of development, theory and practice. *Journal of Marital and Family Therapy, 10,* 113–125.

Tomm, K. (1984b). One perspective on the Milan systemic approach: Part II. Description of session format, interviewing style and interventions. *Journal of Marital and Family Therapy, 10,* 253–271.

Tomm, K. (1987a). Interventive interviewing: Part I. Strategizing as a fourth guideline for the therapist. *Family Process, 26,* 3–13.

Tomm, K. (1987b). Interventive interviewing: II. Reflexive questioning as a means to enable self-healing. *Family Process, 26,* 167–183.

Tomm, K. (1988). Interventive interviewing: Part III. Intending to ask lineal, circular, strategic, or reflexive questions? *Family Process, 27,* 1–15.

Tomm, K. (1989). Externalizing the problem and internalizing personal agency. *Journal of Strategic and Systemic Therapies, 8*(1), 54–59.

Tomm, K. (1990). A critique of the DSM. *Dulwich Centre Newsletter,* No, 3, 5–8.

Tomm, K. (1991a). Beginnings of a "HIPs and PIPs" approach to psychiatric assessment. *The Calgary Participator, 1*(Spring), 25–28.

Tomm, K. (1991b). The ethics of dual relationships. *The Calgary Participator, 1*(Winter), 11–15.

Tomm, K. (1992). *Interviewing the Internalized Other: Toward a Systemic Reconstruction of the Self and Other.* Workshop, California School of Professional Psychology, Alameda, CA.

Tomm, K. (1993a). The courage to protest: A commentary on Michael White's "Deconstruction and Therapy." In S. Gilligan & R. Price (Eds.), *Therapeutic Conversations* (pp. 62–80). New York: Norton.

Tomm, K. (1993b). *Constructivist Therapy.* Videotape, Distinguished Presenters Series. Denver, CO: International Association of Marriage and Family Counselors.

Tomm, K. (1996). *Bringing Forth Healthy Interpersonal Patterns (HIPs) to Replace Pathologizing Interpersonal Patterns (PIPs).* Workshop, Therapeutic Conversations 3 conference. Denver.

Tomm, K., Cynthia, Andrew, & Vanessa. (1992). Therapeutic distinctions in an on-going therapy. In S. McNamee & K. J. Gergen (Eds.), *Therapy as Social Construction* (pp. 116–135). Newbury Park, CA: Sage.

Tomm, K., Dolan, Y., & Furman, B. (1994). *Sequencing Questions to Enable Change.* Panel discussion, Therapeutic Conversations 2 conference, Reston, VA.

Tomm, K., & Wright, L. M. (1979). Training in family therapy: Perceptual, conceptual and executive skills. *Family Process, 18,* 227–250.

Tomm, W. (1989). (Ed.) *The Effects of Feminist Approaches on Research Methodologies.* Waterloo, ON, Canada: Wilfrid Laurier University Press.

Tomm, W. (1995). *Bodied Mindfulness: Women's Spirits, Bodies and Places.* Waterloo, ON, Canada: Wilfrid Laurier University Press.

Tomm, W. (1996). Case story: Experiences with complementary health workers. *Making the Rounds in Health, Faith, & Ethics, 9*(1), 1–4 (plus commentaries on pp. 5–8). Chicago, IL: Park Ridge Center.

Tomm, W., & Hamilton, G. (1988). (Eds.) *Gender Bias in Scholarship: The Pervasive Bias.* Waterloo, ON, Canada: Wilfrid Laurier University Press.

White, M. (1993). Deconstruction and therapy. In S. Gilligan & R. Price (Eds.), *Therapeutic Conversations* (pp. 22–61). New York: Norton.

CHAPTER

Direction and Discovery: A Conversation about Power and Politics in Narrative Therapy With Michael White and Jeff Zimmerman

Attention to the politics of experience and to the politics of therapeutic conversation has been a hallmark of the narrative therapy approach, as reflected in the work and personal ethics of one its founders, Michael White (see Chapter 3). Joining us for this conversation was Jeff Zimmerman, the director of the Bay Area Family Therapy Training Associates (BAFTTA) and co-author (with Vicky Dickerson) of *If Problems Talked: Narrative Therapy in Action* (1996) and a number of valuable papers (e.g., Dickerson & Zimmerman, 1992, 1993, 1995; Dickerson, Zimmerman & Berndt, 1994; Zimmerman & Dickerson, 1994a, 1994b, 1995).

The following edited discussion took place on March 16, 1998, in Jeff's BAFTTA office in Cupertino, California. White had just completed the first half of a two-day workshop on "Re-Membering, Definitional Ceremony, and Rich Description."

Hoyt: I'd like to begin by asking you to reflect on how to balance the ideas of *direction* and *discovery*. How do you balance the idea that on the one hand the therapist isn't in charge, is de-centered, but, on the other

An abridged version of this conversation appeared in M. White (2000), *Reflections on Narrative Practice: Essays and Interviews* (pp. 97–116). Adelaide, Australia: Dulwich Centre Publications. Used by agreement.

hand, is still responsible and is actively doing something in therapy? I'm interested in how this is different than having some sort of treatment plan and trying to march the client to a certain place. What do you listen for? Is there a way to listen so that you're participating but not leading? Or are you leading?

White: We're certainly playing a part that is directive in terms of what gets taken up, from these conversations, for further exploration. We do play a significantly directive role in that. But that's not to say that we are directing things in the sense that we are authoring the actual accounts of people's lives that are expressed in these conversations. In all of these conversations we do hear, in people's stories, a whole range of expressions that provide points of entry to different accounts of their lives. Take the videotape of Alice. [Alice, a woman who had been consistently subject to abuse in her childhood and adolescence, had appeared in a videotape that was shown in the workshop.] In these conversations we hear certain expressions that draw our attention to knowledges of life and skills of living that can be relatively invisible to the people who consult us, and the recognition of these knowledges of life and skills of living shapes our responses in these conversations. So, it is the case that we will be playing a part in the identification and in the rich description of these other knowledges and skills of living, but we don't radically construct these. In reflecting on how Alice began to describe these knowledges and skills, and on her unique naming of them, I believe that it is quite evident that this is not something that I could have come up with. The whole of her account of her "passion for justice," including the history of this as a theme in her life, and the ways that this has sustained her through all of the trauma that she has been subject to, was built in a context that presented Alice with options for a re-engagement with her own life. This account of Alice's life, including the general naming of it as "passion for justice," and the identification of the particularities of her life that constitute this theme, is not one that I could have independently or substantially authored.[1]

---

[1]White's response to an audience member's question at a public dialogue (White & Meichenbaum, 2000) held during the 4th Evolution of Psychotherapy Conference illuminated this point:

> The therapist in most narrative practices is *decentered but influential*. I think that these are two very distinct ideas; and they're sometimes collapsed together. I can be asking questions that privilege the people who are consulting me as the primary author of the stories of their lives and their accounts of their identity, but they wouldn't be giving this account if it wasn't for the questions I was asking. These are highly influential questions, but I'm decentered in that I am not at the center. What's at the center are the descriptions and the accounts of life and identity that are built in these conversations. . . . We can be *centered and influential*—if we're centered and influential it means that progress is dependent upon the knowledges of the professional worker, the expert knowledges. That also can be quite a burden, a huge responsibility, and can lead to fatigue and burnout. It's a very problematic place to be.

Zimmerman: In some ways I suppose we direct a certain kind of discovery. We direct a kind of conversation that constructs contexts which invite certain kinds of discoveries to be made. I feel like I'm doing much better work when I'm thinking in terms of *discovery* than when I'm orientated towards being *directive*. Personally, I find it easier to remain in this discovery-mode when working with children. At times with adults I can waver towards the directing end and I don't like the effects this can have.

White: I think we are all capable of being directive at times. There are all sorts of ways that we can be engaged in practices that take us away from what Jeff is calling "discovery." Perhaps some consciousness of this is a partial remedy as it can assist us to avoid engaging in therapy in a way that simply contributes to a confirmation of what we, as therapists, already know. The *confirmation of the known* is what can take place in the name of therapy. And conversations that just contribute to a confirmation of the known are often dead-ended conversations.

Zimmerman: Right.

Hoyt: How is it that you stay in touch with the person's agenda for seeking consultation in the first place?

White: People's agenda for these conversations frequently change as the conversations develop. So often people change what they want in life as these conversations progress. They might start with a highly specific agenda, and although at times this endures, usually there is some modification in this. As these conversations make it possible for people to stand in different territories of their lives, territories that differently construct their identities and in which different knowledges and skills of living become available for exploration, they identify other purposes for the therapeutic conversation.

Hoyt: These orientations to therapy conversations that you are talking about, how do they relate to poststructuralist inquiry? It would seem to me that there is a significant difference between asking questions in the hope of getting to a particular place, and asking questions to which you genuinely do not know where the answers will lead.[2]

White: I think that engaging in some explicit challenge to structuralist conceptions of life is helpful in relation to this. If there is nowhere particular to arrive at, no previously established destinations that are granted

---

It's also very marginalizing of the knowledges and skills of living that people actually come into our consultations with. We can be *centered and noninfluential*—and that's even more painful. Or we can be *decentered and noninfluential*—in which case we're just irrelevant. . . . I think a lot of my questions provide that scaffolding for people to experience being knowledged in matters that they would never otherwise experience being knowledged about, but these are not knowledges that I have offered or initiated.

[2]See Hoyt and Friedman (1998/2000)

some normative or "truth" status, then there are many possibilities for us to speak about things that we have never spoken about, and to journey to places that we could never have imagined journeying to.

Zimmerman: I find the distinction of coming from a place of *curiosity*, rather than a place of "I'm going to build a landscape," a helpful one. If I can follow the client's experience and stay curious in relation to it, I feel I'm doing good work.

Hoyt: In our last published conversation [in Hoyt & Combs, 1996—see Chapter 3], you said: "If I knew where we would be at the end of the session, I don't think I would do this work." There wouldn't be discovery, there wouldn't be the excitement, there wouldn't be imagination.

White: We'd just be confirming what we already know.

Hoyt: Let me read you two quotations and then ask your reflections. They are both related to this consideration of the balance between *direction* and *discovery*. The first comes from the *Newsweek* [Cowley & Springen, 1995, p. 74] article featuring narrative therapy in which David Epston said: "Every time we ask a question we're generating a possible version of a life." The second is from an interview in the *Family Therapy Networker* in which Salvador Minuchin was quoted:

> I remember seeing Michael White do a very masterful session of narrative therapy, but it was like watching a sheep dog at work. He kept pushing people through a series of constructed questions into the groove of seeing their stories in the more positive way that he wanted for them. The therapist changes the old story and convinces the client that the new story is more true than the old. We all offer our patients a language, and we say, "Let's begin to see your life in this language, and I will give you solutions in this language." I do it. Everybody does it. [in Simon, 1996, pp. 55–56]

What do you think of these characterizations?

White: I have always admired Minuchin's questioning of therapeutic practices, and his efforts to encourage people to acknowledge and to name the power relations of therapy. And, although I don't see myself or my work in the description of Minuchin's that you quoted, I think the issue of the role and meaning of questions in therapeutic conversations is a really good one to consider. I am interested in how we can talk about this issue in ways that do not blur distinctions around different practices. This is important because if all acts of power in the name of therapy are equal— if it is not possible to differentiate between those acts that are more imposing from those that are less imposing—then we don't have anywhere to go in terms of questioning therapeutic practice, and there will be no impetus for us to find ways of making what we do more accountable to the people who consult us.

So, let's talk about the meaning and role of questions within narrative therapy. We could start by considering the context in relation to David Epston's comment that you quoted: "Every time we ask a question we're generating a possible version of a life." I believe that David is here refer- ring to the fact that a well-formed narrative question can be highly evoca- tive of alternative images of a person's identity. But David is not referring to the sort of questions that are imposed from out of the blue. Rather, he is referring to questions that are formed by therapists in response to people's expressions. How do these questions generate a possible version of life? These images often generate reverberations that reach down through a person's history, reverberations that touch on historical experiences, that set off resonances. Suddenly the person finds themselves speaking of some of their experiences of the events of their life that line up with and that support the image that was evoked by the question. At times these are experiences of events of life that the person has never previously given voice to. In regard to developing an understanding of this process, I have found Gaston Bachelard's (1969) work on the image to be quite helpful.

Zimmerman: I want to say that having done the therapy that would be more structuralist at one point in my life, the experience of doing the two are entirely different for me as a therapist, in just the ways you were talking about. When I did those structuralist therapies, I felt like I was in a great position of power and that I was orchestrating everything that happened. When I do narrative therapy, I don't feel that way. I don't have that experience as a therapist and I don't think my clients have that experience as clients. I gain knowledges from the people that I am seeing that I wouldn't have any access to the other way, that I wouldn't have a clue about. I lost some burdensome feeling from having to be the one who had to figure it all out. So, I would say it was a positive gain and a positive loss. That's why I wondered about what Minuchin's connecting to in the work. What is influencing his reading of it?

Hoyt: Elsewhere, Minuchin [1992] made another statement in relation to control within therapy conversations:

> Control does not disappear from family therapy when it is re-named "co- creation." All that happens is that the influence of the therapist on the family is made invisible. Safely underground, it may remain unexamined. . . . The bottom line is that the constructivist approach, by bracketing the idiosyncratic story, obscures the social fabric that also constructs it. [pp. 7– 8]. . . . Constructivist practice, with some exceptions, robs the therapist of human complexity. [p. 10]

White: I think it would be fair to say that Minuchin and I share an inter- est in exploring the practices of power involved in therapeutic conversations. Minuchin says some things here that I agree with. I have heard accounts given of a practice that is referred to as "constructivist" practice that does appear to obscure the power relations of therapy and what he refers to as the "social fabric." To deny the power relations of therapy in this way makes the therapist less accountable for exercises of power and for the real effects of this in the shaping of people's lives. And to obscure "social fabric" that shapes the stories of people's lives would surely contribute to a personal burden. So, what Minuchin is saying here really strikes a chord for me. I would agree with his comments on the therapeutic practices that he calls "constructivist—I emphasize *calls* here, because I don't know whether or not "constructivists," whomever they might be, would agree that Minuchin is reasonably representing their position on these matters. Like Minuchin, I would be interested in the responses of constructivist thinkers to these important questions about power and about the social fabric.

Zimmerman: I notice that you are quite particular in identifying different traditions of thought and how they influence therapeutic practice.

White: Well, yes, I believe that this is important. In this quote of Minuchin's, for example, I don't take his comments to be a critique of poststructuralist informed practices as I know them. I have never considered what I think and what I do to be "constructivist." I don't have much familiarity with constructivism, and I don't have an appreciation of the history of this tradition of thought. I am not suggesting that Minuchin is representing as constructivist the sort of poststructuralist inquiry that shapes narrative explorations, but it is not unusual these days to see different traditions of thought and practice collapsed on to each other in ways that actually obscure what is being proposed in each of these distinct traditions. For example, in the literature I have read accounts of my thought and practices that represent me as an"anti-realist," despite the fact that I have little sympathy for what is proposed in this tradition, and despite the fact that I believe the realist/anti-realist debate to be irrelevant to what I know of poststructuralist inquiry and narrative practice.[3]

---

[3]For example, in her book *Back to Reality: A Critique of Postmodern Theory in Psychotherapy*, Barbara Held (1995, p. 132—also see Chapter 9, this volume) has written:

> [T]o see or treat people's actions, including their utterances, as literary texts to be deconstructed is to apply a metaphor that brings with it some danger that the therapist will be tempted to ignore or minimize the importance of the (extralinguistic) reality of the real person sitting before the therapist, with all her real life experiences. These include real psychological, social, and economic circumstances, for instance, poverty, oppression, abuse, and even, contrary to the narrative view, real mental illness, such as schizophrenia or depression. For if all we need to do to solve the client's problem is change her (antirealist) narrative/view of it, then we need not put any efforts and resources into trying to change the real circumstances of that extralinguistic reality.

I have also been represented as a social constructionist and a postmodernist. While I can relate to and appreciate many of the ideas that are represented as social constructionist, in this tradition of thought there is also much that leaves me unsatisfied. And I know just little fragments of the specificity of postmodernism, which has its roots in art and literature. Perhaps this specificity is now becoming lost, as the term *postmodernism* is now often employed to categorize any idea and practice that does not reproduce foundationist thought. But even the specificity of *this* description is at risk. I have recently seen postmodernism represented as a form of "anything goes" moral relativism, as the achievement of simultaneously holding multiple beliefs or views or theories about life, and even as a "new eclecticism." I think that this is an unfortunate turn, because in it postmodernism has come to represent what it contradicts.

On any account, this running together of distinct traditions of thought and practice is unhelpful. It leads to the false representation of the position of different thinkers. It destroys a climate of thought by manufacturing a soup that is so thick that it is indigestible, and one in which the different flavors can no longer be distinguished. As an outcome, discerning action in the name of therapy becomes impossible. And therapists are deprived of any clarity in regard to the development of proposals for the further exploration of specific ideas and practices.

It can also become quite amusing! Sometimes, because of the blurring of distinct traditions of thinking, it is claimed that, in what I have written about what I think and do, I haven't properly acknowledged certain thinkers. Simultaneously, it is sometimes said that if I did acknowledge these thinkers then I wouldn't have written what I have written about what I think and do because I wouldn't then think these ways and do these things in the way that I do them!

Hoyt: And you believe that conundrums of this sort are the product of this blurring of different and distinct traditions of thought?

The very title *Narrative Means to Therapeutic Ends* (White & Epston, 1990) indicates that "story reauthoring" is the vehicle, not the destination. This is spelled out in *Experience, Contradiction, Narrative and Imagination* (Epston & White, 1992) when White (p. 81) writes:

> Thus, the stories that we enter into with our experience have real effects on our lives. The expression of our experience through these stories shapes or makes-up our lives and our relationships; our lives are shaped or constituted through the very process of the interpretation of experience within the contexts of the stories that we enter into and that we are entered into by others.
>
> This is not to propose that life is synonymous with text. It is not enough for a person to tell a new story about oneself, or to assert claims about oneself. Instead, the position carried by these assertions about the world of experience and narrative is that life is the performance of texts. And it is the performance of these texts that is transformative of person's lives.

White: Often this seems to be the case. At times even the poststructuralist-informed proposals of narrative practice are run together with those that are based on linguistic analyses which are informed by structuralist ideas. I believe that to question this lumping together of these different traditions, and to untangle these, is important, as it makes it more possible for all of us to see a way ahead, irrespective of our persuasions.

I think it's really important that the distinctions remain clear, and that yet more of these be drawn. For these distinctions to be blurred makes it very difficult for therapists in our field to experience a degree of conscious choice in terms of the ideas and practices that they wish to engage with, and to reflect on these ideas and practices as they monitor the effects of these in their work with people who seek consultation. Also, when these distinctions are blurred we cannot find a place in which we might sit together, regardless of our differing persuasions, and engage in conversations with each other in which we might all extend on the limits of what we already think.[4]

Zimmerman: I would be interested in how we can have these conversations. Especially as when we view the work of others, from an outsider's

---

[4]Elsewhere, White (1999, pp. 58–59) expands on some of the implications of the structuralism/poststructuralism distinction for identity formation:

Poststructuralist understandings account for identity as a social and public achievement—identity is something that is negotiated within social institutions and within communities of people—and is shaped by historical and cultural forces. In exploring the mechanisms that give rise to identity within these contexts, the structure of narrative frequently comes under scrutiny, for people routinely negotiate meaning within the context of narrative frames—they attribute meaning to their experiences of the events of their lives by locating these in sequences that unfold through time according to certain themes or plots. And more than this: it is in this 'storying' of experience that people derive identity descriptions that are filed into the identity categories of modern culture—motive, need, attributes, traits, properties, and so on. According to this poststructuralist take on life, it is not one's motive that shapes action, but one's account of one's motive that has been socially derived in narrative negotiations that does so.

In comparison to structuralist conceptions of life that are informed by the surface/depth contrast, a characteristic of poststructuralist thought is the contrasting of the metaphors 'thin' and 'thick.' In engaging with this thin/thick contrast, rather than reproducing the time-honored therapeutic practices of interpreting people's expressions of living through recourse to the expert knowledge discourses of the culture of therapy, and of remedial action on the part of the therapist (which contribute to thin description), the practices of narrative therapy assist people to break from thin conclusions about their lives, about their identities, and about their relationships. But more than this: these narrative practices also provide people with the opportunity to engage in the thick or rich descriptions of their lives, of their identities, and of their relationships. As people become more narratively resourced through the generation of this thick or rich description, they find that they have available to them options for action that would not have otherwise been imaginable.

perspective, what we see is often quite different from that which is seen by those who are actually practicing it. For example, I am sure that my view of structural therapy from an outsider's perspective is quite different from those who are structural therapists. We bring our own interpretations and understandings. Finding ways to make further distinctions between certain practices I think would be very helpful.

Hoyt: In terms of making these sorts of distinctions, I want to ask you, Michael, an historical kind of question. I read some of your earlier papers [White, 1984, 1986]. At one time you were writing more in a cybernetics and strategic frame. What do you think you gained in the shift?

White: I have gone through different phases in my explorations, and in these have framed my work in various ways, including in the ways that are informed by some of the schools of family therapy. Several experiences assisted me to break from these efforts. And some of these breaks were in the form of a U-turn. For example, in the latter part of the 70's, Cheryl White expressed concerns about the direction of my explorations in therapy—that these were engaging me in relational politics that were taking me away from my preferred values and preferred ways of being in my life, and limiting of my considerations of the power relations of local culture, including those considerations shaped by a feminist consciousness, one that Cheryl had introduced me to in the first place at the beginning of the 70's. So, Cheryl's expression of these concerns, her identification of and naming of them, and her faith in the fact that I could find another way, was instrumental in my return to the spirit of my earlier engagement with therapeutic practice.[5]

---

[5]In another recent interview (with Jill Freedman), White (2000, pp. 120–121) elaborates:

> But I do strongly value my engagement with family therapy. It is clear to me that in this field it has been possible, to an extent, for people to think outside of what was otherwise being taught at the time. In fact, I believe this has been encouraged. Perhaps this could be identified as a tradition, or as a spirit of adventure and exploration. So, for me, standing on the inside of what I think and do, what I appreciate most strongly is the contribution of those figures that have shaped such a fertile context—to the shaping of a context that is fertile in the sense that it accomodates a whole range of ideas that are often discontinuous, at times contradictory, and frequently novel. This is a context in which ideas are not spontaneously rejected because they don't fit well with what has already been established. I believe this to be something that we can celebrate.
>
> When I think about the figures that have contributed to this tradition, so many come to mind: Jay Haley, Virginia Satir, Salvador Minuchin, Mara Selvini Palazzoli, Luigi Boscolo, Gianfranco Cecchin, Peggy Papp, Olga Silverstein, Lynn Hoffman, Paul Watzlawick and John Weakland, to name just a few. And most of these people continue to contribute to this tradition, and to the further development of ideas and practices. At these times when I am naming names I always feel disconcerted—I find myself thinking of all the other names that should also be in here.

And there were many singular events that were significant. For example, around 1980 I sent Eleanor Werthiem a manuscript that I had been working on, and soon after had the pleasure of meeting her on a visit to Melbourne. She said that she appreciated those parts of the manuscript that provided an account of what actually happened in my therapeutic conversations with families of young children, but confronted me on my attempts to formalize an understanding of this by engaging with theory. Eleanor's challenge to me was powerful and direct. She chose her words carefully, and they kept ringing in my ears for quite some time.

Hoyt: You said that you made a U-turn and that you renewed your engagement with certain values and practices. Could you say something about the history of these—do you mean your personal history?

White: Personal and communal, a history of standing a bit outside of some of the institutions of our culture—not on the periphery in the sense that groups of marginalized people stand on the periphery and can look back on culture—but to an extent outside some of the institutions and cultures.

I grew up in a working class family and always had a strong awareness of the power relations of class. Many experiences contributed to this awareness. For example, the high school that I went to was huge and forced some order on the masses through a system of "streaming." The working class kids were in the lower streams, and were mostly seen as hopeless by the school—these students didn't warrant the expenditure of much in the way of attention and general resources. These classes were unruly, poorly taught, and the cane was consistently resorted to in efforts to establish a semblance of order. Needless to say, the culture of the school yard was violent.

In my second year at this school, an English teacher by the name of Alison Siliakis was assigned to my class. In response to the uproarious atmosphere, she did something very unusual. She brought a record player into the class, and, ignoring the chaos, began to play Joan Baez records, all the while encouraging us to speak about what we had heard in this music. At the onset, no one knew quite what to make of this. I was mermerized by both of them, Alison Siliakis and Joan Baez. This was an extraordinary development—such powerful respect for us and others being expressed in what seemed a sea of disqualification and abuse. Mrs. Siliakis went on to ignite my interest in poetry and novels, and in other possible worlds.

Toward the latter part of my life as a student I joined the protest movement against the Australian and United States involvement in the Vietnam war. For me, this was galvanizing of lots of lived experiences, and was also, in part, an expression of Alison Siliakis's and Joan Baez's contribution to my life. And, in turn, this involvement in the protest movement contributed further to a consciousness of the power relations of local culture.

Hoyt: This reminds me of a passage written by Lynn Hoffman (1993, p. 7). She wrote:

> I became particularly aware [in the early 1980s] of the unconscious sexism of all styles of family therapy. Up to that time, most family therapists had accepted them without question. Even when colleagues of mine applied feminist principles to their practice, they focused upon particular injustices like mother-bashing but did not question very much the models they had been trained in. Mainly pioneered by men, these styles went from a benign paternalism to an extreme focus on hierarchy, secrecy, and control. Even feminist versions kept therapists in a power position in relation to the people the therapists saw. How else could they "empower" them?
>
> I began to ask questions. . . . To become another activist seemed too close to becoming another kind of expert, so for the moment I stayed quiet on the subject. I still continued to search for a less hierarchically organized family therapy that would enlarge the options for all.

Do you have any thoughts about this?

White: I know that Lynn Hoffman has made a very significant contribution towards this search for less hierarchically organized family therapy—in fact, a very significant contribution to many explorations of a whole range of questions in this field. And, as well, Lynn, along with other feminist family therapists, has raised the relations of gender and power within therapeutic conversations. I believe that this has made very real differences to the ways in which family therapy is practiced.

Hoyt: Indeed.

White: But I was curious, Michael, what was interesting to you in that question about shifting from a strategic-directive approach?

Hoyt: I'm struggling with it personally on many levels: How to be with without being in control. That maybe says it in a sentence, and then all of the professional mantle gets wrapped around that. What am I supposed to do as a therapist, as a doctor, as an interventionist? And particularly when I see people who I think I have a good idea of something *I* think would be helpful to them and they seem in dire straits and they need a hand quickly and I don't want to hold back and let them suffer, but I also see the other side of it that in some ways I may be disabling them if I jump in and sort of impose my ideas. Plus, it fits into my personality in some ways: I struggle with not being in the center; to be de-centered and stay involved is not an easy thing for me. As a professional, there are so many canons of authority, like the *DSM* [*Diagnostic and Statistical Manual*, APA, 1994], and you look at them and you know there is something terribly wrong. So I'm kind of questioning, like the bumper sticker says: *Question Authority.*

Zimmerman: *[points above bookcase]* See the one I've got up there: *Subvert the Dominant Paradigm! [laughter]* Stephen [Madigan] sent me that one.

Hoyt: There are so many taken-for-granted sorts of things. I work in a medical center and so there's a structure of *patient-doctor* imposed and they are like petitioners and sometimes they're sent and sometimes they come, but there's already all sorts of these assumptions of "deficit" and "they're broken" and "they need to go to Psychiatry." It's very hard to try to reverse that in a quick way. I think one of the ways I've seen you do that, Michael, is just by the way you listen, what you listen for. You used a phrase today, "rescuing the said from the saying."

White: Yeah, I borrowed that from Clifford Geertz [1973; see White, 1997, p. 15].

Hoyt: Hearing what is vital and not getting lost in all the words, in the way it is sometimes said. In *Narratives of Therapists' Lives* [White, 1997, p. 94] you refer to "many of the significant expressions of life that would otherwise pass like a blip across a person's screen of consciousness, and disappear off the edge into a vacuum." You have an amazing ear, you detect it. It's in there somewhere and you'll find it. Like that article called "Panning for Gold" [Wylie, 1994].[6] You find those nuggets—and I'm trying to figure out how I'm going to do more of that.

White: In response to your question, it is my preference to ask you a question. So, what is the history of you asking these questions like "How am I going to do more of that?" What is the history of you asking questions of some of the taken-for-granted practices of the culture of psychotherapy, of some of the regular and generally accepted ways of speaking with people about their lives?[7] What is the history of you confronting your own assumptions about what is helpful and unhelpful in therapeutic conversations? And what is the history of your interest in these "nuggets," and of your attribution of value and meaning to these other expressions of living that are so often neglected in therapeutic conversations?

Hoyt: What is it about?

---

[6]Also see White's discussion (in Hoyt & Combs, 1996—see Chapter 3, this volume, p. 85) about "the little sacraments of daily existence. . . . the sacred significance of the little events of people's lives; those little events that lie in the shadows of the dominant plots of people's lives, those little events that are so often neglected, but that might come to be regarded with reverence, and at times with awe."

[7]A discussion about the role of power and influence that followed the "Narrative Solutions/Solution Narratives" conference presented by White and de Shazer (1996) was the direct predecessor of the conversation reported here.

White: Yeah.

Hoyt: There was something you mentioned today [in the workshop] about if you know the history of an idea it doesn't capture you the same way. In some ways I've always been . . . I'm like the loyal opposition, I'm participating but I'm not quite taken by it. I'm not alienated to the point where I'm out, but I'm not a true believer and so I'm always kind of looking for what's the edge and the inconsistency and where doesn't it fit and what do you gain and what do you lose? Some of the approaches I've studied—and at different times have practiced—have come to seem to me either discouragingly pathologically preoccupied and/or too involved with enhancing the therapist's power and authority. So I've been on a project for the last several years of interviewing people, asking questions. Some of it involves personal reasons for connecting with certain people, some of it is much more an intellectual curiosity kind of interest, some of it is my continuing quest to find ways to more efficiently assist clients.

Also—and I think I may have written this to you—in the meeting with Gene [Combs] and you and I [see Chapter 3] , there was something that transpired that was something of a turning point for me, empowering or renewing my sense of choice. We were talking about which path we step on and building the path as we go. Something about the image or the moment of us being there became very profound for me. We co-created it, although I think I owe it to you at the same time. It wouldn't have happened had you not been there.

White: Could you say a bit more about that?

Hoyt: I have different ways of being and one of the things at that Therapeutic Conversations conference [Therapeutic Conversations 2, Reston, VA, July 1994] where we spoke with Gene Combs was there was a wonderful sense of love and respect in the air. It was very sweet and it was very appealing to me, and that is one way I can be. And then there is another way I can be that is very sharp and sarcastic, clever but very cynical. It's entertaining but at times it can be, I think, more destructive than anything. I struggle with it, back and forth, and it's played out in different parts of my life. That conversation sort of crystallized it. While we were talking about "building the path as we go," I was thinking of it consciously and it became really clear. There's still a process, but I have a choice. So, when we did the first little introduction at the workshop this morning, when you asked us to turn to the person next to us and tell him or her something about why we're here, I said "I'm here to be reminded about choice." And it seems so refreshing to me to be able to say, "Hey, I have a conscious choice about this," rather than just having to sort all of this out endlessly and endlessly and endlessly. It's an ethical choice in a sense. So that's some history of my questioning.

I became aware of narrative, if you will, not narrative therapy but of the social construction of reality, as a child. My family was at the bottom of the middle class and secular Jewish. I grew up feeling myself to be an American but also knew we weren't quite mainstream. I was raised with something of an 'outsider's' perspective, which contributes to my distrust of dominant, totalizing descriptions. (For me, a suspicion of appearances and a tendency to look behind things, a tendency to deconstruct, can be a positive aspect of cynicism.) My parents had friends of different religious backgrounds and ethnicities and races and my father had an interest in anthropology and archaeology, so that also helped reinforce the idea that there are many ways to be human rather than there being one truth or one right way. Early on I was "multi-versed," if you will. So I kind of have it back there somewhere, but it also felt like, "Oh, I get to choose again," sort of coming home to it in a way.

White: Sounds a bit like re-engagement with history for you as well. Or some aspects of history.

Hoyt: Yes. I've also had a recent experience of my mother becoming ill. She's developed Alzheimer's disease—she's still somewhat functional, but she's fading.[8] She's moved into a care-giving institution, and I was cleaning out her place and I spent a weekend there by myself and found all the old family photographs, cartons of them. I looked at my great, great, grandfather. I saw things from a hundred years ago and 50 years ago, pictures of me as a child, pictures of me with my father and grandfather, and began to remember things they said and what parts of what they stood for or represent for me—such as honesty and fair play and letting other people be themselves and respecting other people's ways of doing things— did I like and can re-engage with. (My wife, Jennifer, also strongly encourages these values.) It was wonderful. It had a mourning, a sadness about it, too—times lost. But it was also, to use some terms, "hullo, again" and "re-membering" [see White, 1988, 1995, 1997] .

White: Yes.

Hoyt: Michael, I know that the works of certain anthropologists have been influential in your work. For example, in "Deconstruction and Therapy" [White, 1989/1993, p. 38] you quoted Clifford Geertz [1986, p. 380]:

> The wrenching question, sour and disabused, that Lionel Trilling somewhere quotes an eighteenth-century aesthetician as asking—"How Comes It that we all start out Originals and End up Copies?"—finds. . . . an answer that is surprisingly reassuring: it is the copying that originates.

How do you understand this?

---

[8]Ruth Hoyt passed away on her 80th birthday, 29 May 1999.

White: It is a lament that very much speaks to a humanist essentialism, one that asserts the existence of certain elements and substances that make up a self that is at the center of who we are. It is a lament that takes for granted not only the existence of this self, but that there is a "truth" of human nature to be found in these essences, and that this represents what is "original" about being human. What is lamented is that this original is lost to processes of socialization and enculturation, to the forces of repression. There are many contemporary versions of this lament, and, in the culture of therapy, these inspire the development of practices that supposedly assist people to become more truly who they really are by challenging whatever it is that is considered to be repressive and by "liberating" what it is that is deemed to be original about the self—so that a life can be more exactly an expression of these essences.

Clifford Geertz is a cultural anthropologist who has a non-essentialist understanding of identity formation. Non-essentialist understandings are a challenge to the modern idea that there is a self that is at the center of who we are. Geertz would have us invert this lament that we have been speaking of, and in this inversion it is recast as: "How Comes It that we all start out Copies and End up Originals?" This turns out to be a far more interesting question, one that breaks us from naturalistic accounts of identity. It is a question to which Geertz responds: "It is the copying that originates." In this sense, rather than to become more truly who we really are, "originating" refers to identity-shaping activity that contributes to us becoming other than who we are.

To invert this lament engages us in a fascination with the specificity of and consequences of people's acts of living as they go about reproducing the stories of their lives, as they go about the social negotiation and renegotiation of accounts of their identity. It draws our attention to people's self-shaping activities: to the extent to which people's responses to the contingencies of their lives takes them past the previously known limits of their existence; to the way that people's efforts in maintaining coherent expressions of their identity as they navigate through the different contexts of their lives contributes to revisions of their accounts of and experience of this very identity; to how people's management of the predicaments, dilemmas, and contradictions of their lives contribute to possibilities for them to think outside of what they would have otherwise thought, and so on. To engage with the inverted version of this lament centers meaning-making as an achievement that is constitutive of life. In their attempts to reproduce identity in acts of living, people wind up originating—the reproduction of identity encapsulates the copy that went before, but it is more than that.[9]

---

[9]See Gary Snyder's (1983) poem, "Axe Handles," and other epigraphs that open this volume.

Hoyt: Is it similar to the idea of *re-telling*, where thickening layers of description take it to another level? [see White, 1997; Geertz, 1973; Meyerhoff, 1982, 1986].

White: Yes.

Zimmerman: What I want to comment on is the real effects of Geertz's construction. For me, the effect of reversing this lament is to take all the pressure off. If there is no person or thing I'm supposed to live up to, be compared against, even if I'm attempting to copy or working in a similar way then I am freed from the sort of judgment based on some "imagined" hard criteria. I am freed up to celebrate differences.

White: People who come here for training [Bay Area Family Therapy Training Associates] don't wind up being a carbon copy of Jeff Zimmerman. In watching your practice they would get a first-hand account of what you do, and would be drawn to certain expressions of it. And many would then go off and do their best to engage with the ideas and practices that they explored in this training with you. But in their efforts to reproduce these ideas and practices they would become something else—through these people's own expressions, these ideas and practices would become other than what they were.

Zimmerman: I'm aware of turning down invitations to be in that position, and I'm aware of asking questions of the people who come here to work that invite them in the other direction. To taking their own ideas more seriously. That's an intentional stance that I think has really good effects when you're in a "supervisory" position with students.

Hoyt: There's a parallel process, a meta-message of becoming an original rather than trying to become a Jeff Zimmerman or Michael White.

Zimmerman: And it's isomorphic to the work, to the work you're doing in therapy.

White: This intentional stance that you speak of means that people who come for training are more likely to find opportunities to value their own expressions of poststructuralist practice. If you didn't intentionally arrange a context for opportunities of this sort the people who come here would be attempting to reproduce the ideas and practices explored in the training context, but their unique expression of these ideas and practices would not be visible to them. Under these circumstances it would be very difficult for these people to embrace the unique aspects of their expressions of these ideas and practices, aspects that could not be traced back to your own expressions.

Zimmerman: Right.

Hoyt: Do you mind if I shift the direction a bit and ask a different question? Let me frame it as a quotation from something you said in an earlier conversation, Michael, in relation to *transference and technologies of power*.

> But these technologies of transference are not just the historical conditions for the constitution of the transference phenomenon. Transference can also be read as the 'trace' of very present power relations. . . . So, a strong and ongoing experience of transference can cue people to the fact that they are in a subject position in an inflexible power relationship that could lead to domination. This reading of transference opens possibilities for action that can include a refusal of this power relation.
>
> I don't want to be misrepresented on this point. I'm not saying that there is no such phenomenon as transference. And I do understand that there are those who would justify bringing forth this phenomenon with the idea that this establishes a context for working through issues of personal authority, and so on. But I do think that there is a politics associated with this phenomenon, and [I] would raise questions about the deliberate and not so deliberate reproduction of these politics in the therapeutic context. And I would also want to explore the sort of questions that could contribute to a dismantling of the therapeutic structures that reproduce this phenomenon. [White, in Hoyt & Combs, 1996—see Chapter 3, p. 87, this volume]

So, how do you see the politics associated with the phenomenon and then, what questions would you raise about it?

White: If someone experiences transference in relation to me, then I want to understand in what ways I might be complicit in the reproduction of certain power relations. I want to explore how we can establish a therapeutic context that contributes to an awareness of the contribution I might be making, wittingly or unwittingly, in the reproduction of power relations that could drift towards relations of domination. It may be that I am speaking with taken-for-granted privilege and that I'm not aware of this. It may be the way that I sit or generally arrange my body in space that is an expression of the power relations of gender. Whatever. I am interested in the options available for rendering more visible these sort of practices of power, as well as the real and potential effects of these, so that they can, to some extent at least, become available to us to modify. What are your thoughts about this?

Zimmerman: I'm interested in how de-centering practices can assist in reducing the chances of what is known as transference. I'm also curious about the effect of the stories that people might bring with them about the counseling process and what a difference this can also make.

White: And it's not just certain people's private stories either. In seeking therapy people often come to an office which is a formal space in which the therapist's authority is assumed. There are many factors which contribute to the sort of power relations that can create a context for what is known as *transference*.

Hoyt: Perhaps particularly with a male therapist and a female client, it's all too easy to fall into a reproduction of stereotypic gender politics. This potential reproduction also exists in doing therapy with persons who have been subject to sexual abuse, as Rachel Hare-Mustin (e.g., 1992, 1994; Hare-Mustin & Marecek, 1990) and others have written about.

White: Rachel Hare-Mustin has had, and continues to have, a very significant and eloquent voice in this field on the power relations of local culture, including on the power relations of gender in therapy. She consistently works to encourage this therapy field to acknowledge these power relations and to prioritize them in consideration of therapeutic practice.

Hoyt: You have also spoken and written about the importance of making this a priority.

White: I have written about the potential for the inherent power differential within the therapeutic context to have negative effects on the lives of those who have survived abuse and about some of the *practices of accountability* that are possible for male therapists to engage with when working in these contexts (White, 1995). I believe these are very relevant and significant concerns.

It is also possible for us to engage with other practices of accountability throughout all therapeutic conversations. For example, there are questions we can ask that might reduce the potential for the sort of power relations that we are talking about to become toxic in their effects. We can routinely consult people about the direction of the therapeutic conversation:

- *"How is this conversation going for you?"*
- *"Are we talking about what is important for us to be talking about, or are we off track in this?"*
- *"How does this conversation fit with the agenda that you came here with?"*
- *"Would you catch me up with how this conversation is going for you. This will help us to figure out where to go next."*
- *"It seems to me that we are at a point where there are a number of possible directions for our conversations. These would all take us into different explorations of your life and relationships. I would like to share my thoughts about these possibilities with you, and then consult you about a couple of things: other ideas that you might have for the direction of our conversation, and which of all of these possibilities most interest you."*

Apart from all else, consultations of this sort make it clear that the therapist can't assume to know what might be the relevant and appropriate conversations to be having with others, and that she or he is not an authority on what is best for others.[10]

Zimmerman: I absolutely agree, and this takes me back to the conversation about transference. If I think back to the couple of times that I have had the experience of transference happening, I would see myself as 100% complicit in it. In deconstructing what had occurred I would have seen that I had positioned myself in a way in which I placed myself in a position of power, or one of monitoring the experience of those that had come to consult with me. I think it would be interesting to consider what are the practices of therapy and therapists that construct the phenomenon of transference.

Hoyt: As a part of deconstructing these practices I'd be interested in how therapists can proceed so as to learn about and from the people consulting us rather than appearing to be "assessing" them or checking them out. How can we ensure that we are not engaging in "grading" these people?

White: I'm really interested in what you are saying. We have a culture of evaluation. These times could be called the "grading times." This is the "rating-table" era. Our present era is the era of the developmental continuum. When we trace the history of this culture of evaluation we can see how modern processes of the judgment of people's actions are intimately associated with, and in the service of, reproducing our society's constructed norms.

Even just norms for living. Modern systems of power engage people in disciplines of the self. It is through the disciplining of the self that people might close the gap between where they stand and the constructed norms of our culture. It is through the sort of practices of evaluation and grading that you speak of that therapists can become agents of this disciplinary technology.

---

[10]Recall also White's comments in Chapter 3, p. 77:

> [W]e can't pretend that we are not somehow contributing to the process. We can't pretend that we are not influential in the therapeutic interaction. There is no neutral position in which therapists can stand. I can embrace this fact by joining with people to address all of those things that they find traumatizing and limiting of their lives. . . . And, because the impossibility of neutrality means that I cannot avoid being "for" something, I take the responsibility to distrust what I am for—that is, my ways of life and my ways of thought—and I can do this in many ways. For example, I can distrust what I am for with regard to the appropriateness of this to the lives of others. I can distrust what I am for in the sense that what I am for has the potential to reproduce the very things that I oppose in my relations with others. I can distrust what I am for to the extent that what I am for has a distinct location in the worlds of gender, class, race, culture, sexual preference, etc. And so on.

Zimmerman: I notice I do this. We all do this. Today I recall in the workshop that you said to someone, "That was a good question." There are practices like that which we say out of habit without reflection which inadvertently represent grading or evaluation. If you don't say that to someone else, what do they think: "Well, maybe mine wasn't a good question." What I sensed you really meant was "That's interesting to me" or something like that.

White: Yes, it's certainly a different response, to say: "That is very interesting," or "That captures my imagination."

Zimmerman: Yeah, that for me is situated more in yourself.

Hoyt: To me, when I find myself saying "That's a good question," it usually means it stretched me. It made me think and it wasn't in my repertoire already—it wasn't just confirming the known.

White: To say "That question stretched me" rather than "That was a good question" is associated with very different real effects.

Zimmerman: Right, on the person asking it—and on the other people in the room who may have asked questions to which you didn't say "That was a good question."

Hoyt: Even positive affirmations, although well intended, still serve to maintain the idea of performance evaluation. It's more of the same.

White: I agree.

Zimmerman: On another note, you were talking today, Michael [White], about the *performance of preferred claims*. When someone consults with us and speaks of their hopes and desires for change, there is much within the therapeutic culture that can invite us to disregard these claims, to be cynical about them. What you seemed to be saying was that as therapists we could create a context for a performance of these claims. What a different way that is to think about what you're getting from people and what a different response you would make back, than if you were thinking about what they were saying as a reflection of some motives or something out of awareness.

White: Can you say a little more about this, Jeff?

Zimmerman: I remember seeing you do an interview, this was 1987 or 1988, in Tulsa, and Gail Lapidus and I were sitting behind the mirror watching and a woman came in, and she was one of those people who was an outcast of the system. She had many so-called "disabilities" and she was in about eight different marginalized positions. She came in and was saying, "Oh yes, I really want to get better and I really want this," and I looked at Gail and she looked at me, like "Oh yeah, we've heard this before." You responded to her in a way that suggested that you saw what the woman was saying as a reflection of her preferred claims. That was one of the three or four most transformative things for me in doing this work, because I saw the effect of that, that by the end of the interview she was taking her claims much more seriously herself. She entered into it.

White: Yeah.

Zimmerman: I got to thinking, "Well, what would have been the effect of me listening to that and thinking, 'Oh yeah, sure, you're just saying that and it doesn't mean much, maybe what you're really after is this or that.'" She never would have entered into it in the same way.

White: I believe that to take up the opportunity to more richly describe one's quest has the effect of advancing one's quest. In this way, therapy can become a context for the performance of preferred claims about identity, about ways of being in the world—and that's our business, isn't it, to open up space for people to express these claims and to contribute to establishing contexts in which these claims might be performed and acknowledged by others in ways that are authenticating of them. I understand this to be powerfully shaping of people's lives. I don't believe that it is all that helpful, to the people who consult therapists, for us to traffic in cynicism. Unfortunately young people are regularly subject to this in relation to their preferred identity claims—"They are just saying that they want to break from all of this trouble because that is what they want you to think," or "In entering this undertaking to change their ways, they are just pulling the wool over your eyes. This is just what they want you to believe."

But we don't have to engage with this doctrine of doubt. We can respond to such identity claims in ways that are honoring of these, in ways that contribute to possibilities for people to more richly describe them, and to participate in the identification and creation of forums in which these claims might be performed. We can then consult the people concerned about what they consider to be the consequences, to their lives and relationships, of the performance of these claims, and encourage them to evaluate these consequences.

Hoyt: An alternative approach elevates us as The Expert who interprets their motivations.

Zimmerman: It just doesn't seem like a helpful idea to me. None of us, I think, would get into any debate about interpreting "truths."

Hoyt: I want to ask a question that comes out of the contrast on one point that Steve de Shazer wrote about your work, Michael. In his discussion of Chang and Phillips' [1993] paper from the Tulsa [Therapeutic Conversations] Conference, he said:

White draws a "pro-problem"/"anti-problem (unique outcomes)" distinction, while I draw a "problem"/"solution (exception)" distinction. It is clear to me now that his "anti," his concept of "unique outcomes" is on the "problem" side of my distinction. His clinical practice of constructing the historical predictability of the "unique outcome" undermines its *uniqueness* and emphasizes the *outcome* or the end of a long process. The "unique outcome" is now just as historical as the problem of which it becomes just one part. Since the "unique outcome" is constructed as a historically predictable event, then it is just as causally determined as the rest of the problem, rather than the turning point that I had thought he was describing. As such, it leaves the concept of "anorexia" intact.

Thus Michael White's view is a very traditional one. . . . That is, externalizing the problem and the unique outcome, objectifies and reifies them: In practice, "anorexia" exists as a real thing. [de Shazer, 1993, pp. 118-119]

That's his view, at least as he wrote it then. How do you respond to it?

White: Well, there's a lot of things to respond to in this.

Zimmerman: My reaction is that we ought to talk to people with anorexia and see what they think about whether anorexia is a real thing or not. They might have some things to say about that. What their experience of it is. I'd say they experience it as pretty real, and pretty mean. [see White & Epston, 1990; Zimmerman & Dickerson, 1994]

White: And life-threatening. When young people talk about their experience of anorexia nervosa, it is common for them to identify it as a force or multiplicity of forces that keep them small, that, in a myriad of ways, have the effect of rendering them invisible to others and to themselves. I think it probably would be a good question to ask or a good comment to share with people who struggle with things like anorexia nervosa.

Zimmerman: Like the Anti-Anorexia/Anti-Bulemia League[11]— Lorraine Grieves and Stephen Madigan (and others) might have some things to say about that, that would be quite strong. One of the bigger points, to me, is *who's deciding?* Is Steve [de Shazer] deciding about what experience is to be labeled in what way, or whether the problem experience is the one that's relevant to the client? Who's directing that course, in that instance?

Hoyt: I took what Steve was saying was you externalize it, but it's still more of the same. Anorexia is alive and well and that the construction of anorexia is reified.

White: Because I'm not a "constructivist" in that sense, it is difficult for me to appreciate that argument. There is a whole range of experiences that people consult us about that cannot be simply assigned the status of

---

[11]The Anti-Anorexia/Anti-Bulemia League organized in Vancouver, Canada, (see Madigan, 1997; Madigan & Epston, 1995; Madigan & Goldner, 1998).

constructs that are either radically invented by people, or that can be radically dissolved by engaging with other constructs. Sure, we might consider anorexia nervosa a product of some of the more dominant discourses of our culture, but this consideration will invite us to apprehend anorexia nervosa as a product of a particular type of rationality. It will invite us into an appreciation of the extent to which anorexia is something that is produced through the coordinated actions of various parties and institutions. It will invite us to consider some of the actual relational practices and techniques of the self that are associated with anorexia as a mode of life and thought, relational practices and techniques of the self that are very much shaped by the normalizing-judgment imperative of our culture, one that has been instrumental in the social control of women. It will invite us to join with others in the identification of the instruments of these normalizing judgments—for example, the grand narratives of human development, and the tables and continuums that are associated with these.

This rationality, these coordinated actions, these relational practices and techniques of the self, and these instruments of normalizing judgment cannot be subsumed under the notion "construct." And we can consider these "real" without engaging with any claims about the objective nature of the world and life.

Hoyt: So, when you say that you *externalize* something [White, 1988/1989], how do you answer the question, "Where did the problem go?"

White: It is *situated*. To externalize the problem is to situate it, to deconstruct it. To situate it in culture, in language, in the power relations of local culture, in modes of life and thought that are shaping of life and that are venerated in our culture. It is to exoticise the familiar and taken for granted.

Zimmerman: To go back to the Steve de Shazer thing: I think what he's doing is really different, I mean in the sense that he's not in the same kind of conversation with his clients that I think we try to be. He is, I think, operating from a more constructivist perspective, and I think it has different effects on his work. He's moving people along in ways that he is figuring out would best move them along. I always think of his work as the other side of the coin from doing the MRI [Mental Research Institute] work. So the group he's connected to [the Brief Family Therapy Center, in Milwaukee], they're not breaking the "problem" and bringing in the "solution," but it's still from that same position of directing in a way that you first started this interview asking about. The *discovery* is much more, I think, in his head than in the conversation. Like, "Okay, this looks like this might work, I'm going to pull it out here"—and I'm not saying that it's a bad thing, but I do think the process is different. He might or might not relate to what we're saying from that perspective. I'm interpreting it that way.

Hoyt: I want to ask another basic question, if I could. I hear these days some people referring to narrative therapy as a kind of social movement, or a kind of liberation philosophy. It is being identified in some circles as politically "left-wing." Have you heard these sorts of things? Is it your intention for narrative therapy to be perceived in these ways?

White: I have heard people reflect on narrative therapy in these ways and have some concern that such descriptions could be trivializing and diminishing of the courage expressed in, and of the very significant contributions and achievements of, various social movements. I do not know of any therapists who have risked their lives and the safety of their families, who have totally compromised their security, or who have been exiled due to their involvement in narrative therapy. And yet these experiences are often had by people who participate in social movements, and in initiatives that are informed by liberation philosophy.

And there are other reasons why the description of narrative therapy as a social movement does not fit for me. I don't know how it is that narrative therapy could be constructed as a social movement, or as a kind of liberation philosophy. Social movements, in my understanding, are broad-based and issue focussed, very often addressing wider social justice issues from a variety of political platforms. In this sense, I don't believe that there is anything about what I understand to be narrative therapy that would allow it to make any claim to be a social movement or a liberation philosophy.

As well, the liberation philosophies principally focus on the forces of oppression and repression. And, as an outcome of their association with liberal humanism, these movements usually incorporate a strong vision or narrative about how things could otherwise be in the world. Contrast this with the agenda that is explicit in narrative therapy. This is to engage in some local inquiry into what is happening, into how things are becoming other than what they were, or into the potential for things to become other than what they are. It is to engage in the rich description of the knowledges and skills of living expressed in this, and in an exploration of the possibilities, limitations and possible dangers associated with how things are and with how they are becoming other than what they were. Although I believe that this emphasis provides for a socially and politically sensitive practice, I want to reiterate that I don't believe that there is anything about these practices that could constitute narrative therapy as a social movement.

Hoyt: It seems to me, if I'm following you, that one distinction comes back to the ways in which narrative practices seek to provide a context for people to identify their own preferences for life and to evaluate the effects of these preferences. The people consulting therapists are making choices as to the directions in which they go rather than following an agenda or direction set by the therapist.

White: I think that is part of it. It is like saying: "Well, everything is not exactly what it seems to be," or "Things don't have to be the way they've been," or "There are these settled certainties that really are not all that settled."

Hoyt: I have one further question. In discussing your paper, "Deconstruction in Therapy" [White, 1989/1993] , Karl Tomm [1993, pp. 64–65] commented:

> What I would like to see more of in Michael's workshop presentations and in his written work is a readiness to openly and explicitly apply his critique of knowledge and power during his teaching. This desire arises from my interest in the second-order perspective of observing systems. Perhaps it is unreasonable of me to expect this from him in that such a critique could undermine the effectiveness of his protest against those theories and practices that he considers pathologizing. On the other hand, I often wonder whether the receptiveness of other professionals could be enhanced if he became more open and self-reflective in this respect. I must add, however, that in his clinical work Michael is very attentive to and critical of his own power. He has always carefully monitored the effects of his influence on clients and recently even began inviting clients to interview him about his questions. In doing so, he invites them to become more aware of the influence he is having upon them. Nevertheless, this attention to his own power during therapy has not yet become an integral part of his workshop teaching, nor has a critique of his own power as a major contributor in the field become a part of his major presentations. Perhaps these are developments we shall see in the future.

How would you respond to Karl's concern?

White: I always appreciate Karl Tomm's attention to the power relations of therapy. He is a good friend who is always offering challenges in a field where there hasn't been anywhere near enough effort put into addressing these power relations. And I don't believe that such a critique in anyway undermines my refusal of the pathologizing discourses. In fact, any reflections on the power relations in this field can only support such a critique. I agree that it would be helpful for all presenters who are in an influential position to address this influence through critique, in a way that contributes to an exploration of the power relation that is associated with this influence, whether this be across the therapist/service seeker interface or the presenter/workshop participant interface—an exploration partly shaped by questions like:

- *"What are possibilities that are associated with this power relation?"*
- *"What are its limitations?"*
- *"And what are the dangers of this power relation?"*

I have been working on different approaches to this critique in relation to my own consultations and presentations, and have been encouraged in this by Karl Tomm's reflections on these consultations and presentations. Rather than contributing to an "anything goes" sentiment, poststructuralist inquiry contributes to a "nothing goes" sentiment—nothing goes without question, including all of the narrative practices referred to here and elsewhere, and our participation in the power relations that Karl Tomm is drawing attention to here.

Hoyt: Do you ever feel as if you're pathologizing the pathologizers? That you're putting down the psychiatrists (and others) who diagnose people as having "ADHD" or "Borderline Personality Disorder"?

White: To pathologize anyone requires an engagement with the discourses of psychopathology and with very distinct, very well know, structuralist practices. I do my best not to engage with either (although this does not mean that I am not engaged in the reproduction of power relations). I have not "put-down" psychiatrists, psychologists, social workers, counsellors or professional schools or the particular affiliations of any professional discipline. And I have not taken a position for or against labels. Rather, I have been interested to understand what these labels mean to people, what they make possible, who they serve best and least, and to explore the real and potential limitations and dangers of these labels. But I have always questioned the pathologizing discourses that are so routinely dishonoring of people's lives, and that marginalize and disqualify the knowledges and skills that people bring with them into the therapeutic arena, knowledges and skills that have been generated in the history of their lives and their relationships with others. And I have continued to challenge the taken-for-granted practices of immodesty of the culture of psychotherapy.

Zimmerman: I think it's important to think through how we challenge pathologizing practices. I know that once I did not take such care in this, but now I'm very careful to be respectful in this process.

White: Let me just add, that in the questioning and challenging of pathologizing practices, I have not been at all interested in playing any part in the construction of new norms around which therapists might be encouraged or required to measure and evaluate themselves. To continue to raise these questions and to take up this challenge is not specifying of other therapists' practices. There is a world of options for engaging with people seeking consultation that don't reproduce the discourses of psychopathology.

Hoyt: That seems a good note to finish up on! Thank you, Michael and Jeff. I really appreciate having the opportunity to join with you in this discussion.

☐ References

American Psychiatric Association [APA] (1994). *Diagnostic and Statistic Manual of Psychiatric Disorders*. (4th ed., Rev.) Washington, DC: Author.

Bachelard, G. (1969). *The Poetics of Space*. Boston: Beacon Press.

Chang, J., & Phillips, M. (1993). Michael White and Steve de Shazer: New directions in family therapy. In S. Gilligan & R. Price (Eds.), *Therapeutic Conversations* (pp. 95–111). New York: Norton.

Cowley, G., & Springen, K. (1995, April 17). Rewriting life stories. *Newsweek*, pp. 70–74.

de Shazer, S. (1993). Commentary: de Shazer and White: Vive la différence. In S. Gilligan & R. Price (Eds.), *Therapeutic Conversations* (pp. 112–120). New York: Norton.

Dickerson, V. C., & Zimmerman, J. L. (1992). Families with adolescents: Escaping problem lifestyles. *Family Process, 31*, 341–353.

Dickerson, V. C., & Zimmerman, J. L. (1993). A narrative approach to families with adolescents. In S. Friedman (Ed.), *The New Language of Change: Constructive Collaboration in Psychotherapy* (pp. 226–250). New York: Guilford.

Dickerson, V. C., & Zimmerman, J. L. (1995). A constructionist exercise in anti-pathologizing. *Journal of Systemic Therapies, 14*(1), 33–45.

Dickerson, V. C., & Zimmerman, J. L. (1996). Myth, misconceptions, and a word or two about politics. *Journal of Systemic Therapies, 15*(1), 79–88.

Dickerson, V. C., Zimmerman, J. L., & Berndt, L. (1994). Challenging developmental "truths": Separating from separation. *Dulwich Centre Newsletter, 4*, 2–12.

Epston, D., & White, M. (1992). *Experience, Contradiction, Narrative and Imagination: Selected Papers of David Epston and Michael White, 1989–1991*. Adelaide: Dulwich Centre Publications.

Geertz, C. (1973). Thick description: Toward an interpretive theory of culture. In C. Geertz, *The Interpretation of Cultures*. New York: Basic Books.

Geertz, C. (1986). Making experiences, authoring selves: In V. Turner & E. Bruner (Eds.), *The Anthropology of Experience*. Chicago: University of Illinois Press.

Hare-Mustin, R. (1992). Cries and whispers: The psychotherapy of Anne Sexton. *Psychotherapy, 29*, 406–409.

Hare-Mustin, R. (1994). Discourses in the mirrored room: A postmodern analysis of therapy. *Family Process, 33*, 19–35.

Hare-Mustin, R., & Marecek, J. (Eds.) (1990). *Making a Difference: Psychology and the Construction of Gender*. New Haven, CT: Yale University Press.

Held, B. S. (1995). *Back to Reality: A Critique of Postmodern Theory in Psychotherapy*. New York: Norton.

Hoffman, L. (1993). *Exchanging Voices: A Collaborative Approach to Family Therapy*. London: Karnac Books.

Hoyt, M. F., & Combs, G. (1996). On ethics and the spiritualities of the surface: A conversation with Michael White. In M.F. Hoyt (Ed.), *Constructive Therapies, Volume 2* (pp. 33–59). New York: Guilford Press. [see Chapter 3, this volume]

Hoyt, M. F., & Friedman, S. (1998). Dilemmas of postmodern practice under managed care and some pragmatics for increasing the likelihood of treatment authorization. *Journal of Systemic Therapies, 17*(3), 1–11. Reprinted in M.F. Hoyt, *Some Stories Are Better than Others: Doing What Works in Brief Therapy and Managed Care* (pp. 109–117). Philadelphia: Brunner/Mazel, 2000.

Hoyt, M. F., & Nylund, D. (1997). The joy of narrative: An exercise for learning from our internalized clients. *Journal of Systemic Therapies, 16*(4), 361–366. Reprinted in M. F. Hoyt, *Some Stories Are Better than Others: Doing What Works in Brief Therapy and Managed Care* (pp. 201–206). Philadelphia: Brunner/Mazel, 2000.

Madigan, S. P. (1997). Re-considering memory: Re-remembering lost identities back towards re-membered selves. In C. Smith & D. Nylund (Eds.), *Narrative Therapy with Children and Adolescents* (pp. 127–142; with commentary by L. Grieves). New York: Guilford Press.

Madigan, S. P., & Epston, D. (1995). From "spy-chiatric gaze" to communities of concern: From professional monologue to dialogue. In S. Friedman (Ed.), *The Reflecting Team in Action: Collaborative Practice in Family Therapy* (pp. 257–276). New York: Guilford Press.

Madigan, S. P., & Goldner, E. (1998). A narrative approach to anorexia: Discourse, reflexivity, and questions. In M. F. Hoyt (Ed.), *The Handbook of Constructive Therapies* (pp. 380–400). San Francisco: Jossey-Bass.

Minuchin, S. (1992). The restoried history of family therapy. In J. K. Zeig (Ed.), *The Evolution of Psychotherapy: The Second Conference* (pp. 3–12). New York: Brunner/Mazel.

Myerhoff, B. (1982). Life history among the elderly: Performance, visibility and remembering. In J. Ruby (Ed.), *A Crack in the Mirror: Reflexive Perspectives in Anthropology.* Philadelphia: University of Pennsylvania Press.

Myerhoff, B. (1986). Life not death in Venice: Its second life. In V. Turner & E. Bruner (Eds.), *The Anthropology of Experience.* Chicago: University of Chicago Press.

Simon, R. (1996). It's more complicated than that: An interview with Salvador Minuchin. *Family Therapy Networker, 20*(6), 50–56.

Snyder, G. (1983). "Axe handles." In *Axe Handles* (pp. 5–6). San Francisco: North Point Press.

Tomm, K. (1993). The courage to protest: A commentary on Michael White's work. In S. Gilligan & R. Price (Eds.), *Therapeutic Conversations* (pp. 62–80). New York: Norton.

White, M. (1984) Marital therapy: Practical approaches to longstanding problems. *Australian and New Zealand Journal of Family Therapy, 5,* 27–43.

White, M. (1986). Anorexia nervosa: A cybernetic perspective. In J. Elka-Harkaway (Ed.), *Eating Disorders* (pp. 117–129). New York: Aspen. Reprinted in M. White, *Selected Papers* (pp. 5–28). Adelaide: Dulwich Centre Publications, 1989.

White, M. (1988). Saying hullo again: The incorporation of the lost relationship in the resolution of grief. *Dulwich Centre Newsletter,* Spring. Reprinted in M. White, *Selected Papers* (pp. 29–36). Adelaide: Dulwich Centre Publications, 1989.

White, M. (1988). The externalizing of the problem and the re-authoring of lives and relationships. *Dulwich Centre Newsletter,* Summer. Reprinted in M. White, *Selected Papers* (pp. 5–28). Adelaide: Dulwich Centre Publications, 1989.

White, M. (1993). Deconstruction and therapy. In S. Gilligan & R. Price (Eds.), *Therapeutic Conversations* (pp. 22–61). New York: Norton. (Original work published in the *Dulwich Centre Newsletter,* 1991, 3, 1–21.)

White, M. (1995). *Re-Authoring Lives: Interviews and Essays.* Adelaide: Dulwich Centre Publications.

White, M. (1997). *Narratives of Therapists' Lives* . Adelaide: Dulwich Centre Publications.

White, M. (1999). Reflecting-team work as definitional ceremony revisited. *Gecko: A Journal of Deconstruction and Narrative Ideas in Therapeutic Practice, 2,* 55–82.

White, M. (2000). Then and now . . . [interview with Jill Freedman]. In *Reflections on Nar-*

rative Practice: Essays and Interviews (pp. 117–127). Adelaide: Dulwich Centre Publications.

White, M., & de Shazer, S. (1996, October 11-12). *Narrative Solutions/Solution Narratives.* Conference sponsored by Brief Family Therapy Center, Milwaukee.

White, M., & Epston, D. (1990). *Narrative Means to Therapeutic Ends.* New York: Norton.

White, M., & Meichenbaum, D. (2000, May). *Dialogue: Nature and Challenge of a Narrative Perspective of Psychology.* Held at the Evolution of Psychotherapy Conference sponsored by the Milton H. Erickson Foundation, Anaheim, CA.

Wylie, M. S. (1994). Panning for gold. *Family Therapy Networker, 18*(6), 40–48.

Zimmerman, J. L., & Dickerson, V. C. (1993). Separating couples from restraining patterns and the relationship discourses that support them. *Journal of Marital and Family Therapy, 19*(4), 403–413.

Zimmerman, J. L., & Dickerson, V. C. (1994a). Tales of the body thief: Externalizing and deconstructing eating disorders. In M. F. Hoyt (Ed.), *Constructive Therapies* (pp. 295–318). New York: Guilford Press.

Zimmerman, J. L., & Dickerson, V. C. (1994b). Using a narrative metaphor: Implications for theory and clinical practice. *Family Process, 33,* 233–246.

Zimmerman, J. L., & Dickerson, V. C. (1995). Narrative therapy and the work of Michael White. In M. Elkaim (Ed.), *Panorama des Therapies Familiales* (pp. 533–554). Paris: Editions du Seuil.

Zimmerman, J. L., & Dickerson, V. C. (1996). *If Problems Talked: Narrative Therapy in Action.* New York: Guilford Press.

CREDITS

Opening Epigraph: The poem "Axe Handles" from *Axe Handles* by Gary Snyder. Copyright 1983 by Gary Snyder. Reprinted by permission of North Point Press, a division of Farrar, Straus and Giroux, LLC.

Chapter 1: The chapter by M.F. Hoyt, "On the Importance of Keeping It Simple and Taking the Patient Seriously: A Conversation with Steve de Shazer and John Weakland," which appeared (with changes) in *Constructive Therapies* (M.F. Hoyt, Editor, 1994), is used by permission of Guilford Publications and Steve de Shazer.

Chapter 2: The chapter by M.F. Hoyt, "Welcome to Possibilityland: A Conversation with Bill O'Hanlon," which appeared (with changes) in *Constructive Therapies, Volume 2* (M.F. Hoyt, Editor, 1996), is used by permission of Guilford Publications and Bill O'Hanlon.

Chapter 3: The chapter by M.F. Hoyt and G. Combs, "On Ethics and the Spiritualities of the Surface: A Conversation with Michael White," which appeared (with changes) in *Constructive Therapies, Volume 2* (M.F. Hoyt, Editor, 1996), is used by permission of Guilford Publications and Michael White and Gene Combs.

Chapter 4: The chapter by M.F. Hoyt, "Cognitive-Behavioral Treatment of Posttraumatic Stress Disorder from a Narrative Constructivist Perspective: A Conversation with Donald Meichenbaum," which appeared (with changes) in *Constructive Therapies, Volume 2* (M.F. Hoyt, Editor, 1996), is used by permission of Guilford Publications and Donald Meichenbaum.

Chapter 5: The chapter by M.F. Hoyt, "Contact, Contract, Change, Encore: A Conversation about Redecision Therapy with Bob Goulding," which appeared (with changes) in *Transactional Analysis Journal*, 1995, 25(4), 300–311, is used by permission of the International Transactional Analysis Association. In addition, portions by M.F. Hoyt, "Foreword," which appeared (with changes) in *Redecision Therapy: A Brief, Action-Oriented Approach* (C.E. Lennox, Editor, 1997), are used by permission of Jason Aronson Publications.

Chapter 6: The chapter by M.F. Hoyt and P. Watzlawick, "Constructing Therapeutic Realities: A Conversation with Paul Watzlawick," with appeared (with changes) in *The Handbook of Constructive Therapies* (M.F. Hoyt, Editor, copyright 1998, Jossey-Bass Publisher), is used by permission of Jossey-Bass, Inc., a subsidiary of John Wiley & Sons, Inc., and Paul Watzlawick.

Chapter 7: The chapter by M.F. Hoyt, "Solution Building and Language Games: A Conversation with Steve de Shazer (and Some After Words with Insoo Kim Berg," which appeared (with changes) in *Constructive Therapies, Volume 2* (M.F. Hoyt, Editor, 1996), is used by permission of Guilford Publications and Steve de Shazer and Insoo Kim Berg.

Chapter 8: The chapter by M.F. Hoyt, "Postmodernism, the Relational Self, Constructive Therapies, and Beyond: A Conversation with Kenneth Gergen," which appeared (with changes) in *Constructive Therapies, Volume 2* (M.F. Hoyt, Editor, 1996), is used by permission of Guilford Publications and Kenneth Gergen.

Chapter 9: The article by M.F. Hoyt, S.D. Miller, B.S. Held, and W.J. Matthews, "About Constructivism: Or, If Four Colleagues Talked in New York, Would Anyone Hear It?" which appeared (with changes) in *Journal of Systemic Therapies*, 2000, 19(4), 76–92, is used by permission of Guilford Publications and Scott Miller, Barbara Held, and William Matthews.

Chapter 10: The article by M.F. Hoyt and J.M. Carlson, "Interview: Michael Hoyt," which appeared (with changes) in *The Family Journal: Counseling and Therapy for Couples and Families*, 1997, 5(2), 172-181, is used by permission of *The Family Journal* and J. Matthew Carlson.

Chapter 11: The chapter by M.F. Hoyt and S.P. Madigan, "Honoring Our Internalized Others and the Ethics of Caring: A Conversation with Karl Tomm," which appeared (with changes) in *The Handbook of Constructive Therapies* (M.F. Hoyt, Editor, copyright 1998, Jossey-Bass Publishers), is used by permission of Jossey-Bass, Inc., a subsidiary of John Wiley & Sons, Inc., and Stephen Madigan and Karl Tomm.

Chapter 12: The chapter by M. White, M.F. Hoyt, and J.L. Zimmerman, "Direction and Discovery: A Conversation about Power and Politics in Narrative Therapy," which appeared (with changes) in *Reflections on Narrative Practice: Essays and Interviews* (M. White, 2000, Dulwich Centre Publications), is used by permission of Dulwich Centre Publications and Michael White and Jeff Zimmerman.

INDEX

ABOUT THE EDITOR

Michael F. Hoyt, Ph.D. (Yale '76), is a senior staff psychologist at the Kaiser Permanente Medical Center in San Rafael, California, and serves on the clinical faculty of the University of California School of Medicine, San Francisco. An expert clinician and internationally respected teacher and lecturer, Dr. Hoyt is the author of *Some Stories Are Better Than Others: Doing What Works in Brief Therapy and Managed Care* and *Brief Therapy and Managed Care*; the editor of *The Handbook of Constructive Therapies and Constructive Therapies, Volumes 1 & 2*; and co-editor (with Simon Budman and Steven Friedman) of *The First Sessions in Brief Therapy*. Dr. Hoyt has been honored as a Woodrow Wilson Fellow, as a Continuing Education Distinguished Speaker by the American Psychological Association, and as a Distinguished Presenter by the International Association of Marriage and Family Counselors. With his wife and son, Dr. Hoyt resides in Mill Valley, California.